ABOLITIONIST VOICES

Edited by
David Gordon Scott

With a Foreword by
Johannes Feest

First published in Great Britain in 2026 by

Bristol University Press
University of Bristol
1–9 Old Park Hill
Bristol
BS2 8BB
UK
t: +44 (0)117 374 6645
e: bup-info@bristol.ac.uk

Details of international sales and distribution partners are available at bristoluniversitypress.co.uk

© Bristol University Press 2026

British Library Cataloguing in Publication Data
A catalogue record for this book is available from the British Library

ISBN 978-1-5292-2403-0 hardcover
ISBN 978-1-5292-2404-7 paperback
ISBN 978-1-5292-2405-4 ePub
ISBN 978-1-5292-2406-1 ePdf

The right of David Gordon Scott to be identified as editor of this work has been asserted by him in accordance with the Copyright, Designs and Patents Act 1988.

All rights reserved: no part of this publication may be reproduced, stored in a retrieval system, or transmitted in any form or by any means, electronic, mechanical, photocopying, recording, or otherwise without the prior permission of Bristol University Press.

Every reasonable effort has been made to obtain permission to reproduce copyrighted material. If, however, anyone knows of an oversight, please contact the publisher.

The statements and opinions contained within this publication are solely those of the editor and contributors and not of the University of Bristol or Bristol University Press. The University of Bristol and Bristol University Press disclaim responsibility for any injury to persons or property resulting from any material published in this publication.

Bristol University Press works to counter discrimination on grounds of gender, race, disability, age and sexuality.

Cover design: Liam Roberts Design
Front cover image: Stocksy/kkgas

Bristol University Press' authorised representative in the European Union
is: Easy Access System Europe, Mustamäe tee 50, 10621 Tallinn, Estonia,
Email: gpsr.requests@easproject.com

Contents

Notes on Contributors		v
Foreword by Johannes Feest		ix
Preface		xii
1	The Abolitionist Rhizome *David Gordon Scott*	1

PART I Voices of the Oppressed

2	Kropotkin and the Anarchist Case for Prison Abolition *Ruth Kinna*	25
3	Angela Davis and the Contributions and Contradictions of Abolition *Joy James*	43
4	Phenomenology, Abolition and the Lived Experience of Incarceration *Lisa Guenther*	64

PART II Abolitionist Ideas

5	Liberation and Reconciliation: The Christian Tradition and Prison Abolition *Hannah Bowman*	85
6	The Daybreak of Abolition: The Overcoming of Punishment and Promotion of Therapy in Nietzsche's Philosophy *Caius Brandão*	103
7	Marxism and the Political Economy of Abolitionism *Jon Burnett*	121
8	Foucault and Prison Abolition *Chloë Taylor*	138

PART III The Scope of Oppression

9	The Slavery Industrial Complex *Viviane Saleh-Hanna*	157
10	Abolition and the Colonial Carceral Archipelago *Thalia Anthony and Harry Blagg*	181
11	Southerning Nonpunitive and Abolitionist Feminism *Valeria Vegh Weis*	200

PART IV Struggles for Liberation and Justice

12	Eco-Abolition: Policing Environmental Injustice *Nathan Stephens-Griffin and Andrea Brock*	223
13	Abolitionist Activism in Post-Mass-Media Societies: Moral Panic and the Amplification of Abolitionist Voices *Michael Dellwing*	245
14	Libertarian Socialism and the Struggle for Liberative Justice *David Gordon Scott*	270

Index 292

Notes on Contributors

Thalia Anthony is Professor of Law at the University of Technology Sydney. Her research has specialized in colonization and the criminalization of Indigenous peoples. Her books include *Indigenous People, Crime and Punishment* (Routledge, 2013) and (with Harry Blagg) *Decolonising Criminology* (Palgrave Macmillan, 2019).

Harry Blagg is Professor of Criminology and Director of the Centre for Indigenous Peoples and Community Justice in the Law School of the University of Western Australia.

Hannah Bowman is the founder and director of Christians for the Abolition of Prisons (christiansforabolition.org), and writes and teaches on the Christian theology supporting prison abolition. She has an MA in Religious Studies from Mount Saint Mary's University, Los Angeles.

Caius Brandão is a Brazilian philosopher who holds bachelor's, master's and doctoral degrees in moral philosophy. His scholarly pursuits are deeply entrenched in the oeuvre of Friedrich Nietzsche and his scholarly writings encompass a collection of erudite volumes and articles, spanning a broad spectrum of philosophical themes. Particularly noteworthy is his recent book, *Penal Abolitionism: The Overcoming of Punishment in Friedrich Nietzsche's Philosophy*, originally published in Portuguese (Editora Científica Digital, 2022).

Andrea Brock is a political ecologist at the University of Sussex. She researches the relationship between extractivism, corporate power and state violence. She has written about the criminalization, policing and repression of anti-coal and anti-fracking resistance, the political ecology of (green) extractivism, and counterinsurgency. Her edited volume (with Alexander Dunlap) *Enforcing Ecocide: Power, Policing & Planetary Militarization* (Springer, 2022) features case studies from across the globe that explore the links between militarization, policing and ecological destruction.

Jon Burnett is Lecturer in Criminology at the University of Hull. His research focuses on and interrogates carcerality, the political economies of work and punishment, and state violence. He has published extensively in a range of academic and nonacademic fora, and he is the author of *Work and the Carceral State* (Pluto Press, 2022). He has previously worked in research-based roles at Positive Action for Refugees and Asylum Seekers (PAFRAS), Medical Justice and the Institute of Race Relations. He has been a witness at the Permanent Peoples' Tribunal on the Human Rights of Migrant and Refugee Peoples and is a former co-editor of the international journal *Justice, Power and Resistance* (published by Bristol University Press).

Michael Dellwing has undertaken work in dramaturgical sociology, symbolic interaction, media and cultural sociology. He now studies digital society and the nexus of play and decentralized culture. His recent work includes an introduction to ethnography in digital societies and a volume on research as play.

Johannes Feest is Emeritus Professor at the University of Bremen. He has published widely on prisons and prison abolitionism. In Germany, he initiated a 'Manifesto for the abolition of penitentiaries and other prisons' (https://strafvollzugsarchiv.de/abolitionism/manifesto?lang=en).

Lisa Guenther is Queen's National Scholar in Political Philosophy and Critical Prison Studies at Queen's University in Canada. She is the author of *Solitary Confinement: Social Death and Its Afterlives* (University of Minnesota Press, 2013) and co-editor of *Death and Other Penalties: Philosophy in a Time of Mass Incarceration* (Fordham University Press, 2015). From 2012 to 2017, she facilitated a discussion group with men on death row in Tennessee called the REACH Coalition. She is currently a member of the P4W Memorial Collective Advisory Board and is researching the relationship between slavery, settler colonialism and incarceration in Canada and the US.

Joy James is Ebenezer Fitch Professor of Humanities at Williams College. Her books include *Resisting State Violence* (University of Minnesota Press, 1996) and *Seeking the 'Beloved Community'* (State University of New York Press, 2014). She is the editor of *The Angela Y. Davis Reader* (Wiley Blackwell, 1998), *Imprisoned Intellectuals* (Roman and Littlefield, 2003), *The New Abolitionists* (State University of New York Press, 2005) and *Warfare in the American Homeland* (Duke University Press, 2007). Her current writing on the 'Captive Maternal' began with the article 'The womb of western theory' (*Carceral Notebooks*, Vol. 12, 2016) and will be published in book length form by Pluto Press in 2025.

Ruth Kinna works at Loughborough University as a political theorist and historian of ideas specializing in anarchism. She is a co-founder and member of the Anarchism Research Group and co-editor of the journal *Anarchist Studies*. She is the author of *The Government of No One* (Pelican, 2019) and *Kropotkin: Reviewing the Classical Anarchist Tradition* (Edinburgh University Press, 2016).

Viviane Saleh-Hanna is Full Professor of Crime and Justice Studies and Director of Black Studies at the University of Massachusetts, Dartmouth. She has been involved in penal abolition movements and international abolitionist work for almost 30 years. Her research and scholarship focus on Black feminist hauntology, penal abolition, anti-colonialism, wholistic justice, structurally abusive relationships, and freedom-driven dreams and understandings guided by Toni Morrison, Octavia E. Butler and N.K. Jemisin. She has spent the last few years immersed in trainings and teachings by Anishinaabe and Haudenosaunee elders and professors at the Centre for Indigegogy at Wilfred Laurier University in Canada. She recently co-edited and contributed chapters in the anthology *Abolish Criminology* (Routledge, 2024) and serves on the board of editors for the *Journal of Prisoners on Prisons* and the *African Journal of Criminology and Justice Studies*.

David Gordon Scott works at The Open University. His recent books include *Against Imprisonment* (Waterside Press, 2018), *For Abolition* (Waterside Press, 2020), *International Handbook of Penal Abolition* (Routledge, 2021, co-edited with Michael Coyle) and *Demystifying Power, Crime and Social Harm* (Palgrave Macmillan, 2023, co-edited with Joe Sim). He is a former coordinator of the European Group for the Study of Deviance and Social Control and co-founding editor (with Emma Bell) of the international journal *Justice, Power and Resistance* (published by Bristol University Press). His latest book is *Envisioning Abolition* (Bristol University Press, 2025, co-edited with Emma Bell), which explores the emergence and development of penal abolitionism in anarchist and socialist thought and is published as a companion text to this volume.

Nathan Stephens-Griffin is Senior Lecturer at Northumbria University. He primarily works across the disciplines of sociology, criminology and critical animal studies. His most recent published work has focused on exploring abolitionist applications in political ecology and green criminology. He also has a longstanding interest in state/corporate power and the repression of social movements (for example, through his research and writing about the undercover policing of ecological and other forms of protest in Britain). Methodologically, he enjoys using biographical, visual and graphic narrative approaches to social research. He is the author of *Understanding Veganism: Biography and Identity* (Palgrave Macmillan, 2017).

Chloë Taylor is Professor of Women's and Gender Studies at the University of Alberta in Canada. Her research interests include prison abolitionism, 20th-century French philosophy, the philosophy of gender and sexuality, critical animal studies, Anthropocene studies and critical disability studies. She is the author of 20 articles and three monographs, and the editor or co-editor of six books, including, with Kelly Struthers Montford, *Building Abolition: Decarceration and Social Justice* (Routledge, 2021).

Valeria Vegh Weis is a senior researcher at the University of Konstanz, Germany and Associate Professor of Criminology, Buenos Aires University. She has published widely and her books include *Bienvenidos al Lawfare!* (Capital Intellectual, 2021), *Criminalisation of Activism* (Routledge, 2021) and *Marxism and Criminology. A History of Criminal Selectivity* (Haymarket, 2018).

Foreword

Johannes Feest

In the 1970s, penal abolitionism seemed a promising new force in criminology and criminal policy. In Western Europe, it spread by means of the *European Group for the Study of Deviance and Social Control*. The idea had a substantial following in the UK, but also in Germany, the Netherlands and Scandinavia. Its unquestioned leaders were Herman Bianchi (the Netherlands), Nils Christie (Norway), Louk Hulsman (the Netherlands) and Thomas Mathiesen (Norway). They represented very different approaches to the question of how to get rid of the criminal (in)justice system, especially the prison institution. Bianchi's ideas had a religious foundation, Hulsman and Christie represented different hues of humanism, and Mathiesen had a Marxist background. Together, they made some inroads into academic thinking on crime and even into practical politics.

One generation later, these founding fathers were all dead and the movement was put on the defensive by a renewal of law-and-order politics in Europe. The idea did, however, survive because of some residual support mainly in Germany, Italy, Spain, Portugal, the UK and the Americas. The biggest push came eventually from platforms like 'Critical Resistance', launched in Berkeley, California, in 1998 (see James, Chapter 3 in this volume). This also helped the *International Conference on Penal Abolition* (ICOPA), founded in 1982 (see Morris, 1997) to survive.

In the UK, David Gordon Scott has been, over the last ten years, the most active and visible penal abolitionist, both as an academic and as an activist. His activities and publications have helped to keep the abolitionist agenda alive, both in the UK and elsewhere in a time when it was struggling both inside and outside the UK. I first encountered him in Padua, Italy, when we met to plan the edited volume *No Prison* (Ferrari and Pavarini, 2018). But his major international achievement so far is co-editing the first truly *International Handbook on Penal Abolition* (see Coyle and Scott, 2021).

The present volume is a most convincing selection of contributions, demonstrating the 'multitude of different and diverse abolitionist voices' as he calls it in his Preface. The lineup includes scholars from Argentina,

Australia, Brazil, Canada, Germany, the US and (of course also) the UK. And most of them are new voices, at least for me. Furthermore, while the 'founding fathers' of penal abolitionism mentioned previously were all men, the majority of the voices presented here are women. And the one person, who could qualify as 'founding mother', the abolitionist/pacifist Faye Honey Knopp, is not only mentioned twice in the chapter on the Christian tradition (see Bowman, Chapter 5 in this volume), but peace making is rightly seen by many contributors as a corollary of abolition.

Instead of trying to duplicate David's magisterial presentation of these contributions, I will restrict myself to a few remarks on his preface, his introductory and his concluding chapter.

Let me start with the term 'rhizome', a surprising and striking metaphor to indicate the diversity and manifold origins of penal abolitionism. But metaphors are always at risk of being misleading. A closer look may show that a rhizome is characterized by sprouting out of one common rootstalk. David himself is cautioning us 'to resist the temptation to claim that all penal abolitionist arguments and lines of reasoning find their roots in one tradition or movement' (see Chapter 1 of this volume). On second thoughts, maybe the prison institution itself is more rhizome-like, sprouting from the same root. This would 'explain' why it is raising its ugly head everywhere. This would also have the practical advantage that the system could be eliminated once and for all by eradicating it root and stem. So much for the utility of metaphors.

But apart from such small quibbles, David's introduction demonstrates convincingly that while the prison institution was not always present in human history, abolitionism in a wider sense was. It was always present as the perennial 'struggle for freedom and a dignified life' and specifically 'struggles against the injustice, wrongdoing and unfairness of the institutions and practices of the criminal law'. If this is indeed the core element of penal abolitionism, it interfaces with many other struggles against oppression and for justice. This generalization of the term 'abolitionism' as a common denominator for different causes and movements is a relatively new development. A recent German reader on abolitionism (based mainly on American sources) lists the following disciplining and carceral institutions as candidates for abolition: 'family, school, university, factory, welfare and employment offices, psychiatric clinics, police' (Loick and Thompson, 2022: 42). The unlimited possibilities as well as the practical difficulties of such a list are brought together in Ruth Wilson Gilmore's (2024) famous dictum: abolitionism presupposes 'that we change something, namely everything'.

In his concluding chapter, David talks about 'socialist-inspired abolitionism' and the struggle for liberative justice. But obviously not every kind of socialism can be seen as abolitionist, be it in theory or in practice. David describes the kind of socialism he has in mind and calls it, somewhat irritatingly, 'libertarian'. However, what he describes amounts to what an old teacher of mine, Hal Draper (1966), used to call 'Socialism from Below' and I think that David could agree on the following definition:

> The heart of 'Socialism from Below' is its view that socialism can be realized only through the self-emancipation of activised masses in motion, reaching out for freedom with their own hand, mobilized 'from below' in a struggle to take charge of their own destiny, as actors (not merely subjects) on the stage of history. (Draper, 1966: 4)

Again, apart from terminological questions, I found this chapter most convincing. There can indeed be, as he says, 'no doubt that any radical transformation of the penal field can only be successfully brought about in conjunction with a radical overturning and transformation of the current social system and its political economy'. And there also should be agreement that the struggle for liberative justice will be necessarily unfinished, which, as David put it, is 'a promise of something still to come – a freedom always on the horizon but never quite within our grasp' – a perfect link between Thomas Mathiesen's philosophy of the unfinished and Enrique Dussel's liberation philosophy.

This book is a wonderfully polyphonic achievement. Every reader should be able to find their own access to the great abolitionist concert.

References
Coyle, M. and Scott, D. (eds) (2021) *International Handbook of Penal Abolition*, Abingdon: Routledge.
Draper, H. (1966) 'The two souls of socialism', *New Politics*, 5(1): 57–84 (see also pamphlet version published by the International Socialists and the University of Berkeley).
Ferrari, L. and Pavarini, M. (eds) (2018) *No Prison*, Bristol: EG Press.
Gilmore, R.W. (2024) *Change Everything*, Chicago: Haymarket Books.
Loick, D. and Thompson, V.E. (eds) (2022) *Abolitionismus; Ein Reader*, Berlin: Suhrkamp Verlag AG.
Morris, R. (1997) *Penal Abolition: The Practical Choice*, Ottawa: Canadian Scholars Press.

Preface

David Gordon Scott

There is no one single abolitionist voice. Rather, there are a multitude of different and diverse abolitionist voices that have arisen in different times, traditions and places. Penal abolitionist thought has many roots and is perhaps best referred to as a 'rhizome' (Deleuze and Guattari, 1987; Glissant, 2020). Some of these roots of abolitionism are interlinked from the start, whereas others take a very different line of reasoning, but end up in the same place: that state punishments are morally and politically bankrupt and cannot be easily justified, if at all. Yet, it is likely that over time, most lines of abolitionist reasoning at some point or other will have influenced each other, albeit in different ways.

A key element of the abolitionist rhizome is its focus on a particular outcome – the massive reduction, defunding, delegitimation or total ending of the use of prisons, policing, criminal laws, courts and punishment. Penal abolitionists question the validity and justification of legal coercion, and maintain that society would be better served looking for alternative nonpenal responses in its place. As the promotion of penal abolition is closely tied to that of liberation and emancipation, it should come as no surprise that different reasons have been put forward as to why we should aspire to such a goal of decarceration. Thus, whereas the destination may be the same for all penal abolitionists, their journey there may not be. Abolitionists can have quite different reasons for questioning the penal apparatus of the capitalist state and be motivated by quite different ethical, political and theoretical concerns. To assume that all penal abolitionists today share exactly the same motivations or worldview would be a mistake. But at the same time, to assume that penal abolitionist ideas exist in a vacuum unaffected by other lines of abolitionist reasoning would equally be incorrect.

While there is an increasing acknowledgement that penal abolitionisms are now found across all parts of the world (Coyle and Scott, 2021), reflections on the historical and contemporary diversity of penal abolitionist thought remain relatively rare (see Scott and Bell, 2025). Even among the recent groundswell of penal abolitionist publications and community interventions since the early 2020s (Kurti and Brown, 2023), there remains little appreciation of the diverse inspirations of radical critiques of policing, punishment and legal coercion. This volume aims to help address this deficit in the literature. The book situates penal abolitionisms within different political, ethical, sociological, philosophical and theological perspectives. The following chapters bring together critical thinkers from Europe, North America, Australasia and South America to reflect upon the diversity and interconnectedness of penal abolitionisms, sometimes through consideration of the emergence of abolitionist ideas and sentiments in the past, and at other times as statements of the priorities of the present and future. Each chapter is written by author(s) who are closely associated with a different abolitionist approach.

The intention of this collection is to shed new light on the depth and diversity of penal abolitionist voices, while at the same time highlighting their continuities, interconnections and overlaps – the abolitionist rhizome. In so doing, this volume does not reveal a fragmented or incoherent picture of penal abolitionisms, and nor does it undermine the hybridity of much of penal abolitionist thought. Rather, it demonstrates that acknowledgement of its diversity, plurality and long historical presence can only strengthen the case for penal abolition. Penal abolitionisms interconnect like a patchwork quilt, where each approach offers a different way of reflecting on the failings of the penal law, but when considered collectively, they reveal a picture of the intricacy, diversity and strength of critique. They also reveal a raft of creative alternatives to the penal rationale. There are more people advocating penal abolition and more reasons to critique prisons, punishment and legal coercion than many give credit. Penal abolitionism has a lot of friends, advocates and sympathizers, with these allegiances stretching back over many centuries.

Undoubtedly, it is important for penal abolitionists to ground their thought within a given standpoint or theoretical tradition. Such an ethico-political grounding provides the intellectual scaffolding and reasoning for the call for abolition. But problems arise when there is a failure to acknowledge the partiality and contingency of such standpoints, especially if any given standpoint is portrayed as the *only* approach to penal abolition. Such a placing of exclusionary boundaries around the roots and intellectual development of penal abolitionist thought is unhelpful and ultimately diminishes the vitality, durability and renewability of abolitionist critiques. It is important to resist the temptation to claim that *all* penal abolitionist arguments and lines of reasoning find their roots in one tradition or movement.

By visibilizing the diverse and nuanced nature of penal abolitionisms, this volume aims to indicate how sometimes neglected or forgotten abolitionist ideas of the past can be of assistance for those engaging in emancipatory struggles against penal and social injustice in the present. There has long been a bias towards 'immediatism' and the clustering of abolitionist thought around a given thinker or tradition at a given moment in time. To some extent, this may be inevitable – authors want to connect with the ideas in their present moment and this aspiration can be helpful for creating a shared language and the development of new concepts. However, at the same time, it is important that we are conscious of other lines of penal abolitionist thought from the past. This can help prevent the 'reinvention' or repackaging of pre-existing abolitionist ideas and can lead to stronger, hybrid penal abolitionist thinking that draws upon the very best lines of reasoning available – the 'middle' of the abolitionist rhizome (Deleuze and Guattari, 1987; Glissant, 2020). Appreciation of other earlier penal abolitionisms can highlight key weaknesses, gaps, omissions and previous exclusions. It can help prevent a liberation movement from repeating the mistakes from the past and identify where there is common ground for building alliances.

It should be noted from the outset that *Abolitionist Voices* is not a textbook charting the intellectual development of all lines of penal abolitionist reasoning, or all their nuances or interconnections. A fully comprehensive account of the abolitionist rhizome would be neither desirable nor feasible for a short volume such as this. It would not be desirable because not every single line of penal abolitionist reasoning carries the same moral and political weight: there are some arguments calling for penal abolition that simply have not been particularly well made,[1] and nor would a truly comprehensive volume at this time be entirely feasible. There are lines of abolitionist thought which exist in languages or cultures inaccessible to this editor; and the range of liberation movements inspiring them are multiple and spread across the globe. This collection of contributions does not aim to bring an end to the discussion on voices contributing to the abolitionist rhizome, but instead, this volume is intended to help initiate a greater appreciation of the diversity of abolitionist voices and the furthering of contemporary struggles for revolutionary praxis, emancipation and the securing of sustainable life on our planet.[2]

Notes

[1] I am thinking here of the advocation of penal abolition by the Marquis de Sade (see Phillips, 2005) or more recent calls for alternative punishments grounded in the latest surveillance technology (Daw, 2020). Some may find such foundations for abolition persuasive, but this author does not.

[2] This book should be read (if possible) alongside its companion volume, *Envisioning Abolition* (Scott and Bell, 2025), which is also published by Bristol University Press.

References

Coyle, M. and Scott, D. (eds) (2021) *International Handbook of Penal Abolition*, Abingdon: Routledge.

Daw, C. (2020) *Justice on Trial*, London: Bloomsbury.

Deleuze, G. and Guattari, F. (1987) *A Thousand Plateaus: Capitalism and Schizophrenia*, Minneapolis: University of Minnesota Press.

Glissant, E. (2020) *Introduction to a Poetics of Diversity*, Liverpool: Liverpool University Press.
Kurti, Z. and Brown, M. (2023) 'Carceral reckoning and twenty-first century US abolition movements: generational struggles in the fight against prisons' in *Punishment and Society*. Available from: https://journals.sagepub.com/doi/10.1177/14624745231171364 [Accessed 3 September 2023].
Phillips, J. (2005) *The Marquis de Sade: A Very Short Introduction*, Oxford: Oxford University Press.
Scott, D. and Bell, E. (eds) (2025) *Envisioning Abolition*, Bristol: Bristol University Press.

1

The Abolitionist Rhizome

David Gordon Scott

Introduction

There are many different roads to penal abolition. However, rather than creating a tension, this multiplicity is something that should be celebrated as it can help inspire the cross-fertilization of liberatory ideas. There can be little doubt, for example, that the emancipatory praxis of anti-chattel-slavery abolition and the philosophical perspective of phenomenology are very different in origin, and yet both, when considered in terms of their contributions to abolitionist ideas, have been very significant. What they represent are two different roots of, and routes to, penal abolition.

Following the insights of Giles Deleuze and Felix Guattari (1987) and Eduard Glissant (2020), penal abolitionisms can be conceived as a 'rhizome'. Glissant (2020) defines a rhizome as something which is multi-rooted and reaches out and interconnects with other roots. As this volume testifies, there are many roots of penal abolition. Yet, at the same time, these roots often draw upon and incorporate insights from other lines of abolitionist reasoning. For Glissant (2020: 37) in *Introduction to a Poetics of Diversity*, 'the single root is the one that kills around it, while the rhizome is the root that extends to meet other roots'. The penal abolitionist rhizome thus grows stronger through its diversity and willingness to reach out across different traditions and perspectives – the greater the variety and interconnections of the different theoretical and political origins of penal abolition, the greater its overall strength and utility as a direct intervention in the present against penal and social injustice. The aim of this volume is to shine a spotlight on some of this diversity of penal abolitionist voices.

As a rhizome, penal abolitionist thought does not remain static and the same, but rather constantly metamorphosizes, grows and evolves. Abolitionist lines of reasoning have transformed over time by absorbing and developing through encounters with other radical ideas, liberation movements and traditions of emancipatory praxis. Sometimes this is explicit and fully acknowledged, but at other times it is implicit and may only become obvious when analysing abolitionist thought in retrospect.

Glissant (2020) draws heavily upon the ideas of Giles Deleuze and Felix Guattari (1987) and their influential text *A Thousand Plateaus: Capitalism and Schizophrenia* when conceiving of the rhizome. In a helpful summary of what they mean by the 'rhizome', Deleuze and Guattari (1987: 21) note: 'A rhizome connects any point with any other point ... [and] cannot be reduced to either the one or the multiple. ... It has no beginning or end but always a middle through which it grows and overflows.'

The rhizome is a 'subterranean stem' (Deleuze and Guattari, 1987: 6) characterized by 'heterogeneity and connection' (Deleuze and Guattari, 1987: 7). The 'essence of the rhizome [is] to intersect roots and sometimes merge with them' (Deleuze and Guattari, 1987: 13). It is decentred and nonhierarchical, and 'operates by variation, expansion, conquest, capture, [and] offshoots' (Deleuze and Guattari, 1987: 21). When people refer to penal abolitionism as one single perspective, it is perhaps a reflection of the strength of the ideas emerging through the multiple interconnections of the melting pot which Deleuze and Guattari (1987: 21) call the 'middle' and its goal of generating 'productive outgrowths' (Deleuze and Guattari, 1987: 14): 'A new rhizome may form in the heart of a tree, the hollow of a root, the crook of a branch. Or else it is a microscopic element of the root-tree, a radicle [primary root], that gets rhizome production going' (Deleuze and Guattari, 1987: 15).

Certainly, to argue that penal abolitionisms have developed along a singular or linear trajectory negates its hybridity and interconnectedness. However, there are abolitionist traditions and lines or reasoning that are more developed than others – which Deleuze and Guattari (1987: 15) referred to as the 'radicle'– which are the 'primary roots' that get things going. Some of these primary roots are explored in this volume. Yet it is perhaps the 'middle' which many of those unfamiliar with the historical and contemporary nuances of penal abolitionisms see most easily. To be sure, there are many similarities in penal abolitionist thinking, but this should not negate the multiple roots that feed into it.[1]

Although a timeline of different liberation movements and theoretical and conceptual breakthroughs in abolitionist thought can be charted, penal abolitionisms have not evolved like building blocks, one on top of the other. Rather, they have come together from different directions, with the abolitionist rhizome evolving, over-flowing and interconnecting in multiple and different ways and different times. To suggest that there is *only one root of abolitionist thought* is therefore misleading. There are a multitude of abolitionist ideas and sentiments dating back many centuries that cannot (and should not) be grounded in one single liberation movement or intellectual tradition. However, when penal abolitionists reflect upon the multiple roots and interconnections of different lines of abolitionist reasoning, this may mean considering specific lines of thought in isolation (referred to here as the primary root or 'radicle' – see, for example, the companion volume, Scott and Bell [2025]) as well as through a consideration of how they help constitute, and in turn are constituted by, each other (something which can be referred to as the 'middle').

The ideas of absorption, evolution and metamorphosis in a penal abolitionist rhizome draws parallels with the arguments of the great Italian socialist Antonio Gramsci (1971). While locked in a fascist prison cell, Gramsci reflected on the evolving nature of socialist/Marxist praxis. For him, it was important for socialism to grasp and assimilate new cultural ideas, and infuse them with socialist meanings. Socialism was thus ever-evolving and renewing itself within the culture and politics of the times, ensuring its relevance and applicability to contemporary struggles for emancipation. Following Gramsci (1971), it is important for any liberation movement to absorb and infuse contemporary language and concepts into its politics and praxis. Only by doing so can it remain topical and have cross- generational appeal. This remains true for penal abolitionisms. The different pathways, roots and routes to penal abolition are not isolated and fragmented. Though they may start in different times and places, abolitionists often reach out and gain new cultural and political impetus through connecting with the key issues of the day, as has happened recently following the death of George Floyd in the US in 2020, most notably about 'defunding the police'. Abolitionism and contemporary struggles for liberation can inform each other in a myriad of different ways, resulting in renewal and innovation in emancipatory politics and praxis.

As well as its diverse rootedness, it is also important for penal abolitionists in the present to grasp the fact that abolitionism has been around for a very long time indeed (see Scott and Bell, 2025). The influential Dutch abolitionist Herman Bianchi (1991: 9) argues that abolitionism can be found in 'the earliest periods of human culture'. For Bianchi (1991: 9):

> Abolitionism is one of the most important manifestations of the general human urge to do away with and the struggle against those phenomena or institutions of a social, political or religious nature that at the given time are considered to be unjust, wrong, unfair or undue. All crusades and actions for political reforms, for democracy or socialism are in their origins abolitionist movements.

Abolitionism is ever-present in human history. It represents a universal human aspiration to be free of the yoke of oppression, exploitation and domination. At its core, abolitionism is a struggle for freedom and a dignified life. It requires the establishment of a framework of values – a moral compass – informing how a civilized society should operate if it aspires to justice. Penal abolition refers specifically to those struggles against the injustice, wrongdoing and unfairness of the institutions and practices of the criminal law. This critique (and the promotion of emancipatory alternatives) is just one strand of wider liberation struggles and the pursuit of revolutionary praxis.

The following 13 substantive chapters that comprise this volume can all be considered as contributions to diverse abolitionist traditions, perspectives and theories, but that collectively contribute to the penal abolitionist rhizome. This includes chapters rearticulating abolitionism within influential recent theoretical writings and contemporary liberation movements. Each chapter is written by an author or authors closely associated with a different intellectual tradition or movement. The intention of bringing these diverse thinkers together is to help highlight the variety and interconnectedness of abolitionist voices.

What follows introduces the ensuing chapters. This is done in four parts, which reflect the four parts of the book. The first part entails a discussion of the strategic importance of hearing the voices of people directly oppressed, introducing the first three substantive chapters (Chapters 2–4). The second part considers the next four contributions in this volume, which highlight the development and diversity of penal abolitionist ideas (Chapters 5–8). The third part introduces three chapters detailing the scope of oppression and abolitionist responses (Chapters 9–11) and the fourth part concludes with a consideration of the final three chapters of the book (Chapters 12–14), which are focused on the ongoing struggle for liberation and justice.

Hearing oppressed voices

The voices of the oppressed have informed abolitionist ideas for centuries and remain pivotal in struggles against oppression. Hearing the voices of people in prison and their critique of power is also a central plank in penal abolitionist ethics (Scott, 2020a). Penal abolitionism is a living revolutionary philosophy with the explicit aim of radically transforming society through the direct actions and lived agency of individuals and communities currently experiencing legal repression and state violence (James, 2005). Oppressed voices of people in prison have borne witness to the destructive tendencies of penal power for literally hundreds of years.

The following are extracts from some letters written by people in prison advocating penal abolition that were originally sent to this author and one other in 2018:[2]

Thirteen years ago, I walked right into the pit of hell. Once you begin to do your time in here you can really just watch your years wither away with no remorse. Reconviction rates are so high because no one enjoys being locked up, but the turmoil and stress that prison takes on people creates a malice that builds up in the soul. No one can truly know the psychological harms of being incarcerated until they have been incarcerated. (Adrian)

Later, when back in prison, I slit my wrists due to a deep depression that had descended upon me. The officers found me unconscious in my cell from blood loss and had to life-flight me from the prison. When I came around, I was in a suicide-watch cell. (Douglas)

On suicide watch I was stripped naked, given a flimsy and short paper gown and placed in a cold cell without sheets or blankets. I spent my first night in prison naked and afraid ... I ended up in a prison known as 'the fort' on block 1, housing a mixture of disabled people. Everyone took psych meds and many slept for 10–16 hours a day, doing little in their waking hours aside from eating and smoking. Most had no family in contact with them. The simple truth is that prison is not the place to treat mental ill-health or drug addiction: the two main reasons why people end up in prison ... The overall effect of incarceration is to take those who have problems (poverty, addiction, mental health problems, learning disabilities, etc) and place them in a setting which is known not to help, or exacerbates those kind of problems. The dubious satisfaction of seeing 'bad people' punished should not lead us to support a system which is not helping people, or preventing help to future victims. (Richard)

My abolitionist thinking and praxis began to develop from the time I came into contact with systems of oppression that imbricated and pressed a mighty weight on my shoulders, which I continue to bare. I am at war with the carceral state in response to the violence of capital, aided by carcerality. Although I am wounded and my body and soul are bleeding, organizing against the carceral beast allows me to acquire knowledge that one can only gather by looking at its entrails. Personal encounters with the carceral oppression are the foundation of my transformation from a docile body into abolitionist in thought and praxis. This issue is a matter of life and death. The mission of the carceral state is to discipline and dispose of the bodies and the souls of the captives who are deemed inferior, while the role of the prison is to produce docile bodies that conform to the norms established by histories of power struggle, domination and subversion. However, these carceral spaces often miss the mark and produce empowered, albeit traumatized, subversive bodies and souls. I am one of those individuals who personally experienced and witnessed the violence of state-sanctioned oppression. I took a trip to the belly of the beast and I came out the other side: changed, traumatized, yet empowered. (Aisha)

Prisoner voices, like the preceding ones, evidence an institution characterized by violence, suffering and death (Scott, 2020a; Coyle and Scott, 2021). The prison place is firmly grounded in a philosophy of oppression. The revolutionary struggle against the yoke of penal oppression and state power is first and foremost the struggle of those directly impacted by it. Those resisting from the inside of the penal machinery are also though part of the struggle for freedom for all humanity. For those advocating liberative justice (see Scott, Chapter 14 in this volume), there is no real freedom for anyone unless all have genuinely tasted freedom. As Wole Soyinka (1985: 13) notes, when people remain 'silent in the face or tyranny' or 'submit willingly to the "daily humiliation of fear", the man [or woman] dies' – at least in a spiritual sense, if not corporeally. Resisting injustice is important for our dignity, self-respect and wellbeing. Soyinka (1985: 71) continues:

> And it is not merely the injustice within the prison that should be tackled, it is not only the fascist continuum of outside power within the prison that must be defeated though this, naturally, forms the bulk of a prisoner's struggles. Where necessary, where his social conscience is called upon, a commitment to absolute ideals cannot plead the excuse of immobilization to turn his back on the fight for an equitable society.

Certainly, the imprisonment of people from liberation movements focused on *political freedoms* have often led to stark criticism of the penal apparatus of the capitalist state. But as Soyinka (1985) infers, the oppression of political activists and those struggling for freedom can situate resistance to criminal injustice at the forefront of a wider struggle for a more equitable and socially just society.

The historical significance of the writings of autobiographical accounts of political prisoners has been well documented (James, 2003; Summers, 2004; Dearey, 2010; James, Chapter 3 in this volume). There is indeed a very long history of prisoners criticizing the prison place, and these testimonies are important expressions of penal failure over the last 200 and more years (Scott, 2018, 2020a). Peter Kropotkin's reflections on prison life are some of the most well-known abolitionist testimonies in the 19th century. Kropotkin was one of the foremost thinkers in anarchist and libertarian socialist thought and was imprisoned for his political beliefs and actions. In the following chapter Ruth Kinna situates Kropotkin's experience of Russian and French prisons with those of other anarchist prisoner writings, pointing to the systemic failure of the prison to meet its stated aims. Kinna (Chapter 2 in this volume) identifies how Kropotkin reached the abolitionist conclusion that prisons were unnecessary for a just society via a questioning of the legal definition of crime and an understanding that much human wrongdoing is shaped by societal injustice.

The contribution from Kinna (Chapter 2 in this volume) reminds us that abolitionists must be prepared to listen to and learn from the stories and narratives of prisoners, people who in the main are portrayed as possessing a 'suspect humanity' (James, 2005). Alongside Kropotkin's early abolitionist critique, it is also important to hear the calls for radical social change put forward in the writings of revolutionary political prisoners like Eldridge Cleaver, Wole Soyinka and Malcolm X. Engagement with the radical voices of those on the inside of the penal apparatus of the capitalist state can help generate revolutionary consciousness and spur on a wider liberation movement focused on the realization of freedom for all. In this sense, penal abolitionists today can gain inspiration from those who have fought against dehumanization and state repression in the past. The voice of the oppressed, sometimes across different sites of resistance and revolutionary struggle, are an important means of bearing witness to injustice.

It is the revolutionary voices of those who directly experience state repression and the struggles of their families and loved ones who arguably should lead the collective penal abolitionist struggle. Penal abolitionism as revolutionary praxis has found inspiration in the direct struggles for liberation by neo-Marxist activists, such as George Jackson (1941–1971), who spent virtually all his adult life in prison. Imprisoned initially for a minor property offence, while incarcerated he became a leading revolutionary activist against class and racial oppression, publishing his thoughts in 1970 in the book, *Soledad Brother: Letters from Prison* (Jackson, 1973). A year later, on 21 August 1971, Jackson was shot dead by prison officers in the yard of San Quentin Prison; the exact circumstances surrounding his death remain contested to this day. Jackson epitomized revolutionary praxis. When reflecting on the radicalization of his fellow Black prisoners, he wrote:

> They have become aware that their only hope lies in resistance. They have learned that resistance is actually possible. The holds are beginning to slip away. Very few men imprisoned for economic crimes or even crimes of passion against the oppressor feel that they are really guilty. Most of today's black convicts have come to understand that they are the most abused victims of an unrighteous order. (Jackson, 1973: np)

These reimaginings of who are the perpetrators and victims of social harms and the resulting struggle for freedom from penal repression are thus understood with the wider struggle against the racialized dimensions of carceral colonial capitalism. Jackson's (1973) influence on penal abolitionism in the last fifty years is enormous, although the extent of this may not always be fully apparent as his ideas have become absorbed within the abolitionist rhizome. Indeed, Jackson's Black revolutionary ideas appear to have a 'ghosted' presence in contemporary abolitionist writings (James, 2023). His 'delectable' ideas have become a 'contraband delicacy' (Woodward, 2014; James, 2023) that has been widely consumed by academic penal abolitionists. Drawing on the ideas of Vincent Woodward (2014), Joy James (2023) notes that the ideas of Jackson, born through his lived experience and revolutionary praxis, had direct influence on work of the French philosopher Michel Foucault (see also Taylor, Chapter 8 in this volume) and that Jackson was perhaps the greatest single influence on the abolitionist work of Angela Y. Davis (2003).

The contribution of former political prisoner Angela Y. Davis to abolitionist thought is the focus of the chapter by James (Chapter 3 in this volume). Davis, who studied under Herbert Marcuse at the Frankfurt School and was hugely influenced by the Communist Party of the US, was politicized by George Jackson, and this association precipitated her incarceration for nearly a year and a half in the early 1970s. Yet unlike the case of Black revolutionary Jackson, the campaign to free Angela Y. Davis became an international *cause célèbre* among leftists around the world: influential philosophers like Michel Foucault and Gilles Deleuze, and famous musicians, such as Nina Simon, Aretha Franklin, John Lennon and Mick Jagger, all publicly supported her cause (James, 2023; James, Chapter 3 in this volume).

In her chapter, James (Chapter 3 in this volume) acknowledges the crucial role Davis played in the creation of the grass roots liberation movement *Critical Resistance* and subsequent 'prison industrial complex' abolitionist interventions in the 1990s and early 2000s, but also highlights her failure at the same time to sufficiently prioritize Black radicalism and liberation struggles. Despite her achievements, James argues that Davis failed to encapsulate the spirit of the revolutionary legacy of Jackson and other Black political prisoners. This failure has resulted in the marginalization of certain revolutionary voices and the sanitation of political resistance to state oppression within academic abolitionism (James, 2021). Such a dilution of political commitment and liberalization of struggle may have enhanced the global celebrity status of Davis (for example, in December 2020, a deal was announced between Davis and a profit-orientated fashion label, 'Heroes of Blackness', for her image to feature on clothing such as hoodies and t-shirts),[3] but on the face of it does little, if not nothing, to further emancipatory politics and praxis for the most oppressed peoples.

As James has noted in her chapter and elsewhere, there is a clear *presence* of Black radicalism and revolutionary thought in such academic abolitionism and yet at the same time, there is also a profound *absence* of a full-on commitment to revolutionary praxis and the goal of liberation

(James, 2023; James, Chapter 3 in this volume). This concern sits alongside another that James (Chapter 3 in this volume) raises in her chapter – the important concern that abolitionist cadres can sometimes lead to 'narrative appropriation' and erasure of oppressed voices. Abolitionists must listen, learn to learn from and patiently hear the voice of the estranged Other rather than speak for them or, even worse, displace their voice altogether (Scott, 2016). When people fall silent in the face of oppression, 'the [hu]man dies' (Soyinka,1985). Abolitionists must passionately work against the silencing of oppressed voices, and certainly should never be part of the silencing process.

Further caution on the adoption of prisoner lived experience in academic discourse is garnished in the following chapter too by Lisa Guenther (Chapter 4 in this volume), albeit on different grounds. Penal abolitionists, she argues, should act with caution when engaging with notions of prisoner 'lived experience'. It would be a mistake to give epistemic privilege to all voices from the inside, or to forget that prisoners may draw upon existing cultural scripts when giving voice (see also Scott, 2016). In a well-made case, Guenther (Chapter 4 in this volume) argues that phenomenology is perhaps the best-suited framework through which to consider prisoner voice. Like Soyinka, Kropotkin, Jackson and others cited previously, Guenther insightfully notes that personal experience and biographical knowledge of incarceration become valuable when they are directly connected to a critical analysis of power. This questioning of power, when combined with considerations of theory, history and social structures of domination and oppression, is the voice abolitionists should amplify. She advocates a *critical phenomenology*, which, in echoing Karl Marx's famous 'eleventh thesis on Feuerbach', aims not only to understand the world, but also to change it. Guenther (Chapter 4 in this volume) emphasizes throughout her chapter the importance of a critical phenomenological analysis of carceral power for abolitionist interventions today, providing a critical lens through which it is possible to hear and fruitfully engage with oppressed abolitionist voices within the penal machinery and their calls for liberation on both the inside and outside of the prison walls.

Abolitionist ideas

Penal abolitionist ideas have existed since state punishments were first conceived and deployed. Abolitionist sentiments are present in both ancient Eastern and Western philosophies and theologies. One example is the *Tao Te Ching* (Le Guin, 1997), purportedly written by the great teacher 'Lao Tzu', in China in the 6th century BCE and is the foundation text of Taoism. The anti-authoritarian ethics found in Taoism probably derive from prehistoric Chinese folk law and question the merits of human-made laws, state control and legal coercion. Human-made laws create infringements and hence crime and criminals (something now widely incorporated into criminological thought and abolitionist theory, albeit via the labelling theory of the 1960s – see, for example, Becker [1963], Barton et al [2007] and Dellwing [Chapter 13 in this volume] for discussion of its critical criminological application).

Abolitionist sentiments can also be found among early Christian communities and the doctrine of Christianity, which emerged some 2,000 years ago. Such abolitionist sentiments, for example, can be found in the writings of the 4th-century Neoplatonian Christian theologian Gregory of Nazianzus. Indeed, inspired by the life and moral teachings of the historical figure of Jesus Christ, Lee Griffith (1993) argues that there is a scriptural association between the nature of imprisonment and death. Prisons are haunted by the presence of death (incorporating notions of civil death, corporeal death and social death – see Scott, 2018, 2020a) and as such stood in opposition to the doctrine of new life found in the promise of Christianity. Griffith (1993), like Marxist-inspired liberation theologies (see, for example, Miranda, 1977), emphasizes the importance of liberation from oppression and freedom for all people in Christianity. Human-made laws were also seen as profoundly limited and Christians were often advised to avoid recourse to law, including the criminal law (see Scott [1996] for discussion). Like Taoism, the way to virtue in Christianity is through the promotion of values such as forgiveness, compassion and love for other people rather than a focus on punishment and penal law.

A contemporary retelling of Christian abolition theology can found in the chapter by Hannah Bowman. Bowman (Chapter 5 in this volume) notes the interconnecting themes of liberation and reconciliation in Christian theology. Drawing upon both Black liberation and womanist theologies, Bowman (Chapter 5 in this volume) shows how contemporary Christian abolitionist theologies may well be a 'primary root' or 'radicle' of abolitionist thought, but that they are also influenced by other lines of abolitionist reasoning, thus evidencing further the reach of the 'abolitionist rhizome' and the importance of interconnection.

In his scholarly book *Penal Abolition*, Vincenzo Ruggerio (2010) attempts to make deep-rooted connections between the ideas of penal abolitionism and Western philosophy, noting the 'anti-platonic' underpinnings of much of penal abolitionism. Abolitionist sentiments (though not full-blown abolitionist thought), for example, can be found in the virtue ethics of Aristotle and some limited connections can also be made with the critique of free will and blame by Spinoza.[4] Ruggerio (2010) also indicated that the insights of the great German thinker Friedrich Nietzsche were relevant for penal abolitionisms. Caius Brandão (Chapter 6 in this volume) elaborates further on the abolitionist thought of this hugely influential German philosopher. Brandão (Chapter 6 in this volume) argues that Nietzsche aimed to overcome the punitive logic of punishment by advocating an 'alternative *mode of valuation*' for evaluation and responding to crime and criminals. Questioning in particular Christian values and associated moral modes of valuation of blame and guilt, alongside exposing the illusion of free will, Nietzsche argued that we should not punish criminals as 'scoundrels'. Rather, we should aim to understand their behaviour within the constraints placed upon them by social contexts and find a new way of evaluating what they have done, which can facilitate therapeutic interventions based on scientific wisdom (Brandão, Chapter 6 in this volume).

So there are undoubtedly traces of abolitionisms across a broad spectrum of thinking, indicating that the pathway to penal abolition has many different routes (and roots), some of which easily complement each other, and others that do not so easily do. One of the most significant contemporary inspirations of penal abolition is *The Politics of Abolition*, first published over fifty years ago in 1974 by the Norwegian sociologist Thomas Mathiesen. Mathiesen (1974) was inspired by Marxism and laid much of the groundwork for the expansion of penal abolitionist ideas to the present today. Marxist abolitionism also found its roots in *British Prisons*, first published in 1979, by Mike Fitzgerald and Joe Sim (1979), who provided a devastating material analysis of the role prisons play in upholding class inequalities. Jon Burnett (Chapter 7 in this volume) takes the debate on the political economy of abolitionism back to the early writings of Karl Marx, demonstrating how the insights of Marx have relevance to our understanding of the deconstruction of crime in the present. Burnett (Chapter 7 in this volume) argues that the conceptual tools of a Marxist analysis remain integral to grassroots abolitionist organizing in the present and can help realize the goal of prison abolition in the future.

In a manner which sidestepped rather than contradicted the political economies of Marxist and other socialist inspired analysis, the French philosopher Michel Foucault focused on the centrality of the prison in the very emergence of modernity, inspiring future generations with his critical insights into disciplinary power and the 'carceral continuum'. In his hugely influential book *Discipline and Punish* (which may have been better titled in English as 'discipline and surveillance'), first published in English in 1977, Foucault tied together his rich theoretical analysis of the rise of the disciplinary society with his activism for the French abolitionist group GiP. Foucault (1977) emphasized the importance of connecting with prisoner movements and providing a platform for the voice of the subjugated. In this sense, like Mathiesen and other abolitionists before him, the voice of the oppressed was key to the struggle against penal repression.

Bringing this part of the book to a close, Chloë Taylor (Chapter 8 in this volume) provides an overview of the distinct contribution of Foucault to penal abolitionism, including his important claim that whereas the reformed prison has consistently failed to meet its stated goals, it does appear to meet other social functions in advanced capitalist societies. This argument, sometimes known as 'left functionalism' (Cohen, 1985), has provided highly influential and Taylor (Chapter 8 in this volume) details the way in which some of Foucault's ideas and concepts have been deployed and expanded upon in the writings of critical prison studies scholars to critique a 'racist, xenophobic, colonial, sexist, homophobic, transphobic and ableist juridical-legal system.' (Taylor, Chapter 8 in this volume). This recent work has also attempted to address some of the limitations with *Discipline and Punish* and to ensure that Foucault's work continues to speak to present conditions under carceral colonial capitalism.

The scope of oppression

The focus of the book then turns to the scope of oppression. Anti-chattel slavery is often associated with penal abolitionism and the modern prison is often conceived as one aspect of the 'afterlife' of slavery (Davis, 2003, 2005; James, 2005; Saleh-Hanna, Chapter 9 in this volume). Calls for the abolition of chattel slavery have a long history – dating back to those made by Jean Bodin in the 1570s or Antonio Vieira in the 1650s – but chattel slavery was largely taken for granted in moral and political philosophy until the late 1700s. British anti-chattel-slavery abolitionism was inspired by economic concerns around the unproductivity of 'coerced labour' (that is, chattel slavery) and moral arguments that chattel slavery was a 'social evil' that contravened 'English Liberty' (Brown, 2006). The moral arguments only really gained political significance following the defeat of the British in the American War of Independence in 1783 as a form of distancing them from victorious American slaveholders (that is, rejecting the rejectors). Indeed, 'English liberty' (and the moral condemnation of slavery) and free trade were considered as something that could justify further imperial expansion around the globe, especially Africa (Brown, 2006). The bourgeois British anti-chattel-slavery movement, mobilized across 50 years from 1788 to 1838, may well have drawn upon increasing grassroots support against the slave trade, but they were also very much part of the establishment (Brown, 2006). Many of the British anti-chattel-slavery abolitionists, such as Granville Sharp, Thomas Clarkson and William Wilberforce, benefited from aristocratic patronage, wealth and/or had access to the political elite. It was these members of the British establishment who most strongly argued that chattel slavery stood against 'English liberty' and infringed upon basic British freedoms.

Anti-chattel slavery thus differentiated the British from the Americans and appeared to reinstate a sense of 'moral superiority' over their former colony. Yet rather than being tied to emancipatory politics and praxis or calls for radical social transformation, the British anti-chattel-slavery abolitionists were reformers who were looking to strengthen the moral legitimacy of the current social, political and economic order. In so doing, they worked closely with the British state to achieve their aims. By the 1830s, chattel slavery had become the unacceptable face of labour exploitation, state racism and class domination in Britain and its Empire (Brown, 2006). The slave trade was abolished in 1807 in Britain and the delayed introduction of the Slavery Abolition Act (1833) brought an end to slavery in the British Empire in 1838.

The British anti-slavery abolitionist focus was on a distinctly 'British [English] freedom [liberty]' which obscured the problem of 'wage slavery' and the appalling living and working conditions of people exercising their noncoerced 'free labour'. Further, several of the British anti-chattel-slavery abolitionists, including William Wilberforce, Samuel Romily and Thomas Fowell Buxton, were also prominent penal reformers. Indeed, Wilberforce unsuccessfully acted as the advocate for Jeremy Bentham's proposals for building a 'Panopticon prison' with the British Cabinet in the early 1800s (Scott, 2020b). The British anti-chattel-slavery abolitionists did not work on the grounds of revolutionary praxis or ground their critique of dehumanization within the everyday lived struggle and voices of the oppressed, and nor was their ultimate objective emancipation and liberation. The anti-chattel-slavery abolitionists looked to accumulate what has become known as 'moral capital', not liberative justice (Kane, 2001; Brown, 2006; Scott, 2020b).

Yet, the story of anti-chattel-slavery abolition and its links to penal abolitionism in the present is clearly quite different in North America. The connections between the anti-chattel-slavery abolitionism of Frederick Douglas and the prison as an example of chattel-slavery afterlife is very strong in the penal abolitionism of activists such as Angela Y. Davis (2003; 2005). James (2005) also makes this link when reflecting on the importance of conceiving contemporary prisoners as neo-slaves. Drawing on the lived experiences of chattel slaves in the 1800s, who won their freedom through pain, personal struggle and triumph, James (2005) argues that it is important for abolitionists everywhere to understand what is required by caged bodies to resist and survive state violence. It is the voices and narratives of the slaves – the people who directly experienced the oppression of slavery and resisted the dehumanizing power of the slave owners – rather than the British bourgeois abolitionists that should be the inspiration for penal abolitionists working for liberative justice today.

The influence of the Canadian anti-chattel-slavery abolitionism on penal abolition today is also evident. Viviane Saleh-Hanna (Chapter 9 in this volume) in her chapter shows how the shadow of the 'slavery industrial complex' underscored industrialization, the expansion of white settler nation states, and the emergence and consolidation of contemporary carceral colonial capitalist power. She notes how its 'haunting structures and enduring tentacles [continue to] exist within the carceral pathways it paved' (Saleh-Hanna, Chapter 9 in this volume). To support her argument, she historically maps the slavery industrial complex through Canada's maritime fishing industries, New France's fur trade and New England's cotton mills in northeastern regions of the US.

No discussion of penal abolition today can ignore the importance of abolitionist ideas and movements from the Global South or those engaged in unpicking colonial legacies from around the world. The historical advancement of carceral colonial capitalism (itself intertwined with that of slavery and its afterlives) and the legacies of racist social order and white supremacy are central to struggles for liberative justice. Carceral colonial capitalism is an expression of colonial oppression and control of First Nation populations. Colonialism, such as through the British Empire, denied the full humanity of Indigenous populations, criminalizing its people and vilifying their culture and previous ways of life. The imposed white Western colonialist hegemony, and its penal practices, directly contravened longstanding Indigenous responses to harms that focused on the rebuilding and repairing of relationships damaged through harm. The colonial catastrophes of genocide, mass rape and brutal state violence – through internment in concentration camps, massacres, expulsion from land, destruction of cultural heritage and everyday cruelty and physical violence – continue to haunt those resisting oppression and domination today.

Thalia Anthony and Harry Blagg (Chapter 10 in this volume) argue that liberation from the brutal violence of colonization cannot be completed until the prison has been abolished and power, control and sovereignty have been returned to First Nations communities. They note how colonial power has reduced First Nations peoples' lives in countries like Australia to a 'bare life'. They point out how First Nations people are now the most 'hyperincarcerated' population in the world, indicating just how deeply imbricated colonialism and incarceration continue to be (Anthony and Blagg, Chapter 10 in this volume). They highlight the ongoing harms of carceral colonial capitalism by drawing upon an 'Agembian framework' to position the prison within a 'constellation of intersecting carceral camps'.

Another example of ongoing harms of carceral colonial capitalism and the struggle for justice in the Global South is highlighted in the chapter by Valeria Vegh Weis (Chapter 11 in this volume). Feminism has long been associated with penal abolitionism. This has had two main strands: the disproportionate penal harms experienced by women in prison and the need to protect women and children from physical, emotional and sexual violence. Vegh Weis discusses the emergence of a fourth wave of feminism in Argentina, identifying three nonpunitive approaches to violence currently being fostered in that country, as well as detailing some of the lessons and challenges that inform Southern abolitionist feminism today.

Struggles for liberation and justice

This leads us to the fourth and final part of this volume: the struggle for liberation and justice. The struggle for justice is central to multiple liberation campaigns and is key to calls for penal abolition. Penal abolitionist ideas have emerged in and alongside liberation movements as a form of revolutionary praxis (see also earlier discussion of Jackson and Soyinka about the importance of political engagement and resistance for human dignity). In many ways the different roots and routes to penal abolitionism reflect a cry for *liberative justice* – the demand for freedom for the oppressed (see Scott, Chapter 14 in this volume). This is not just because legal coercion, prisons and punishment are one of the key tools used by the state in the suppression of liberation movements. The harms of penal incarceration show how the penal law itself is a manifestation of oppression. Abolitionists cannot remain scientific, neutral, detached and entirely objective observers when faced with so much evidence of the suffering of those with the least power initiated through violence by, for or in the interests of, the powerful (Scott and Sim, 2023). Direct engagement in the struggle for liberation is ethically and politically imperative for libertarian socialists and abolitionists (Scott and Bell, 2025). As the critical insights of Joy James discussed earlier in this chapter remind us, the penal abolitionist rhizome and revolutionary liberative praxis are conjoined. Penal oppression – and the indignities, violence and deprivations of both positive and negative freedom that characterize the penal system – stand in direct contrast to the ethics and politics of liberative justice (Scott, 2020a; Scott, Chapter 14 in this volume). Thus, when struggling for liberation, the lack of freedom of those held in captivity and suffering under the yoke of the penal law directly contradicts the freedom fighters' commitment to a broader emancipatory logic.

The liberation struggles and movements associated with penal abolitionisms aim to change the way people think about the institutions of the penal law. As indicated previously, penal abolitionism is as old as any institution of the penal system itself. As will be shown in the following chapters, criminal and penal laws have always followed the interests of privilege, status and power, and as such have always been resisted by the powerless and disenfranchised communities they have victimized. State violence has led to anti-colonial, anti-slave, anti-racist liberation movements and other uprisings promoting the liberation of humanity. Under the yoke of carceral colonial capitalism, such revolutionary praxis remains as urgent as ever (Soyinka, 1985).

In the 21st century, penal abolitionism has flourished through its connections with liberation movements. One key struggle today is around preventing impending climate catastrophe and ecocide (Scott, 2022). Led by climate rebels, such as *Extinction Rebellion* and *Just Stop Oil* in the UK, this struggle is not just about having a better future, but having any kind of future at all. The existential problem we face today is not just climate heating, but full-scale ecocide (Whyte, 2020). The concept 'ecocide' was first coined by the international lawyer Richard Falk, who drafted the first ever ecocide convention back in 1973. His proposals were never adopted in international law, but as global warming has become increasingly evident (and indeed, accelerating as half of the CO_2 in the air has been produced since 1990), questions about what the world is going to do about impending ecocide have become some the most important and debated in the world today (Whyte, 2020; Scott, 2022).

Ecocide is basically the deliberate destruction of the capacity to sustain human life on planet earth (Whyte, 2020). Ecocide involves several different forms of planetary destruction, including annihilating longstanding natural habitats resulting in the extinction of large numbers of animal and plant species; the toxic pollution of the air and water, including by plastics, household and industrial waste; the death of ecosystems on land and sea; and the rapid increase in carbon gases that are raising the temperature of the planet to dangerous levels for future life on earth (Whyte, 2020).

There have been literally thousands of attempts all around the world to use the law, including the criminal law, to prevent environmental disasters. In the main, they have failed. A civil legal approach is important but alone not enough. The legal response currently gaining the most publicity and financial support is the introduction of a new criminal offence of ecocide in international criminal law. The main global advocates of the new crime of ecocide are *Stop Ecocide International*, a group that wants to add a fifth crime of ecocide to the Rome Statute of the International Criminal Court (ICC). As David Whyte (2020) has powerfully argued, the problem is that not only is this new international law, if it is ever enacted, destined to fail because the criminal law cannot effectively control the deeply ingrained ecocidal tendencies of the capitalist corporation, but that it may even make things worse. Whyte (2020) indicates to us four reasons why this is the case.

First, as penal abolitionists have long noted, there is no evidence that the criminal law is an effective way of sending a message of deterrence (Scott, 2018). There is a difference between what *Stop Ecocide International* intends for the law and how the law would be interpreted by corporations and states. Further, the major oil and fossil fuel companies have known about the deadly harms of their work since at least the 1970s. Their response so far has not been to change their focus or operational practices, but to renew their efforts to exploit even greater profits (Whyte, 2020).

Second, the law would likely focus on a few 'bad apple' corporations and their chief executives. This may have the perverse effect of actually adding legitimacy to those companies and states that are not prosecuted.

Criminalization of corporations, for example, may work in the interests of the global corporate elite as it will only focus on outliers when the problem of ecocide is much more widespread and deeply ingrained in the organization and structure of the global economy and its markets (Whyte, 2020).

Third, the ICC is almost completely ineffective in terms of responding to serious and deadly global harm and wrongdoing. Several industrialized nations (such as the US) are not under the jurisdiction of the ICC. Further, up until now, the nations most likely to be prosecuted by the ICC were from Africa (and had lost a civil war), which is not where the people who run or own those corporations destroying the planet reside (Whyte, 2020).

Fourth, the ICC and other instruments of the criminal law will fail to hold those who benefit the most to account. Through complex chains of ownership and the legal rules and protections which limit the liabilities of the owners of corporations, the corporate structure effectively creates virtual immunity from any possible corporate punishments that can be sentenced by the law courts. Worse still, the new law could give the impression that something is being done to prevent ecocide and thus result in complacency or distract attention and resources away from those interventions that might actually stop the onset of the age of extinction (Whyte, 2020).

The philosophical roots of *Stop Ecocide International* in British anti-chattel-slavery abolitionism are hugely revealing of its limitations. There are clearly similarities between the British slavery abolitionists in the past (as previously discussed) and *Stop Ecocide International* today (Scott, 2022). This insight sheds new light on why the calls for an ecocide criminal law may prove to be counterproductive. Earlier, it was noted that the call for anti-chattel-slavery abolition in Britain was not rooted in emancipatory moral principles, but was rather about attempting to reinstate a sense of 'moral superiority' and 'moral capital' to the British ruling elite, and such a conception of establishing the moral superiority and moral capital of the 'global elite' today is something which may be an aspiration of some of those advocating the proposed ecocide law. Any prosecutions that arose from the ICC ecocide law would probably be limited and restricted to only those corporations that are the very worst and most obvious offenders; and most likely smaller companies based in relatively impoverished nations.

The British anti-slavery abolitionists 200 years ago wanted to aid rather than restrict the accumulation of economic capital. Today *Stop Ecocide International* wishes to do nothing to damage shareholder profits and economic growth. The British anti-slavery abolitionists advocated the ending of 'slave labour', but not 'wage slavery' and other more subtle forms of coerced labour, which generated 'moral capital'. Today *Stop Ecocide International* highlights the importance of discarding only environmentally destructive forms of capitalist accumulation. In recent years there has been sustained high-level media advertising and 'greenwashing' policies to convince the consumer that they are buying ecologically sustainable products. The stakes – the very existence of a planet that can sustain life – are too high for a law that merely further greenwashes corporate power. This is a long way from a commitment to revolutionary praxis. As Whyte (2020) reminds us, not only have 20 corporations collectively produced 35 per cent of all fossil fuel emissions since 1965, but also that since 1988, just 100 have collectively produced 71 per cent of all fossil fuel emissions. Whereas the focus on saving the planet in the media is often on what ordinary people can do, the massive profits of the rich, who are literally bleeding the earth dry, are barely highlighted. It is estimated that 737 corporations control about 80 per cent of the wealth and a mere 147 corporations control about 40 per cent of it (Whyte, 2020). Many of these corporations are directly implicated in ecocide and it is here where our focus should be for radical change (Scott and Sim, 2023).

The lessons are clear for both anti-chattel-slavery abolitionists and those looking to promote the criminal law as a way of controlling the ecological harms of power. Both can be co-opted and utilized in the interests of the capitalist state and can inform and bolster the moral sensibilities of the ruling elite. These examples of how 'moral capital' (Kane, 2001; Brown, 2006; Scott, 2020b; Scott, 2022) can be accumulated demonstrate that it is essential that connections are made across a wide range of sites of exploitation, repression and domination, as indicated in Part III of this book. Engagement with the political, social and economic elite will not deliver liberative justice, radical social and economic transformation, or prevent ecological destruction *unless* it is strongly tied/connected to the 'view from below' and infused with socialist emancipatory politics and praxis. What we can learn from the British anti-chattel-slavery abolitionists is that when the ruling elite champion a given moral cause, it may well be for the 'moral capital' that can be transferred to them rather than an honest and noble intervention, such as trying to prevent the further deepening of planetary wide ecocide (Scott, 2020b).

Liberation never comes from above. It always comes from below, and this is very much the perspective of Part IV of the book and the chapter by Stephens-Griffin and Brock (Chapter 12 in this volume), who argue that carceral and ecological harms, such as ecocide, go hand in hand. They suggest that it is essential that the struggles for 'ecological justice', human and other species liberation from oppression and penal abolitionisms are deeply interconnected. They call for the development of an explicitly ecological abolitionist framework – an 'abolition ecology' – as a means of resisting carceral colonial capitalism. They argue that as carceral and ecological harms are closely entwined, any such struggle for liberation must also be so. Significantly, they call for a 'total liberation perspective' as a means of 'unifying diverse and disparate liberation movements' under one coherent revolutionary struggle for emancipation and justice.

The abolitionist struggle for justice *must come from below* – from the oppressed and their families and loved ones – and requires the commitment of ordinary rebels to revolutionary praxis. Radical emancipatory politics must be rooted in a philosophy of hope that can generate motivation and with a will for change. This necessitates consideration of activist voices, who engage directly in the struggle, and how their voice can be amplified and heard. Michael Dellwing (Chapter 13 in this volume) offers a considered analysis of the implications (both pitfalls and possibilities) for abolitionist activist voices to be heard in the time of a post-mass media society. Drawing on the tradition of labelling theory and social problem studies, Dellwing charts the downturn of the influence of centralized state/corporate media systems and a resurgence in critical challenges to state power, including punitive power. He argues that counterhegemonic activism, including the revolutionary praxis of penal abolitionisms, has rarely been as strong as it is today, but that the centralized media organizations are attempting to claw back their power by denouncing leftist activism through a 'moral panic' around the dissemination of 'fake news'. Only the state/corporate media (so the state/corporate media argue) can deliver the news in a trustworthy manner! However, Dellwing, like many sociology of media scholars in the past, strongly contests this view, arguing that it is essential that abolitionist activists/activist-scholars maintain their commitment to decentralized forms of social media and the amplification of their voice outside of the state-corporate media machine.

Further, it is important to recognize that struggles for liberative justice remain unfinished. Struggles for freedom from oppression, domination and exploitation are constant and ongoing. Political commitments grounded in the philosophy of hope for progressive change need to be constantly renewed (Gramsci, 1971; Scott, 2020a). Scott (Chapter 14 in this volume) argues that abolitionists and must engage in 'subversive thinking' – that is, lines of thought that can be of assistance in the upending of the existing social order. This aspect of revolutionary praxis means subverting and reframing the focus of harm so that serious harms are understood as being generated through the criminogenic nature of power. Subversive thinking should be in the service of liberation movements, and for Scott, this means connecting penal abolitionisms with the emancipatory politics and praxis of libertarian socialism (see also Scott and Bell, 2025).

Abolitionist activist-scholars should ensure they meet their ethical 'response-abilities' and bear witness to injustice, while at the same time remaining part of the political dialogue (Scott, Chapter 14 in this volume; Scott 2020a). Penal abolition is a philosophy of hope standing directly in the pathway of the philosophy of oppression. Penal abolitionists therefore need to find ways so that they can meet the (contradictory) ethical demand of responding to and ameliorating the pain and suffering of the oppressed in the here and how, while at the same working towards their genuine liberation in the future through revolutionary praxis. Such is the hope and aspiration that sits very much at the centre of the penal abolitionist rhizome.

Notes

1. For Deleuze and Guattari, (1987: 21), this focus on the middle can be referred to as a 'plateau'. In their words, 'a plateau is always in the middle, not at the beginning or the end. A rhizome is made of plateaus'.
2. Between 2017 and 2018, Michael Coyle and I received more than 120 letters from people in prison all around the world. All the people in prison cited here are from North America (the US or Canada) and the extracts are drawn from letters we received but were not published in the *International Handbook of Penal Abolition* (Coyle and Scott, 2021). Consent to publish extracts of the letters was given by the authors.
3. A portion of the profits from the sales go to a group called 'Dream Defenders', which is working towards defunding the police, and a further prison abolition organization called 'Underground Grit'.
4. Though Spinoza questioned many aspects of free will and blameworthiness, he still appears to offer a defence of punishment in his writings.

References

Barton, A., Corteen, K., Scott, D. and Whyte, D. (2007) 'Conclusion: expanding the criminological imagination', in A. Barton, K. Corteen, D. Scott and D. Whyte (eds) *Expanding the Criminological Imagination: Critical Readings in Criminology*, London: Routledge, pp 198–213.

Becker, H. (1963) *Outsiders*, New York: Free Press.

Bianchi, H. (1991) 'Abolitionism in the past, present and future', in Z. Lasocik, M. Płatek and I. Rzeplińska (eds), *Abolitionism in History: On Another Way of Thinking (Papers from the IV International Conference on Penal Abolition)*, Warsaw: Uniwersytetu Warszawskiego, pp 9–15.

Brown, C. (2006) *Moral Capital: Foundations of British Abolitionism*, Chapel Hill: University of North Carolina Press.

Cohen, S. (1985) *Visions of Social Control*, Cambridge: Polity Press.

Coyle, M. and Scott, D. (eds) (2021) *International Handbook of Penal Abolition*, Abingdon: Routledge.

Davis, A. (2003) *Are Prisons Obsolete?*, New York: Seven Stories Press.

Davis, A. (2005) *Abolition Democracy*, New York: Seven Stories Press.

Dearey, M. (ed.) (2010) *Radicalisation: The Life Writings of Political Prisoners*, Abingdon: Routledge.

Deleuze, G. and Guattari, F. (1987) *A Thousand Plateaus: Capitalism and Schizophrenia*, Minneapolis: University of Minnesota Press.

Fitzgerald, M. and Sim, J. (1979) *British Prisons*, Oxford: Basil Blackwell.

Foucault, M. (1977) *Discipline and Punish*, Harmondsworth: Penguin.

Glissant, E. (2020) *Introduction to a Poetics of Diversity*, Liverpool: Liverpool University Press.

Gramsci, A. (1971) *Selections from the Prison Notebooks*, London: Lawrence & Wishart.

Griffith, L. (1993) *The Fall of the Prison: Biblical Perspectives on the Prison*, New York: W.B. Eerdmans Publishing Company.

Jackson, G. (1973) *Soledad Brother: Letters from Prison*, Harmondsworth: Penguin (online version, unpaginated). Available from: https://www.historyisaweapon.com/defcon1/soledadbro.html [Accessed 19 September 2023].

James, J. (ed.) (2003) *Imprisoned Intellectuals: America's Political Prisoners Write on Life, Liberation and Rebellion*, Lanham, MD: Rowman & Littlefield.

James, J. (2005) 'Introduction', in J. James (ed.) *The New Abolitionists: (Neo) Slave Narratives and Contemporary Prison Writings*, Albany: University of New York Press, pp xx-xxiii.

James, J. (2021) 'Foreword', in M. Coyle and D. Scott, (eds) *International Handbook of Penal Abolition*, Abingdon: Routledge, pp xx–xxiii.

James, J. (2023) '"The delectable negro": George Jackson, Michel Foucault, Angela Davis and the consumption of Black rebellion'. Unpublished English-language version of a paper published in a French-language journal in 2023.

Kane, J. (2001) *The Politics of Moral Capital*, Cambridge: Cambridge University Press.

Le Guin, U. (1997) *Lao Tzu: A Book about the Way and the Power of the Way*, London: Shambhala Publications.

Mathiesen, T. (1974) *The Politics of Abolition*, Oxford: Martin Robertson.

Miranda, J.P. (1977) *Marx and the Bible: A Critique of the Philosophy of Oppression*, London: Orbis Books.

Ruggerio, V. (2010) *Penal Abolition*, Oxford: Clarendon Press.

Scott, D. (1996) *Heavenly Confinement?*, London: LAP.

Scott, D. (2016) 'Hearing the voice of the estranged other: abolitionist ethical hermeneutics', *Kriminologisches Journal*, 3: 184–201.

Scott, D. (2018) *Against Imprisonment*, Hook: Waterside Press.

Scott, D. (2020a) *For Abolition*, Hook: Waterside Press.

Scott, D. (2020b) 'Abolitionism must come from below: a critique of British anti-slavery abolition', *HERC*, Open University. Available from: https://oucriminology.wordpress.com/2020/06/23/abolitionism-must-come-from-below-a-critique-of-british-anti-slavery-abolition/ [Accessed 15 September 2024].

Scott, D. (2022) 'Stopping ecocide and climate catastrophe: a critique of the criminal law', *HERC*, Open University. Available from: https://www.open.ac.uk/researchcentres/herc/blog/stopping-ecocide-and-climate-catastrophe-critique-criminal-law [Accessed 15 September 2024].

Scott, D. and Sim, J. (eds) (2023) *Demystifying Power, Crime and Social Harm*, London: Palgrave Macmillan.

Scott, D. and Bell, E. (eds) (2025) *Envisioning Abolition*, Bristol: Bristol University Press.

Soyinka, W. (1985) *The Man Died: His Classic Prison Writings*, London: Arrow Books.

Summers, J. (ed.) (2004) *Late-Medieval Prison Writing and the Politics of Autobiography*, Oxford: Oxford University Press.
Whyte, D. (2020) *Ecocide*, Manchester: Manchester University Press.
Woodward, V. (2014) *The Delectable Negro: Human Consumption and Homoeroticism within US Slave Culture,* New York: New York University Press.

PART I

Voices of the Oppressed

2

Kropotkin and the Anarchist Case for Prison Abolition

Ruth Kinna

Introduction: Prison testimonies

Anarchism has a substantial body of literature attesting to the harshness and corruption of prison life. Firsthand accounts include Louise Michel's description of the penal colony in New Caledonia (1981 [1886]), David Nicoll's *Life in English Prisons* (2005 [1895]), Clément Duval's *Outrage: An Anarchist Memoir of the Penal Colony* (2021 [1907]) and Alexander Berkman's *Prison Memoirs of an Anarchist* (1992 [1912]). Berkman's depiction of the 'monster shapes' that haunted his release vividly capture the nature of the ordeal: the 'cries of pain', the 'agony of the dungeon', the 'sickening thud of the riot clubs on the prisoner's head' and the 'harrowing' solitude (Berkman, 1992 [1912]: 97). His account is echoed by contemporary writers. The Black liberation activist Assata Shakur (b. 1947) records an encounter with Mrs Butterworth, warden of the Middlesex County Jail, New Jersey. Shakur was being held on murder charges following a shootout with police in 1973:

> Two or three days after i started, the warden, Miss Bitch, accompanied by some male guards, visited me.
> 'We hear that you are running around your cell', she said.
> 'You will have to stop this activity at once.'
> 'What? Why?'
> 'Because you are disturbing the people downstairs.'
> 'What people?'
> 'There is an office underneath you and you are disturbing the workers.'

'Are you crazy? They'll just have to be disturbed. I don't run for that long anyhow. If you let me out into the yard to exercise with the other women, i'll stop running around by cell.'

'I order you to stop running around your room.'

'I don't remember joining you army', i said. 'When i join your army, then you can order me around.' (Shakur, 1987: 55)

Maria Alyokhina (b. 1988) remembers her arrival in 2012 at a prison colony in the Perm region of the Ural Mountains. She was serving a two-year sentence for hooliganism aggravated by religious hatred after taking part in Pussy Riot's 'punk prayer' in Moscow's Christ the Saviour Cathedral:

'Attention, women!' shouts a prisoner attendant ...

Whenever we hear 'Attention!', we have to stand up and say, 'Good day!' in chorus. These are the rules. It is the first lesson in politeness, which I must master, because to reform is to know and fulfil the orders ...

'Who was sleeping during the recitation of regulations?' the guard shouts, entering the barracks. We remain silent.
...
In the corner of the room there is a surveillance camera. This is how they were able to see that one of us sitting on the wooden benches had discreetly rested her head on her palm and dozed off. We all wear identical checked uniforms. We look so much alike it must be hard to distinguish whose head had dipped down. We stand in our places, not budging, and look at each other. Someone smiles, another whispers, and a third sighs wearily. Someone else stares at the others' faces with interest. I am not interested, and I don't think this is funny. Because I know who was caught on camera sleeping for ten minutes. It was me ...

'Out of the room, everyone! It's time for a search' ... and it becomes suddenly clear to everyone why the guards are here. It is not about who was sleeping. It's the search.

The first rule of every search is that it's unexpected. Russia has known this since the 1930s ... This is so that they can take you by surprise, disarm you. Then they can take whatever they want from you with no resistance. So they drop into our barracks, somewhere in Russia in the middle of nowhere, to check whether we're hiding an extra sweater or a T-shirt or a dress that 'doesn't meet the standards'. (Alyokhina, 2017: 121–123)

If, as Nils Christie argues, personal experiences provide 'near' and 'indirect' (Christie, 1997: 21) data for social science research (Christie, 1986: 17), these accounts help furnish a case for abolition. But they do not make the argument. This chapter seeks to explain the anarchist case by examining Peter Kropotkin's seminal text, *In Russian and French Prisons* (1887). Kropotkin is described as a pioneer of humanistic and insurgent criminology (Tifft and Stevenson, 1985). Yet his book remains neglected, apparently falling outside the 'purely anarchist context' of his earlier work (Woodcock, 1991: xix) and not landing squarely within the mainstream. Drawing on his experiences in St Petersburg's Peter Paul Fortress (1874–1876), the St. Paul prison in Lyons (1882) and Clairvaux's 'Maison Centrale' (1883–1886), Kropotkin rejected the possibility of reform, concluding that imprisonment compounded the problem of anti-social behaviour. The chapter provides an analysis of Kropotkin's account and explains his scepticism about reform and the reasons why he concluded that the only possible answer to the question 'are prisons necessary?' was 'no'. The concluding section shows how two lines of Kropotkin's abolitionist thesis were developed in later anarchist thought: the first 'environmental' strand focuses on the systemic injustices that incentivize wrongdoing and the second 'ethical' thread emphasizes the faultiness of the concept of crime.

In Russian and French Prisons: Kropotkin's case against reform

In Russian and French Prisons, Kropotkin (1887) interweaves findings of official reports with his personal recollections of incarceration. The following analysis uses themes of environment, culture and social relationships to uncover the concerns that led him to advocate abolition.

Environment

In her fictionalized account of prison, *Wife of Prisoner 4,287*, Kropotkin's soulmate Sophie described Clairvaux as a '[f]ormidable, sombre ... mass of stone' that 'extended quite beyond ... view, running through the valley and climbing the hill' (Kropotkin, S., 1886: 4). Kropotkin's account of the environment also had a strong architectural aspect, though he used the term 'cellular confinement' to describe the dominant design principle and he added an administrative and spatial dimension.

Kropotkin described the physical estate as an imperfect expression of an ideational shift in prison philosophy from 'vengeance' to 'deterrence' and 'improvement' (Kropotkin, 1887: 24; 349). Philanthropic notions of social responsibility, he argued, had driven this change. Yet its transformative potential had been kept in check by pervasive beliefs that explained wrongdoing as the result of individual failure, '"bad will" and "sin"' (Kropotkin, 1887: 349). Modern analysts use different terms to describe the evolution of prison architecture. For Jewkes and Johnston, the cellular prison represented a change from 'reform' to 'repression' (Jewkes and Johnston, 2007: 178, 182). But their assessment of the relationship between separation, punishment and atonement bolsters Kropotkin's view that prison was intended to enforce seclusion to enable moral reflection while also reproving wrongdoing by restricting social interaction (Kropotkin, 1887: 99, 320). This was his overriding impression: the wagon that took him to Clairvaux was arranged in two rows of 'small cupboards' fitted with a barred window to avert the risk of suffocation while preventing prisoners from 'seeing one another and talking' (Kropotkin, 1887: 273); the outstanding feature of the cells of the Trubetskoi Bastion, the holding centre for political prisoners in the Peter and Paul Fortress, which opened in 1872, was numbing silence. The cells, measuring 25 feet on the diagonal, were padded with layers of felt and iron mesh to thwart social interaction (Kropotkin, 1887: 92–94). Equally deadening was the high-vaulted, dimly lit visitors' reception hall in Lyon prison. Constructed in the 1840s, this engulfed prisoners and visitors in cacophonous, 'infernal' noise (Kropotkin, 1887: 269).

The unwillingness of legislators to attend to the wellbeing of individuals they saw as felons and outlaws explained these imperfections: both the prison at Clairvaux, a remodelled ancient abbey, and the purpose-built prison at Lyon were characteristically cramped, dark, damp and dilapidated. Overcrowding was a persistent problem. The prison at Tomsk, a holding station for exiles in Western Siberia, had space for 960 prisoners; Kropotkin estimated that the population regularly topped 2,200 (Kropotkin, 1887: 139). Poor management exacerbated the toxic conditions of the estate. Lyon's 'star-shaped' St Paul Prison was known for its insanitary accumulations of filth; the cells 'full of bugs and never heated' were sometimes 'literally covered with human excretions' (Kropotkin, 1887: 259, 271). In St Petersburg's House of Detention, a remand centre built in the 1870s, the relentless polishing of asphalt floors produced 'suffocating', 'asphyxiating' clouds of polluting dust (Kropotkin, 1887: 60). Prisoners were meant to suffer; slopping-out, poor ventilation and bad light achieved this and also made prisons ideal incubators for sickness and disease (Kropotkin, 1887: 55–59).

Kropotkin's reflections on the environment flipped prevailing views about 'contagion'. Moralists worried about the transmissibility of 'criminality', justifying imprisonment as containment. Kropotkin diagnosed prison as a primary source of infection and traced the spread of transmissible repressive practices. Anticipating modern ideas of carceral space, he correlated prison with emergent predatory subcultures (Gill et al, 2018). For every jailer, he argued, there was a 'detective trained as a blood-hound' and a 'police spy'; each contributed to 'corruption, erected into a system' (Kropotkin, 1970 [1882]: 201). In Clairvaux, 'a tiny hamlet ... of less than a dozen houses', the prison had degraded the social ecology (Kropotkin, 1899: 461). Once an abbey, it had become a magnet for a host of dodgy legal professionals and hangers-on, 'detectives, spies, petty solicitors, informers, people preying on simpletons, and the like' (Kropotkin, 1899: 469). Similarly noxious cultures flourished in Lyon. Looking at the environs of the Palais de Justice, Kropotkin saw a 'world' defined by 'petty thefts, petty swindlings, spying and corruption of all sorts'. The prison, he argued, had created an atmosphere which 'spread like a blot of oil round the prison' (Kropotkin, 1899: 470).

In the Russian exile system, Kropotkin linked these flows to processes of colonization, territorialization and empire building. If prison expansion was intended to project state power or majesty, these projects in fact exemplified the state's disintegrative energy (de Vito, Anderson and Bosma, 2018). Those who survived the 4,500-mile trek into exile provided a steady source of labour for a range of state and private enterprises. But the system was characterized by weak infrastructure and ramshackle administration. The family separations it fostered caused social breakdown and dysfunction.

To explain, Kropotkin divided the population into 'forced' and 'free' migrant groups. The former were recent convicts and families. The latter were established colonizers, divided into three categories: those resettled from the end of the 16th century to bolster Tsarist control; various categories of refugees, such as anti-Tsarist rebels, religious nonconformists or rural workers fleeing bureaucracy and serfdom; and 'Siberyaks', former convicts who had joined the 'regular ranks' of the local population (Kropotkin, 1887: 127–130, 377). The forced migrants, who constituted the 'great mass' of migrant population, spent the first third of their sentences in hard labour camps and the rest of their exile settled in the surrounding villages (Kropotkin, 1887: 166). This settlement policy benefited neither the convicts nor the free migrants. The forced migrants were a 'floating population, mostly starving and quite unable to do any useful work' (Kropotkin, 1887: 175). Lacking the requisite skills and motivation to support themselves in the new landscape, they lived in 'wretchedness' and made a negligible contribution 'to the colonization of the country' (Kropotkin, 1887: 205). They became a burden on the settled migrant communities. The resulting tensions were not eased by the administrative bungling that enabled around 15 per cent of the forced migrants to break for freedom. Siberyak bounty hunters, Kropotkin noted, considered the escapees fair game, branding them 'criminal' (Kropotkin, 1887: 182, 223). The net result of prison, he concluded, was social division, mistrust and aggression.

Culture

Evoking Hobbes' famous depiction of the state of nature, Kropotkin described prison life as one of '[o]aths, filth, brutality, bribery, blows, hunger' (Kropotkin, 1887: 54). Prisons, he argued, were laboratories of violence and of regimented routine: the prisoner was 'a numbered thing, which must move according to regulations' (Kropotkin, 1887: 330). Correlating this punitive mix with the exercise of arbitrary authority, he claimed that prison officers used their position to destroy the prisoners' sense of self and capacity for judgement.

Arbitrary authority is associated with executive caprice, social dependence and the lack of transparent rules. In Maria Aloykhina's testimony, arbitrariness arises from the guards' power to interpret and apply complex rules – to 'point to a rule at some level of the hierarchy as the basis for any action that they take' (cited in Loucks, 2000: 1). Kropotkin recorded both bureaucratic and autocratic practices. Officials, he argued, applied rules as 'small persecutions' (Kropotkin, 1887: 332). Prisoners' lives depended on the guards' 'good or bad humour' and the 'depth of their psychological deductions' (Kropotkin, 1887: 274). This was true even of French warders, who were generally less brutal than their Russian counterparts. The guards relished their commanding position. Siberian colonies were exemplary in this respect: mine superintendents were 'kings' in their 'dominions' (Kropotkin, 1887: 168). Likewise, the real 'curse' of the privately run mines was the 'absolute arbitrariness of the gaolers' (Kropotkin, 1887: 187). Captain Zagarin, Governor-General of Krasnoyarsk Prison, reputedly told his prisoners that he was their governor, minister and Tsar (Kropotkin, 1887: 188).

Kropotkin speculated that the prison service attracted a high proportion of narcissists and sadists (Kropotkin, 1887: 69, 188). Yet the 'mad brutality' of the prison system was not adequately explained by the presence of 'bad apples' (Kropotkin, 1887: 188). Officers were prone to abuse their authority 'like all those who hold power in their hands' and the hierarchical order of the prison intensified this tendency. As Kropotkin put it, authority 'will be more unscrupulous, and the more felt by the abused, the more limited and narrow is the world they live in' (Kropotkin, 1887: 333). Prison, like the military, was organized as a formal hierarchy. Neither rationalization nor flattening would substantively alter it. Nor would the appointment of an 'honest jailer' resolve the problem, even supposing one could be found (Kropotkin, 1887: 14). 'Put a Pestalozzi' in charge of a prison, Kropotkin remarked, nodding to the famous educationalist and pedagogue, and he 'would soon become a prison warder'. He continued: '[the] institution makes them what they are, petty and vexatious persecutors of the prisoners' (Kropotkin, 1887: 333).

Kropotkin acknowledged that guards' powers were legally constrained. The 'flogging which goes on still in English prisons', he remarked in his memoirs, was 'absolutely impossible in France' (Kropotkin, 1899: 462). Yet they had considerable scope to inflict vicious punishment. Kropotkin reported how a prisoner had been driven mad after spending two months chained in isolation (Kropotkin, 1887: 297). Prisoners were regularly shackled, birched, put on starvation diets, made to kneel on 'bare flags' for hours on end, forced to sleep in cells without bedding, hosed and left to chill in icy cells, and kept in stiflingly hot or freezing black holes (small lock-ups without sunlight) (Kropotkin, 1887: 67, 73, 293, 297). Boys held in French reformatories endured field punishment, being laid flat on their stomachs with their hands and feet tied to meet behind their backs (Kropotkin, 1887: 382). It was all too easy for guards to exceed their regulatory powers. Women were frequently raped by 'drunken officials' en route to Siberia (Kropotkin, 1887: 198) and sometimes held hostage to incentivize the cooperation of the men they followed into exile (Kropotkin, 1887: 168, 170). It was common knowledge that guards in Clairvaux, a prison which Kropotkin considered 'one of the best in Europe' (Kropotkin, 1899: 462), had murdered a prisoner and arranged his hanging to disguise the killing as suicide (Kropotkin, 1887: 292; 1899: 469).

For Kropotkin, physical violence was the most dramatic manifestation of arbitrary rule. Yet daily supervision was equally pernicious. The simplest actions were disciplined and coerced: prisoners were not permitted to walk; they marched in file to rhythms shouted by guards as galley slaves had once rowed. One of the ironies of cellular confinement was that prisoners were constantly monitored; isolated but 'never alone, as an eye is continually kept upon you' (Kropotkin, 1887: 94). Seventy-five years before anti-nuclear campaigners complained that prisoners were 'dressed like freaks' to satisfy the guards' urge to make them feel 'ridiculous and inferior' (Prison Reform Council, 1962: 20), Kropotkin observed that warders issued 'fool's dress to those whom they pretend to moralize' (Kropotkin, 1887: 328). These petty humiliations depersonalized prisoners. Inmates became emotionally detached. Complex feelings were forbidden:

> Tears may choke him; he must suppress them ... human feelings are not allowed in prisons ... all is crushed by the force which denies him the right to be a man. Condemned to bestial life, all that might suggest better feelings will be carefully suppressed. He must *not* be a man, so it is ordained by the prison rules. (Kropotkin, 1887: 330–331)

Work, supposedly a remedial, educative tool, was also coerced. Everyday life was characterized by hardship, boredom or a combination of the two. In *The Ballad of Reading Gaol*, Oscar Wilde wrote despairingly about tearing 'tarry rope', sewing sacks, breaking stones and sweating 'on the mill' (Wilde, 1898, sec. III v. 8). Kropotkin also highlighted the debilitating monotony of prison work, distinguishing 'free labour' (work which 'makes man feel himself a part of the immense life of the world') from degrading 'forced labour' – work undertaken only from 'fear of a worse punishment' (Kropotkin, 1899: 315; 462). Prison labour fell into the second category. In Clairvaux, prisoners were woken at

5 or 6 am and marched to steamy machine rooms where they laboured until it was dark (Kropotkin, 1887: 280–281). In Russia workshops were reserved for 'skilled craftsmen'. The rest were condemned to useless pursuits. Kropotkin witnessed teams organized to 'shovel snow into heaps' before being ordered to flatten it (Kropotkin, 1887: 67). Siberian exiles worked punishing hours in deadly salt and gold mines. On Sakhalin, the Tsarist penal colony established in the 1850s, exiles were forced to dig coal or cultivate barren land. Unable to recoup loans advanced to farm this infertile soil, they were reduced 'to a kind of perpetual serfdom' (Kropotkin, 1887: 179). Acknowledging the privileges that he enjoyed as a political prisoner (Kropotkin, 1887: 90, 93, 285, 321; 1899: 461), Kropotkin noted that ordinary 'criminals' were often 'carefully maintained in absolute idleness'. Kharkov Central Prison permitted '[n]o books, no writing materials, and no implements for manual labour. No means of easing the tortured mind, nor anything on which to concentrate the morbid activity of the brain' (Kropotkin, 1887: 75).

Kropotkin compared the deadening effects of prison life to Arctic exploration. The difference between prison and exploration, he remarked, was that there was no prospect of success or achievement in prison, only increasing 'physical and mental depression'. Using the same analogy in 1970, Stanley Cohen and Laurie Taylor (Fielding and Fielding, 2008: 77) quoted a prisoner serving a life sentence: 'Your dreams turn into nightmares and your castles into ashes, all you think about is fantasy and in the end you turn your back on reality and live in a contorted world of make-believe' (cited in RAP, nd.: 5). Kropotkin's earlier assessment was that prison caused 'low passions' and 'shallow and futile desires' (Kropotkin, 1887: 177). Prisoners lost the ability to concentrate. Thought became 'less rapid, or, rather less persistent: it loses it depth' (Kropotkin, 1887: 321). Hopelessness bred dissipation and frustration, often resulting in sexual assault (Kropotkin, 1887: 262, 336).

Prison culture demeaned and dehumanized, impeding prisoners' capacity to decide courses of action. Indeed, prisons were 'institutions based on a false principle' *designed* to curb the possibility of 'exercising and reinforcing the firmness of … Will' (Kropotkin, 1887: 324). Ill-conceived notions of administrative efficiency, compounded by inadequate funding, exacerbated the problem: the quest to keep and maintain the 'greatest number of prisoners with the least possible amount of warders' reduced men 'to the level of unreasoning machines'. Kropotkin imagined a dystopian future where 'electric currents transmitted to them by a single warder' would control 'a thousand automatons rising and working, eating and going to bed' (Kropotkin, 1887: 325).

Relationships

Prison cultivated what Kropotkin called 'false relations', marked by social division and rivalry. Assata Shakur's description of her encounter with

Mrs Butterworth/Miss Bitch captured the 'them' and 'us' division he had in mind. However, Kropotkin's commentary suggested that few prisoners were able to defy the authorities and that far more were psychologically crushed by the guards. He noted how in Clairvaux, all new arrivals were immediately categorized by warders as 'soumis' or 'insoumis' – submissives or insubordinates. The classification determined how intolerable the prisoner's life would be (Kropotkin, 1887: 294).

Kropotkin's account of the enmity between guards and prisoners echoed the social divisions described by William Godwin in *Caleb Williams* (2009 [1794]), a fictionalized account of civilized and outlaw society. In one scene the eponymous hero stumbles into a den of thieves; its leader, a model of benevolence and integrity, guarantees his security, even though Caleb is an outsider and regarded with suspicion by other group members. After chiding the band for attacking Caleb, the leader reminds them that they are 'thieves without licence' at 'open war with another set of men, who are thieves according to the law'. Thus, in distinction to the oppressor group they were virtuous and just; they treated others without 'cruelty, malice and revenge' (Godwin, 2009 [1794]: 209).

In this vein, Kropotkin observed the mutual antagonism between guards and prisoners, and how the guards' perception of themselves was determined almost exclusively by their disparagement of the prisoners: 'Compelled as they are to live in the midst of a hostile camp of prisoners', the guards functioned as a 'league' in opposition to the 'league of the prisoners' (Kropotkin, 1887: 333). Yet modifying Godwin's thesis, Kropotkin described guards and convicts as two categories of prisoner and downplayed the possibility of finding virtue in either camp (Kropotkin, 1887: 332). For the guards, the social stigma attached to prison work was the chief barrier. Citizens paid warders 'for performing a function for which no educated man would like to prepare his own children' (Kropotkin, 1887: 353). So despised, they made the prisoners feel their resentment.

Prisoners constituted themselves as communities against 'outlaw society', just as Godwin had imagined. In Clairvaux, Kropotkin was told that the 'real thieves' were 'those who keep us here' (Kropotkin, 1887: 318). Noting that prisoners frequently blamed themselves for having been caught and rarely expressed remorse for their actions, he observed that the consensus among the imprisoned was that they lacked the 'cunning' of their political masters (Kropotkin, 1887: 311). However, the prisoners' shared loathing of the guards rarely translated into camaraderie. Kropotkin reported instances of solidarity and mutual aid in women's prisons, but contended that most prisoners competed for the guards' favours (Kropotkin, 1887: 50). Discretion thus cemented hierarchies and distrust. Habits of conformity cultivated during incarceration and the high incidence of mental illness further undermined companionship.

Like the guards, prisoners knew that they were generally regarded as the 'foe of society' and that the 'liberated prisoner' was generally regarded as 'something plague-stricken' (Kropotkin, 1887: 327). This only intensified their sense of alienation and resentment. Yet in reality, ex-prisoners were disadvantaged and marginalized. They struggled to find work and build intimate relationships. Their isolation persisted, Kropotkin commented, precisely when they most needed 'fraternal support' and a 'brotherly hand' (Kropotkin, 1887: 327). The relationships prisoners formed on release were typically founded on a common hatred of law-abiding citizens. Kropotkin quoted Zola to sum up the mindset: 'what swine respectable people are!' (Kropotkin, 1887: 334). Society, 'represented by the governor, the warders, the employers', became the freed prisoners' adversary:

> Everything which may be done to deceive them is right. The prisoner is an outlaw to them; they become outlaws to him. And, as soon as he is free, he will put this morality into practice. Before having been in prison, he may have committed faults without reflection. Prison education will make him consider society as an enemy. (Kropotkin, 1887: 334)

Kropotkin's account of social relationships indicated that prison transformed prisoners in perverse ways, entirely contrary to the aspirations of reformers and philanthropists. Prisons, he argued, 'have not moralized anybody, but have more or less demoralized all those who have spent a number or years there' (Kropotkin, 1887: 309). He repeatedly called prisons 'nurseries of crime' (Kropotkin, 1887: 263, 309, 336). Elsewhere, he described schools 'prisons for little ones' (Kropotkin, 1912 [1898]: 378). The implication was that prison forced compliance after instruction had failed to instil respect for authority. In this sense, prison was the ruling classes' second line of attack against the oppressed.

The case against reform

Kropotkin admitted that he had once believed that prisons could serve as 'reformatories' (Kropotkin, 1887: 18). But his mature view came closer to Wilde's conception of prison as 'the result in our days of hard-and-fast rules, and of stupidity' (Wilde, 2000 [1897]: 848). He concluded that prison brought a netherworld of criminality into being, engendered institutional violence, nurturing mistrust and social enmity. Prisons 'do *not* moralize their inmates; they do not deter them from crime' (Kropotkin, 1887: 304–8). On the contrary, prison was a 'deteriorating influence' which left prisoners 'less' rather than more equipped to live in society (Kropotkin, 1887: 357). Eager to lessen the hardship of prison life, Kropotkin continued to support proposals for reform. But he did so not as a reformist, but as an abolitionist. For as long as prisons '*remain prisons*', he argued, modification would 'not substantially ameliorate them' (Kropotkin, 1887: 301).

Kropotkin's abolitionism questioned the legitimacy of law and the justification of punishment. His objections to law were threefold: against the principle of command, the internal regulation of legal systems and the moralization of law. In the first place, he argued, law functioned as 'a religion' or an opiate (Kropotkin, 1970 [1886]: 197). Defended as 'a remedy for evil', it stymied public discussion of justice and compelled obedience to rules without regard to their general acceptance (Kropotkin, 1970 [1886]: 196). The rules regulating legal procedures further detached law from the social systems it underpinned. Kropotkin painted a ghoulish picture of the judge as 'a visionary in a world of legal fictions, revelling in the infliction of imprisonment and death' (Kropotkin, 1970 [1886]: 200). Finally, he argued, law was never impartial since it fused 'moral goodness and the law of the masters ... into one and the same divinity' (Kropotkin, 1970 [1886]: 197). For example, in capitalism, law provided 'security for exploitation' (Kropotkin, 1970 [1886]: 213). Yet, partiality was a factor of the law's moral character, not solely its class function. Here, Kropotkin's critique chimed with Godwin's description of law as a 'stagnant condition ... of permanence' (Godwin, 1985 [1798], bk. VII, ch. VIII: 688), and it anticipated the 'new criminology' of the 1960s, which challenged the 'theoretical notion that the definition of crime was morally fixed and unquestionable' (Cohen, 1979: 4).

Kropotkin's critique of punishment centred on the principle of moral responsibility, which he labelled egoistic, 'unintelligent' individualism (Kropotkin, 1887: 367). Seeing it embedded in Victorian criminology and psychiatry, he argued that the punishment of 'crime' and the medicalization of 'deviant' behaviour relied on the same mistaken assumption, namely that individuals were praiseworthy or blameworthy for their choices and behaviours unless there was evidence to indicate mental incapacity. Kropotkin's counter to this was that these assessments of 'criminality' or 'madness' ignored the environmental conditions affecting free will. To pursue the point, he picked an argument with Cesare Lombroso, perhaps the most influential criminologist of the day. Lombroso classed 'criminals and the feeble-minded' as 'evolutionary deprived people' (van Swaaningen, 1997: 31). Kropotkin argued that his 'biological theory' (Kropotkin, 1887: 345–347) simply ignored the strong correlation between social deprivation and the so-called 'criminal class', and the disproportionate representation of the poor in the prison population (Kropotkin, 1887: 356). Lombroso's concept of 'inherited criminality', Kropotkin remarked, had only gained purchase because 'hard and blackened hands' were 'considered as a sign of inferiority, and a silk-dress and the knowledge of how to keep servants under strict discipline' had become 'a token of superiority' (Kropotkin, 1887: 365). In a later critique, he advanced an alternative 'anthropological' view which treated the criminal as '"a manufactured product", a product of society itself' (Kropotkin, 1912: 77).

In support of abolition, Kropotkin proposed communist ethics and what he called 'wilfulness'. The ethics was predicated on a principle of interdependence which treated individuals as socialized rather than atomized agents. Applied to capitalism, it countered concepts of individual right and desert, and promoted production as a collective endeavour: genius and talent, he argued, were nurtured in social contexts (Kropotkin, 1907: 230–231). Applied to social relations, communist ethics construed individual wrongdoing as a social problem. Individuals could no more be held individually responsible for transgressions than they could claim their distinctive skills as possessions.

Kropotkin used a concept of 'false relations' to frame 'wilfulness'. It referred to the capacity to reflect on moral rules rather than an obligation to obey them. Wilfulness was an acquired practice of judgement and deliberation which acted as a brake on 'passions'. Reasoning that no one was immune to the 'feelings and thoughts' that prompted 'acts considered as criminal', he correlated the lack of 'firm Will' with the 'want' of the 'best passions' in society: love, compassion, empathy and solidarity (Kropotkin, 1887: 352). Habits of obedience, giving free rein to the promotion of the worst passions – loathing, fear, antipathy and mistrust – explained why individuals surrendered to 'temptations' and flouted 'established principles of morality' (Kropotkin, 1887: 323). Imprisonment was a prime example. For Kropotkin, it was a manifestation of a perilous, self-perpetuating logic of annihilation. To illustrate this, he reminded participants of the 1912 London Eugenics Conference that Fyodor Dostoevksy, whose book *House of the Dead* criminologists much admired, had been epileptic and, according to eugenicist norms, 'unfit' and 'deviant' (Kropotkin, 1912: 77–78). Dostoevksy's exceptional status tested the morality of initiatives, already underway, to eliminate congenital 'defects' by sterilization and selective breeding and to remove those suffering from mental illness to the new asylums, institutions that were 'nothing else but prisons' (Kropotkin, 1887: 350).

As Colin Ward notes, Kropotkin's abolitionism was part of his wider critique of institutionalization, a tradition of social welfare that Ward described as 'a service given grudgingly and punitively by authority' (Ward, 1982: 112). In the theory of mutual aid, he proposed association as the antidote to institutionalization and advocated the rekindling of voluntary grassroots and community organizations. Writing in 1902 about the principles of justice encouraged by the associations of the European medieval city states, Kropotkin reported:

> The cities make their *Conjuration*. At first the citizens swear to drop all contests arising from the *lex talionis* (law of retaliation) and, if

new contests arise, never to appeal to external powers, but to settle everything among themselves. The Guild, the Parish, the Town Community are the different degrees of jurisdiction. Bailies, chosen by the members of the guild, the street, the parish or the town, decide the compensation to be granted to the wronged party. In specially important cases, the guild, the street, the parish or the town, convoked to a general meeting, pronounce the sentence. Besides, *Arbitration* in all the stages between individuals, between guilds, between parishes and cities takes a very large extension. (Kropotkin, 1902: 5–6)

Appealing to a concept of ethics 'without sanction or obligation', adapted from the philosopher Jean-Marie Guyau (1898), he imagined the duty to obey giving way to a habit of care, where anti-social behaviour stimulated holistic reflection on rules of justice (Kropotkin, 1887: 310, 363, 370). Tifft and Sullivan have labelled the approach 'direct justice' (Tifft and Sullivan, 1980: 71–75). Returning to the topic at the end of his life, Kropotkin described justice as a social practice of mutual aid elaborated by wilful individuals 'for *sociality*, for life harmonizing with the life of society as a whole' (Kropotkin, 1968 [1924]: 326).

The balder argument of *In Russian and French Prisons* rejected reformism because it automatically stipulated social exclusion as the price for offending. As Sophie Kropotkin pointed out, this practice penalized prisoners' families as well as the prisoners themselves: women not only endured enormous 'privations' to fund prison visits, but they were also usually ostracized (Kropotkin, S. 1886: 6). Kropotkin concurred (Kropotkin, 1887: 268), but his main objection was that the removal of individuals from society normalized social irresponsibility by institutionalizing obedience, repression and punishment. The inference was that the question typically asked by reformers, 'What is to be done with criminals?' (Baker, nd: np), wrongly assumed that normative questions posed by the law and notions of transgression or deviation could be treated as self-evident, settled or irrelevant. Anti-social behaviour begged questions about social context, individual wellbeing, structural incentives and their modification. From Kropotkin's perspective, reform represented an attempt to 'mitigate the evil' of imprisonment without confronting 'the principles of penal institutions' or grappling with the problem of antisocial behaviour 'at source' (Kropotkin, 1887: 3).

Abolitionism and prison abolition

Joe Sim argues that 'abolitionism emerged from the political schisms that gripped Western Europe and North America in the late 1960s' (Sim, 2017: 422). Yet 19th-century anarchists used the term to call for the dismantling of the infrastructure of the state, including the prison system. The critique supported two interrelated analyses of 'crime': an 'environmental' approach that highlighted the injustices mirrored by wrongdoing and an 'ethical' perspective that underlined the illegitimacy of punishment. Both resonate with Kropotkin's position.

Anarchists adopted the language of abolition in the mid-19th century when it was still current in anti-slavery campaigns. Yet whereas anti-slavery campaigners applied the term narrowly to demand the abolition of chattel slavery, anarchists used it to advance a broad critique of domination or 'mastership'. Thus, Leo Tolstoy distinguished 'the cause of slavery' as 'the casual temporary seizure by the Southerners of a few millions of negroes' from the 'ancient and universal recognition … of the right of coercion by some men in regard to certain others' (Tolstoy, 1924 [1904]). Tolstoy's terminology is problematic, but his distinction chimed with the thesis outlined by P.J. Proudhon in *What is Property?* (1840). Proudhon had argued for 'an end to privilege, the abolition of slavery, equality of rights, and the reign of law. Justice nothing else' (Proudhon, 1969 [1840]: 39).

The environmental argument for abolition drew attention to the perpetuation of mastership after emancipation. As W.C. Owen argued, the prison system was a primary mechanism: in the US, chain gangs and convict leasing arrangements were a direct offshoot of emancipation (Prison Reform League, 1910: ch. VI; see also Davis and Rodriguez, 2000: 214; Davis, 2003: 29–30; Gilmore, 2009: 73–87). The wider conclusion anarchists drew was that constitutionalism signified not the inauguration of justice, but the transfer of arbitrary legal power from monarchy to bureaucracy (Nocella, Seis and Shantz, 2018, 2020). This contrasts significantly with the view adopted by most contemporary constitutional theorists. For example, the political philosopher Philip Pettit argues that: 'Neither a tax levy, nor even a term of imprisonment, need take away someone's freedom' (Pettit, 1997: 56). Likewise, Quentin Skinner contends that: 'Citizens who are imprisoned for falling foul of laws to which they have given their consent can be said to retain … their underlying status as free-men, although they have obviously been deprived of one of their civil liberties' (Skinner, 2008: 88). Rejecting appeals to consent and autonomy, anarchists argued that the freedoms described were negated by the persistence of law and authority. As Helen Blagg and Charlotte Wilson put it in their investigation of British women's prisons, crime 'is an arbitrary legal term' (Blagg and Wilson, 1912: 16). Similarly, Voltairine de Cleyre rejected the idea that crime was 'a thing-in-itself' (de Cleyre, 1914 [1903]: 173). In her view, nature 'knows nothing about crime and nothing ever was a crime until the social Conscience made it so' (de Cleyre, 1914 [1903]: 184). The protection of uneven distributions of property and the maintenance of the state's monopoly of violence haunted its construction. This was Tolstoy's view too. His novel *Resurrection*, a fictionalized account of the Tsarist legal and judicial system, included this exchange between the lawyer Rogozhinsky and his sceptical brother-in-law Nekhlyudov:

> '[E]very thief knows that stealing is wrong, and that we should not steal – that it is immoral', said Rogozhinsky, with a quiet, self-assured slightly contemptuous smile which specially irritated Nekhlyudov.
> 'No, he does not know it; they say to him 'don't steal', and he knows that the master of the factory steals his labour by keeping down his wages; that the Government, through all its officials, robs him continually by taxation.
> 'Why, that is Anarchism', Rogozhinsky said, quietly defining his brother-in-law's words. (Tolstoy, 1947 [1899], bk. II, ch. XXXII: 328)

Abolitionism was elaborated both to explain the incidence of criminality and to reframe punishment as repression. The inequalities arising from property distributions formed a central part of the anarchist argument. Voltairine de Cleyre's succinct view was: 'THE REASON MEN STEAL IS BECAUSE THEIR RIGHTS ARE STOLEN FROM THEM BEFORE THEY ARE BORN' (de Cleyre, 1914 [1903]: 192). Likewise, Emma Goldman referred to 'our cruel social and economic arrangements' and ranked 'social and economic influences' as 'the most relentless, the most poisonous germs of crime'. Complicating Lombroso's discovery that crime had innate 'biologic, physiologic or psychologic' causes (Goldman, 1979 [1911]: 291), she identified capitalism as a social pathogen and tied abolitionism to the eradication of impoverishment, coerced marriage and forced pregnancy.

The ethical arguments against punishment revolved around notions of responsibility. However, the elaboration of the concept suggested different responses to wrongdoing. Like Kropotkin, Blagg and Wilson argued that wrongdoing was a lapse of judgement which punishment was ill-equipped to correct: the 'collective force of society should be used to stimulate and support the exercise of individual will power under a sense of personal responsibility, and to make every effort to strengthen and restore it where it is enfeebled or lost' (Blagg and Wilson, 1912: 6). While detaching wrongdoing from institutional practice and giving more scope to free will than Kropotkin had done, they also emphasized care to bolster willpower. Tolstoy argued that forgiveness and humility were the proper responses to wrongdoing. Nekhlyudov, the hero of *Resurrection,* is struck by the wisdom of an old prisoner: 'Do thine own business and leave other alone ... God knows whom to execute, whom to pardon, but we do not know' (Tolstoy, 1947 [1899], bk III, ch. XXVIII: 454). He arrives at the 'simplest, truest certainty' that 'the dreadful evil he had been witnessing in prisons and jails, and the quiet self-assurance of the perpetrators of this evil, resulted from men attempting to do what was impossible: to correct evil while themselves evil'

(Tolstoy, 1947 [1899], bk III, ch. XXVIII: 458). In contrast, W.C. Owen recommended 'reformation' to ease relationships between wrongdoers and the wronged. His grim reports of prison life in early 20th-century America bore a striking resemblance to Kropotkin's descriptions of Russian and French prisons. Echoing Kropotkin's view that the 'primitive' idea of vengeance had given way to a philosophy of 'deterrence', he also downplayed the practical significance of this change. Deterrence, he argued, was 'terrorism' which sprang from a faulty logic 'to stamp out criminality by fear' (Prison Reform League, 1910: 19). Yet rather than rely exclusively on care and mutual aid, Owen proposed social alternatives to incarceration, for example, probation and community service orders, enabling atonement without punishment.

As Larry Tifft and Dennis Sullivan argue, Kropotkin's core thesis was that *'lawful harms'* caused far more misery in the world than the 'social harms punishable by law' (Tifft and Sullivan, 1980: 9). Invoking the concept of mutual aid or 'the struggle to be human', they further argue that 'anti-person, anti-nature, and anti-social acts need not be feared' in an 'environment' of freedom (Tifft and Sullivan, 1980: 179). Kropotkin's often-quoted remark that 'two thirds of all breaches of law' are 'so-called "crimes against property"' (Kropotkin, 1887: 366) bolsters the environmental thrust of this anarchist analysis. Yet this should not distract from the richness of anarchist abolitionism, which combines ethical with environmental approaches.

References
Alyokhina, M. (2017) *Riot Days*, Harmondsworth: Penguin.
Baker, C. (nd) *Against Prisons*, D. Imrie and M. William (trans.), Portland: Venomous Butterfly.
Berkman, A. (1992 [1912]) *Prison Memoirs of an Anarchist* (extracts), in G. Fellner (ed.) *Life of an Anarchist: The Alexander Berkman Reader*, New York: Four Walls Eight Windows. Available from: https://theanarchistlibrary.org/library/alexander-berkman-prison-memoirs-of-an-anarchist [Accessed 15 September 2024].
Blagg, H. and Wilson, C. (1912) *Women and Prisons*, London: Fabian Society.
Christie, N. (1986) 'The ideal victim', in E.A. Fattah (ed.) *From Crime Policy to Victim Policy*, London: Palgrave Macmillan, pp 17–30.
Christie, N. (1997) 'Four blocks against insight: notes on the oversocialization of criminologist', *Theoretical Criminology*, 1(1): 13–23.
Cohen, S. (1979) *Crime and Punishment: Some Thoughts on Theories and Policies*, London: Radical Alternatives to Prison.
Davis, A.Y. (2003) *Are Prisons Obsolete?*, New York: Seven Stories.
Davis, A.Y. and D. Rodriguez (2000), 'The challenge of prison abolition: a conversation', *Social Justice*, 27(3): 212–218.
De Cleyre, V. (1914 [1903]) 'Crime and punishment', in A. Berkman (ed.) *Selected Writings of Voltairine de Cleyre*, New York: Mother Earth, pp 173–204.

De Vito, C. Anderson, C. and Bosma, U. (2018) 'Transportation, deportation and exile: perspectives from the colonies in the nineteenth and twentieth centuries', *International Review of Social History*, 63(S26): 1–24.

Duval, C. (2021 [1907]) *Outrage: An Anarchist Memoir of the Penal Colony*, M. Shreve (trans.), Oakland, CA: PM Press.

Fielding, N. and Fielding, J. (2008) 'Resistance and adaptation to criminal identity: using secondary analysis to evaluate classic studies of crime and deviance', *Historical Social Research*, 33(3): 75–93.

Gill, N., Conlon, D., Moran, D. and Burridge, A. (2018) 'Carceral circuitry: new directions in carceral geography', *Progress in Human Geography*, 42(2): 183–204.

Gilmore, R.W. (2009) 'Race, prisons and war: scenes from the history of US violence', *Socialist Register*, 45: 73–87.

Godwin, W. (2009 [1794]) *Caleb Williams*, Oxford: Oxford University Press.

Godwin, W. (1985 [1798]) *Enquiry Concerning Political Justice and its Influence on Morals and Happiness* (3rd edn), Harmondsworth: Penguin.

Goldman, E. (1979 [1911]) 'Prisons: a social crime and failure', in A.K. Shulman (ed.) *Red Emma Speaks*, London: Wildwood, pp 286–300.

Guyau, J.M. (1898) *A Sketch of Morality Independent of Obligation or Sanction*, 2nd ed. trans. Gertrude Kapteyn, London: Watts & Co.

Jewkes, Y. and Johnston, H. (2007) 'The evolution of prison architecture', in Y. Jewkes (ed.) *Handbook on Prisons*, Cullompton: Willan Publishing, pp 174–196.

Kropotkin, S. (1886) *Wife of Prisoner 4,287*, S.E. Holmes (trans.), reproduced from *Liberty*. Available from: http://dwardmac.pitzer.edu/anarchist_archives/kropotkin/wifeofnumber4287.pdf [Accessed 15 September 2024].

Kropotkin, P. (1887) *In Russian and French Prisons*, London: Ward & Downey.

Kropotkin, P. (1899) *Memoirs of a Revolutionist*, Cambridge: Riverside Press.

Kropotkin, P. (1902) *Organised Vengeance Called Justice*, London: Freedom Press.

Kropotkin, P. (1907 [1898]) *Anarchism: Its Philosophy and Ideal*, London: Freedom Press.

Kropotkin, P. (1912) 'The sterilisation of the unfit', *Freedom*, October: 77–78.

Kropotkin, P. (1912 [1898]) *Fields Factories and Workshops: Or, Industry Combined with Agriculture and Brain Work with Manual Work* (new edn), London: Thomas Nelson & Sons.

Kropotkin, P. (1968 [1924]) *Ethics: Origin and Development*, L.S. Friedland and J.R. Piroshnikoff (trans.), New York: Benjamin Blom.

Kropotkin, P. (1970 [1882]) 'Law and authority', in R. Baldwin (ed.) *Kropotkin's Revolutionary Pamphlets*, New York: Dover, pp 196–218.

Loucks, N. (2000) *Prison Rules: A Working Guide*, London: Prison Reform Trust.

Michel, L. (1981 [1886]) *The Red Virgin: Memoirs of Louise Michel*, B. Lowry and E. Ellington Gunter (trans.), Alabama: University of Alabama Press.

Nicoll, D. (2005 [1895]) *Life in English Prisons (100 Years Ago), Mysteries of Scotland Yard – Startling Revelations*, London: Kate Sharpley Library.

Nocella II, A.J., Seis, M. and Shantz, J. (eds) (2018) *Contemporary Anarchist Criminology: Against Authoritarianism and Punishment*, New York: Peter Lang,

Nocella II, A.J., Seis, M. and Shantz, J. (eds) (2020) *Classic Writings in Anarchist Criminology: A Historical Dismantling of Punishment and Domination*, Edinburgh: AK Press.

Pettit, P. (1997) *Republicanism: A Theory of Freedom and Government*, Oxford: Oxford University Press.

Prison Reform Council (1962) *Inside Story*, London: Housmans.

Prison Reform League (1910) *Crime and Criminals*, Los Angeles: Prison Reform League.

Proudhon P.J. (1969 [1840]) *What Is Property? An Inquiry into the Principle of Right and of Government*, B.R. Tucker (trans.), London: William Reeves

Radical Alternatives to Prison (RAP) (nd) *The Case for Radical Alternatives to Prison*, London: Christian Action.

Shakur, A. (1987) *Assata: An Autobiography*, London: Zed Books.

Sim, J. (2017) 'Abolitionism', in A. Brisman, E. Carrabine and N. South (eds) *The Routledge Companion to Criminological Theory and Concepts*, Abingdon: Routledge, pp 422–426.

Skinner, Q. (2008) 'Freedom as the absence of arbitrary power', in C. Laborde and J. Maynor (eds) *Republicanism and Political Theory*, Oxford: Blackwell.

Tifft, L. and Stevenson, L.E. (1985) 'Humanistic criminology: roots from Peter Kropotkin', *Journal of Society and Social Welfare*, 12(3): 488–520.

Tifft, L. and Sullivan, D. (1980) *The Struggle to be Human: Crime, Criminology and Anarchism*, Orkney: Cienfuegos Press.

Tolstoy, L. (1924 [1904]) 'Letter on the question of William Lloyd Garrison'. Available from: https://www.marxists.org/archive/tolstoy/1924/william-lloyd-garrison.html [Accessed 15 September 2024].

Tolstoy, L. (1947 [1899]) *Resurrection*, L. Maude (trans.), London: Geoffrey Cumberlege/Oxford University Press.

Van Swaaningen, R. (1997) *Critical Criminology: Visions from Europe*, London: Sage.

Ward, C. (1982) *Anarchy in Action*, London: Freedom Press.

Wilde, O. (2000 [1897]) 'To the editor of the *Daily Chronicle*', in M. Holland and R. Hart-Davis (eds), *The Complete Letters of Oscar Wilde*, London: Fourth Estate, pp 847–855.

Wilde, O. (1898) *The Ballad of Reading Gaol*. Available from: https://www.poetryfoundation.org/poems/45495/the-ballad-of-reading-gaol [Accessed 15 September 2024].

Woodcock, G. (1991) 'Introduction', in P. Kropotkin, *In Russian and French Prisons*, Montréal: Black Rose.

3

Angela Davis and the Contributions and Contradictions of Abolition

Joy James

A radical academic abolitionist emerges from state violence

As a doctoral student working on her dissertation at the University of California-San Diego, mentored by philosopher Herbert Marcuse, Angela Y. Davis accepted a teaching position in philosophy at the University of California-Los Angeles (UCLA). In 1969, a UCLA student working as a Federal Bureau of Investigation (FBI) informant outed Davis as a member of the Communist Party USA (CPUSA). Governor Ronald Reagan publicly pronounced that Angela Davis would never again teach in the University of California (UC) system after she had publicly acknowledged that she was a member of the CPUSA. Governor Reagan worked with the UC Regents to remove Davis from her teaching post as UC's first Black philosophy professor. Davis had joined the CPUSA at a time when she was also working on educational materials for the Oakland Black Panther Party (BPP). During the employment ordeal, Davis would also work closely on the Soledad Brother Defense Committee for incarcerated Black men, including George Jackson (BPP Field Marshall), facing the death penalty. She was profoundly radicalized during this time and for several decades afterwards. Although sectors of the public and iconography scholarship depicted Davis as a Black Panther, Davis does not appear to have identified herself in her previous editions of her autobiography and writings as a 'Panther' until nearly several decades after the Oakland-based Black Panther Party closed in 1982.

Davis consistently identified herself as an 'abolitionist' against the death penalty, mass incarceration, and persecution of political prisoners. As noted earlier, she worked with three high-profile Black men accused of killing a white prison guard after a guard(s) shot and killed several Black prisoners in the prison yard. George Jackson, Fleeta Drumgo, and John Clutchette were known as the 'Soledad Brothers'. Named after the prison, they were on trial and facing the death penalty. All of the Soledad Brothers would be acquitted at trial in March 1972, except for George Jackson, who was killed in August 1971 by a prison guard.

While working on the Soledad Brothers case, Angela Davis faced her own peril. Her bodyguard was Jonathan Jackson, the 17-year-old brother of George Jackson. The teen had access to Davis' weapons, which were kept in a house where Black radicals, but not Davis, lived. In a risky attempt to free and save the life of his older brother and other Black prisoners, Jonathan Jackson took several of Davis' weapons to the Marin County Courthouse on 7 August 1970 and took several people hostage in the courtroom. Black prisoners testifying in front of the court at the time included Ruchell 'Cinque' Magee, William Arthur Christmas, and James McClain. During the attempted escape, prison guards shot into the getaway van in the parking lot, killing Jonathan Jackson, Christmas and McClain, killing hostage Judge Harrold Haley and seriously injuring hostage Deputy District Attorney Gary Thomas. The following day, learning that her weapons had been used in the raid, Angela Davis, with the assistance of the CPUSA, fled into a CPUSA 'railroad' (distinguished here from a revolutionary underground such as the ones created by the Black Liberation Army or Republic of New Afrika). Due to her flight out of the state of California, Davis was placed on the FBI Most Wanted List. Largely led by Charlene Michell, who mentored and recruited Davis into the CPUSA, Davis was shepherded from California to Chicago, New York and other cities until her peaceful October arrest – FBI agents did not draw their guns – with her CPUSA-assigned companion David Poindexter, in a mid-town Manhattan hotel.

Angela Davis became an internationally known political fugitive and prisoner following the 1970 Marin County Courthouse raid led by Jonathan Jackson. Extradited back to California, she was an active participant in her trial. The defence committee grew into an international force, leading to the creation of the 'National United Committee to Free Angela Davis' (NUCFAD). Later the title was extended to include the phrase 'and All Political Prisoners'. Davis was acquitted in June 1972 by an all-White jury. Her one-time co-defendant Ruchell Magee, a Black prisoner who was shot at Marin County by prison guards, was also acquitted of major charges in 1973 by a jury. Tragically, Magee was kept in prison for an additional fifty years because the judge presiding over his trial refused to enter the jury verdict into the court records.

Magee appears to have had little public or intellectual impact on Davis' political thought and abolition. Magee considered himself a 'slave' who had a right to resist incarceration, while Davis and her legal team identified her as a 'citizen' who had a right to a fair trial. Davis was therefore more likely to be acquitted if her trial was severed from Magee's. Ironically, they both received nearly the same level of exoneration by their juries (Davis' was all-white and led by a woman, Magee's jury included Black men).

Unlike Magee, George Jackson had a profound impact on Davis during that era, half a century ago. While she was incarcerated, Davis could visit Jackson and their relationship became a personal one. Prison guards shot George Jackson in the back and killed him on 21 August 1971, while Davis was still on trial and detained in jail. Jackson had politicized Davis into a radical form of abolitionist that engaged material struggle. Co-founder of the Black Panther Party (originally named the 'Black Panther Party for Self-Defense'), Huey P. Newton, with whom Davis worked and allied herself, had also been incarcerated, faced the death penalty, and written influential books. However, George Jackson was considered to be the guerrilla fighter whose militancy, intellect, and analyses had a global impact. Jackson's highly influential *Soledad Brother: The Prison Letters of George Jackson* (Jackson, 1970) was written at the suggestion of his attorney Faye Stender. According to some scholars, Stender was also Jackson's lover. She requested French playwright Jean Genet to write the foreword for *Soledad Brother*. Stender believed that if Jackson became a literary sensation his celebrity status might save him from execution and/or assassination in prison.

However, while Jackson's impact on Davis was significant in terms of political theory, their political alignments and divergences remain largely unknown to the public. Davis supported and mourned Jackson as a revolutionary and a martyr. Yet, as an academic and author she largely rejected his militant analysis of US fascism and assertion that oppressed people have the right to all forms of resistance against predatory states and policing. The 1974 memoir *Angela Davis: An Autobiography*, edited by Toni Morrison and published by Random House, is less confrontational and militarist than Jackson's writing, particularly his posthumous *Blood in My Eye* which Morrison led Random House to publish a year after George Jackson was killed, which depicted him as a guerrilla intellectual and fighter, and BPP Field Marshall. Davis, who had briefly worked with the BPP on educational materials before joining the CPUSA through its Che-Lumumba Club, did not appear to embrace the militaristic aspect of the BPP (hence she joined the CPUSA in 1968 after several weeks/months working with the BPP). The romantic alliance between Davis and Jackson appears to be the most popular aspect of their association; however, their different political perspectives on liberation struggles would lead to different versions of abolition as radical or revolutionary engagements.

Elevating academia as a site for abolition

After her June 1972 acquittal, Angela Davis gradually returned to teaching as a visiting professor at prominent or prestigious universities in the US and in other nations. Despite Governor Reagan's declaration that she would never teach in the UC system, Davis became a UC-Santa Cruz (UCSC) lecturer in the History of Consciousness Department in 1984 and a full professor by 1991. In 1994, she was appointed UC Presidential Chair in African-American and Feminist Studies, one of the most prestigious positions in UC. She co-led the UCSC Feminist Studies Department, working with Bettina Aptheker. Davis and Aptheker, friends at the private Manhattan Elizabeth Irwin high school, both became UCSC professors. Aptheker left CPUSA several years before Davis.

In 1991, the CPUSA, led by Gus Hall, banned Angela Davis, Charlene Mitchell and some 200 reformers and leaders from the party. This led Davis and her comrades to create the Committees of Correspondence. After the collapse of the Soviet Union in 1991, and with her no longer being a member of the CPUSA central committee, Davis' academic stature and politics became more acceptable to (and aligned with) liberals, academics and funders. At the same time, the radical rebellions of the Black Power movements, American Indian Movement (Davis travelled to support the American Indian Movement [AIM] at Pine Ridge, but was turned back by police forces), anti-war protesters, Puerto Rican Independentistas, Brown Beret, Black Liberation Army, revolutionary environmental protestors became less visible as abolition became more prominent in academic studies. Davis' colleagues, former CPUSA members, became more focused on building abolition formats. Powerful non-profits began to contribute funds and shape political education. Connections among academics and conferences at prestigious institutions became increasingly public, for example 'Critical Resistance: Beyond the Prison Industrial Complex' (or 'CritResist') in 1998.

The Soviet Union fell in 1991, largely due to US escalation of militarism and nuclear warheads during the administration of President Ronald Reagan, who had hounded Davis when he was the governor of California. Seen as a 'non-communist' by some, Davis became less controversial. Her political views embraced 'integrationist' and liberal politics that affirmed US culture as being capable of being reformed. Within several decades of the founding of *Critical Resistance*, the language of 'industrial prison complex' (originally used by Mike Davis) and later 'nonreformist reforms' (orginally used by Andre Gorz) became popularized in academic abolition. Feminism and abolitionist reformism became part of standard discourse in abolition studies and progressive speech within mainstream and elite academia. Davis had met with and worked with the West Coast Panthers and leaders such as

Huey P. Newton in the late 1960s and early 1970s. After her 1972 acquittal and 1991 departure from the CPUSA, she became the most prominent of Black radicals, although Panthers in New York/Harlem were seen as the most militant. Davis, as was the case with most academics and abolitionists, denounced, dismissed or re-interpreted militant formations that advocated for the right to self-defence in order to build a prominent or dominant narrative that popularized academic abolition.

Cultural studies and abolition

Academic-based abolition became popular with multicultural studies, feminism and LGBTQ studies on the rise in the 1990s. Within academia, the definition of 'abolition' focused less on working-class militants and radical imprisoned leaders, including the agency of political prisoners and prisoners of war. In the 1990s, the radicalism of the Black liberation struggles focused often on political prisoners; yet, Davis' works became more directed towards historical studies and events. Her focus on the historical, feminism and intersectionality shaped influential trajectories in academic studies. Davis wrote about the antebellum era, 19th- to 20th-century Black feminists referencing chattel slavery, the 13th Amendment, convict prison lease system abolition resistance, and their links and formations shaped by racism or anti-Blackness as the architecture of contemporary mass incarceration (James, 1998). These were themes that were also central in Davis' academic work and teaching at UCLA, as well as her experience and courage in advocating for the Soledad Brothers Defence Committee.

1998 academic conferences launch abolition

In 1997, with (assistant) professors, doctoral students and organizers, Davis began drafting plans for *Critical Resistance* (CritResist or CR). In its early years, CR was funded by nonprofit donors, who provided seed money and allegedly proposed the concept. CR was known for its popular and well-attended academic conferences held at prestigious state and private universities. The organization attracted, trained and mentored prominent abolitionists, such as Andrea Smith, Davis' former doctoral student. The first decade of CR conferences at Research I or prestigious institutions included the University of Colorado-Boulder (CU-Boulder) (March 1998); the University of California-Berkeley (UC-Berkeley) (September 1998); and a few years later, Columbia University. Conferences at elite public and private universities shaped CritResist until nonacademics directed it to become more engaged with nonelite communities. After the first decade, organizers began to develop conferences focused increasingly on material struggles and 'conditions on the ground'. Originally, academia was the setting for CritResist's emergence.

Prior to the September 1998 launch of CritResist at UC-Berkeley, Davis had requested that another Research I state institution, CU-Boulder, host a March 1998 launch for academic-led abolition. Davis named that conference after her historic UCLA 6 October 1969 Royce Hall lecture 'Unfinished Liberation'. That lecture, or paper, was delivered when Governor Reagan and UC Regents sought to fire her as a member of the CPUSA. The March 1998 conference at CU-Boulder (reportedly at the time the most expensive conference held at CU, with costs mounting to around $100,000) would be followed by another, even more expensive formal launch of *Critical Resistance* (Gloria Steinem was considered to have been a key fundraiser) at UC-Berkeley that September. 'Critical Resistance: Beyond the Prison Industrial Complex' was funded by influential liberal nonprofit(s).

Prominent liberals and nonradicals shaped abolitionist politics through nonprofits and academia. Angela Davis' autobiography (Davis, 1974), her personal narrative of incarceration, her writings and her activism brought massive attention to prison abolition. From 1998 and for several decades, 'Critical Resistance: Beyond the Prison Industrial Complex' or 'CritResist' became central to Davis' stature as an academic, author, and advocate for civil and human rights. CritResist developed a platform for influential critics of US politics and state-sanctioned violence. Its leadership and membership also supported the Boycott, Divestment and Sanctions (BDS) movement to end apartheid and the occupation and state-sanctioned violence against Palestine. Despite the important work, prisoners of war and political prisoners, as well as militancy and rebellions, were not that prominent in Davis' leadership cadre of CritResist. A political prisoner's critique of academic abolition leadership and conferences such as 'Unfinished Liberation' led this author to edit anthologies on revolutionaries and political prisoners for over a decade (James, 2000, 2003, 2008).

Davis focused on both mass incarceration and political imprisonment, but mass incarceration, linked to chattel slavery, was a main focal point in her analyses. In 'Racialized Punishment and Prison Abolition', she emphasizes the importance of social justice as tied to abolition that confronts racism and captivity:

> An effective abolitionist campaign will have to directly address the role of race in the criminalization process. I emphasize the need to disarticulate notions of punishment from crime because I want to argue for a serious consideration of abolitionist strategies to dismantle the prison system in its present role as an institution which preserves existing structures of racism as well as creates more complicated modes of racism in US society. (Davis, 1998)

Davis explores the historical past to discern the trajectory of current movements which she helped to create. In *Are Prisons Obsolete?* (2003), Davis writes: 'I have introduced three abolition campaigns that were eventually more or less successful to make the point that social circumstances transform and popular attitudes shift, in part in response to organized social movements' (Davis, 2003). She values the historical campaigns that targeted racism: chattel slavery, lynching and Jim Crow segregation. Mass campaigns were multiracial, multiclass and Black-led. They were also anti-violence campaigns in which armed struggle was still a component, although not a primary one. In the post-civil rights movement era, from the 1966 Stokely Carmichael chant for 'Black Power!' to the 1972 National Black Political Convention several months before Angela Davis' acquittal in June, the 'revolutionary era' was led by Black militants, who would become political prisoners, and their attorneys. Davis was aligned with or co-led the Soledad Brothers Defence Committee (SBDC) and was a key leader of the 1970–1972 National United Committee to Free Angela Davis (NUCFAD). The year following her acquittal, NUCFAD became the National Alliance Against Racist and Political Repression (NAARPR) which would close in 1986 and re-emerge over thirty years later at a re-founding in Chicago, IL.

Replacing NAARPR, co-lead by Davis and influential organizers and academics, CritResist grew from 1998 to 2008, promoted through academic leadership and by foundation grants. The major focus remained on mass incarceration; the emphasis on political prisoners was not as prominent as it had been in the late 1960s and early 1970s when mass movements fought to save the lives of – or resist the murders of – Panthers such as Fred Hampton, Mark Clark and George Jackson, while also protesting the captivity of political prisoners such as Panther Geronimo Pratt, Mumia Abu-Jamal and American Indian Movement (AIM) leader Leonard Peltier, as well as other political prisoners. (Some abolitionists and academics argue that all imprisoned Blacks – despite their varied political beliefs – are political prisoners based on being a targeted race.) By its ten-year anniversary in 2008, the year that Professor Davis retired from academia, 'Critical Resistance: Beyond the Prison Industrial Complex' leadership had become more decentralized and focused on impoverished, working-class communities and organizing them.

Contrasts: 'Unfinished Liberation' Conference and Jericho '98: Free Political Prisoners!

Several weeks after the March 1998 CU-Boulder 'Unfinished Liberation' conference, the Jericho '98 mass protest (reportedly attended by over 5,000 people) took place in Washington DC. Davis' keynote at the Boulder conference made no mention of political prisoners or this upcoming protest to free political prisoners that would be staged in Washington DC. No public announcements about the protest or requests that conference attendees travel to Washington or support imprisoned organizers was raised. Political prisoners such as Peltier, Mumia Abu-Jamal, Geronimo Pratt, Ruchell Magee (Davis' former co-defendant) were among these. Although Davis' list of invitees to the CU-Boulder conference did not include Black Panthers, this author reached out to Kim Holder, Harlem BPP veteran. Holder suggested that speaker invitations also be sent to three other NYC Panther veterans: Safiyah Bukhari, Gabe Torres, and Lew Lew Lee. Bukhari and Torres were incarcerated as political prisoners. All four East Coast Panther vets attended the Boulder conference.

Boulder's 'Unfinished Liberation' conference on mass incarceration and Washington DC's Jericho March to free political prisoners took place in the same month with little to no connections between the abolitionists. The four NYC Panthers, as did Davis, while at the Boulder conference, appear to have failed to share publicly or promote information on the DC Jericho movement to encourage people to support or attend the Jericho '98 March 27th gathering in DC. The academic-led abolition conference was educational but distanced from political prisoners (Davis herself was a former political prisoner but not a 'Panther vet'). Although Panther vets and political prisoners appeared on campus, they lectured and talked but perhaps did not mobilize an audience that was not seen as publicly aligned with militant struggles. Academia as an educational site seemed to have muted contemporary revolutionary abolitionist struggles. Contradictions concerning organizing and mobilization appeared but were not addressed.

In addition to that missed opportunity, Oakland or California leadership attempted to oust documentarian Lee Lew Lee, an Afro-Asian Panther and filmmaker, and ban his 1996 documentary *All Power to the People! The Black Panther Party and Beyond!* from the Boulder conference. During a late-night phone call shortly before the Unfinished Liberation conference, Davis conveyed that Elaine Brown, the first woman leader of the BPP, promoted by Huey Newton, had contacted Davis to demand that the documentary be banned from the conference because in the documentary a Panther vet/political prisoner briefly states that Brown allied with state operatives or police agents. In her 1992 memoir *A Taste of Power*, Brown describes her long-term romantic relationship to a White operative who had spied on Black civil rights and liberation organizations. The attempts to block the documentary failed and the screening took place in Boulder (James, 2000).

Jericho confronts the state: free political prisoners!

Several weeks after leaving Boulder, Kim Holder, Safiyah Bukhari, and Angela Davis all attended the Washington DC protest led by the Jericho movement to end political imprisonment and to free political prisoners.

Davis' CU-Boulder keynote, before 2,000 people, focused on gender, race, and equality, mass incarceration and prison abolition; the keynote did not address political prisoners incarcerated because of their affiliations with radical organizations such as the BLA (Black Liberation Army), RNA (Republic of New Afrika), AIM (American Indian Movement). At the Jericho event Davis spoke at the platform before the White House, repeatedly using the phrase 'prison industrial complex' (PIC), language coined in Mike Davis' 1990 *City of Quartz*. The Jericho Movement event focused on imprisoned radical and rebel organizers, as targets of COINTELPRO, FBI and local police. The Jericho Movement was organized by political prisoner Safiya Bukhari and then-held Panther vet Jalil Muntaqim (who served 49 years in prison before his release). *All Power to the People! The Black Panther Party and Beyond!* featured speakers at the Washington DC event: Safiyah Bukhari, Kim Holder, and Kathleen Cleaver. The documentary suggested that Elaine Brown worked with state operatives (see earlier) and largely failed to depict Davis (Davis did not publicly identify as a Panther during those decades in which the BPP existed as a [splintered] party; decades later, Davis did however pen the foreword to the memoirs of Black Panther women leaders Assata Shakur and Safiya Bukhari.)

According to the Jericho digital platform, Safiya Bukhari of the Provisional Government of the Republic of New Afrika (RNA) and the New Afrikan Liberation Front made the original call in October 1996 to create the Washington DC protest against President Bill Clinton administration's refusal to offer clemency for political prisoners. Political prisoner Muntaqim also called for a national march on the White House for March 1998. Bukhari (who transitioned in 2003) was incarcerated from 1975 to 1983. Muntaqim, who was in prison during the conference and the mass march, was incarcerated from 1971 to 2020.

Jericho's motto was patterned on Jericho's biblical walls tumbling down: the Jericho March focused on advocacy groups such as AIM and MOVE, and individuals such as AIM leader Leonard Peltier and the human rights journalist Mumia Abu-Jamal. At the Jericho event, militants controlled the microphone with fiery declarations for freedom. Davis presented more as an academic and scholar educating about the prison industrial complex. The Jericho Movement petition was co-signed by some 50 organizations. Defence committees, some 64 Jericho Organizing Committees and Students for Jericho demanded that the Clinton administration offer 'Recognition and Amnesty for US held Political Prisoners and Prisoners of War':

> There are hundreds of people who went to prison as a result of their work on the street against oppressive conditions like indecent housing and inadequate or complete lack of medical care, lack of quality education, police brutality and murder, and struggling for

independence and liberation. These people belonged to organizations like the Black Panther Party, La Raza Unida, FALN, Los Macheteros, North American Anti-Imperialist Movement, May 19th, AIM, the Black Liberation Army, etc., and many were incarcerated because of their political beliefs and acts in support of and/or in defense of freedom. (Jericho Movement, 2015)

During the Washington DC event, a Black protester advocating for political prisoners distracted from Angela Davis' presentation by performing African drumming during her speech. The speech mentioned the need to free Ruchell Magee, her former co-defendant, and cited statistics on mass incarceration as she repeated the phrase which would be popularized by CR: 'the prison industrial complex'. Other speakers included Puerto Rican, Black, American Indian, Chicano, Asian and White radical attorneys and advocates for revolutionary political prisoners. University conferences had spent or would spend hundreds of thousands of dollars for campus political education on incarceration and abolition. Yet a different form of pedagogy and militant thought had created revolutionary abolition among radicals who were largely not academics. Speakers at 'Jericho '98' made demands, quoting from Malcolm X's 'Message to the Grass Roots', delivered on 10 November 1963, in which he stated that oppressed peoples must put aside their differences and unite based on common struggles. However, a stark contrast between abolition for revolutionaries and abolition for the mass incarcerated remained. The latter would be seen as reformist and thus more acceptable to the state, whereas the former would signal the uprisings and rebellions prohibited and punished by the state and its counter-revolutionary policing agencies.

Jericho speakers at the March 1998 protest included former political prisoner Geronimo Pratt.[1] Geronimo Pratt was released in 1997 after his conviction was overturned (Kathleen Cleaver was one of his attorneys; Cleaver earned her JD from Yale Law School and served as an attorney for Pratt, exposing the malfeasance of the Los Angeles Police Department [LAPD] and FBI). Pratt had been framed by the FBI and LAPD for a murder that he did not commit. The US would ultimately pay financial compensation for his 27 years of incarceration without ever admitting that the government and FBI COINTELPRO had framed him in order to destabilize Black liberation struggles. Pratt recalled that Amnesty International had refused to support his case because he was not a 'prisoner of conscience'; the decorated Vietnam solider refused to renounce armed self-defence during the decades of COINTELPRO and police torture and assassinations of Black radicals. Pratt's response to Amnesty was that all political prisoners have conscience so they should qualify as 'prisoners of conscience'. At the Jericho '98 gathering at Washington DC, Pratt spoke about Californian political prisoners Hugo

Pinnell and Ruchell Magee (released from prison in 2023, Magee transitioned after several months of 'freedom' [James and Changa, 2023]).

Kathleen Cleaver, the first woman to sit on the BPP central committee, also spoke at the Jericho gathering. The former Student Nonviolent Coordinating Committee (SNCC) organizer had wed Eldridge Cleaver. (By 1969, the Cleavers had split from Huey Newton and the Oakland BPP leadership and left the country). Other speakers at the Jericho gathering included Ramona Africa of MOVE who shared that Meryl Africa had died after 20 years in prison. Josefina Rodriguez spoke about the Puerto Rican independence struggle against colonialism. Attorney Bob Boyle, who had worked with the Panther 21, was also present. When Safiya Bukhari took the microphone to explain the work of Jericho '98 on behalf of US political prisoners, she called out the name of the slain George Jackson.

AIM leader Dennis Banks, advocating for Peltier and others, offered a long view and theory of imprisonment that argued that given genocidal violence against and the captivity of indigenous peoples, the history of colonization rendered political prisoners as a mass: 'To be born native is to be born a political prisoner.' Banks referenced the leader Geronimo (1829–1909) being tricked after meeting with state officials, only to be incarcerated for decades. Banks also described how Chief Joseph was also tracked down and put in prison and never allowed to return home. From the podium before the White House, Banks narrated how President Andrew Jackson's 1830 Indian Removal Act allowed the US military to impose a forced march on Indigenous people in order to move them west of Mississippi; thousands died from disease, exhaustion and starvation in genocidal violence that created mass political prisoners. Banks told the gathering: 'Let's shout to the White House, let's shout to the White House Free Leonard Peltier!' In the closing days of his second term, President Clinton offered clemency to Puerto Rican *Independentistas* to increase voter turnout among New York Puerto Rican communities for the First Lady Hillary Clinton, during the 2000 election. She went on to become the first female Senator from New York State. No US President has provided clemency to a member of the BPP or BLA or RNA. As of November 2024, Peltier remains a political prisoner.

Anthologizing abolition: states of confinement – policing, detention, and prisons

In 1998, after the 'Unfinished Liberation' and Jericho Movement protest took place, *The Angela Y. Davis Reader* was published. This author had consulted Davis about the Introduction and agreed to delete information that highlighted contradictions within abolition activism (for example, fundraising from individuals aligned with the CIA or state). The *Reader* became an influential anthology, one that sold out quickly but soon after became expensive and largely unaffordable for most readers; in 2023, as *Contextualizing Angela Davis: The Agency and Identity of an Icon* (James, 2024) was preparing for publication, *The Angela Y. Davis Reader* was made affordable in print. Two years after the anthology was originally printed, *States of Confinement* was published in 2000. This anthology would also not exist except for Davis' contributions. *States of Confinement* is largely comprised of papers and presentations delivered at the 1998 'Unfinished Liberation' conference, the conference that Davis had requested to be held in Boulder. Davis did not request an anthology from the conference. However, this author negotiated with a white, feminist editor at a prominent centrist/liberal press to collect chapters and edit the anthology, in which Davis made substantial contributions. Published in 2000, *States of Confinement* consisted of the essays of CritResist founders and other participants at the CU-Boulder March 1998 conference.

This author had negotiated books for incarcerated people. Thus, 50 copies of *States of Confinement* were mailed to largely political prisoners. One political prisoner, Jalil Muntaqim, informed this author that the anthology did not reflect the analyses and abolitionist demands and desires of revolutionaries. As mentioned above, that led this author to a decade of anthologizing only political prisoners and political resistors to the state. The US Department of Justice, Office of Justice Programs (2000) posted *States of Confinement* on its platform. Ironically, the government amplified the book on its state platforms, which identified the collected writings from the 1998 CU conference as a text worthy of government scrutiny.

The US government catalogued the anthology contesting carceral systems. The annotation reads: 'This book explores racial, sexual, and class inequalities tied to criminal justice in the United States and raises such issues as inequities in prosecution, sentencing, and exploitation and abuse in policing and imprisonment.'

The abstract asserts:

> Contributors to the book critique the death penalty, racism and the criminal justice system; confinement based on gender and sexuality; police misconduct and brutality; and state punitive responses to political radicalism and resistance. The book's 26 chapters explore the limits of a democratic society that has dedicated immense resources to policing and punishment. The chapters are organized into five parts: (1) executions – capital punishment and sentencing children to death; (2) Blacks and criminal justice – Black radicalism and the economy of incarceration, young Blacks and the criminal justice system, and Black gangs; (3) gender, sexuality and confinement – programming and healthcare for incarcerated women, imprisoned native women,

military prostitution, AIDS and rape in Texas prisons, and ritual killings; (4) policing – lynching, police militarization, state violence, the criminalization of immigrant workers, and surveillance; and, (5) political repression and resistance – the grand jury and jail activists, Arab Americans and civil liberties, political prisoners.

The *States of Confinement* anthology would not have existed without Davis requesting that the 'Unfinished Liberation' conference be organized at CU-Boulder. The compilation of talks and papers presented at the conference included Davis' 'From the Convict Lease System to the Supermax Prison'. Transitioning from CU-Boulder to Brown University, using personal research funds to invite political prisoner veterans/prisoners of war to Brown for conferences, this author began to organize conferences and edit volumes focusing on political prisoners: *Imprisoned Intellectuals*, *The New Abolitionists*, *Warfare in the American Homeland*. These anthologies included the writings of Geronimo Pratt, George Jackson, Assata Shakur, Mumia Abu-Jamal and Angela Davis.

Following Muntaqim's critique this author left Boulder for Providence RI to teach at Brown University. The task there was to shift the abolition focus to expand and to engage more with political prisoners and revolutionaries. At first, Brown University was apprehensive or disaffected concerning political prisoners. However, some twenty years later, in 2023, Brown purchased Mumia Abu-Jamal's papers. Literature and art by political prisoners was becoming central to academia (Radcliffe/Harvard purchased Angela Davis' archives in 2018). Keynote speakers at the Mumia Abu-Jamal 2023 conference included Abu-Jamal (who spoke by phone), Angela Davis, Johanna Fernandez and Pam Afrika (who was unable to attend the gathering due to health issues). The acquisitions of political prisoners' writings, art, music, speeches became more prominent on campuses, especially so for elite schools, in which non-profit organizations and academic abolitionists might converge.

Critical resistance evolves in 21st-century abolitionism

California's extensive flagship or elite public universities reflected a vast public system for influential and gifted intellectuals. Davis' stature in that system helped to open doors for CR by stabilizing it through a cadre of undergraduate, graduate students and faculty developing the framework on campuses. The campuses included the incarcerated, liberals, radicals and militants. Before Davis' retirement from the academy, she contributed over a decade to building CR and mentoring its cadres. On its 10th anniversary in 2008, the C10 gathering of 'Critical Resistance: Beyond the Prison Industrial Complex' developed multi-racial activist-academic leadership. Davis' former status as a political prisoner, as well as her scholarship, publications and prominent status as an academic, allowed her to help leverage influential platforms and publications to focus on abolition, anti-racism and feminism largely within academic settings. Let us now return to the two 1998 academic conferences and the emergence and development of CR.

In the 1998 spring and autumn, from CU-Boulder 'Unfinished Liberation' through to UC-Berkeley's CritResist, the concept of abolition expanded. Mike Davis spoke at the UC-Berkeley CR conference, popularizing his phrase 'prison industrial complex' taken from his 1990 *City of Quartz* (Critical Resistance's statement 'Rest in Power Mike Davis' following Mike Davis' passing in 2022 and paid tribute to his political phrases and analyses [Critical Resistance, 2022]).[2] The UC-Berkeley *Critical Resistance* conference was expansive, its invited speakers also included US Congresswoman Maxine Waters.[3] CritResist gathered diverse abolitionists and over years began expanding analytical frameworks. The emergent organization provided critical language that defined the 'prison industrial complex' (PIC) as 'the overlapping interests of government and industry that use surveillance, policing, and imprisonment as solutions to economic, social and political problems.' CR analyses how the PIC's economic and racial power stabilizes corporate and state as 'the authority of people'. CR maintains that racist stereotypes target and criminalize the impoverished, nonconforming and undocumented as 'deviants'. Public and private prisons as well as police forces use 'tough on crime' narratives to monetize suffering and support oppressive police unions. CritResist views abolition as a 'political vision with the goal of eliminating imprisonment, policing, and surveillance and creating lasting alternatives to punishment and imprisonment' (Critical Resistance, nda).[4] For CritResist, a future without prisons is imperative: 'Abolition isn't just about getting rid of' cages; it includes 'undoing the society we live in'. Thus abolition becomes a strategy that is both a 'practical organizing tool and a long-term goal':

> An abolitionist vision means that we must build models. Today that can represent how we want to live in the future. It means developing practical strategies for taking small steps that move us toward making our dreams real and that lead us all to believe that things really could be different. It means living this vision in our daily lives. (Critical Resistance, nda)[5]

CR does not mention its predecessor and 'trial run' – the March 1998 CU-Boulder conference Davis requested and named 'Unfinished Liberation' after her 1969 UCLA lecture delivered while under siege by the Governor of California and the UC Regents (see detailed discussion above).

What, if anything, was beneficial from the CU-Boulder conference and was any of the CU content relevant to the UC-Berkeley launch? The official genealogy 'disappears' the pre-conference requested by Davis which presumably shaped perceptions of what type of abolition was desirable and viable. In the official records, Davis' 'Unfinished Liberation' as a mass gathering in March 1998 is notably absent when the timeline is set in September 1998, with no memories or data reflecting the two events in March 1998: CU-Boulder and Jericho '98 in Washington DC. The UC-Berkeley massive conference became the origin story of CritResist. However, memories of its predecessor point to the importance of studying internal contradictions:

> over 3,500 activists, academics, former and current prisoners, labor leaders, religious organizations, feminists, gay, lesbian and transgender activists, youth, families, and policy makers from 50 states and several countries. The three-day event hosted 200 panels and workshops, cultural events, and a film festival. The following year, Northeast academics and activists dialogued with 1998 CR conference coordinators to create a Northeast Regional Conference for the Bay Area. The focus on feminist leadership was and remains prominent within Critical Resistance; leadership was diverse and dedicated, such as the co-founded leaders Rose Braz, who became the first staffer of Critical Resistance following the UC-Berkeley Conference in September 1998. (Critical Resistance, ndb)

CR continued to develop and lean towards grassroots organizing. According to CR archives, in December 1999, 20 planners met in Philadelphia to plan Critical Resistance East (CR East). Later, a 9–11 March 2001 conference at Columbia University in Manhattan drew over 2,000 people to address the prison industrial complex (PIC). While CR 'prioritized the participation and leadership of those most vulnerable to the prison industrial complex', it began to move beyond elite academia-based conferences after its early years and increasingly focused on collective strategies and skilled local organizing and expectation of conference organizers:[6]

> this was only a jumping-off point for a regional component of CR's movement building project, and for smaller groups to find their way into organizing locally in their areas. As CR East planners were putting the regional conference together, Critical Resistance continued to grow nationally ... planning for Critical Resistance South, and local groups getting involved in CR East outreach and organizing. ... CR needed to develop a national structure and to come up with a strategic plan. (Critical Resistance, nda)[7]

The May 2001 CritResist gathering worked with varied states to develop national structure and ideology relevant to the local chapters, and to support autonomous structures through national chapters in Oakland, Los Angeles, New York City, Portland.[8] Abolitionist labour included other carceral settings: public housing residents, surveillance and gentrification, juvenile detention centres, and political education programmes for women in residential treatment centres. The CritResist South conference de-emphasized large (academic) conferences; a Southern Regional Coordinator emerged to support new chapters;[9] a Louisiana conference was held in April 2003 in New Orleans' Treme sector, a historically Black community. Distancing from elite academia, CritResist South increased educational endeavours about the massive growth of mass incarceration:

> From 1980 to 2002, the number of people imprisoned in the nation's prisons, jails, juvenile facilities and detention centers quadrupled in size – from roughly 500,000 to 2.1 million people. The US now has the largest prison system in the world and its impact influences the social, economic and political life of all regions and sectors in the US. Along with the United States' 2.1 million people behind bars, 2.2 million individuals are now employed in policing, corrections and courts, overshadowing the 1.7 million Americans employed in higher education, and the 600,000 employed in public welfare. With 6.6 million people in prison and jail, or on probation and parole, there are now 8.8 million people either under the control of the correctional system or working in the criminal justice sector in the US. (Herzing and Burch, 2003)

CritResist and its academic cadres, and prominent (co-)founder Angela Davis, consistently link antebellum slavery, postbellum convict prison leasing, Jim Crow segregation, contemporary mass incarceration, immigration policing, domestic violence, closing prisons and stopping new prison developments, and sexual/racial violence. CritResist's battles against contemporary imprisonment span multiple states:

> ... Critical Resistance, a national grassroots group that fights to end this nation's reliance on prisons, police, and surveillance as an answer to social, political, and economic problems [created work] groups made up of community organizers from across the South (from Alabama, Arkansas, Florida, Georgia, Kentucky, Louisiana, Mississippi, North Carolina, South Carolina, Tennessee, Virginia, and West Virginia) [which] joined together to organize everything from site logistics, to outreach, lead-up events, written materials, a media strategy and a wide-ranging program. (Herzing and Burch, 2003)

CR South originally met at the historic Highlander Centre in Tennessee. The gathering included performances, films, discussions and workshops focused on strategies to curtail predatory and racially fashioned policing that included the school-to-prison pipelines, familial dysfunction and disintegration through poverty and state agencies. Strategies also addressed abolitionist support for political prisoners (Herzing and Burch, 2003: 1).

Solidarity and candour in abolition circles?

CritResist, Angela Davis, and abolitionist collectives brought new forms of activism to the academy. Their analyses and contributions were amplified through countless articles, podcasts, webinars and publications. Influential authors linked abolition, academia, anti-racism, feminism and LGBTQIA+ rights. Davis' key books include the 2016 *Freedom Is a Constant Struggle: Ferguson, Palestine, and the Foundation of a Movement* and the most recent two volumes of *Abolition: Politics, Practices, Promises*. There is also *Abolition. Feminism. Now.* authored by Angela Davis, Gina Dent, Erica Meiners and Beth Richie. The academics and authors also created a 2023 digital 'reading and discussion guide' with the book, posted on the Haymarket Books publisher platform. The text reflects decades of contributions by authors, organizers, CritResist and INCITE! Women of Color against Violence. (INCITE was renamed 'Women, Gender Non-conforming, and Trans People of Color against Violence'.) The authors embrace a collective vision of radical abolition and feminism linked to anti-racism and anti-capitalism as key components for study and struggle amid a range of ideological frameworks from liberal to anti-imperialist. The *Abolition. Feminism. Now.* digital study guide raises queries to help clarify feminist abolition; some of the questions appear below:

> Why is it important to recognize that abolition and feminism are both political methods and practices?
> Why is it important to acknowledge that harm will still occur, even with a robust ecosystem of networks and tools?
> Why is feminism central to abolition and abolition indivisible from feminism? Why must gender violence be included in the fight for abolition?
> How do you think about the connections between colonialism, imperialism, gender violence, and abolition feminism?
> How did Critical Resistance's use of new vocabulary, including the terms 'prison industrial complex' and 'abolition,' impact the movement for social change?
> .... How are child and family services used to harm poor families? How does this disproportionately impact Black and Indigenous women?
> Why are feminist, queer, women of color histories of resistance often erased by systems and institutions? What actions can you take to prevent this erasure in current movement work?

How did INCITE! build a collective political consciousness of gender violence over time, and what challenges did the organization experience? (Davis et al, 2023)

Conclusion: Identity, contradiction and cooptation

INCITE! Women of Color against Violence evolved alongside CritResist and the emergence of influential academic abolitionists. However, contradictions emerged. INCITE and *Critical Resistance* co-founder Andrea Smith, who attended the Unfinished Liberation conference as Davis' doctoral student, wrote an influential dissertation on gender violence against Indigenous women; the text became a well-received book: *Conquest: Sexual Violence and American Indian Genocide* (Smith, 2015). Falsely claiming to be an Indigenous scholar, Smith garnered academic admissions, positions, and publications and became a prominent abolitionist within the network built from *Critical Resistance*. She helped to build networks of 'women of colour' abolitionists, including INCITE, CritResist.

After years of controversy, Indigenous women and scholars posted the 7 July 2015 'Open Letter from Indigenous Women Scholars Regarding Discussions of Andrea Smith' (Barker, 2015). The letter was signed by Joanne Barker, Jodi A. Byrd, Jill Doerfler, Lisa Kahaleole Hall, LeAnne Howe, J. K'haulani Kauanui, Jean O'Brien, Kathryn W. Shanley, Noenoe K. Silva, Shannon Speed, Kim TallBear and Jacki Thompson Rand. In order to defend Smith, who belonged to the prominent circle of academics who promoted academic-led abolition, academics dismissed the concerns of Indigenous women scholars, intellectuals and communities as 'disposability politics' or 'cancel culture'. Indigenous women who objected to white people reinventing themselves as Indigenous were chastised by some feminist abolitionists. Despite *Indian Country Today* publishing the 2015 'Open letter from Indigenous women scholars regarding discussions of Andrea Smith', an academic abolition firewall built by influential networks maintained. Only when the major liberal/centrist press covered the controversy did the concerns of Indigenous women became a priority. After the *New York Times* published 'The Native Scholar Who Wasn't' in May 2021 (Viren, 2021), Andrea Smith negotiated an early retirement from UC-Riverside, which terminated her standing as a professor in August 2024, based on Smith's use of false and unsubstantiated claims of indigeneity to promote her academic career and prominence as an abolitionist. The issue concerning abolition agency is not about a single scholar; rather, the question is: how might the contradictions embedded in progressive or liberal or radical abolition be addressed in ways that are productive and that stop exploitation and narrative domination?

Platformed in elite academia, foundations and nonprofits, contemporary abolition has benefited from the struggles and leadership of wo/men,

LGBTQIA+ feminist scholars and organizers of all ethnicities, yet abolition contains contradictions rarely critiqued in public. Even abolition's 'intersectionality' and feminism have not consistently built a stable foundation for accountability to communal, nonelites, and transformative radical politics. Millions of dollars of funding from foundations to academic abolitionists has created a political firewall that makes transparency and accountability more difficult given the prominent roles of elites, directors and writers.

The very understanding of identity and belonging can be corrupted by political brands and power tied to funders and the liberal state. Vigilance against identity theft is essential yet insufficient public space has been created to address contradictions within abolitionist formations that foster or ignore the narrative capture of marginalized peoples. Navajo Nation citizen/Yankton Sioux Tribe descendant Jacqueline Keeler offers an important warning about concentrated power residing within elite abolitionist formations: 'It is the ultimate form of colonization, where they actually become us instead of actually listening to us' (Quinn, 2023).

Notes

[1] This author had in fact invited Pratt to deliver the second keynote for 'Unfinished Liberation' following Davis' primary keynote. CU-Boulder faculty leadership and the Ethnic Studies chair, who were promoting Unfinished Liberation, had been nervous about Pratt's appearance on campus, as Newton had supported Davis when she was on trial but had told Black Panther members not to corroborate Pratt's innocence of murder charges (Coleman, 2011). Pratt had never responded to the invitation.

[2] For further details, see https://criticalresistance.org/updates/rest-in-power-mike-davis/ [Accessed 15 September 2024].

[3] For further details, see https://criticalresistance.org/updates/rest-in-power-mike-davis/ [Accessed 15 September 2024].

[4] For further details, see http://criticalresistance.org/about/history/ [Accessed 15 September 2024].

[5] For further details, see http://criticalresistance.org/about/history/ [Accessed 15 September 2024].

[6] For further details, see http://criticalresistance.org/about/history/ [Accessed 15 September 2024].

[7] For further details, see http://criticalresistance.org/about/history/ [Accessed 15 September 2024].

[8] For further details, see http://criticalresistance.org/about/history/ [Accessed 15 September 2024].

[9] For further details, see http://criticalresistance.org/about/history/ [Accessed 15 September 2024].

References

Barker, Joanne et al (2015) 'Open letter from Indigenous women scholars regarding discussions of Andrea Smith', *Indian Country Today (ICT)*, original 7 July 2015, updated 18 September 2018, Available from: https://ictnews.org/archive/open-letter-from-indigenous-women-scholars-regarding-discussions-of-andrea-smith [Accessed 15 September 2024].

Bukhari, S. (2010) *The War Before: The True-Life Story of Becoming a Black Panther, Keeping the Faith in Prison, and Fighting for Those Left Behind*, Laura Whitehorn (ed.), New York: Feminist Press.

Coleman, K. (2011) 'Elmer "Geronimo" Pratt: the untold story of the Black Panther leader, dead at 63'. Available from: https://newrepublic.com/article/90735/black-panther-geronimo-pratt-murder-conviction-prison-huey-newton [Accessed 18 October 2024].

Critical Resistance (nda) 'History'. Available from: http://criticalresistance.org/about/history/ [Accessed 15 September 2024].

Critical Resistance (ndb) 'Honoring Rose Braz: CR co-founder and abolitionist leader'. Available from: https://criticalresistance.org/6125-2/ [Accessed 15 September 2024].

Critical Resistance (2022) 'Rest in power, Mike Davis!'. Available from: https://criticalresistance.org/updates/rest-in-power-mike-davis/ [Accessed 18 October 2024].

Davis, A. (1974) *The Autobiography of Angela Davis*, New York: Random House.

Davis, A. (1998) 'Racialized punishment and prison abolition', in J. James (ed.) *The Angela Y. Davis Reader*, Chichester: Blackwell.

Davis, A. (2003) *Are Prisons Obsolete?*, New York: Seven Stories Press.

Davis, A., Dent, G., Meiners, E. and Richie, B. (2023) *Abolition. Feminism. Now*, Chicago: Haymarket Books.

Davis, M. (1990) *City of Quartz*. Chicago: Haymarket Books.

Herzing, R. and Burch, M. (2003) 'Critical Resistance South: challenging the prison industrial complex', *USA Today Magazine, The November Coalition*.

Jackson, G. (1970) *Soledad Brother: The Prison Letters of George Jackson*. Brooklyn, NY: Lawrence Hill.

Jericho Movement (2015) 'The Jericho Movement: amnesty and freedom for all political prisoners'. Available from: http://www.thejerichomovement.com/sites/default/files/resource_file/jericho_3-fold_2015.pdf [Accessed 15 September 2024].

James, J. (1996) *Resisting State Violence*, Minneapolis: University of Minnesota Press.

James, J. (ed.) (1998) *The Angela Y. Davis Reader*, New York: Wiley Blackwell.

James, J. (ed.) (2000) *States of Confinement: Policing, Detention, and Prisons*, New York: St Martin's Press.

James, J. (ed.) (2003) *Imprisoned Intellectuals*, Lexington: Rowman & Littlefield.

James, J. (ed.) (2005) *The New Abolitionists*, Albany, NY: SUNY Press.

James, J. (ed.) (2008) *Warfare in the American Homeland*, Durham, NC: Duke University Press.

James, J. (2024) *Contextualizing Angela Davis: The Agency and Identity of an Icon*, London: Bloomsbury Press.

James, J. and Changa, K. (2023) 'Slave rebel or citizen?', *Inquest*, Harvard Law School, 2 May.

Lew Lee, L. (1996) *All Power to the People! The Black Panther Party and Beyond* (documentary). Available from: https://www.youtube.com/watch?v=pKvE6_s0jy0 [Accessed 18 October 2024].

Muntaqim, J. (2003) *We Are Our Own Liberators*, Binghamton, NY: PM Press.

Newton, H. (1972) *To Die for the People: The Writings of Huey P. Newton*. New York: Random House Press.

Quinn, R. (2023) 'Professor leaving university after being dubbed "pretendian" for years', *Inside Higher Education*, 18 August. Available from: https://www.insidehighered.com/news/faculty-issues/diversity-equity/2023/08/18/professor-leaving-after-being-dubbed-pretendian [Accessed 15 September 2024].

Shakur, A. (1988) *Assata: An Autobiography*, London: Zed Press.

Smith, A. (2015) *Conquest: Sexual Violence and American Indian Genocide*, Durham, NC: Duke University Press.

US Department of Justice, Office of Justice Programs, James J. (ed.) (2000) *States of Confinement, Policing, Detention, and Prisons*, New York: St Martin's Press. Available from: https://www.ojp.gov/ncjrs/virtual-library/abstracts/states-confinement-policing-detention-and-prisons, NCJ Number 18321 [Accessed 15 September 2024].

Viren, S. (2021) 'The native scholar who wasn't', *New York Times*, 25 May.

West, C. (1993) *Race Matters*, Boston: Beacon Press.

4

Phenomenology, Abolition and the Lived Experience of Incarceration

Lisa Guenther

Many abolitionists affirm the importance of lived experience for our critical analysis of carceral systems and for social movements to dismantle these systems. But the meaning of 'lived experience' is by no means clear. Not everyone who spends time in prison shares the same perspective, nor do they analyse their experience in the same way or to the same extent. Olúfẹ́mi Táíwò (2020) warns against reifying and tokenizing lived experience, as if it automatically yielded deep insights into the meaning of systems and structures. And yet, given the degree to which the perspectives of people in prison have been systematically silenced or discredited in advance, many abolitionist activists and scholars rightfully emphasize the importance of amplifying the voices of those who are directly impacted by prison systems.[1] As a method that begins with first-person experience, but also reflects on the conditions under which this experience yields true knowledge about the world, phenomenology seems particularly well suited to engage with these questions about the significance of lived experience for abolitionist theory and practice. In this chapter, I offer an overview of four different approaches to phenomenological research in prison studies, reflecting on their strengths and limitations for abolitionist movements: 1) first-person testimony from people in prison; 2) qualitative social science research on the lived experience of prisoners; 3) phenomenological reflection on lived experience in prison; and 4) critical phenomenologies of carceral power. I conclude with some reflections on the possibility of an abolitionist practice of phenomenology.

Four approaches to phenomenology and prison studies

Phenomenology and prison studies intersect in at least four different ways. In this section, I will review each of these approaches with several examples to elucidate their strengths and limitations.

First-person testimony about prison experience

The most direct source of research on the lived experience of people in prison is writing by prisoners themselves. This may take the form of letters, journals or diaries, poems or articles written for prison newsletters or for publications outside of prison, memoirs, autobiographies and academic journals. Prison writing by Malcolm X (1987), George Jackson (1994), Angela Davis (1989), Assata Shakur (1999), Leonard Peltier (2000), Jack Henry Abbott (1991), Jacobo Timerman (2002), Reginald Dwayne Betts (2010) and many others share detailed descriptions of their lived experience of incarceration, deep reflections on this experience, and incisive critiques of the racism, heterosexism, capitalism and other forms of structural violence that have shaped the prisons system (see also Chapter 1 in this volume). Many prison memoirs engage with questions and ideas that overlap with the phenomenological tradition in philosophy, such as the experience of time, space and embodiment, without needing to engage with this philosophical tradition directly; a notable exception is James Davis III's article 'Law, prison, and double-double consciousness' (2019), to which I will return later.

In a 1970 letter to his lawyer, George Jackson writes about the intergenerational temporality of his experience in solitary confinement:

> My recall is nearly perfect, time has faded nothing. I recall the very first kidnap. I've lived through the passage, died on the passage, lain in the unmarked, shallow graves of the millions who fertilized the Amerikan soil with their corpses; cotton and corn growing out of my chest, 'unto the third and fourth generation', the tenth, the hundredth. My mind ranges back and forth through the uncounted generations, and I feel all that they ever felt, but double. I can't help it; there are too many things to remind me of the 23½ hours that I'm in this cell. Not ten minutes pass without a reminder. In between, I'm left to speculate on what form the reminder will take. (Jackson, 1994: 233)

Jack Henry Abbott writes in his prison memoir about the impact of prison time on his embodied experience of sensation:

> I have been made oversensitive – my very flesh has been made to suffer sensations and longings I never had before. I have been chopped to

pieces by a life of deprivation of sensations; by beatings so frequent I am now a piece of meat and bone; by lies and by drugs that attack my nervous system. I have had my mind turned into steel by the endless smelter of time in confinement. (Abbott, 1991: 37)

Angela Davis reflects on the interplay between her own experience of racist criminalization and the political forces that have shaped both her experience and her decision to write about this experience:

[T]he forces that have made my life what it is are the very same forces that have shaped and mis-shaped the lives of millions of people ... I was reluctant to write this book because concentration on my personal history might detract from the movement which brought my case to the people in the first place ... When I decided to write the book after all, it was because I had come to envision it as a *political* autobiography that emphasized the people, the events, and the forces in my life that propelled me to my present commitment. (Davis, 1989: xv–xvi)

Whether or not these texts were written as 'research', they are among the most authoritative works in prison studies. But their epistemic authority does not follow automatically from the fact that they were written by people with firsthand experience of incarceration; after all, members of the Aryan Brotherhood have a 'lived experience' of prison, and this does not grant them the right to have their voices validated and amplified by prison scholars or abolitionist activists. Rather, the epistemic and political authority of the prison writing I have mentioned here stems from the degree to which these authors have reflected on their personal experience and connected this experience to a critical analysis of power. They are crucial touchstones for abolitionist organizing, not because they convey a direct, unmediated experience of the prison system and therefore reveal some essential truth about it, but rather because they have thought very carefully about the meaning of their experience in relation to world-historical structures that shape this experience, such as slavery, heteropatriarchy and colonization. As such, these authors are already doing what I would call 'critical phenomenology', with or without reference to the phenomenological tradition.

Qualitative social science research on the lived experience of prisoners

Another important source of phenomenologically rich data on the lived experience of people in prison is qualitative social science research based on ethnographic observations of prison life and/or interviews with people in prison, the latter of whom are asked to describe their lived experience and sometimes prompted to reflect on a specific aspect of their experience, such as space or time. Examples of this research include Cohen and Taylor (1972), Grassian (1983), Leder (1999), Medlicott (2001) and Rhodes (2004). While such work may not explicitly define its method as phenomenological, and while it may engage with other methods beyond phenomenology (such as Foucauldian genealogy in the case of Rhodes), the through-line of this approach to prison research is a commitment to listening carefully to what people in prison say about their own experience, affirming them as 'knowledgeable agents' and 'valuable sources of information about prison life and death' (Medlicott, 1999: 215), and conveying their reflections in their own words.

As with prison memoirs, these studies do not generally engage with the phenomenological tradition in philosophy, but they offer qualitative research on the first-person experience of people in prison and/or on the prison environment as a context for lived experience. Such research can be valuable for more explicitly phenomenological analyses of prison life. For example, Lorna Rhodes shares this testimony from a prisoner in a Washington state supermax:

> Your lights are on all day … it really kind of dulls all your senses … It makes you numb. You get easily mad. You feel that everything they do is just to make you mad … It's terrible in here. I think they go out of their way to turn this into hell. (Rhodes, 2004: 30)

John Woodland, a prisoner at Maryland Penitentiary, tells philosophy professor Drew Leder:

> One thing I noticed when I first came to the penitentiary is that the penitentiary design is similar to the high-rise projects in West Baltimore or East Baltimore or wherever. In prison it's the tiers; in the projects it's the floors … It's just enough room to live in. No more. Nothing for relaxation. Nothing for feeling comfortable. Just enough room to live in. (Baxter et al, 2005: 208)

When we read these reflections on carceral space and sense perception in phenomenologically inspired social science research alongside memoirs written by prisoners themselves, some important questions arise about the relation between first-person testimony, second-person (I-You) exchanges and third-person reflection on the experience of others. It might seem like a truism that first-person testimony is the most direct, reliable material for phenomenological research, second-person exchanges are the next best thing as long as they are grounded in genuine 'empathy', and third-person reflection is valuable mainly as a context to set the stage for lived experience or to explicate its meaning. But I want to argue that phenomenological research in prison is, or at least ought to be, more complicated than this. Abolitionist voices speak for themselves, but they also speak to other people about a world whose meaning and structure is at stake in the conversation.

Consider, for example, Cohen and Taylor's (1972) study of Durham prison in the UK, in which researchers shared with their imprisoned informants a passage from Victor Serge's 1970 description of his own lived experience as a political prisoner in French penitentiaries. Serge writes:

> Here I am back in a cell. Alone. Minutes, hours, days slip away with terrifying insubstantiality. Months will pass away like this, and years. Life! The problem of time is everything. Nothing distinguishes one hour from the next: the minutes and hours fall slowly, torturously. Once past, they vanish into near nothingness. The present minute is infinite. But time does not exist. (Serge, cited in Medlicott, 1999: 212)

Not only are Cohen and Taylor's (1972) research participants deeply moved by Serge's description of prison time, but even decades later, one of Medlicott's research participants shares his own strikingly similar reflections on time:

> It's just like a matter of waiting for the end of waiting, you know. Killing time before time kills you. Like I say, I am able to retreat into an inner world. And I do write a bit… sometimes I'll just sit there, still, for three or four hours … I'm self-contained in a way. (Medlicott, 1999: 220)

While it may be tempting to see this consistency as a confirmation of the 'essence' of prison temporality, it seems just as likely that people in prison, like people outside of prison, interpret their own experience through the testimonies of others. But if this is the case, then there is no simple, direct access to the meaning of an experience through first-person introspection. We learn how to make sense of our own perspective through an ongoing engagement with multiple forms of what we could call context, including literary archives, institutional structures, cultural scripts and social relations of power between researchers who offer a certain selection of readings as prompts and research participants who engage to a greater or lesser extent with the questions and prompts of an interviewer. In prison, like anywhere in the world, the distinction between 'my own' experience and my interpretation of that experience through the lens of other people's experiences is ambiguous. Even if I take great pains to perform the phenomenological method by bracketing my assumptions about the world and reflecting directly on the evidence of my first-person experience, one of the most important insights I will discover if I am honest with myself is that there is no I without the many others, near and far, whose words, actions and interpretations have influenced my own. A phenomenological study of my own lived experience discovers a multitude of voices, not all of which can be explicitly recovered and disentangled by even the most rigorous phenomenologist.

Even the passages I have chosen to share in this chapter are mediated by my own interest in space, time and embodied perception. These passages stand out to me as particularly insightful about an experience of incarceration that I have never undergone personally, and yet, as I will argue, even if I were sharing my own first-person testimony, it is not clear that this would yield any more straightforward access to the 'truth' of carceral power. This is not a reason to fall into scepticism, but rather to engage critically with all phenomenological research, even or especially if we are committed to abolishing carceral systems.

Phenomenological reflection on lived experience in prison

Both first-person testimony and qualitative social science research generate rich and varied descriptions of life in prison, usually without engaging directly with the phenomenological tradition in philosophy. But there is another genre of prison writing that brings these archives together, drawing on concepts and methods from thinkers such as Edmund Husserl, Martin Heidegger, Maurice Merleau-Ponty, Alfred Schutz, Frantz Fanon and Hannah Arendt to reflect on the transcendental (and sometimes also the material) conditions of possibility for experiences described by people in prison, either in their own first-person testimony or in interviews with social scientists. Examples of such research include Meisenhelder (1985), Doyle (2006), Guenther (2013), Gallagher (2014), Polizzi (2017) and Davis III (2019).

While the phenomenological tradition is wide-ranging, some common epistemic and ontological commitments include the following: consciousness is consciousness of… (in other words, consciousness is relational); there are nested levels of personhood from the transcendental ego that form the most basic condition for the possibility of meaningful experience to the concrete specificity of embodied, social, historical personhood or being-in-the-world; perceptual experience is perspectival and therefore always partial; my own first-person perspective is singular and unsharable at the level of the transcendental ego, but it is mutually co-constituted with others at the level of concrete personhood; and so on.

Researchers who engage with prison studies through this philosophical tradition typically draw on phenomenological concepts to elucidate first-person testimony and third-person social science research, for example, by helping us pick out patterns in this data that we might have otherwise overlooked without a phenomenological concept to 'name' what is going on.

Laura Doyle (2006) draws on Merleau-Ponty's phenomenological concept of the chiasm, or the intercorporeal reciprocity of touching and being touched, to engage with the prison memoirs of Jacobo Timerman and Lena Constante and with Alan Feldman's ethnographic research on the Irish hunger strikes at Long Kesh prison. She argues that while the incarceration and torture of political prisoners aims to exploit this intercorporeal reciprocity in order to destroy the prisoner's capacity for resistance, an 'inscape' (Doyle, 2006: 186) or 'breathing space' (Doyle, 2006: 188) remains as a site of 'intercorporeal resistance' (Doyle, 2006: 195) that helps to sustain the prisoner's psychic, physical and political life.

Shaun Gallagher (2014) brings together social scientific research in developmental psychology with phenomenological concepts such as Heidegger's Being-with Others and Husserl's account of the intersubjective conditions for a meaningful experience of the world to argue that solitary confinement is a form of 'cruel and unusual' punishment that deprives prisoners of the psychological and phenomenological conditions of meaningful experience. In his view, phenomenological accounts of being-in-the-world as a relational complex rather than a separate individual help to explain the cognitive, affective and other symptoms of prolonged isolation in prison, and lends support to legal and political critiques of solitary confinement as a degradation of human dignity. Here, the emphasis is less on the first-person testimony of prisoners (although such testimony is included) and more on the explanatory power of phenomenological concepts to clarify and deepen empirical research in social psychology.

James Davis III's (2019) analysis of double-double consciousness stands out as unique, to my knowledge, in offering an explicitly phenomenological reflection on his own lived experience of imprisonment. In this essay, Davis draws on W.E.B. du Bois' account of double consciousness, in which a Black person in an anti-Black world experiences that world both from their own perspective and through an anticipation of the way in which white people – from whom they are separated by a kind of veil – are likely to perceive them and behave towards them. Double consciousness is an expression of racist oppression that divides the awareness of Black people against themselves, forcing them to see the world through the eyes of another, but it also offers a more complex awareness of how the world works and how to navigate it in order to survive. Davis reworks du Bois' account of double consciousness, arguing that the experience of doubleness is redoubled for Black people in prison: not only must they navigate the white world as such, but they must also navigate the institution of the prison, which seeks to invalidate the perspective of all prisoners, but especially those who are racialized as Black. And yet, by developing a sense of double-double consciousness that navigates oppositions between Black and white, prisoner and 'human', the Black man in prison is able to move beyond the impasse of racist antagonism to develop a 'critically reflective consciousness' (Davis III, 2019: 1140) and to find the meaning of his own humanity 'as a reflection of the humanity of others'

(Davis III, 2019: 1143). In Davis' own words: 'Double-double consciousness allows the prisoner to recognize the fiction of his surroundings [in the racist structure of incarceration] and, even further, the false perceptions that created the social structure within which the prison is situated' (Davis III, 2019: 1139).

Davis (2019) approaches phenomenology not merely as a descriptive science, but as a critical tool for intervening in the world he describes. In this sense, his method resonates with what I call *critical phenomenology*: a practice of phenomenological reflection that seeks not only to understand the world but also to change it. While many of the texts I have listed in this section share this approach to phenomenology, there is a significant enough methodological difference between classical and critical phenomenology to warrant a more focused discussion.

Critical phenomenologies of carceral power

Critical phenomenology is a hybrid method that brings together a philosophical reflection on the conditions of possibility for meaningful experience and a critical reflection on the material and historical conditions that shape this experience – for example, through configurations of power like white supremacy, colonialism and heteropatriarchy (Guenther, 2019a, 2021c). As such, critical phenomenologies of carceral power not only reflect on the lived experience of people in prison, but also analyse and critique the carceral logics that structure time, space and personhood in prison societies such as the US. Again, there is no such thing as raw lived experience in this approach to phenomenological research; any engagement with testimony or ethnography must take into account the way sedimented historical structures shape how we describe and reflect on our own experience or the experience of others. This critical reflection on the relationship between individuated experience and collective histories of domination and resistance can never be completed; even as I reflect on the context of power and history, this context changes, and I can never exhaust the depth or complexity of my own pre-reflective investments in dominant power. For these reasons, critical phenomenology requires specific methods and concepts to account for the interplay between the 'who' and the 'where'/'when'/'how' of experience. Classical phenomenology may focus on the transcendental structures that make experience possible and meaningful for *anyone*, anytime, anywhere and anyhow, but critical phenomenology cannot assume such universality; rather, it borrows a plurality of methods and concepts from other discourses such as Black studies, feminism, queer theory, disability studies and critical theory broadly construed to trace the interconnections between power, knowledge and experience.

Examples of such an approach include James Davis III's (2019) essay on double-double consciousness (an essay that crosses so many of the categories I have proposed in this chapter), Pitts (2018), Weiss (2018),

Philippe-Beauchamp (2021), Ludwig (2021) and my own efforts both to clarify the method of critical phenomenology (Guenther, 2019a, 2021c) and to bring this method to bear on carceral power, both within the prison – through critical phenomenologies of solitary confinement (2013), private prisons (2018a) and prisoner resistance (2015, 2017) – and beyond the prison – through critical phenomenologies of gated communities (2018b), racist policing (2019b, 2021a) and carceral-colonial power (2021b).

For example, Andrea Pitts (2018) engages with Jennifer Poteet's first-person testimony of her experience of harmful and abusive medical treatment in prison to critique the 'specifically phenomenological harms' of carceral medicine (Pitts, 2018: 14). For Pitts, this harm is phenomenological not only because Poteet describes her first-person experience and reflects on the embodied temporality of trauma in insightful ways, but also insofar as this testimony discloses a complex intersection of multiple forms of structural and interpersonal violence. Pitts elaborates on the sociohistorical dimensions of Poteet's testimony through an engagement with research in the phenomenological tradition, such as work by Frantz Fanon, Drew Leder and Mariana Ortega. But what makes this analysis a critical phenomenology of carceral power is not primarily the engagement with lived experience or with phenomenological theory per se, but the analysis of these complex connections between experience, theory and historically sedimented relations of power. Likewise, Xavier Philippe-Beauchamp's article 'A meagre world' brings together the first-person testimony of people in prison, a philosophical engagement with the work of Merleau-Ponty and a more explicitly political reflection on prisoner resistance; as such, it offers a subtle, complex analysis of how 'the contained body testifies both of its imprisonment and of its will to overcome it' (Philippe-Beauchamp, 2021: 432).

Rather than summarizing my own work in detail, I will point out a few distinctions that may be helpful in moving the conversation from a *critical* practice of phenomenology that seeks to describe and analyse the historically sedimented social structures that (re)produce carceral logics at the level of both lived experience and the historical-material world, to an *abolitionist* practice of phenomenology that seeks to alter these structures. It would be hubris to assume that academic scholarship can change the world, but I do think critical phenomenologists of carceral power should be accountable to abolitionist movements, so I will point out a few ways that I have struggled to do this in my own work.

Search for a method: from critical phenomenology to abolitionist praxis

My first attempt to engage philosophically and politically with the lived experience of people in prison was my book *Solitary Confinement: Social Death and Its Afterlives* (2013). Beginning with first-person testimony of solitary confinement as a 'living death' or a feeling of being 'buried alive', I sought to explicate the meaning of this testimony through a critical analysis of civil death and social death (concepts I learned from the work of Colin Dayan and Orlando Patterson), through a Foucauldian genealogy of the US prison system, and through a phenomenological reflection on the relational structure of personhood and the importance of intersubjectivity for a coherent experience of the world, and even of oneself. My original title for this book was *Social Death and Its Afterlives: A Critical Phenomenology of Solitary Confinement*, but I did not yet have a clear sense of what I meant by 'critical phenomenology'. At the time, it was a way for me to signal that I wanted to bring together critical concepts and methods from Foucault, Black studies and phenomenology, even if these concepts and methods did not always sit well with each other.

In this book I was critical of the Thirteenth Amendment as an incomplete abolition of slavery that reinscribed its logic in the US prison system, and I was committed to the abolition of solitary confinement, but I was still a bit wobbly on prison abolition. For example, in the final chapter I argue:

> We must make the rhetoric of prison reform live up to its promises and its avowed ideals, and we must work to keep these promises and ideals open to critical engagement. Or we must dare to take prison abolition seriously as an ethical and political response to a system that, from the beginning, has harmed prisoners in the name of helping them'. (Guenther, 2013: 220)

Today, I would no longer entertain such hopes for the rhetoric of prison reform.

As I struggled to write the introduction to *Solitary Confinement*, I became increasingly ambivalent about my engagement with prisoners' testimony about an experience I had not undergone myself. While I sought to counterbalance my description of the suffering of people in prison with accounts of their strategies for survival and resistance (hence the 'afterlives' of social death named in both versions of the title), by the time I sent the final version of the manuscript to the publisher, I felt the need to shift the focus of my research from the suffering of people in prison to the creative power of prisoner resistance (Guenther, 2015, 2017). This shift was influenced by Saidiya Hartman's (1997) critique of the way in which white abolitionists in the 19th century deployed narratives of Black suffering to support the abolitionist cause, and later by Eve Tuck's (2009: 409) analysis of 'damage-centred research' which compounds colonial violence by describing it in ways that emphasize the victimization of communities rather than their desires and strategies for survival and resistance. Not only does such research subordinate the epistemic and political authority of those who are targeted for violence to the scholar who amplifies their voices and explicates their meaning, but it also risks fetishizing 'informants' as morally and epistemically unimpeachable as long as they are suffering and as long as their testimony provides evidence to support the abolitionist cause. As such, it risks silencing or sidelining the voices of people whose experience in prison is not one of unmitigated suffering, who manage to find some form of agency or even empowerment in prison, and who may or may not support movements for prison abolition.

This line of critical analysis underlines the complexity of engaging with the first-person testimony of people in prison from the perspective of a non-incarcerated scholar. In my research for the solitary confinement book, I was drawn to testimony that confirmed my hunch that solitary confinement was a form of civil and social death, and I no doubt overlooked the testimony of prisoners who found relief or even power in solitary confinement (see, for example, Malcolm X, 1987). This is yet another indication that first-person testimony should not be mistaken for raw truth. A critical phenomenology of reading and listening would teach us that we are most highly attuned to testimony that speaks to us, and the reasons for this differential attunement are difficult – perhaps impossible – to determine; we may look for signs of radical abolitionist resistance in a movement for moderate reform, or we may overlook signs of radical abolitionist resistance because we expect it to take a particular form.

Another set of methodological and political concerns arose for me as I became less and less comfortable with my phenomenological interpretations of prisoner testimony. What were the grounds of my own authority to explicate the meaning of experiences in prison that were not my own? And whom was this explication intended to educate or enlighten? People in prison did not need to be told that you could lose your grip on reality if you did too much time in the hole; neither did abolitionist organizers on either side of the prison walls. The main audience for this book was other philosophers, in particular other phenomenologists, some of whom found it interesting as a 'case study', or as evidence that phenomenology was relevant to 'the real world'. As long as people with no experience of incarceration or forced isolation were gathering in lecture halls or seminar rooms to reflect on the relevance of Husserl's epistemology to the experience of people in prison, I feared that we were continuing to replicate the divisions upon which carceral power rests.

And so, the focus of my research had to shift from a phenomenological reflection on the testimony of others – whether about their disempowering experiences in prison or their empowering experiences of collective resistance – to a critical phenomenological reflection on my own experience as a white, middle-class woman in a world shaped by carceral structures designed to protect people like me, if only nominally. If carceral power divides the world into those who deserve protection and those who deserve punishment, then it makes more sense for those of us who are framed for protection to describe, analyse and dismantle these systems from our own side of this structure rather than from the other. If lived experience offered direct, unmediated access to knowledge, this should be easy! All I would need to do is to bracket the natural attitude, which takes for granted the world as it is given to me, shift into the phenomenological attitude in order to reflect on how the world is given to me and to clarify the conditions of possibility for this givenness, jot this all down in a notebook and share my insights with the world. Instead, I have found this approach to critical phenomenology by far the most challenging, given the degree to which my conscious perspective is complicated by unconscious desires, fears and investments. It is difficult – perhaps impossible – to plumb the depths of one's own lived experience, entangled as it is with power and ideology, but this dizzying confrontation with the complexity of my own experience also calls into question my relatively neat and tidy interpretations of other people's experiences. Even in my critical phenomenologies of whiteness (Guenther, 2018b, 2019b), I have found it easier to reflect on the testimonies and ethnographies of others than to reflect on my own lived experience. This may be a personal limitation, of course, but I also think it points to the stubborn complexity of lived experience, the keen sense that one has not quite captured all the nuances of one's own experience, and the relative ease with which one connects the dots between selected passages from another person's memoir, testimony or ethnography, compared to sorting through the jumble of one's own ongoing experiences.

These methodological reflections on critical phenomenology have implications for my account of the relevance of phenomenology for abolition. To cut a long story short:

- *Life is complicated*. Phenomenology gives us a philosophical language for expressing this complexity to some degree, but it also provides tempting shortcuts to name or explain the meaning of lived experience through reference to concepts in the philosophical canon in a way that forecloses the radical potential of a patient, rigorous and relentlessly honest reflection on one's 'own' experience in relation to others and in the context of an historical material world.
- *Lived experience is tricky*. Both in phenomenological research and in abolitionist movements, it is often held up as a clear, unproblematic source of true knowledge, but it takes only a moment's reflection to see how it is mediated in endlessly complicated ways, both for listeners or readers and also for the subject of experience themselves.
- *Lived experience is also indispensable for abolitionist theory and practice*. We *all* have a lived experience of carceral power, whether we are targeted for

surveillance and punishment or nominally protected by the surveillance and punishment of others. Whether or not we engage with the phenomenological tradition in philosophy, it is useful for each and every one of us to reflect on our 'own' lived experience of carceral power and to listen to the testimony, reflections and analysis of others who are situated in both different and similar ways to the way in which carceral power structures the lifeworld.

I will now elaborate on these intuitions about the relevance of phenomenology for abolition, beginning with a fairly general discussion of what abolition means to me.

Towards an abolitionist phenomenology

As Angela Davis (2003) teaches us abolition is not just a movement to shut down prisons, but also to build up the institutions, practices and relationships that would make prisons obsolete. The struggle is not just to dismantle the institution of the prison but also to transform the conditions under which carceral power reproduces itself, both within and beyond prisons, jails and detention centres. For Ruth Wilson Gilmore (2007: 242), 'prison is not a building "over there" but a set of relationships that undermine rather than stabilize everyday lives everywhere'. To abolish carceral power, then, it is not enough to close the buildings we call prisons; we must alter the set of relationships that make prisons possible and plausible. But if this is the case, then there is arguably a transcendental dimension to prison abolition: it's not just a matter of intervening at the level of 'actual' prisons, although this is important. But in order to prevent prison closures from engendering newer, more insidious forms of carceral surveillance and control, we must also intervene at the level of the *possible* to change the conditions under which incarceration is perceived as a practice of justice and accountability rather than punitive state violence. To put this a bit differently: the challenge of abolition is to create the conditions of *impossibility* for carceral power, the conditions under which this form of state violence may be recognized as *intolerable* (Zurn and Dilts, 2015).

Since phenomenology is a method to shift our attention from the register of the actual to the possible, it may be a useful theoretical framework for abolitionist theory: a reminder not to mistake the closure of this or that institution for the transformation of carceral common sense, or what we could call the carceral 'natural attitude'. In this sense, a phenomenological critique of carceral power may help us to resist foreshortening abolitionist horizons, such as by tolerating a shift from custodial supervision in prison to more diffuse networks of carceral surveillance through digital monitoring technologies. And yet, the jargon of phenomenology and the inaccessibility of phenomenological texts for many readers remains a barrier that even concerted efforts to translate theory into action struggle to overcome.

Abolition is above all a *praxis*; it calls for 'a million experiments' to create, support and amplify the conditions for nonviolent, nonpunitive forms of conflict resolution, harm reduction and repair, safety and accountability that do not rely on state violence (Kaba, 2020). This is the world-building dimension of prison abolition: the commitment to building and sustaining concrete alternatives to a justice system built on racist, colonial state violence. Here, too, phenomenology may have something to teach us about worlding, where 'world' refers not to the totality of entities on planet earth, but rather to an open-ended context for meaning and mattering that exceeds any individuated being and offers interpretive horizons for beings to show themselves as such (Heidegger, 1962). While Heidegger himself was by no means a prison abolitionist, some important insights might emerge through a conversation between abolitionists and critical phenomenologists who understand worlding as a collective praxis of creating, sustaining and altering the horizons through which we make sense of our lived experience, including experiences of carceral state violence.

Abolition, understood as a collective project of world building that makes carceral power obsolete, is impossible without both sustained reflection on one's own lived experience as a situated being-in-the-world, and an ethical-epistemic attunement to the lived experience of others, in particular to those who are most negatively impacted by punitive state violence. This is where the more familiar aspects of phenomenological method might come into play. Abolitionist theory and practice call for the *epochē* or bracketing of both 'common sense' and 'expert' assumptions about justice, safety and accountability. This bracketing of the given helps to shift our attention from the world as it is handed down to us through generations of carceral capitalism to the way in which we apprehend this world; in other words, it challenges us to shift from the 'what' to the 'how' of lived experience, generating a thick description of our first-person experience and/or a careful engagement with the way in which other people describe their experience. Finally – although this task can never be completed, for the reasons discussed previously – an abolitionist approach to critical phenomenology calls upon us to reflect on the historical and transcendental structures that make these experiences possible and meaningful, experimenting with ways of collectively altering these structures.

Conclusion

This chapter has provided an overview of four different approaches to phenomenological research on prisons and has reflected on some of the implications of this research for prison abolition. In my view, the method of critical phenomenology and the praxis of abolition have much in common and much more to learn from one another. While first-person testimony is important for both, it should never be regarded as a direct expression of the truth about a situation; not only is such testimony highly mediated, but personhood itself also emerges through complex relations to the situation(s) in which one finds oneself and the power relations that structure this situation. When engaged as a qualitative research method, phenomenology's focus on first-person accounts of lived experience helps to orient researchers towards listening to the subjugated voices of people with a first-hand experience of incarceration. This is important, given the epistemic injustice that marginalizes and silences the perspectives of people in prison as well as people who, whether or not they ever do time in a penal institution, are routinely criminalized and punished on the basis of their race, class, gender, gender presentation, sexuality, disability and so forth. But we should also remember that this engagement with first-person accounts of prison experience is not, in itself, liberatory or abolitionist. Depending on the way in which first-person testimonies are gathered and interpreted, phenomenological or ethnographic research in prison may be complicit in, or lend credibility to, punitive narratives or logics, thus compounding both the epistemic injustice of selective listening and the social injustice of carceral power. They may also engage in 'damage-centered research' (Tuck, 2009: 409), extracting stories of pain and suffering in order to enlighten the rest of us. This is the case even when the researcher is motivated by empathy and a sincere desire to amplify the voices of people behind bars. As the critical practice of phenomenology teaches us, every act of perception and interpretation is partial and limited. These acts are always already shaped by the finitude of a situated historical and social perspective, by the desires and interests of the researcher, by their evaluation of which details are relevant or irrelevant, and by many other factors that exceed the scope of conscious awareness. To make good on its abolitionist promise, critical phenomenology would have to become more than just a philosophical or empirical research method; it would need to engage in concrete forms of collective praxis to make prisons obsolete and to build or reclaim less punitive worlds.

Note
[1] See, for example, DeWeaver, 2017; Doyle, Gardiner and Wells, 2021; and Amplify Voices Inside (https://amplifyvoices.com/).

References
Abbott, J.H. (1991) *In the Belly of the Beast: Letters from Prison*, New York: Vintage Books.
Baxter, C., Brown, W., Chatman-Bey, T., Johnson, Jr., H.B., Medley, M., Thompson, D., Tillett, S. and Woodland Jr., J. (with Leder, D.) (2005) 'Live from the panopticon: architecture and power revisited', in J. James (ed.) *The New Abolitionists: (Neo) Slave Narratives and Contemporary Prison Writings*, Albany, NY: SUNY Press, pp 205–215.

Betts, R.D. (2010) *A Question of Freedom: A Memoir of Learning, Survival, and Coming of Age in Prison*, New York: Avery.

Cohen, S. and Taylor, L. (1972) *Psychological Survival: The Experience of Long-Term Imprisonment*, London: Penguin.

Davis, A. (1989) *Angela Davis: An Autobiography*, New York: International Publishers.

Davis, A. (2003) *Are Prisons Obsolete?*, New York: Seven Stories Press.

Davis III, J. (2019) 'Law, prison, and double-double consciousness', *Yale Law Journal* Forum (30 April). Available from: https://www.yalelawjournal.org/forum/double-double-consciousness [Accessed 9 October 2024].

DeWeaver, Emile (2017) 'The prison reform movement must center the voices of incarcerated people', *ColorLines* (31 October). Available from: https://www.colorlines.com/articles/prison-reform-movement-must-center-voices-incarcerated-people-op-ed [Accessed 15 September 2024].

Doyle, C., Gardner, K. and Wells, K. (2021) 'The importance of incorporating lived experience in efforts to reduce Australian reincarceration rates', *International Journal for Crime, Justice and Social Democracy*, 10(2): 83–98.

Doyle, L. (2006) 'Bodies inside/out: violation and resistance from the prison cell to the bluest eye', in D. Olkowski and G. Weiss (eds) *Feminist Interpretations of Maurice Merleau-Ponty*, University Park, PA: Penn State University Press, pp 183–208.

Gallagher, S. (2014) 'The cruel and unusual phenomenology of solitary confinement', *Frontiers in Psychology*, 5.

Gilmore, R.W. (2007) *Golden Gulag: Prisons, Surplus, Crisis, and Opposition in Globalizing California*, Berkeley and LA: University of California Press.

Grassian, S. (1983) 'Psychopathological effects of solitary confinement', *American Journal of Psychiatry*, 140(11): 1450–1454.

Guenther, L. (2013) *Solitary Confinement: Social Death and Its Afterlives*, Minneapolis: Minnesota University Press.

Guenther, L. (2015) 'Political action at the end of the world: Hannah Arendt and the California prison hunger strikes', *Canadian Journal for Human Rights*, 4(1): 33–56.

Guenther, L. (2017) 'A critical phenomenology of solidarity and resistance in the 2013 California prison hunger strikes', in L. Dolezal and D. Petherbridge (eds) *Body/Self/Other: The Phenomenology of Social Encounters*, Albany, NY: SUNY Press, pp 42–74.

Guenther, L. (2018a) 'Dwelling in carceral space', *Levinas Studies*, 12.

Guenther, L. (2018b) 'Prison beds and compensated man-days: the spatio-temporal order of carceral neoliberalism', *Social Justice*, 44(2/3): 61–82.

Guenther, L. (2019a) 'Critical phenomenology', in A. Murphy, G. Salamon and G. Weiss (eds) *50 Concepts for a Critical Phenomenology*, Evanston, IL: Northwestern University Press, pp 11–16.

Guenther, L. (2019b) 'Seeing like a cop: a critical phenomenology of Whiteness as property', in E. Lee (ed.) *Race and Phenomenology*, Lanham, MD: Rowman & Littlefield, pp 189–206.

Guenther, L. (2021a) 'Police, drones, and the politics of perception', in E. Mendieta and B. Jones (eds) *The Ethics of Policing*, New York: New York University Press, 248–267.

Guenther, L. (2021b) 'Settler colonialism, incarceration, and the abolitionist imperative: lessons from an Australian youth detention centre', in C. Taylor and K.S. Montford (eds) *Building Abolition: Decarceration and Social Justice*, New York: Routledge, 97–109.

Guenther, L. (2021c) 'Six senses of critique for critical phenomenology', *Puncta: Journal of Critical Phenomenology*, 4(2): 5–23.

Hartman, S. (1997) *Scenes of Subjection: Terror, Slavery, and Self-Making in Nineteenth-Century America*, Oxford: Oxford University Press.

Heidegger, M. (1962) *Being and Time*, J. Macquarrie and E. Robinson (trans.), San Francisco: Harper & Row.

Jackson, G. (1994) *Soledad Brother: The Prison Letters of George Jackson*, Chicago: Lawrence Hill Books.

Kaba, M. (2020) 'We need a million experiments...', *Twitter* (15 June). Available from: https://twitter.com/prisonculture/status/1272548582139330566 [Accessed 15 September 2024].

Leder, D. (1999) *The Soul Knows No Bars: Inmates Reflect on Life, Death, and Hope*, Lanham, MD: Rowman & Littlefield.

Ludwig, A. (2021) 'From criminal man to carceral body: an ethnography of intake in New York City jails', *Catalyst: Feminism, Theory, Technoscience*, 7(2). Available from: https://catalystjournal.org/index.php/catalyst/article/view/34994/28288 [Accessed 15 September 2024].

Malcolm X. (1987) *The Autobiography of Malcolm X, as Told to Alex Haley*, New York: Ballantine Books.

Medlicott, D. (1999) 'Surviving in the time machine: suicidal prisoners and the pains of prison time', *Time & Society*, 8(2): 211–230.

Medlicott, D. (2001) *Surviving the Prison Place: Narratives of Suicidal Prisoners*, Aldershot: Ashgate.

Meisenhelder, T. (1985) 'An essay on time and the phenomenology of imprisonment', *Deviant Behavior*, 6(1). Available from: https://www.tandfonline.com/doi/abs/10.1080/01639625.1985.9967658 [Accessed 15 September 2024].

Peltier, L. (2000) *Prison Writings: My Life Is My Sun Dance*, H. Arden (ed.), New York: St Martin's Press.

Philippe-Beauchamp, X. (2021) 'A meagre world: phenomenological corporeity in prison', *The Humanistic Psychologist*, 49(3): 423–434.

Pitts, A.J. (2018) 'Examining carceral medicine through critical phenomenology', *IJFAB: International Journal of Feminist Approaches to Bioethics*, 11(2): 14–35.

Polizzi, D. (2017) *Solitary Confinement: Lived Experiences and Ethical Implications*, Bristol: Policy Press.

Rhodes, L.A. (2004) *Total Confinement: Madness and Reason in the Maximum Security Prison*, Berkeley: University of California Press.

Shakur, A. (1999) *Assata: An Autobiography*, Chicago: Lawrence Hill Books.

Táíwò, O. (2020) 'Being-in-the-room privilege: elite capture and epistemic deference', *The Philosopher* (30 November). Available from: https://www.thephilosopher1923.org/post/being-in-the-room-privilege-elite-capture-and-epistemic-deference [Accessed 15 September 2024].

Timerman, J. (2002) *Prisoner without a Name, Cell without a Number*, T. Talbot (trans.), Madison, WI: University of Wisconsin Press.

Tuck, E. (2009) 'Suspending damage: a letter to communities', *Harvard Educational Review* 79(3): 409–428.

Weiss, G. (2018) 'Doing time in a for-profit space: renegotiating identity in the prison-industrial complex', in S. Cohen-Shabot and C. Landry (eds) *Rethinking Feminist Phenomenology: Theoretical and Applied Perspectives*, Lanham, MD: Rowman & Littlefield, pp 69–83.

Zurn, P. and Dilts, A. (2015) *Active Intolerance: Michel Foucault, the Prisons Information Group, and the Future of Abolition*, New York: Palgrave Macmillan.

PART II

Abolitionist Ideas

5

Liberation and Reconciliation: The Christian Tradition and Prison Abolition

Hannah Bowman

Why would, or should, Christians be prison abolitionists? Liberation and reconciliation are focal points where the Christian tradition and abolition of the prison industrial complex meet: where the theorizing of abolition can be informed by Christian theology and where theological reflection is enlivened by considering actual practices of abolition. Christian theologies of liberation and reconciliation help Christians understand abolition as God's work, and abolitionist insights and praxis force Christianity to face the challenges, limits and radical potential of its commitment to liberation and reconciliation. To insist on liberation and reconciliation as real promises for those who are imprisoned, punished and estranged in this life forces Christianity to take its theological claims seriously. Abolition is the concretization of Christian hope.

Theologies of liberation and reconciliation related to the practice of prison abolition have been developed within the Christian tradition over the last half a century. Sources for anti-prison theology within Christianity include Black liberation and womanist theology, which engages with mass incarceration as a tool of racial control and works in conversation with 'secular' movements for prison abolition and alternative ways of creating justice; Christian efforts to promote restorative justice, and 'peace churches', where opposition to prisons forms part of an overall commitment to anti-violence work, as in Quaker author Faye Honey Knopp's 1976 book *Instead of Prisons: A Handbook for Abolitionists*;[1] the work of the American Friends Service Committee (AFSC), which opposes the warlike violence of our retributive systems (Magnani and Wray, 2006: 5); and Lee Griffith's 1993 book *The Fall of the Prison: Biblical Perspectives on Prison Abolition*, which was influenced by peace church traditions.

The purpose of tracing such 'abolition theology' in the Christian tradition is not simply to give credit to the thinkers who have been formative in presenting abolitionist tendencies within Christianity. Instead, it is to see the shape and sources of abolitionist and abolition-adjacent thought in order to ask ourselves how and where attention to what is perhaps the most important moral scandal of our time can find a further foothold in the mainstream of the church. At its heart, prison abolition – which for purposes of this chapter means a commitment to a world without incarceration[2] – should have a central place in the Christian tradition because its primary concerns, liberation and reconciliation, are indispensable to the Christian gospel. In its analysis of and resistance to systems of oppression, abolition theology draws on threads of liberation theology, Black and womanist theologies, and postcolonial/decolonial theologies which insist on the importance of embodied realities to the longstanding liberatory texts of the New Testament. Meanwhile, in its approach to interpersonal harm, abolition theology pushes the boundaries of traditional Christian conceptions of mercy, forgiveness and reconciliation – not to mention judgement and condemnation. Put simply, abolition requires attention to the 'preferential option for the poor' and vindication of the oppressed which formed the mission of Jesus, as well as to the 'ministry of reconciliation' (2 Cor. 5:18) for which, Christians believe, Jesus lived, died and rose (Myers and Enns, 2009: 11–12). This doubled attention within abolition theology mirrors the productive ambiguity within the practice of 'transformative justice' – a way of responding to harm and violence which insists upon prioritizing and changing the social conditions which lead to harm, while also holding space within it for profound, relational, community-based accountability work to address acts of harm when they occur (Mingus, 2019). It also reflects the deep unity between liberation and communal care found in womanist theology (for example, Douglas, 1994: 108).

This chapter will consider the distinctive contributions of Christian thought to this doubled locus of liberation and reconciliation: first, the abolitionist thought appearing in Black liberation theologies, as well as that appearing among interpreters who see concepts such as resurrection as pointing towards prison abolition; second, the contributions of womanist theology to an understanding of abolition and liberation as requiring communal flourishing; and, third, the connections between Christian theologies of reconciliation and mercy and the practices of restorative justice. Finally, the chapter will explore some limitations to Christian thought on the topic of prison abolition and propose next steps articulating a Christian 'abolition theology' building on the long tradition that comes before it.

Liberation

For the Christian concept of 'liberation' to be effective in promoting a theology supporting abolition, it must be grounded in the realities of racial and economic oppression from which liberation is necessary.[3] Mass incarceration in the American context functions as a system of racial control, a 'new Jim Crow' (Alexander, 2010; see also Davis, 2003). This system is what abolitionist organization *Critical Resistance* (nd) calls the 'prison industrial complex'.

Because of the racialized function of the prison industrial complex in the American context, Black liberation theology offers the primary resources for fusing Christian notions of liberation with real resistance to the prison industrial complex. Black liberation theologian James Cone addresses the role of incarceration in the oppression of Black people in America in stark terms, 'explor[ing] today's criminal justice system as a modern-day lynching' (Robert, 2018). Cone (2011: 163) writes: 'The lynching of black America is taking place in the criminal justice system', citing the disproportionate percentages of Black people subject to criminalization, incarceration and correctional supervision. Nikia Smith Robert builds on Cone's work to engage in a deeper analysis of the whole system of mass incarceration and criminalization as a system of oppression that she calls 'lockdown America' (Robert, 2017: 41).[4] She traces incarceration alongside Christian theologies of sacrifice, concluding that: 'Calvary's cross and modernity's prison industrial complex are the same. They each require a sacrifice that victimizes Black bodies to preserve the oppressive authority of dominant society' (Robert, 2017: 48).

Robert's emphasis is on the mutual construction of a sacrificial underclass 'required' by Christian sacrificial atonement theology and a racialized subaltern class held captive first by enslavement and then after emancipation through a series of legal strictures, including imprisonment, aimed at the construction of 'criminality' as characteristic of Blackness. Similarly, Jason Lydon, as summarized by Joshua Dubler and Vincent Lloyd, attributes American incarceration to 'a dangerous sacrificial theology,' requiring a racialized scapegoated class (Dubler and Lloyd, 2020: 203).

Rima Vesely-Flad (2018) and Kelly Brown Douglas (2015) similarly emphasize how Blackness, specifically, is constructed as a criminal threat. Vesely-Flad (2018: 19) traces the association between criminality and Blackness to Puritan covenant theology and the distinction made between 'covenanted children' and 'creatures'; she describes how Blackness is first posited as 'social pollution' and then this supposed threat is moralized, so that Blackness is seen as 'moral pollution' (Vesely-Flad, 2018: 9 and 3). Or as Douglas (2015: 70) puts it, 'a free black body poses an ontological danger to an Anglo-Saxon exceptionalist social order. It also presents an existential danger'. For this reason, she argues, Black bodies are constructed as inherently threatening or violent. We cannot talk about violence without interrogating the way in which racial dynamics affect who is seen as violent and how. Or, to paraphrase Vesely-Flad (2018), the cultural construction of a racialized Black underclass that is seen as a 'threat' to whiteness is moralized. In this way the prison, which is often characterized as an attempt to address 'crime' or harm, is revealed as a tool of racial control. What these concepts emphasize is the impossibility of separating the ideal of a prison as a way of addressing interpersonal harm in a race-neutral way from the reality of the intertwining of racist social constructions of criminality and the ways we define crime, harm and even violence.

Black Liberation theologians thus remind Christians that opposition to imprisonment in Christian theology is morally required because of the actual function of prisons as tools of racial control. Abolition theology must be grounded in anti-racist praxis. Douglas (2015: xiv and 41–42) identifies the prison industrial complex as part of a 'stand your ground culture' that aims to exclude Black people from 'white space' which is defined by 'the right to exclude'.[5] Whiteness, she argues, is defined by keeping others out of certain spaces, and the prison industrial complex serves this end. Abolition theology must resist such a 'right to exclude' by insisting on liberation in terms which make it clear that liberation can be nothing less than the right of Black people (and other marginalized people) to exist in spaces which have previously been claimed by/for whiteness.

Ultimately Robert (2017: 62) finds in Jesus' transcending of criminality through the cross and resurrection 'a space of resistance where there is life and liberation beyond the defeat of death-dealing circumstances in a Carceral State'. The system of sacrifice which figures in Robert's analysis of 'lockdown America' is overcome by Jesus' victorious solidarity with those who are criminalized and imprisoned (Robert, 2017: 57) as Jesus overcomes criminalization by 'recast[ing] Black bodies as divine and not degraded. Restored and not condemned. Transformed and not criminal' (Robert, 2017: 62). Robert uses the powerful witness of Christ's resurrection as a source of liberation against systems of criminalization.

Additional biblical and theological resources provide further ways of framing these concepts which theologians such as Robert and Douglas present as characteristic of Black liberation in response to mass incarceration: divine solidarity with those who are criminalized and the vindication of one's personhood over against criminalization and of one's right to exist in spaces claimed by oppressive structures. For Lee Griffith (1993), Scripture leads him to abolitionist conclusions based on three foundational ideas: 1) the concept of 'jubilee' in Leviticus 25 and Deuteronomy 15, quoted by Jesus in Luke 4:18; 2) the biblical association of prisons with 'the power of death'; and 3) Jesus' self-identification with prisoners in Matthew 25 and in his own imprisonment and crucifixion. Griffith's opposition to imprisonment is based not only on the ethics of more compassionate ways of responding to 'crime' or harm, but also on God's desire for freedom for prisoners:

> We are so placed that we cannot talk about prisoners without a clear recognition that it is precisely these men and these women who have a right to freedom, who have the *only possible* right to freedom – the right that is based in the Word and activity of God. (Griffith, 1993: 126)

The freedom he identifies is victory over criminalization/death, proclaimed through the liberation of captives provided for in the biblical 'jubilee' laws and enacted through Jesus' identification with those criminalized in solidarity – taken together, this victory resembles closely the vindication of selfhood that Black theologians, such as Robert, find to be a primary liberating response against criminalization.

Jubilee is an essential concept for Griffith; he identifies the 'jubilee' laws – which provide for the remission of debt; the return of land to its original owners, and the freedom of those enslaved due to indebtedness at the end of seven or 50 years – as based in the originary myth of Israel's deliverance from Egypt:

> It was on the basis of God's liberation of the slaves that a covenant was established with Israel, and it was also on the basis of that history of liberation that Israel was to observe the Sabbath and Jubilee ... The proclamations of liberty to the captives were concrete social responses to God's liberating activity in the exodus of Israel from Egypt. Thus, the Jubilee and Sabbath years were a type of social counterpart to Jewish Passover or Christian communion – do this in remembrance of me. (Griffith, 1993: 99)

Griffith argues that during the time of the Babylonian Exile, the idea of liberation from enslavement was extended to imprisonment as well (Griffith, 1993: 102). So, he concludes, when Jesus declares in a quotation from Isaiah 61 that he has come to 'proclaim release to the captives, And recovery of sight to the blind, To set free those who are downtrodden, To proclaim the favorable year of the Lord (Luke 4:18–19)', he is expressing God's will of liberation for all people held captive as 'a renunciation of the power of death…[that] points to the resurrection itself' (Griffith, 1993: 107–108).

In Griffith's analysis, liberation is founded in the promises and law of God, and the foundational religious symbol of liberation is enacted in the reality of prison abolition. Griffith identifies 'the spirit of the prison' with 'the spirit of death' so that, from a Christian perspective, abolition images Jesus' resurrection and victory over death (Griffith, 1993: 109). The power of the prison is broken by Jesus' resurrection: a similar theme to that reflected in Robert's (2017: 61) analysis, by which 'Jesus transformed criminality on the cross. On Good Friday, he was charged as a criminal and defeated by the State. Three days later he arose in victory as the resurrected Savior'.[6]

This view of God's liberating/vindicating solidarity with those who are incarcerated has ecclesiological implications. Jason Sexton (2019: 8) argues for the primacy of '*ecclesia* incarcerate', writing that rather than a model of the churches outside of prison walls 'going' to prisoners, the church as a whole must recognize that the Holy Spirit 'ministers to prisoners in unrestrained ways' and that:

> within this movement the church is constituted as such, as a creaturely entity both generated and constructed by the Spirit and thus embodying the Holy Spirit's action within the ecclesial community. Consequently, this action of embodying the Spirit's work in the ecclesial community demonstrates that a church already exists *there*, inside the prison. (Sexton, 2019: 7)

The nature of the church itself is challenged by the presence of the Holy Spirit with and in those who are incarcerated. Similarly, Mark Lewis Taylor (2001) suggests that the church should be involved in 'adversarial politics', 'dramatic action' and 'organizing of peoples' movements' to participate in what he calls a 'theatrics of counterterror' in opposition to systems of carceral oppression.

The authors mentioned in this chapter so far present a commitment to liberation and abolition that engages with the prison as a modern institution of racial difference and control, and also as an ancient symbol of death which is opposed to the liberating power of God. Scripture and social realities work together to demand liberation for those who are incarcerated. Prisons must be abolished because of the moral obligation to work for racial justice and against racist systems of oppression, on the basis of the powerful myth of divine liberation which enlivens the history of Israel and the Christian community, and on the basis of the liberating/vindicating presence of God (in the person of Jesus and/or the Holy Spirit) with incarcerated and criminalized people.

Communal flourishing

Liberation requires not only opposition to oppression but also vindication of selfhood. This aspect of liberation is expressed well in womanist theology and its concept of what Douglas describes as liberation-as-wholeness (Douglas, 1994: 108). Douglas identifies womanist theology as 'includ[ing] a socio-political analysis of wholeness' that 'seek[s] to eliminate anything that prevents Black people from being whole, liberated people, and from living and working together as a whole, unified community' (Douglas, 1994: 108–109). Evident in Douglas' conception of womanist theology is a similar duality to that which I also see in abolition theology: the twin goals of liberation and unity/reconciliation.

However, the primary context of liberation/unity in womanist theology is much broader than the specific struggle for prison abolition, while abolition theology draws on sources beyond those of womanist theology. Abolition theology and womanist theology are two mutually informative perspectives that share some common emphases.

Correlations between womanist theology and abolitionist ways of discussing communal flourishing can in any case be helpful. Abolitionist Mariame Kaba (2021: 2) describes abolition as 'a positive project that focuses, in part, on building a society where it is possible to address harm without relying on structural forms of oppression or the violent systems that increase it'. Therefore, the Christian perspective on abolition should focus not only on liberation in terms of tearing down structures of oppression, but also on the work of constructing different ways of addressing harm and encouraging 'wholeness' (Douglas, 1994: 108) in community.

Such a focus on communal wholeness is reflected in the goals and practices of the transformative justice movement. Transformative justice practitioner Mia Mingus (2019) writes: 'This is why it is critical that TJ is not simply the absence of the state and violence, but the presence of the values, practices, relationships and world that we want'. Building healed and 'accountable communities' (Burk, 2016) is an essential part of abolitionist work. The Christian theological tradition speaks to this necessity in part through womanist theology.

In practice, encouraging the theological imperative of communal wholeness requires addressing interpersonal harm. Rejecting theological anthropologies that understand 'crime' as 'moral pollution' that requires harmdoers to be removed from a community for its safety – an understanding which is inextricable from the racialized dynamics of criminalization and who is constructed as 'harmful' (Vesely-Flad, 2018) – also requires abolition theology to engage with different ways of addressing harm in the community (see, for example, Christie, 1977: 1–15). Transformative justice seeks to prevent and heal harm both through addressing systemic conditions that lead to harm (Mingus, 2019) – a goal reflected in the womanist emphasis on creating conditions of flourishing and wholeness for the *entire* community – and through community/interpersonal interventions that do not rely on the state violence of the prison industrial complex (Mingus, 2019).

What theological resources can be brought specifically to such interventions to address harm? This question forces us to consider the Christian theological emphases on reconciliation and restoration – although reconciliation is not always a comfortable term to bring to abolitionist work. Theologies that address interpersonal harm are developed in the history of Christian engagement with restorative justice.

Reconciliation

The practices of restorative justice, which has Indigenous roots, were popularized in white and Christian circles by Howard Zehr in his 1990 book *Changing Lenses*. Zehr presents restorative justice as a 'new paradigm for justice' (Zehr, 1990: 97), in which instead of the focus being on a law broken for which the state requires punishment as a response, emphasis is placed on the victim of harm and the surrounding community, and the response centres on meeting the needs of the victim and 'a search for solutions which promote repair, reconciliation, and reassurance' (Zehr, 1990: 183). In practice, restorative justice processes often take the form of 'Victim-Offender Dialogue', in which the person harmed and person responsible for harm meet in a facilitated encounter and agree on a plan for restitution (Zehr, 1990: 161–163; Sered, 2019).

What then is generally theologically characteristic of what this chapter considers as the restorative justice strand of 'abolition theology'? Such a theology focuses on harm and punishment. Its method is correlative, drawing on the moral challenge of the evil of incarceration and the insights of restorative justice, and reading them in correlation with biblical texts to develop models of justice. For Laura Magnani and Harmon Wray of the AFSC, for example, the recognition that 'punishment, by its very nature, causes harm' (Magnani and Wray, 2006: 5) drives opposition to the prison industrial complex because of its inherent violence as well as its role in racial oppression.[7]

Zehr (1990: 135) turns to scriptural roots of restorative justice, such as the concept of 'shalom' as the way 'God intends people to live': 'in a condition of "all rightness" in the material world; in interpersonal, social and political relationships; and in personal character'. He suggests a biblical model of 'covenant justice' – a 'holistic' view of justice which incorporates what we might call 'criminal' or 'retributive justice' as well as 'social justice' or 'distributive justice' – as a precursor of restorative justice (Zehr, 1990: 140); while he does not deny the place of retribution in biblical justice, he views such punishment as aimed at restoration of shalom (Zehr, 1990: 144–145). Christopher Marshall (2001), like Zehr, also sees divine justice as primarily aimed at the creation of shalom.

Richard Buck (2017) also finds sources of restorative justice in the Torah, writing that Talmudic and rabbinic discussion of the 'cities of refuge' (Numbers 35:6–28; Deuteronomy 19:1–13), where unintentional killers could seek sanctuary, emphasizes that 'the purpose of these cities was not to punish through isolation, but rather to provide for the killer a safe and easily accessible place to reflect on what had been done and to embark on a process of *teshuva*, leading, ultimately to atonement' (Buck, 2017: 93).[8] Buck (2017: 97) concludes that in the Hebrew Bible 'the purpose of punishment is not to harm the offender, but rather to repair what has been broken and bring the offender back into the community'.

Even where these authors do not find a complete rejection of punishment, the goals of healing and restoration to community are starkly opposed to the actual function of the prison industrial complex today. The emphasis on restoration of shalom as communal wholeness or right relationship[9] also reflects the communal wholeness sought by womanism and 'remain[ing] in right relationships with each other, with the land, [and] with the environment' that Kaba (2021: 148) describes as part of an 'expansive view of restorative justice'.

From the New Testament, Ched Myers and Elaine Enns identify the Christian call to be 'ambassadors of reconciliation' (2 Corinthians 5:19) with the call to restorative justice (Myers and Enns, 2009). They identify this restorative impulse as grounded in God's work in Christ:

> The cross represents a fundamentally restorative initiative by the divine victim toward the human offender ... In the narrower sense, God is one with Jesus-the-victim of imperial crucifixion; but in the more cosmic sense, God is victimized by *every* expression of human injustice and violence. Yet this God absorbs the violent injustice of the offender, and offers the gift of forgiveness. The powerful notion of 'moral authority of victim initiative' is central to restorative justice. (Myers and Enns, 2009: 11)

Marshall (2001) also insists that the New Testament presents overall a rejection of retribution.

Like Marshall (2001) and Myers and Enns (2009), but perhaps going further, this chapter argues that the absolute rejection of punishment/retribution is central to the restorative justice 'strand' of abolition theology.[10] The opposition to prisons in restorative justice theology is grounded primarily in God's models of restorative justice as shown in the Torah and in God's rejection of retribution and desire for reconciliation. The appeal for abolition reflects the mercy of God.

Catholic theologian Amy Levad (2014) similarly argues against mass incarceration from within the restorative-justice tradition. Levad's emphasis is not only on biblical but also on sacramental theology; as she suggests, sacraments shape 'moral character' and 'create a new sort of community bound together in a common public work. By creating this community, liturgy and sacraments provide a foretaste of God's reign' (Levad, 2014: 87–90).

On this basis, she seeks resources against incarceration in the sacraments of Reconciliation (confession) and Eucharist. She writes that Reconciliation provides resources for communal responses to harm by its recognition that harmdoers remain part of the community and its 'view [of] sin as a violation of relationship [which] leads to an effort to transform those relationships and the character of the offender, rather than an effort merely to compel the offender to comply with the law' (Levad, 2014: 106–107). Meanwhile in the Eucharist's 'visions of God's justice', she writes, Christians see the 'call to seek social justice' for those harmed by any interpersonal or structural violence, including that imposed by unjust systems of punishment and incarceration (Levad, 2014: 97).[11]

As with liberation, reconciliation/restorative justice Christian theology combines recognition of the social dynamics of real situations with groundedness in the character, actions and promises of God. Levad (2014: 106) writes: 'The reason for the preeminence of forgiveness is that we recognize our solidarity in sinfulness and appreciate the forgiveness already extended to us through Jesus Christ. Based upon this experience of forgiveness, the church, the reconciled community, becomes a reconciling community'.

The reconciling nature and action of God are central to the moral argument against incarceration in restorative justice theology, just as God's liberating character is central to the arguments against carceral systems developed from liberation theology.

Taken as a whole, is restorative justice theology part of abolition theology? Its emphasis on alternative ways of envisioning harm and accountability are an essential part of the abolitionist 'positive project' (Kaba, 2021: 2): restorative and transformative justice interventions for addressing harm offer resources towards creating an abolitionist future.

At the same time, restorative justice theology has its limitations. For one thing, reconciliation and forgiveness are fraught concepts in justice work. Reconciliation is a major Christian theological theme that certainly has a place in theological arguments for restorative justice, yet in secular circles there is ongoing debate over the place of forgiveness in a restorative justice process.[12] Indeed, one difference between restorative and transformative justice is that transformative justice insists that there may not be a pre-existing healthy relationship to 'restore'.[13]

Reconciliation is good where it is possible, but at the same time, an emphasis on communal flourishing and wholeness (as seen in womanism, among other sources) is a necessary corrective for interpreting it. Transformation towards communal healing may be a better reflection of Christian reconciliation than forgiveness or reconciliation within any particular relationship could be. While both restorative and transformative justice emphasize the importance of healing for the entire community (Kaba, 2021: 148), restorative justice is generally seen as having more of a focus on relationships within a particular instance of harm, while transformative justice focuses more on systemic conditions.[14] Christian restorative justice theology must balance its theological focus on forgiveness with the systemic changes necessary for communal 'shalom' (Zehr, 1990).

Sarah Jobe (2022) suggests, from her work as a prison chaplain, that a 'moral injury framework' can help address this tension. She writes that understanding why someone commits an action against their own moral code requires recognizing 'a matrix in which individual decisions are being made in a pressure cooker of social, economic, and political factors, and the moral injury framework insists that those individual decisions and broader, structural factors must all be apportioned a percentage of responsibility for any given violation' (Jobe, 2022: 340–341). Within this context, the insights of restorative justice theology about restoration, reconciliation and atonement can be situated alongside the realities of harm and violence *and their systemic causes*, so as to provide a theology of healing adequate to the 'moral agency' of those who have done harm.

Another limitation worth exploring is that restorative justice theology sometimes countenances incarceration. Zehr (1990: 183) admits some ongoing need for prisons, although he says restorative justice 'ought to be the norm'. Levad (2015) also suggests that despite the overall injustice of incarcerating most people, there may still be a need to incarcerate a few people 'for the purposes of public safety'.[15]

For Magnani and Wray (2006) – whose work is explicitly abolitionist – the distinction between 'prison abolition' and 'penal abolition' captures this tension. For Magnani and Wray (2006: 175), 'penal abolition' is an attempt to broaden our conceptions to recognize the 'punishment, revenge, and violence at [the] core' of 'the entire legal apparatus' – a systemic understanding driven primarily by a restorative justice-inflected rejection of retribution and secondarily by an analysis of its socioeconomic and racial functioning. They identify 'the root of the problem: the coercive and violent reality of punishment, which is the linchpin of the retributive justice system, as well as the racial and economic incentives that drive it' (Magnani and Wray, 2006: 175). Yet Magnani and Wray also recognize the tension by which a turn to penal abolition can in fact undermine the radical demand of prison abolition:

> At the same time, good arguments can be made for sticking with prison abolition as the more radical stance, because it would preclude any use of separation or isolation as a sanction. Penal abolition, while challenging the violence of the entire legal apparatus, could permit selective, short-term incarceration in a narrow number of cases for the purpose of treatment or incapacitation. (Magnani and Wray, 2006: 175)

My own rejection of any use of incarceration as a sanction is why I prefer the term 'prison abolition' to 'penal abolition', and why I insist that abolition theology must be theology that supports a world *without* prisons, as well as one that rejects broader systems of policing, criminalization and carceral control (see also the writings of Louk Hulsman and other European abolitionists for an alternative understanding of the difference between penal and prison abolition, questioning how an overly reductionist focus on prisons can detract from critiques of the broader applications and harms of punishment and the logic of crime).

Whichever term is used, Magnani and Wray's (2006) framing sees restorative justice as one step towards such a world without prisons, proposing incremental and intermediate steps towards a horizon of abolition. Similarly, Levad (2015), despite reservations about a complete rejection of imprisonment, 'call[s] for a multi-racial, cross-class, interreligious movement to dismantle mass incarceration' – a step towards an abolitionist future.

Maintaining clarity towards the goal of abolition is a productive challenge drawing restorative justice theology forward.

Conclusions: Towards the radical horizon of abolition

What has not always been in evidence in Christian traditions is the word 'abolition' (although it is becoming more prevalent) – yet when we look more closely, abolition theology has its roots in a variety of theological sources. By broadening our view beyond simply those sources which claim the name of abolition theology, we see the emphases that characterize theological reflection on abolition: theology of liberation (Cone, 1997) and a theological anthropology that accounts for racialized sociopolitical oppression (Vesely-Flad, 2018); analysis of the interconnections between Christian doctrines and the scapegoating system of incarceration (Robert, 2017; Dubler and Lloyd, 2020: 203); reconstructions of scriptural and theological doctrines to support resistance to incarceration and punishment (for example, Griffith's [1993] work on scripture; Sexton's [2019] theology of the 'ecclesia incarcerate' or a variety of different reconstructions of atonement theologies[16]); and ethical reflection on forgiveness and communal care, in sacramental (Levad, 2014), restorative justice (Zehr, 1990) and womanist (Douglas, 1994) thought. And, of course, actions of resistance to the prison industrial complex through activism, solidarity and mutual aid have long been present within local expressions of Christianity, even where an overarching abolitionist framework has not always been articulated.

Why did the term 'abolition' not come into more common use in mainline Protestant and Catholic circles until recently, as it became visible in mainstream culture in the wake of the 2020 uprisings over police violence? I suspect one reason is the concern Amy Levad (2015) raises that 'the term can be alienating when trying to build coalitions to dismantle mass incarceration'. As Brandy Daniels (2015: 3) notes, Christian responses have often analysed the problems of mass incarceration and the theological imperative for change more fully than providing practical ideas for 'what that change might look like or how to engender it'. The ethical radicalism of abolition – its refusal to accept anything less than a complete end to the death-dealing systems of prisons and police – remains a challenge for Christian theology to face.

As Christians continue to live into this radicalism, we can be guided by the multiplicitous approach of the broader secular abolition movement. Abolition opposes the prison industrial complex because it is a tool of racial oppression *and* because of the inherent violence of responding to harm with, as Kaba (2021: 155) puts it, 'deathmaking and harmful institutions' that 'reproduce … reinforce [and] … maintain' harm.[17] Instead, abolition demands holistic systemic *and* interpersonal responses, a juxtaposition of perspectives that presents a locus of ongoing productive tension. Similarly, in abolition theology, whatever its starting point, the questions of theological anthropology concerning the socioeconomic and racial functions of prisons, police and the ways in which Christian theology supports and maintains them *and* the theological questions about forgiveness and reconciliation raised by harm and punishment must both be addressed.

Abolition theology, as explored in this chapter, must draw on secular and theological abolitionist analysis of how prisons and criminalization function as systems of racial control in order to resist them. It must draw on theological resources that support communal wellbeing in order to transform the conditions that lead to harm. The radical 'horizon' of abolition (Kaba, 2021: 93) – a theology that demands the end of prisons – requires that abolition theology provide guidance in addressing the worst of the interpersonal harm and violence that occur. The question most commonly posed to abolitionists is: 'What do we do about serious harm? What about rapists? What about murderers?' While secular abolitionist thought addresses this question in practical and ethical terms, Christianity's theological resources supporting forgiveness, reconciliation and nonretribution also have a relevant role in responding to it. So do theologies such as those of Cone (1997), Robert (2017) and Griffith (1993) that point to freedom as an absolute good, grounded in the liberating character of God.

A Christian abolition theology adequate to responding to this question must draw on the concept of divine liberation in response to a systemic understanding of incarceration, the role that communal healing plays in violence prevention *and* the interpersonal focus of the restorative justice tradition. To truly address harm means recognizing that even the distinction between 'interpersonal' and 'systemic' harm is a function of what, and who, is classified as violent or harmful. Rejecting the construction of certain people as 'morally polluted' (Vesely-Flad, 2018: 3) or inclined to harm means holding interpersonal harm and its systemic causes, including all the oppressions that prevent a community from healing and flourishing, side by side; refusing to place the responsibility for harm entirely on individuals without denying their moral agency (to paraphrase Jobe [2022]). To address harm in this way requires drawing on the concepts of 'liberation', 'flourishing' and 'reconciliation' simultaneously. A Christian response also sees atonement theology and God's action of justice as 'a power that heals restores, and reconciles rather than hurts, punishes, and kills' (Marshall, 2001: 33) – a power that supports 'wholeness' for the whole community (Douglas, 1994: 108) – as central to a holistic response to harm.

The radical horizon of abolition is an ethical challenge. Kaba (2021), along with other secular abolitionists, points out that 'there are a million alternatives' to prisons, not one singular alternate system, and that one need not have fully worked-out solutions in order to insist on abolition's liberating vision (Kaba, 2021: 167; see also Davis, 2003). This means abolition theology must be a theology of epistemological humility, which can move towards abolition's radical horizon in faith without needing a fully worked-out comprehensive system. Abolition theology is open to a multiplicity of liberating possibilities.[18]

The goal, then, is to draw on the longstanding theological resources which support abolition to form Christian communities capable of holding such radical spaces of liberation, flourishing and reconciliation. Robert (2017: 62) argues for such a church:

> this Church embraces a Christian community that includes a criminal element. It is committed to the liberation of the captives and mutuality with the least of these. This Church understands the cross, not on sacrificial terms, but conceives it as a life-altering space of resistance to restore social breaches and call into unity God and the oppressed. (Robert, 2017: 62)

Levad (2014: 97–98) emphasizes the role of liturgy and sacraments in such moral formation, writing that the Eucharist, in particular, 'nourishes' an 'eschatological imagination' opposed to the 'degrading' and 'demeaning' systems of mass incarceration.[19] Sexton's (2019) ecclesiology of an 'ecclesia incarcerate' that prioritizes the church as it already exists within and led by incarcerated people offers another such vision of Christian community aimed at abolition.

At the centre of all the strands of such abolition theology is Jesus: the criminalized one who, Christians believe, 'dies a malefactor but is raised as the Messiah' in opposition to the powers that scapegoat Black bodies (Robert, 2017: 54–55); the one who in response to the murderous harm done to him speaks a word of forgiveness from the cross in what Enns and

Myers (2009: 11) call 'an act of victim-initiated reconciliation'; the one who Griffith (1993: 118) identifies as 'Jesus the Prisoner' who calls us to the abolitionist future of Christian practice to which the sources in Christian tradition point.

Notes

1. Joshua Dubler and Vincent Lloyd discuss Knopp's Quaker background, but note that the book itself makes arguments largely on secular rather than theological grounds (Dubler and Lloyd, 2020: 128). *Instead of Prisons* is available online: https://www.prisonpolicy.org/scans/instead_of_prisons/
2. Police abolition is included as part of this commitment.
3. A pre-eminent source of Black liberation theology, which emphasizes the importance of material liberation to Christian theology, is Cone (1997).
4. This phrase was first used by Christian Parenti in 1999.
5. The language of the 'right to exclude' is drawn from Cheryl Harris. Another important source on the language of 'criminalization' as a way of excluding from spaces preserved for whiteness is Krinks (2024).
6. Willie Jennings finds similar anti-prison themes in the book of Acts in his liberationist commentary: Jennings (2017).
7. Another helpful source that combines Black liberation theology sources and restorative justice ideas is Gilliard (2018).
8. Zehr also discusses cities of refuge (Zehr, 1990: 149).
9. This is also an emphasis in Griffith (1993: 95) and Marshall (2001: 48).
10. I would include my own work on atonement theology within this strand of restorative-justice-influenced abolition theology. See Bowman (2022). My own journey to abolitionist thought came primarily through the restorative justice tradition and its emphasis on nonpunitiveness and addressing harm.
11. Also essential in considering social justice in relation to the Eucharist is Copeland's essay 'Eucharist, racism, and Black bodies' in Copeland (2010). Jennifer McBride explores abolition in light of liturgical seasons in McBride (2017).
12. For example, restorative justice practitioner Sujatha Baliga says that 'a Restorative Justice process never has forgiveness as a prerequisite or an expected outcome. It may or may not happen, but there is never any pressure on survivors to forgive, because they might not be interested in forgiveness' (Baliga and Robins, 2018).
13. As Kaba says: 'For many people, the situation that occurred prior to the harm had lots of harm in it. So what are we restoring people to?' (Kaba, Rice and Smith, 2019).
14. A helpful source on the differences between restorative and transformative justice and the limitations of both is Rasmussen and Shah (2022).
15. This source, Levad (2015), is an online written 'symposium' in which Levad engaged in back-and-forth discussion with critics and commentators on her book. Another useful source which addresses issues in US incarceration without entirely rejecting prisons or punishment is Logan (2008).
16. For example, Taylor (2001); Getek Soltis (2011); Robert (2017); Bowman (2022).
17. Kaba (2021: 149) emphasizes that both restorative and transformative justice approaches require considering the 'mirror[ing] and reinforce[ment]' of the interpersonal and systemic, although transformative justice tends to prioritize systemic change more than restorative justice.
18. Relevant to this epistemological humility is Daniels' (2019: 3) call for a 'negative theology of practice' whereby the church critiques traditional Christian sources and is open to nontraditional ones.

19 As Daniels (2015: 15) notes, Levad's emphasis on the 'radically liberative and transformative' nature of the Eucharist touches on abolition theology without using the term, in its claiming participation in a future reign of God that is not yet fully seen.

References

Alexander, M. (2010) *The New Jim Crow: Mass Incarceration in the Age of Colorblindness*, New York: New Press.

Baliga, S. and Robins, S. (2018) 'The spirit of restorative justice: an interview with Sujatha Baliga', *Daily Good* (5 March). Available from: https://www.dailygood.org/story/1900/thespirit-of-restorative-justice-an-interview-with-sujatha-baliga [Accessed 15 September 2024].

Bowman, H. (2022) 'From substitution to solidarity: towards an abolitionist atonement theology', *Political Theology*, 23(4): 362–380.

Buck, R. (2017) 'Restorative justice in the Hebrew biblical tradition', in T.D. Conway, D.M. McCarthy and V. Schieber (eds) *Redemption and Restoration: A Catholic Perspective on Restorative Justice*, Collegeville, MN: Liturgical Press, pp 88–97.

Burk, C. (2016) 'Think. Re-think. Accountable communities', in C. Chen, J. Dulani and L.L. Piepzna-Samarasinha (eds) *The Revolution Starts at Home: Confronting Intimate Violence in Activist Communities*, Oakland, CA: AK Press, pp 264–79. Available from: https://f12network.files.wordpress.com/2017/06/think-re-think-essay.pdf [Accessed 24 January 2024].

Cameron Rasmussen, C. and Shah, S. (2022) 'Growing justice', *Inquest*, 9 September. Available from: https://inquest.org/growing-restorative-transformative-justice/ [Accessed 24 January 2024].

Christie, N. (1977) 'Conflicts as property', *The British Journal of Criminology*, 17(1): 1–15.

Cone, J.H. (1997) *God of the Oppressed*, Maryknoll, NY: Orbis Books.

Cone, J.H. (2011) *The Cross and the Lynching Tree*, Maryknoll, NY: Orbis Books.

Copeland, M.S. (2010) *Enfleshing Freedom: Body, Race, and Being*, Minneapolis: Fortress Press.

Critical Resistance (nd) 'What is the PIC? What is abolition?' Available from: https://criticalresistance.org/mission-vision/not-so-common-language/ [Accessed 22 August 2022].

Daniels, B. (2015) 'Practical theology and the shift from prison reform to prison abolition: the liberation of theo-ethical reflections on incarceration', *Annual Conference of the American Academy of Religion* (Atlanta, GA), November. Available from: https://www.academia.edu/19474164/Practical_Theology_and_the_Shift_from_Prison_Reform_to_Prison_Abolition [Accessed 24 January 2024].

Daniels, B. (2019) 'Abolition theology? Or the abolition of theology? Toward a negative theology of practice', *Religions*, 10(3): 192. Available from: https://www.mdpi.com/2077-1444/10/3/192 [Accessed 24 January 2024].

Davis, A. (2003) *Are Prisons Obsolete?* New York: Seven Stories Press.
Douglas, K.B. (1994) *The Black Christ*, Maryknoll, NY: Orbis Books.
Douglas, K.B. (2015) *Stand Your Ground: Black Bodies and the Justice of God*, Maryknoll, NY: Orbis Books.
Dubler, J. and Lloyd, V.W. (2020) *Break Every Yoke: Religion, Justice, and the Abolition of Prisons*, New York: Oxford University Press.
Getek Soltis, K. (2011) 'The Christian virtue of justice and the U.S. prison', *Journal of Catholic Social Thought*, 8(1): 37–56.
Gilliard, D.D. (2018) *Rethinking Incarceration: Advocating for Justice that Restores*, Westmont, IL: InterVarsity Press.
Griffith, L. (1993) *The Fall of the Prison: Biblical Perspectives on Prison Abolition*, Grand Rapids, MI: Eerdmans.
Jennings, W. (2017) *Acts: A Theological Commentary on the Bible*, Louisville, KY: Presbyterian Publishing Corporation.
Jobe, S.C. (2022) 'Rethinking responsibility: moral injury from war to prison', *Political Theology*, 23(4): 335–349. .
Kaba, M. (2021) *We Do This 'Til We Free Us: Abolitionist Organizing and Transformative Justice*, Chicago: Haymarket Books.
Kaba, M., Rice, J.D. and Smith, C. (2019) 'Justice in America episode 20: Mariame Kaba and prison abolition', *The Appeal* (20 March). Available from: https://theappeal.org/justice-in-america-episode-20-mariame-kaba-and-prison-abolition/ [Accessed 24 January 2024].
Knopp, F.H. et al (1976) *Instead of Prisons: A Handbook for Abolitionists*, Syracuse, NY: Prison Research Education Action Project. Available from: https://www.prisonpolicy.org/scans/instead_of_prisons/ [Accessed 24 September 2024].
Krinks, A. (2024), *White Property, Black Trespass*, New York: New York University Press.
Levad, A. (2014) *Redeeming a Prison Society: A Liturgical and Sacramental Response to Mass Incarceration*, Minneapolis: Fortress Press.
Levad, A. (2015) 'Redeeming a prison society', *Syndicate* (19 January). Available from: https://syndicate.network/symposia/theology/redeeming-a-prison-society/ [Accessed 24 January 2024].
Logan, J.S. (2008) *Good Punishment? Christian Moral Practice and U.S. Imprisonment*, Grand Rapids, MI: Eerdmans.
Magnani, L. and Wray, H.L. (2006) *Beyond Prisons: A New Interfaith Paradigm for Our Failed Prison System*, Minneapolis: Fortress Press.
Marshall, C.D. (2001) *Beyond Retribution: A New Testament Vision for Justice, Crime, and Punishment*, Grand Rapids, MI: Eerdmans.
McBride, J. (2017), *Radical Discipleship: A Liturgical Politics of the Gospel*, Minneapolis: Fortress Press.

Mingus, M. (2019) 'What is transformative justice? A brief description', *Transform Harm* (11 January). Available from: https://transformharm.org/transformative-justice-a-brief-description/ [Accessed 2 June 2023].

Myers, C. and Enns, E. (2009) *Ambassadors of Reconciliation, Vol. 1: New Testament Reflections on Restorative Justice and Peacemaking*, Maryknoll, NY: Orbis Books.

New American Standard Bible (1977) LaHabra, CA: Lockman Foundation.

Robert, N.S. (2017) 'Penitence, plantation, and the penitentiary: a liberation theology for lockdown America', *Graduate Journal of Harvard Divinity School*, 12: 41–69.

Robert, N.S. (2018) 'James Hal Cone: humble giant in the movement for Black liberation', *Union Theological Seminary* (April). Available from: https://utsnyc.edu/james-hal-cone-humble-giant-in-the-movement-for-black-liberation/ [Accessed 22 August 2022].

Sered, D. (2019) *Until We Reckon: Violence, Mass Incarceration, and a Road to Repair*, New York: New Press.

Sexton, J.S. (2019) 'Experiencing justice from the inside out: theological considerations about the Church's role in justice, healing, and forgiveness', *Religions*, 10(2): 108. Available from: https://www.mdpi.com/2077-1444/10/2/108 [Accessed 24 January 2024].

Taylor, M.L. (2001) *The Executed God: The Way of the Cross in Lockdown America*, Minneapolis: Fortress Press.

Vesely-Flad, R. (2018) *Racial Purity and Dangerous Bodies: Moral Pollution, Black Lives, and the Struggle for Justice*, Minneapolis: Fortress Press.

Zehr, H. (1990) *Changing Lenses: Restorative Justice for Our Times*, Harrisonburg, VA: Herald Press.

6

The Daybreak of Abolition: The Overcoming of Punishment and Promotion of Therapy in Nietzsche's Philosophy

Caius Brandão

Introduction

Friedrich Nietzsche (1844–1900) is one of the most influential philosophers of modernity and the theme of punishment pervades the entire itinerary of his moral philosophy. Nevertheless, his profound criticism of punitive systems has not yet stirred up the same interest as his wider philosophical reception. This may explain why Nietzsche's philosophy of punishment remains unknown to most abolitionist scholars. This chapter brings out some of his abolitionist ideas that unmistakably resonate with state-of-the-art thinking on penal abolitionism.

First, we must bear in mind that Nietzsche rejects moral and religious assessments of criminals. He questions the existence of guilt and moral responsibility through a philosophy that engages in a dialogue with the methods and results of modern science. For him, criminals should not be conceived as 'guilty' and deserving of punishment, but as sick persons who may need medical intervention. He proposes that treatment delivered to criminals must be nonpenal and voluntary.

In this chapter, I offer a reading of Nietzsche's philosophical writings on punishment (*Strafe*), based on his critique of morals. One of the philosopher's greatest controversies was to evaluate the values of Judeo-Christian morality (see Chapter 5), of Platonic descent, as deniers of life itself. It is in the wake of his struggle against morality that Nietzsche addresses punishment as a philosophical matter. Thus, Nietzsche's penal abolitionism takes root and develops within the broader context of his moral philosophy.

Although explicitly calling for the overt elimination of the concept of punishment from the world, Nietzsche did not coin the expression 'penal abolitionism'. In fact, he himself never made use of it in his writings.

However, in this chapter, I explore one facet of the abolitionist horizon unveiled by Nietzsche: the overcoming of punishment through an alternative *mode of valuation*. For Nietzsche, humans are appraising animals par excellence, who create values and evaluate them. In this respect, he points out the variety of modes of valuation. For instance, one may appraise the same behaviour through distinct modes of valuation, such as moral (good or evil), aesthetic (beautiful or ugly) or medical (healthy or ill), to give just a few examples. I carry out this exploration through a critical analysis of a key passage from a book that Nietzsche titled *Daybreak: Thoughts on the Prejudices of Morality*, published in 1881. Other writings from the middle and late periods of his thought support this analysis.

The diversity of writing styles and the unsystematic and, at times, antagonistic form of Nietzsche's philosophy present a significant obstacle to the accurate reading of his works. However, such an effort is worthwhile, for his groundbreaking and challenging scrutiny of modern culture and its moral values offers an invaluable contribution to the contemporary debate on penal abolitionism.

Nietzsche was not committed to improving or offering new foundations for the right to punish. Nor does he look for ways to punish better. As he does in relation to morality, he criticizes punishment as a philosophical problem to be overcome. The main task of his moral philosophy is the 'revaluation of all values' (*Umwertung aller Werte*), which he only concluded with the publication of *The Antichrist* in 1888. In the path of such an accomplishment, he unveils a new horizon and challenges us to conceive of a world where the self-suppression of Platonic-Christian morality and its punitive justice has resulted in the eradication of the concepts of punishment, guilt and revenge.

However, in this scenario, one may rightly question how individuals and societies at large should deal with wrongdoers. A possible answer to this crucial query lies in section 202 of *Daybreak* (1997), which Nietzsche titled 'For the Promotion of Health' (*Zur Pflege der Gesundheit*). For an in-depth interpretation of this memorable section of *Daybreak*, I highlight and explain some key Nietzschean notions, such as 'great health' and 'innocence of becoming'. In doing so, I am able to outline some of the contours, nuances and consequences of the philosopher's punishment abolitionism.

In short, in view of the Nietzschean project of revaluation of all values, the promotion of the health of individuals and culture demands the therapeutics of resentment, the self-suppression of dominant moral values, as well as the creation of new modes of valuation, concerning crime and criminals themselves.

The horizon of punishment abolition: the breaking of new dawns

In section 13 of *Daybreak*, Nietzsche addresses the re-education of the human race. In this passage, he eloquently calls for the eradication of the concept of punishment from the world:

> *Towards the re-education of the human race.* – Men of application and goodwill assist in this one work: to take the concept of punishment which has overrun the whole world and root it out! There exists no more noxious weed! Not only has it been implanted into the consequences of our actions – and how dreadful and repugnant to reason even this is, to conceive cause and effect as cause and punishment! – but they have gone further and, through this infamous mode of interpretation with the aid of the concept of punishment, robbed of its innocence the whole purely chance character of events. Indeed, they have gone so far in their madness as to demand that we feel our very existence to be a punishment. It is as though the education of the human race had hitherto been directed by the fantasies of jailers and hangmen! (Nietzsche, 1997: 13)

Note, in this passage, the strong language used by Nietzsche to express his refutation of the reasoning that conceives of 'cause and effect as cause and punishment': 'dreadful and repugnant'. This logic of punishment is like a weed that infests the field of customs and therefore the way we think and interpret the world and judge each other. Nietzsche, then, proposes the re-education of human beings to replace the punitive logic by another.

By subtracting the innocence from becoming, the mode of moral interpretation and the concept of punishment create a kind of unpayable debt – the existential guilt – to the point that 'we feel our very existence to be a punishment'.

Nietzsche argues that the illusion of a Self, endowed with free will, erroneously grounds our moral interpretations, and that free will is not the true origin of our acts. In order to understand this better, it might be helpful to refer to section 102 of the first volume of *Human, All Too Human* (1879), in which Nietzsche writes the following: 'We do not accuse nature of immorality when it sends us a thunderstorm and makes us wet: why do we call the harmful man immoral? Because in the latter case we assume a voluntarily commanding free will, in the former necessity. But this distinction is an error' (Nietzsche, 1996: 55). This means that both natural events and human actions are subject to the nexus between causality and necessity. Nietzsche holds that the illusion of free will, which erroneously grounds our moral interpretations, is not the actual origin of our deeds.

This notion is essential to understanding the Nietzschean distinct concept of 'the innocence of becoming' (*die Unschuld des Werdens*), which is also articulated between the lines of section 202 of *Daybreak*. Thus, this will now be recalled and analysed, albeit briefly, in this section.

It is my understanding that the title given by Nietzsche to section 202 of *Daybreak* – 'For the Promotion of Health' – offers an important interpretative key. As explained in the forthcoming analysis, Nietzsche advances a new concept of health that calls into question dogmatic notions based on false duality between wellbeing and illness. He then applies this innovative notion of health to criminality issues. As opposed to grounding his moral philosophy on metaphysical explanations, Nietzsche favoured the support of scientific methods and results. Particularly in his writings of the middle and late periods, the close connection between his moral theories with physiology and psychology is notorious.

Under the influence of French physiologist Claude Bernard, Nietzsche argues that there is no essential difference between health and illness. Instead of treating them as two opposing phenomena, he merely recognizes a variance in degrees between them. Thus, exaggeration, disproportion and nonharmony of normal phenomena constitute the unhealthy state. Just as Nietzsche questions the utilitarians' dogmatic view of the notions of *pleasure* and *pain*, he calls into question the belief in absolute values. In the present case, he contests the understanding that *health* is a good in itself and, conversely, that *illness* is an evil in itself.

In this regard, Lara Anastácio (2020) argues that Nietzsche articulates a completely new notion of health. Anastácio writes that this innovative concept is 'first presented in *Daybreak* to acquire an even more radical character in *The Gay Science*. It questions the absolute value of the well-being of the living in favor of the usefulness of illness and pain for life' (Anastácio, 2020: 59).[1] Such 'usefulness of illness and pain for life' resides in the fact that it is precisely in the face of great pain, whether mental or somatic, that people manage to gather and articulate their vital forces, emerging even stronger from the unhealthy state. This implies the necessity or usefulness of suffering for the development of *great health*. As Giacoia Jr. explains:

> Severe illness, bringing with it great pain, can give rise to a restorative perspective of liberation and, therefore, to a certain type of philosophical life. It becomes a precious hook of knowledge, an additional attraction to continue living and thinking, to walk the path of convalescence, leading to a new and great health. (Giacoia Jr., 2020: 24)[2]

Giacoia Jr. also argues that this notion of 'great health' (*grossen Gesundheit*) is the outcome of the physio-psychological therapy of resentment, conceived by Nietzsche both for individuals and for the culture as a whole. In this respect, Giacoia Jr. explains:

> Psychophysiology is a philosophical project that pervades Friedrich Nietzsche's corpus from start to finish. Gradually, the therapy of affects program comes to be presented as Psychophysiology's main goal, taking the form of a *therapia mentis*, which is capable of promoting a purifying correction of our ways of feeling, thinking, and acting. This transformation in turn, constitutes the prerequisite for the liberation of the spirit. The Nietzschean therapy of affects is as a healing treatment, the aim of which is to create favorable conditions for convalescence and restoration of health. More specifically, it generates an increase in strength and resistance, though, by no means the complete absence of illness, which, in the case of a human being, would be an impossible task. (Giacoia Jr., 2019: 202)

This Nietzschean therapy translates into a 'medical and philosophical practice' that allows for the rejection of old and exhausted moral values. It also promotes the renewal of plastic forces, with the establishment of new modes of valuation. Therefore, one should read the title of section 202 of *Daybreak* – 'For the Promotion of Health' – as a harbinger of a dawning of great health within the scope of the punishment problem, which is the central theme of this section. The movement for the creation of new modes of valuation is already evident in the first lines of section 202 of *Daybreak*, which read as follows:

> One has hardly begun to reflect on the physiology of the criminal, and yet one already stands before the irrefutable insight that there exists no essential difference between criminals and the insane: presupposing one *believes* that the *usual* mode of moral thinking is the mode of thinking of *spiritual health*. But no belief is still so firmly believed as this is, and so one should not hesitate to accept the consequence and treat the criminal as a mental patient: not, to be sure, with an arrogant show of being merciful, but with the prudence and goodwill of a physician. (Nietzsche, 1997: 120–121)

The Italian psychiatrist and criminologist Cesare Lombroso developed one of the best-known theories that described a supposed physiological typology of the 'born criminal'. Despite Nietzsche's well-known interest on the subject, there is no concrete evidence that he had direct contact with Lombroso's studies (Brobjer, 2008). Quite in contrast to him, when reflecting upon the physiology of criminals, Nietzsche does not have in mind any kind of physiological determinism that would have the power to make an individual a born criminal. As will be demonstrated later on, he acknowledges that, in the absence of certain sociocultural circumstances, crime itself could not exist. Yet, this does not mean that he exclusively attributes to culture the faculty of generating criminals.

As Frezzatti Jr. (2006) explains, there is no opposition between physiology and culture in Nietzsche's philosophy. Regarding this absence of opposition, Frezzatti Jr. argues as follows:

> There are two perspectives of this problem in Nietzschean philosophy: one that we can denominate of 'physiologic' or 'biological' and other that we can denominate of 'cultural'. In the former, the man is understood through relationships between forces or *quanta* of potency. In the latter, the German philosopher considers that cultural aspects and the education are responsible for the elevation or the decadence of the man. If we just consider one of those perspectives, we should postulate the presence of a biological or cultural determinism in the Nietzschean thought. However, Nietzsche's studies of culture and configurations of forces ('physiology') don't happen isolated one of the other, because they are part of a same philosophical reflection. When the German philosopher considers that the body and the culture suffer the same processes (fight of a hierarchy of forces for more potency), he dissolves the limits between culture and biology. (Frezzatti Jr., 2004: 15)

Naturally, Frezzatti Jr.'s explanation equally applies to Nietzsche's thinking about the physiology of criminals. Likewise, Laura McAllister (2021) seeks to extract some comprehension of criminal physiology from Nietzsche's thought on punishment. According to her:

> Criminality, for Nietzsche, is not only or always related to legality. He recharacterizes the nature and behavior of the criminal as arising from psychological, social, and biological conditions rather than moral failure ... He describes the criminal as a byproduct of civilization, who as a result of having to repress his natural instincts and drives, declines physiologically and psychologically, which causes him to become ill. (McAllister, 2021: 172)

Assuming that there is no essential difference between the physiologies of the criminal and of the mentally ill, in section 202 of *Daybreak*, Nietzsche proposes to offer them both the same type of treatment – that is, medical intelligence and benevolence. A substantially more precise and accurate definition of this treatment proposed by him is subsequently provided. For now, it should be mentioned that in this section, Nietzsche does not intend to address the boundaries around criminals, noncriminals and the mentally ill.

Nowadays, such a comparison between criminals and the mentally ill can cause strangeness or even a certain repulsion. However, as Mazzino Montinari (1997) states, taking into account the 'living and historical environment' is a *sine qua non* condition for reading Nietzsche correctly: 'criminals and prostitutes, alcoholics and neurotics, degenerate and mad ... are popular themes of physiologists from the 19th century' (Montinari, 1997: 86).[3]

In fact, particularly in the 1880s, Nietzsche had direct access to the works of several physiologists who had an important influence on his philosophical work. Among them were notable figures like the Frenchman Charles Féré and the Englishman Francis Galton. Although Nietzsche only had access to several works by these two scientists after the publication of *Daybreak*, it is certain that his interest in physiology is already present in this book. For example, in section 538, entitled 'Moral Insanity of the Genius', he writes that 'three-quarters of all the evil done in the world happens out of timidity: and this is above all a physiological phenomenon!' (Nietzsche, 1997: 213). The overriding emphasis on biology, physiology, psychology and medicine clearly demonstrates his effort to replace the moral mode of valuation with scientific approaches as a means to overcome the culture of punishment.

Thus, what I would like to call attention to in the opening lines of section 202 of *Daybreak* is Nietzsche's determination to substitute *moral judgements* about criminals with new *modes of valuation*. In relation to this comprehension, the following extract of section 453 of the same book, entitled 'Moral Interregnum', confirms such an interpretation:

> Who would now be in a position to describe that which will one day *do away with* moral feelings and judgments! – however sure one may be that the foundations of the latter are all defective and their superstructure is beyond repair: their obligatory force must diminish from day to day, so long as the obligatory force of reason does not diminish! To construct anew the laws of life and action – for this task our sciences of physiology, medicine, sociology and solitude are not yet sufficiently sure of themselves: and it is from them that the foundation-stones of new ideals (if not the new ideals themselves) must come. So it is that, according to our taste and talent, we live an existence which is either a *prelude* or a *postlude*, and the best we can do in this *interregnum* is to be as far as possible our own *reges* and found little *experimental states*. We are experiments: let us also want to be them! (Nietzsche, 1997: 190–191)

Although the sciences of physiology, medicine, society and psychology have not yet developed an extensive knowledge of criminality, for Nietzsche, only they can eventually offer us a more promising approach for the adoption of new modes of valuation, particularly in relation to wrongful behaviours.

Looking back in retrospect, Nietzsche recalls that, in the past, our ancestors used to consider the mentally ill person as a guilty person. They used to view him or her as 'a danger to the community and the abode of some demonic being who has entered into his body as the consequence of a guilt he has incurred – here the rule is: every sick person is a guilty person!' (Nietzsche, 1997: 122).

However, anyone who today wants to take revenge on those sick persons for the losses they cause to individuals and society would be called inhumane. This same turnaround that occurred in the mode of valuation regarding the mentally ill is exactly what Nietzsche advocates for criminals. As he writes in section 66 of the first volume of *Human, All Too Human*, 'our crime against criminals consists in the fact that we treat them as scoundrels' (Nietzsche, 1996: 44).

In a passage from 'On the Pale Criminal' of *Thus Spoke Zarathustra*, Nietzsche expands this idea with the following terms: ' "Enemy" you should say, but not "villain"; "sick man" you should say, but not "scoundrel"; "fool" you should say, but not "sinner"' (Nietzsche, 2006: 26). Bear in mind that the words 'villain' (*Bösewicht*), 'scoundrel' (*Schuft*) and 'sinner' (*Sünder*) are adjectives attributed to criminals based on a *moral or religious* mode of valuation. This is precisely what Nietzsche wants to avoid. Hence, he suggests that criminals are to be treated with medical knowledge and goodwill. In other words, from a mode of valuation that rules out moral and religious prejudices, by replacing them with scientific wisdom. Therefore, instead of advocating punishment, Nietzsche proposes that wrongdoers should have a range of therapeutic measures at hand for a possible recovery of their physio-psychological health.

In section 202 of *Daybreak*, Nietzsche highlights what would be some of the reasonable procedures to promote such a convalescence:

> He needs a change of air, a change of company, a temporary absence, perhaps he needs to be alone and have a new occupation – very well! Perhaps he himself may find it to his advantage to live for a time in custody, so as to secure protection against himself and against a burdensome *tyrannical drive* – very well! One should place before him quite clearly the possibility and the means of becoming cured (the extinction, transformation, sublimation of this drive), also, if things are that bad, the improbability of a cure; one should offer the opportunity of suicide to the incurable criminal who has become an abomination to himself. Keeping this extremest means of relief in reserve, one should neglect nothing in the effort to restore to the criminal his courage and freedom of heart; one should wipe pangs of conscience from his

soul as a matter of cleanliness, and indicate to him how he can make good the harm he has done perhaps to only a single person, and more than make it good, through benefits he could bestow on others and perhaps on the whole community. In all this one should show him the greatest consideration! And especially in allowing him anonymity, or a new name and frequent changes of residence, so that his reputation and his future life shall be as little endangered as possible. (Nietzsche, 1997: 121)

First, in relation to this passage, attention must be paid to Nietzsche's thorough and accurate effort in choosing the terms and expressions, which clearly indicate that therapeutic options should not be at all compulsory. This means that treatment must be offered with 'greatest consideration' (*äusserster Schonung*), in an attitude of full respect and thoughtfulness. Here, the character of voluntariness of such medical treatment is stressed as being of utmost importance for the contemporary abolitionist voices and, in this respect, for public policy development.

Another point worth noting is the possibility that criminals themselves consider 'to live for a time in custody, so as to secure protection against himself and against a burdensome *tyrannical drive*'. This passage reminds us of the anti-hero of *Crime and Punishment*, by Fyodor Dostoevsky (1917) – after committing the murder of two women, Raskolnikov chooses to turn himself in to the police, aware that he would be sentenced to spend long years in a prison in Siberia. In the final lines of the novel, Dostoevsky points to the possibility of regeneration of criminals, as the ability to sublimate that tyrannical impulse that led them to commit their crimes:

But that is the beginning of a new story – the story of the gradual renewal of a man, the story of his gradual regeneration, of his passing from one world into another, of his initiation into a new unknown life. That might be the subject of a new story, but our present story is ended. (Dostoevsky, 1917: 559)

Let our attention now focus on the terms that Nietzsche highlights in italics: 'an annoying *tyrannical impulse*' (*tyrannischen Trieb*), against which the criminal could protect himself, thus avoiding recidivism. For Nietzsche, the possibility of curing the illness that affects a wrongdoer requires the elimination, transformation and sublimation of this tyrannical impulse.

However, if Nietzsche himself concludes, in section 17 of *Beyond Good and Evil*, that 'a thought comes when 'it' wants, and not when 'I' want' (Nietzsche, 2002: 17), how then can people be expected to successfully manage to protect themselves from a tyrannical impulse that involuntarily surfaces in consciousness as a commanding thought?

The answer to this question is in section 109 of *Daybreak*. According to Nietzsche, there exist at least six possible 'methods' to overcome unwanted impulses. In his own words, they can be summarized as follows: 'avoiding opportunities, implanting regularity into the drive, engendering satiety and disgust with it and associating it with a painful idea (such as that of disgrace, evil consequences or offended pride), then dislocation of forces and finally a general weakening and exhaustion' (Nietzsche, 1997: 65).

The appropriate learning of self-mastering and moderating unwanted impulses can prove crucial to promoting criminals' health rehabilitation. In contrast to punitive approaches, such a skill would be far more effective in tackling criminality and anti-social behaviour, thus strengthening the abolitionist movement.

Once again, it is interesting to note the title given by Nietzsche to this section of *Daybreak*: 'Self-Mastery and Moderation and Their Ultimate Motive'. We must bear in mind that 'self-mastery and moderation' (*Selbst-Beherrschung und Mässigung*) are skills that are radically different from the *fable of free will* promoted by 'the hangman's metaphysics'. Nietzsche argues that human will is not free, but determined by causes that are internal (such as instinct and reason) and external to the individuals (for instance, education, culture, censure and praise). A vast array of thinkers, such as Hobbes, Spinoza, Leibniz, Hume, Montaigne, Schopenhauer and Mill, share similar notions of free will.

Nevertheless, regarding the methods of elimination, transformation and sublimation of undesirable tyrannical impulses, Nietzsche clarifies that they are not infallible at all. For this reason, one must duly warn criminals about the 'improbability of a cure'. While he does not deconstruct the traditional category of crime, for him, the incurable criminal who, by chance, has become 'an abomination to himself' should consider 'the opportunity for suicide'. Allowing incurable criminals who have become a monster to themselves to take their own life is, for him, a compassionate attitude, because it sanctions them an 'extremest means of relief'.

In section 88 of the first volume of *Human, All Too Human*, Nietzsche makes an important consideration about the prohibition of suicide: 'There exists a right by which we take a man's life but none by which we take from him his death: this is mere cruelty' (Nietzsche, 1996: 48). In other words, in the present case, it would be too inhuman to prevent criminals – hopelessly subjugated by an incessant '*tyrannical instinct*' – from putting an end to their suffering with themselves.

On the other hand, to those whose illness is curable, Nietzsche prescribes a therapy in which 'one should neglect nothing in the effort to restore to the criminal his courage and freedom of heart; one should wipe pangs of conscience from his soul as a matter of cleanliness' (Nietzsche, 1997: 121). For him, 'courage and freedom of heart' (*den guten Muth und die Freiheit des Gemüthes*) are mental dispositions that criminals require for their convalescence. Furthermore, they need to rid themselves of remorse (*Gewissensbisse*) that deeply degrades their spirit. This means that it is critical for their cure that they become aware of their total unaccountability (*völligen Unverantwortlichkei*) for their actions. It is unmistakable that here Nietzsche brings out a radical consequence of his theory of 'the complete unaccountability of man for his actions and his nature' (Nietzsche, 1996: 57). This theory categorically refutes the existence of free will and therefore denying the validity of blame, blameworthiness and moral guilt. In other words, not only others but also the criminals themselves, who seek restoration of their health must duly recognize their unaccountability and innocence.

The concept of punishment deprives of innocence (*Unschuld*) not only people but also 'the whole purely chance character of events'(*die ganze reine Zufälligkeit des Geschehens*) (*Daybreak*, section 13). In this sense, Nietzsche's notion of 'the innocence of becoming' (*die Unschuld des Werdens*) is indebted to the Heraclitus of Ephesus' philosophy, for whom all entities in the universe flows and nothing remains. Therefore, such a thought is in opposition to the Platonic Idea, of Parmenidean inspiration, of the immutable, timeless, and uniform Being.

Alice Medrado (2021) argues that the Nietzschean conception of becoming calls into question the belief in the concepts of the subject identity and stability. According to her:

> The reality of becoming would dissolve any ontological counterpart that could support the basic terms presupposed in the traditional discourse on freedom, such as the idea of a stable subject, with the capacity for self-determination of his or her own will, as a sufficient cause for actions under moral classification. (Medrado, 2021: 17)[4]

Thus, by opposing the ontological conception of a 'stable subject', whose actions would then be 'under moral classification', Nietzsche articulates his thesis of the innocence of becoming to explain moral, legal, and religious unaccountability. I believe that is essentially the meaning of section 252 of *Daybreak*, where Nietzsche writes: 'Reflect! – He who is punished is never he who performed the deed. He is always the scapegoat' (Nietzsche, 1997: 143).

In *Twilight of the Idols*, Nietzsche reiterates the argument that the notions of guilt and punishment corrupt the innocence of becoming and, for this reason, we must eradicate them, thus purifying psychology, history, nature and social institutions. In section 7, chapter VI of *Twilight of the Idols*, he names his 'most radical opponents': the theologians of Christianity who, based on their hangman's metaphysics, introduced the concepts of sin and punishment into the world. In his own words:

> But now that we have set off in the *opposite* direction, now that we immoralists in particular are trying as hard as we can to rid the world of the concepts of guilt and punishment and cleanse psychology, history, nature, and social institutions and sanctions of these concepts, the most radical opponents we face are the theologians who use the concept of the 'moral world order' to keep infecting the innocence of becoming with 'punishment' and 'guilt'. Christianity is a hangman's metaphysics. (Nietzsche, 2005: 181–182)

With this brief explanation of the Nietzschean notion of the 'innocence of becoming' in its relation to guilt and punishment, we return to the earlier analysis of section 202 of *Daybreak*. Here, attention is drawn to the passage where Nietzsche recommends that one must 'indicate to him how he can make good the harm he has done perhaps to only a single person, and more than make it good, through benefits he could bestow on others and perhaps on the whole community' (Nietzsche, 1997: 121).

For Nietzsche, the victims should be able to perceive this good deed as a way for wrongdoers to demonstrate some goodwill as a kind of counterweight to the ill will manifested through their criminal or unjust action. Underlying this restorative justice approach is Nietzsche's critique of modern criminal law, which reduces the victim to a mere spectator in their own conflict. According to Nietzsche's analysis, the state kidnaps the victim's right to fight for due compensatory reparation, assuming exclusively to itself the role of judging, convicting and punishing the criminal.

As a final point, Nietzsche advises that the criminal be assured, with greatest consideration, 'anonymity, or a new name and frequent changes of residence, so that his reputation and his future life shall be as little endangered as possible' (Nietzsche, 1997: 121). The anonymity and the change of name and address aim to spare wrongdoers from the stigma that one might impose on them, due to any offence they committed in the past. This is necessary because the possibility of a healthy existence requires the total absence of ignominious torture.

Furthermore, for Nietzsche, punishment tarnishes more than the offence itself, as he argues in section 235 of *Daybreak*: 'A strange thing, our kind of punishment! It does not cleanse the offender, it is no expiation: on the contrary, it defiles more than the offence itself' (Nietzsche, 1997: 139).

In relation to the direct victim of an injustice or a crime, Nietzsche ponders the following:

> At present, to be sure, he who has been injured, irrespective of how this injury is to be made good, will still desire his revenge and will turn for it to the courts – and for the time being the courts continue to maintain our detestable criminal codes, with their shopkeeper's

scales and the *desire to counterbalance guilt with punishment*. (Nietzsche, 1997: 121)

It is not surprising that the victim's expectation, when resorting to the courts, is not to compensate for the damage suffered but rather to obtain revenge. As Nietzsche argues in section 33 of 'The wonderer and his shadow', from the second volume of *Human, All Too Human*, judicial punishments are invariably a form of revenge (Nietzsche, 1913). In fact, as seen previously, 'our detestable criminal codes' (*abscheulichen Strafordnungen*)[5] exclude the victims from the conflict and deny them the right to obtain any compensatory reparation for the harm they suffered. In this case, the only expectation left for the injured person is the satisfaction of his or her instinct of revenge.

As for the efforts 'to counterbalance guilt with punishment', Nietzsche argues that the balance of the 'shopkeeper's scales' of criminal law is, in the end, the degree of knowledge that the judge has or can obtain about 'the previous history of the crime' (Nietzsche, 1913: 206). In other words, 'the whole concatenation of circumstances' is what actually leads criminals to commit their crimes. Observe how he elaborates the reasoning behind the attenuation of the criminals' 'guilt':

> The criminal, who knows the whole concatenation of circumstances, does not consider his act so far beyond the bounds of order and comprehension as does his judge. His punishment, however, is measured by the degree of astonishment that seizes the judge when he finds the crime incomprehensible. – If the defending counsel's knowledge of the case and its previous history extends far enough, the so-called extenuating circumstances which he duly pleads must end by absolving his client from all guilt. Or, to put it more plainly, the advocate will, step by step, tone down and finally remove the astonishment of the judge, by forcing every honest listener to the tacit avowal. 'He was bound to act as he did, and if we punished, we should be punishing eternal Necessity.' – Measuring the punishment by the degree of knowledge we possess or can obtain of the previous history of the crime – is that not in conflict with all equity? (Nietzsche, 1913: 205–206)

However, modern criminal law does not seem to leave room for the intellectual probity of a criminal judge to conclude that the wrongdoer 'was bound to act as he did', even when the magistrate is well aware of the most evident 'extenuating circumstances'. Whether for dissuasive or merely vindictive reasons, modern criminal law itself compels the judge to punish 'eternal Necessity'. Nonetheless, Nietzsche leads us to question whether we should not be able to overcome this punitive culture once and for all.

Thus, he anticipates the highest point of his philosophy of punishment, from which he reveals the possibility of a new dawn for humanity, in which guilt, revenge, sin and punishment are utterly eradicated from the world:

> What a relief it would be for the general feeling of life if, together with the belief in guilt, one also got rid of the old instinct for revenge, and even regarded it as a piece of prudence for the promotion of happiness to join Christianity in blessing one's enemies and *to do good* to those who have offended us! Let us do away with the concept *sin* – and let us quickly send after it the concept *punishment*! May these banished monsters henceforth live somewhere other than among men, if they want to go on living at all and do not perish of disgust with themselves! (Nietzsche, 1997: 121)

Although most of section 202 of *Daybreak* is devoted to prescribing treatment for the illness that criminals suffer, in the referenced passage, Nietzsche broadens his intention to promote the health of humanity as a whole. In other words, overcoming the punitive culture aims to alleviate 'the general feeling of life' all among humankind.

In section 186 of 'The wonderer and his shadow', from the second volume of *Human, All Too Human*, Nietzsche alerts us to the production of deleterious effects of this culture on humanity:

> All criminals force society back to earlier stages of culture than that in which they are placed for the time being. Their influence is retrograde. Let us consider the tools that society must forge and maintain for its defence: the cunning detectives, the jailers, the hangmen. Nor should we forget the public counsel for prosecution and defence. Finally we may ask ourselves whether the judge himself and punishment and the whole legal procedure are not oppressive rather than elevating in their reaction upon all who are not law-breakers. For we shall never succeed in arraying self-defence and revenge in the garb of innocence, and so long as men are used and sacrificed as a means to the end of society, all loftier humanity will deplore this necessity. (Nietzsche, 1913: 287)

Here again, Nietzsche presents himself as a kind of doctor of culture when he questions 'whether the judge himself and punishment and the whole legal procedure are not oppressive rather than elevating in their reaction upon all who are not law-breakers'. Therefore, this is one of the reasons, added to those previously mentioned, for us to rid ourselves of 'the belief in guilt' and 'the old instinct for revenge' (Nietzsche, 1997: 122). Thus, we should not overlook the persuasive force of this passage from section 202 of *Daybreak* if we want to grasp its true significance for Nietzsche's philosophy of punishment.

On the other hand, Nietzsche was fully aware of the extemporaneousness of his philosophical thinking on abolition of punishment, as the following passage of 'The wonderer and his shadow' highlights:

> Wrath and punishment are our inheritance from the animals. Man does not become of age until he has restored to the animals this gift of the cradle. – Herein lies buried one of the mightiest ideas that men can have, the idea of a progress of all progresses. – Let us go forward together a few millenniums, my friends! There is still reserved for mankind a great deal of joy, the very scent of which has not yet been wafted to the men of our day! Indeed, we may promise ourselves this joy, nay summon and conjure it up as a necessary thing, so long as the development of human reason does not stand still. Some day we shall no longer be reconciled to the logical sin that lurks in all wrath and punishment, whether exercised by the individual or by society – some day, when head and heart have learnt to live as near together as they now are far apart. That they no longer stand so far apart as they did originally is fairly palpable from a glance at the whole course of humanity. The individual who can review a life of introspective work will become conscious of the *rapprochement* arrived at, with a proud delight at the distance he has bridged, in order that he may thereupon venture upon more ample hopes. (Nietzsche, 1913: 285)

Expressions like 'let us go forward together a few millenniums', 'some day we shall no longer' and 'a glance at the whole course of humanity' do reveal that Nietzsche looks to the horizon of a future still very distant from his own time and, certainly, from ours as well. Despite being an extemporaneous thinker, as Nietzsche himself ponders, it is necessary to predict and invoke the joy of 'the idea of a progress of all progresses' – in other words, the complete and peremptory overcoming of punishment.

Likewise, the recognition of the extemporaneousness of Nietzsche's thought on punishment is also present in the final passage of section 202 of *Daybreak*. There, he argues about institutional immaturity for understanding a criminal as a sick person since the studies of medical art have not yet sufficiently addressed moral, religious and legal issues. When analysing section 202 of *Daybreak*, we must guard ourselves from the inclination to associate the 'promotion of health' with a hypothetical intention of Nietzsche to erect a new ideal or a new morality for the betterment of society. By explicitly and emphatically advocating the abolition of punishment, Nietzsche simply aims to conjecture the possibility of adopting new *modes of valuation* and, consequently, alternative behaviours in relation to criminals. Thus, his purpose is rather to articulate a counterculture's philosophical thought that questions all sorts of punitive theoretical constructs. For Nietzsche, we must eventually replace them with modes of valuation that are affirmative of life. These modes of valuation should also be capable of promoting our great health, as well as recovering our innocence of becoming.

Final considerations on Nietzsche's abolitionism

The crucial point of Nietzsche's philosophy, which is of relevance to contemporary studies on the theme of punishment, is his irreducible defence against punitive systems through the adoption of new modes of valuation in relation to the canons of punitive justice. Visionary? Perhaps, but by problematizing punishment, Nietzsche philosophizes with a hammer in hand. In this regard, his main task was to demonstrate the invalidity of the assumptions of punitive theories, as well as to reveal their harmful outcomes to culture and people's psychological health.

Moreover, it is paramount to note that Nietzsche submitted the problem of punishment to a critical-genealogical analysis, *pari passu* to his struggle against Platonic-Christian morality. By rejecting metaphysical justifications, he revolutionized traditional moral philosophy.

Nietzsche's vast knowledge on some modern sciences, such as history, physiology, psychology, philology, anthropology and ethnological jurisprudence greatly influenced his philosophical works on issues of morality and punishment. In other words, state-of-the-art scientific knowledge of the 1800s informed his writings on these subjects and, for instance, his proposal of nonpenal therapeutic treatment for criminals.

Thus, Nietzsche sought to demonstrate the feasibility of his unprecedented notion regarding the complete overcoming of punishment. Such an endeavour requires the replacement of moral evaluations with medical-scientific knowledge, with a view to restoring the innocence of becoming as well as to attaining humanity's great health.

Nietzsche is a child of his time, attentive to the idiosyncrasies and tendencies of existing punitive systems. He never really expected that there would be 'ears and hands' for his philosophy of punishment, at least not among his contemporaries. Indeed, Nietzsche knew he was an untimely thinker and an extemporaneous visionary. As a philosopher of the future, he presents his abolitionist thought, presumably to influence the future of humanity. Thus, I strongly believe that contemporary abolitionist voices from a broad spectrum of scholars and policy makers can greatly benefit from further research on Nietzsche's writings on punishment.

Notes

[1] Author's own translation.
[2] Author's own translation.
[3] Author's own translation.
[4] Author's own translation.

5   At the time of the publication of *Daybreak* in 1881, the entire unified territory of Germany enforced the so-called Penal Code for the German Empire (Das Strafgesetzbuch für das Deutsche Reich) of 1871. This legislation was largely drafted on the basis of the Prussian Penal Code of 1851, which in turn incorporated a strong influence from the French Penal Code of 1810. All these penal codes aimed at general prevention for just retribution, thus harbouring both utilitarian and retributive justifications for punishment (Grünhut, 1961). The unification of penal laws through the Penal Code for the German Empire, resulted in serious regression for some states of the German Empire. In this regard, Thomas Vormbaum writes: 'For those federal states in which capital punishment had been abolished, its reintroduction was a step backwards. The same went for states in which the now extensive criminal law on moral offences had previously been cut back under the influence of the theory of criminal law of the Enlightenment and the Bavarian Criminal Code of 1813. On the whole, however, the liberal age of criminal law with its constitutional achievements, but also with the typical restrictions of these achievements by authoritarian elements had produced one of its last great works with this unified Reich Criminal Code' (Vormbaum, 2014: 79).

References

Anastácio, L. (2020) 'Funções do patológico em Aurora e a Gaia Ciência: um prólogo para a "grande saúde"', *Estudos Nietzsche*, 11(2): 54–68.

Brobjer, T. (2008) *Nietzsche's Philosophical Context: an Intellectual Biography*, Chicago: University of Illinois Press.

Dostoevsky, F. (1917) *Crime and Punishment*, W.A. Neilson (ed.), C. Garnett (trans.), New York: P.F. Collier & Son.

Frezzatti Jr., W. (2006) 'A fisiologia de Nietzsche: a superação da dualidade cultura/biologia', *Tempo da Ciência*, 11(22): 115–135.

Giacoia Jr., O. (2019) 'Psicofisiologia e terapia dos afetos', *Sofia*, 8(2): 202–18.

Giacoia Jr., O. (2020) 'Saúde, doença e política em Nietzsche', *Estudos Nietzsche*, 11(2): 10–40.

Grünhut, M. (1961) 'The reform of criminal law in Germany', *British Journal of Criminology*, 2(2): 171–177.

McAllister, L. (2021) 'Nietzsche on criminality', PhD thesis, Schollar Commons, University of South Florida.

Medrado, A. (2021) 'Liberdade e imoralismo em Nietzsche', doctoral thesis, Faculdade de Filosofia e Ciências Humanas da Universidade Federal de Minas Gerais.

Montinari, M. (1997) 'Ler Nietzsche: o Crepúsculo dos Ídolos', E. Chaves (trans.), *Cadernos Nietzsche*, 3: 77–91.

Nietzsche, F. (1913) 'Human, all too human II: the wonderer and his shadow', in O. Levy (ed.) *The Complete Works of Friedrich Nietzsche*, P.V. Cohn (trans.), New York: Macmillan, pp 179–366.

Nietzsche, F. (1996) 'Human, all too human: a book for free spirits', in R.J. Hollingdale (ed.) *Cambridge Texts in the History of Philosophy*, Cambridge: Cambridge University Press.

Nietzsche, F. (1997) 'Daybreak: thoughts on the prejudices of morality', in M. Clark and B. Leiter (eds) *Cambridge Texts in the History of Philosophy*, R.J. Hollingdale (trans.), Cambridge: Cambridge University Press.

Nietzsche, F. (2002) 'Beyond good and evil: prelude to a philosophy of the future', in R.P. Horstmann and J. Norman (eds) *Cambridge Texts in the History of Philosophy*, J. Norman (trans.), Cambridge: Cambridge University Press.

Nietzsche, F. (2005) 'The anti-Christ, Ecce Homo, twilight of the idols', in A.A. Ridley and J. Norman (eds) *Cambridge Texts in the History of Philosophy*, J. Norman (trans.), Cambridge: Cambridge University Press.

Nietzsche, F. (2006) 'Thus spoke Zarathustra', in A. Caro and R. Pippin (eds) *Cambridge Texts in the History of Philosophy*, A. Caro (trans.), Cambridge: Cambridge University Press.

Vormbaum, T. (2014) *A Modern History of German Criminal Law*, M. Hiley (trans.), London: Springer.

7

Marxism and the Political Economy of Abolitionism

Jon Burnett

Introduction

It is a truism in some criminological circles that while 'Marxist thought has had a huge impact on the field of criminology, Marx himself actually had very little to say about crime' (Heidt and Wheeldon, 2014: 210; see also, for example, Barlow and Kauzlarich, 2010: 104). However, it is also a truism that is largely untrue, and this chapter argues that demystifying such assumptions is integral to understanding a trajectory of Marxist and neo-Marxist abolitionist praxis. In doing so, what follows first explores Marx's writings in the early 1840s on the theft of wood in the Rhine, exploring how these were crucial in enabling him to realize his ignorance of political economy, and thus further enabling him develop his *critique* of political economy through which analyses of the law and the state under capitalist conditions could be elaborated. These writings were germane to developing understandings of crime and punishment under capitalist conditions, and as they indicate, perceptions that Marx had little to say about crime reside in many ways on taking the category and construct of 'crime' at face value – something which Marx and Marxists did and do not do (see Weis, 2017).

Rather, Marxist praxis has underpinned the development of structural, materialist analyses of crime and punishment, which this chapter subsequently moves on to explore through some of the most germane neo-Marxist bodies of scholarship building from this position: analyses of political economies of punishment. Such works have sought to develop analyses of punishment which problematize such linear crime-punishment discussions and instead hypothesize 'the existence of a structural relationship between transformations of the economy and changes in the penal field' (de Giorgi,

2018: 1). The final sections of this chapter further explore a Marxist and neo-Marxist tradition which locates this broader 'penal field' at the core of its focus. Drawing on critical insights regarding the ways in which prisons and punishment mystify the harms of capitalist power and reproduce forms of social order (Mathiesen, 1974; Fitzgerald and Sim, 1982), it demonstrates how Marxist and neo-Marxist ideas have been vital for interrogating the 'penal question' (Melossi, 1976) well beyond the direct confines of sites of incarceration. Indeed, this chapter argues that, whether explicitly or implicitly, Marxism has been and is a core component abolitionist praxis, and in the Marxist tradition, those working within such frameworks seek not just to interpret the world, but also to change it.

Marxism, crime and criminalization

In October 1842, a young Marx became the editor-in-chief of the liberal newspaper the *Rheinische Zeitung* (*RZ*), and in so doing was rapidly immersed 'in the thick of the most advanced political and economic milieu in Germany' (Draper, 2011 [1977]: 61). The Rhineland's emerging civil society, based on private property and formal legal equality, and inherited in part through the French Revolution, put it in direct conflict with the Prussian state (Bensaïd, 2021: 3). And with the *RZ* having been founded as a 'mouthpiece for Cologne's progressives, who comprised businessmen and professionals' (Sanders, 2009), Marx was 'flanked on the one hand by the practical men of the Government's watchdog agencies, and on the other by the practical businessmen who were shareholders and sponsors of the *RZ*' – or between 'the harassment of the one and screams of the other' (Draper, 2011 [1977]: 61). Indeed, just six months later in March 1843, the paper was shut down, by which point Marx himself had resigned, unable to operate under Prussian censorship. Yet despite his time at the paper being short, Marx nonetheless contributed a range of articles concerned directly with events in the region of his birth which would prove integral to his own political development.

Among them was a short series of articles about wood. Examining how a Bill proposing criminalizing the taking of dead wood (defining it as theft) in the Rhineland was bound to capitalism's appropriation of the commons for the benefit of the bourgeoisie, Marx demonstrated how the proposed law embodied the eradication of the customary rights of the poor at a point when the customary rights of the propertied were being solidified (for discussion, see Draper, 2011 [1977]: 68). At a point where the theft of wood spoke clearly to the growing impoverishment of the peasantry, criminalizing the taking of wood signalled attempts to prevent anyone from independently transforming it into materials to survive (for instance, as firewood), as well as for materials (such as fishing rods, for repairing property and so on) produced outside the dominant mode of capitalist relations and production (see also Bensaïd 2021: 9). Certainly, Marx was at this point yet to become Marx*ist*. As he famously later noted, such was his ignorance of political economy as editor of the *RZ* that he was 'embarrassed at first when [having] to take part in discussions concerning so-called material interests' (Marx, 1904 [1859]: 10). Moreover, through his analysis implying that the private appropriation of fines for wood theft in some ways perverted the role of the state, his frame of analysis was in some respects still working at that point within the confines of bourgeois law rather than transcending it. But the seeds were nonetheless being sown. For it was the immersion into these debates which helped set him on the path to developing analysis of class struggle, his understandings of socialism (see Linebaugh, 1976: 6) and also to the role of the state, the law and of punishment under capitalist conditions.

By the time he would come to write Volume 1 of *Capital* (published 24 years later in 1867), for example, Marx was by that point absolutely clear about the capacity of the law to enforce violent social order(s). He demonstrated that the 'bloody legislation against vagabondage' in England from the end of the 15th century and through the 16th century was directed largely at those who had been forcibly expropriated from their existing forms of life and 'turned *en masse* into beggars, robbers, vagabonds' (Marx, 2013 [1867]: 514), while simultaneously, the law further made legal the appropriation 'of gold and silver in America', the 'enslavement in mines of the aboriginal population', the 'conquest and looting of the East Indies' and the 'turning of Africa into a warren for the commercial hunting' of its populace. Indeed, for Marx, mass violence, dispossession and expropriation were among the momenta of primitive accumulation: the 'rosy dawn' of capitalist production wherein the 'treasures captured outside Europe by undisguised looting, enslavement, and murder, floated back to the mother-country and were there turned to capital' (Marx, 2013 [1867]: 527). And while all of these momenta were certainly different, all nonetheless required and reshaped the 'power of the State, the concentrated and organized force of society' to transform the mode of production; for force 'is the midwife of every old society pregnant with a new one' (Marx, 2013 [1867]: 525–526). As such, analyses of states and of state power, the role(s) of law and conceptualizations of crime and punishment divorced from their political and material contexts were not just inadequate, he made clear; they were fundamentally at odds with liberation (see Marx, 1973).

What Marx recognized, then, was that understanding and disrupting conceptions of crime and the parameters of criminalization were important facets of the broader socialist project. But in doing so, what Marxist praxis further provided was a framework through which to break out from and transcend what have elsewhere been called the 'logics of crime' themselves (see Scott, 2022). Certainly, it was Marx's collaborator Engels who demonstrated the necessity for liberatory movements to engage in this double movement in his earlier exploration of the condition of the working class in England in the 19th century. Having worked in his father's cotton mills in Manchester, and based on extensive investigation, observation and immersion in the processes of urbanization within the city, Engels produced a definitive account of the ravages of industrial capitalism from one of the apexes of the Industrial Revolution. Documenting in forensic detail the immiseration of the working class, Engels (2009 [1845]: 37–38) demonstrated how capitalism's 'barbarous indifference' to much human life manifested itself in a swirling combination of crushing poverty, exposure to illness, starvation and exploitation, all hurrying people 'to their grave before their time' (Engels, 2009 [1845]: 107).

In the processes of industrialization, Engels continued, the 'dissolution of mankind into nomads of which each one has a separate principle and separate purpose, the world of atoms, is here carried out to its most extreme' (Engels, 2009 [1845]: 38). But while for many, he suggested, want 'leaves the working man the choice between starving slowly, killing himself speedily, or taking what he needs where he finds it – in plain English, stealing' (Engels, 2009 [1845]: 126), writing on those segments of the surplus populations who were abandoned to the most virulent, violent forms of destitution, he also noted wryly 'how the poverty of those unfortunates, among whom even thieves find nothing to steal, is exploited by the property-holding class in lawful ways!' (Engels, 2009 [1845]: 41). How 'the police carries on perpetual war' on those with the temerity to allow their poverty to be visible through begging or appealing for help, Engels (2009 [1845]: 98) continued, ensuring that those starving to death would do so 'in a quiet and inoffensive manner'. And as he understood, under the 'social warfare' of industrial capitalism, while 'frauds, thefts, assaults, family quarrels ... crowd[ed] one another' in court reports up and down England (Engels, 2009 [1845]: 142), the violence and harms embedded by capitalist expansion and organization were frequently both absent from these same court reports and facilitated by courts themselves. For the law was 'calculated to protect those who possess property against those who do not'. Enmity 'to the proletariat [was] so emphatically the basis of the law', he argued, 'that the judges, and especially the Justices of the Peace, who are bourgeois themselves, and with whom the proletariat comes most into contact, find this meaning in the law without consideration' (Engels, 2009 [1845]: 286).

However, none of this is to suggest that the state or the law either were or are static entities, existing with one solitary 'function' (for more on this, see Engels, 1969 [1884]). Just as Linebaugh (1976: 5) has argued that it is necessary to 'oppose the view that fossilizes particular compositions of the working class into eternal, even formulaic, patterns', so too is it necessary to avoid fossilizing the capitalist state. Nonetheless, as Pashukanis (1989

[1929]: 176) would later explain, it is entirely possible to foreground the contradictions within the state and criminal justice in bourgeois society while simultaneously asserting that 'class struggle takes place in the form of the administration of justice'. If 'the penal practice of the state power is *by nature* and *in its content* a weapon for the protection of class rule', he suggested, 'then it will appear *in its form* as an aspect of the legal superstructure, and will be absorbed into the legal system as one of its branches' (Pashukanis, 1989 [1929]: 176). In bourgeois society, state power resides in the reproduction of particular class structures – by the police, the courts, the army and so on in conjunction with capital's exploitation of labour – in the long term, even if this needs to be fragmented or other alliances need to be made in the short term to do so.

Political economies of punishment

Thus, as the preceding discussion makes clear, while it is commonly asserted that Marx had little to say about crime and punishment, he was central to contributing a framework through which to question and interrogate notions of crime and punishment under capitalist conditions, as defined through the state and dominant cultural apparatus. Indeed, as de Giorgi (2007: 18) has noted, the Marxist 'materialist approach, which sees processes of social change as shaped by the structural relationship between modes of production and legal/political institutions', has 'represented a powerful framework for critical sociologies of punishment'. And these 'critical sociologies' have proved germane to abolitionist praxis. For they provide one way of interpreting how prisons, and dominant modes of punishment more broadly, operate beyond notions of crime as they are officially defined in the first place.

Central to this mode of analysis has been studies of the political economy (or economies) of punishment, not least *Punishment and Social Structure*, published in 1939 and written by Georg Rusche and Otto Kirchheimer, exiles from Nazi Germany. *Punishment and Social Structure* built on and developed Rusche's earlier 1933 essay, 'Labor Market and Penal Sanction', in which he had argued that: 'Often, legal historians are guided not by an unprejudiced analysis of social laws, but by an evolutionary conception of the development of legal institutions: from barbaric cruelty to the humanitarianism of the relatively perfect legal system which we supposedly enjoy today' (Rusche, 1978 [1933]: 5).

Rusche suggested that such accounts were naïve, failing to comprehend the 'social functions of crime and criminal justice' and the way these 'are shaped by various forces'. Prime among these social forces was the broader fluctuations of labour markets (and indeed dominant modes of production) and the overall position of the lowest strata of the proletariat. 'Naturally, the scarcity or surplus of workers does not unequivocally determine the nature of the labor market', he argued (Rusche, 1978 [1933]: 4), and in the same manner he never suggested that this would unequivocally determine criminal justice either. But his analysis was that as this scarcity or surplus changed, so too would the criminal justice apparatus 'have to meet different tasks'.

Taken up in *Punishment and Social Structure,* the basic proposition was that '[e]very system of production tends to discover punishments which correspond to its productive relationships' (Rusche and Kirchheimer, 2008 [1939]: 5), and what became known as the Rusche-Kirchheimer thesis argued that at times of increased surplus labour, punishment becomes explicitly and expressively violent (with corporal and capital punishments abounding), whereas at points of labour scarcity, punishments utilizing the labour of those convicted of crimes predominate. In a historical overview stretching from the Middle Ages to the point of the book's publication in the 20th century, this schema is utilized to explore punishments including (among other things) banishment, houses of correction and prisons (see Garland, 1990: 93). Embedded within the analysis is an interpretation and attempted demonstration of the function(s) of criminal justice and punishment as instruments of class control, and, as Aviram (2015) states with reference to this analysis:

> Given that criminal enforcement was, and still is, geared almost invariably to the poor, it served as a tool for managing surplus labor or providing access to forced working hands. The uniqueness of criminal law in serving this function lies in its dual role: not only does enforcement and punishment constitute an effective instrument of oppression, but they also come with seemingly class-neutral, moral, ideological justifications, thus giving legitimacy to the prevailing mode of production and quelling protest and uprising. (Aviram, 2015: 16)

Now, the criticisms of *Punishment and Social Structure* have been wide-ranging. As Garland has noted, for example, it is 'sometimes lightly dismissed by critics as nothing more than crude reductionism' (Garland, 1990: 89), while criticisms have also emphasized the ways in which it is not attuned to (for example) the gender dynamics of punishment (see Howe, 1994). But at the same time, it has been integral to a trajectory of Marxist and neo-Marxist thought and organizing which has understood its flaws, built from them and sought to address them. In the 1960s, 1970s and 1980s, for instance, its central messages were taken up within segments of academia – in some cases connected to social movements – challenging the dominant organizing principles of their respective disciplines (in sociology, criminology, social history and so on) in ways reminiscent of Rusche's criticisms of legal historians in the 1930s. For example, Steven Box noted in 1981 that conflict and labelling theories as applied to criminal justice 'need to be supplemented by a wider, more historical and macro view' (Box, 1981: 200) in order to interpret the function of legal systems in preventing 'the weakening of ideological and social hegemony' and facilitating the control of those interpreted as 'problem populations' (Box, 1981: 200). And drawing on Spitzer's analysis of such populations as those whose 'behaviour, personal qualities and/or position threaten the social relations of production in capitalist societies' (Spitzer, 1975: 642), he highlighted how the economically marginalized are 'treated more harshly by the judicial system not simply because of who they are, but also because of what they symbolize, namely the perceived threat to social order posed by the threat of the permanently unemployed' (Box, 1981: 200). In other words, his research was one example of analyses exploring the relationship between labour market conditions, criminalization and punishment (see the discussion in Chiricos and Delone, 1992).

At the same time, a trajectory of work examining the relationships between punishment, labour markets and capitalist conditions has (among other things) demonstrated the dual-regulatory functions of punishment and incarceration. In doing so, this has expanded beyond examining correlations between employment (or unemployment) and punishment, exploring the ancillary functions of punishment more broadly. As Melossi and Pavarini (1981: 17) demonstrated, for instance, in *The Prison and the Factory,* workhouses in the 17th century were utilized to both bend incarcerated peoples to the most precarious strata of the emergent capitalist conditions and also discipline the nascent working class more broadly, who, it was feared, could threaten social order if they engaged in revolt. Coalescing in parts with and developing the analysis of *Punishment and Social Structure,* the principle of less eligibility central to the poor laws was integral to the analysis here, with the shadows of the workhouse and later the prison stretching well beyond their walls (see also Peck, 2001: 41–42). But as would also be foregrounded, it is subordination that was the hallmark of the 'modern' prison as it emerged, a key factor of the 'penitentiary relationship' both then and now (Melossi and Pavarini, 1981: 187). For, as Melossi (2008: 242) would later argue, the 'permanent lesson' of the penitentiary is to 'submit' to the 'bearers of power'.

Indeed, this needs to be borne in mind while the broader rationalities of punishment fluctuate, not least with regard to structural changes within capitalist economies themselves. As de Giorgi (2018) has demonstrated, for example, analyses of political economies of punishment need radical re-examination at points where the dominant modalities of political economy are themselves undergoing shifts. Foregrounding neoliberalism's making explicit of capitalism's class war from above, he highlights how the 'punitive turn' within many countries in the Global North (not least, but not only, the UK and America) from the 1970s onwards was (and is) related to structural shifts in political economy. Certainly, this does not mean that penal policies prior to this point were *not* punitive: a hagiography sometimes sustained by narratives of a 20th-century 'rehabilitative ideal' (for discussion, see Bailey, 2019 and Sim, 2009). However, as de Giorgi and indeed many others have explored, the neoliberal juncture has coalesced with a frontal assault on working conditions, protections and organizing (Bogg, 2016); solidified, reworked and reproduced gendered, racialized and disablist social relations (Ryan, 2019; d'Atri, 2021); and foregrounded and reworked carceral logics and the development of carceral states (Lamble, 2013).

Against this backdrop, prisons operate as one aspect of a much broader assemblage of institutions and dynamics: ranging from the satellite forms of detention, dispersal and deportation of irrregularized migrants (Bowling and Westenra, 2020), to the targeted policing and 'management' of racially minoritized groups (Williams and Clarke, 2016), to the punitive utilization of welfare as a form of control (Mills, 2019) for contemporary surplussed populations (see Burnett, 2015; Haiven, 2020). This is of course not exhaustive, but for de Giorgi (2018: 11–12), one of the most pressing tasks facing analyses of political economies of punishment has been to take stock of such developments, while simultaneously formulating a 'non-reductionist ... structural critique of penal power that is capable of overcoming the false alternative between structure and culture at the same time as it addresses some important theoretical concerns emerging from different theoretical paradigms within the sociology of punishment' (de Giorgi, 2018: 11–12). At a point where the 'dramatic increase under neoliberalism in the capacity of states to carry out policing, carceral, border, and military violence, domestically and globally, is linked to the need to manage surplus populations – and ... is racially coded' (Kundnani, 2021: 65), this is an urgent task.

Marxism and abolitionist praxis

So, drawing from the preceding discussion, how have Marxist ideas informed broader traditions and contemporary forms of penal abolitionism? How are Marxist frameworks situated within penal abolitionism? In the first instance, as Thomas Mathiesen demonstrated more than half a century ago, Marxist frameworks are vital in understanding the ways in which prisons and punishment obscure the harms of capitalist power and the realities of capitalist order(s). In *The Politics of Abolition* (Mathiesen, 2015 [1974]), he explains how prisons perform multiple interrelated ideological functions in capitalist societies: an *expurgatory* function ('housing', managing and in some contexts ridding societies of those deemed 'unproductive' or surplussed); a *power-draining* function (geared towards rendering those incarcerated subservient to the bearers of power); a *diverting* function (from the harms of the powerful); and a *symbolic* function (by stigmatizing those punished, reaffirming the legitimacy of capitalist orders themselves). To that, he later added an *action* function which, through building, expanding and reproducing expansive penal power, confirms to societies that something is 'being done' about crime; while other institutions perform some of these functions, the prison, he argued, coheres them together in a way that is unique. Indeed, despite the persistent failure to perform its stated roles ('rehabilitation', prevention of offending and so on), it is this cohering of functions in real terms which ensures the prison survives as an institution while other institutions performing *some* of these functions are dismantled (see Mathiesen, 2006: 141–142).

As such, Mathiesen's analysis makes clear that when taken together, these functions have the effect of making prisons and dominant forms of punishment appear meaningful and legitimate. Such is the paradigmatic power of the prison, he argues, that it is simultaneously seen as a central reason why and when crime rates fall, while simultaneously articulated as more necessary when crime rates rise. In other words, 'disparate events and actions become meaningful in light of it' (Mathiesen, 2006: 56) and the prison thus maintains its hegemonic position, despite its failures on its own terms. Of course, this process is aided by a whole range of political figures and professionals, and segments of the media and the intelligentsia, working routinely to normalize the prison. But, as he continues, what is distinct in capitalist orders is the materialist underpinnings of these ideological functions. For example, as Joe Sim has demonstrated, Marxist frameworks are integral for deconstructing the notions of crime and criminalization themselves. For prisons are mechanisms for 'punishing the poor', he argues, which 'along with the wider criminal justice system [are] corrosive sites for the "churning" of vast, increasingly racialised, numbers of the dispossessed, pauperised and destitute' (Sim, 2020: 25–26). Criminalization was, and remains central to this process, he continues: often violent, and involving 'state and media-driven focus on policing the behaviour, morals, families and communities of the poor and the powerless' (Sim, 2009: 9). Yet contrast this, he further maintains, with the 'non-criminalisation and non-policing of the powerful, and their systematic criminality' (Sim, 2017).

Tombs (2015), for instance, has documented in detail the concerted deregulation (or *re*-regulation) of corporate harms and violence which have come to exist as hallmarks of Britain's neoliberal project(s): involving a defunding and, in real terms, close to neutering of regulatory agencies such as the Health and Safety Executive and Environment Agency, to the point where they are in many cases no longer able to carry out their statutory duties. Grenfell Tower in London is emblematic of the costs of this assault, with the deaths of more than 70 people and immeasurable damage to hundreds of others as the building burned in 2017 – some of Britain's poorest residents living in one of its wealthiest areas – indistinguishable not just from the local authority cost-cutting leading to palpably unsafe cladding, but also the dismantling of regulatory structures which ultimately facilitated the continued circulation of electrical goods, known to be dangerous, from which the fire most likely originated (Tombs, 2020). Due to the sheer scale of death, Grenfell Tower could not be ignored, although it should be noted that survivors and their families continue to be treated with contempt (see Kale, 2022). But much of the damage, death and violence routinely caused by forms of 'state-corporate violence' (Tombs, 2016: 3) in Britain – the 50,000 deaths a year related to work, the 29,000 deaths a year related to air pollution or the 500 deaths a year due to foodborne illnesses – are 'virtually ignored, not only within the worldview of liberal reform groups but also within mainstream criminology and, not surprisingly, within the state itself' (Sim, 2009: 9).

Some 15 per cent of those in prison are homeless prior to their incarceration. Almost two thirds of those in prison have been unemployed immediately prior to their incarceration. Almost half of those in prison were expelled from school as children. Around 90 per cent have a 'mental disorder', and over half of all women prisoners have previously experienced emotional, physical or sexual abuse (see Birmingham, 2003; Scott and Codd, 2010; Williams, Poyser and Hopkins, 2012; Prison Reform Trust, 2016, 2021; Wyld, Lomax and Collinge, 2018). And that this is the case is related to the way in which the state's focus is frequently trained on the 'poor and the powerless whose depredations, it is argued, need to be controlled through criminal justice interventions, one of which is the prison' (Sim, 2009: 9). As Reiman (2004 [1979]) explained over 40 years ago, 'the rich get richer and the poor get prison', and this is because the functions of the prison cannot be explained simply through crime as a social category. Rather, the prison is connected intimately 'with the reproduction of an unequal and unjust social order divided by the social lacerations of class, gender, "race", age and sexuality' (Sim, 2009: 8).

As such, Marxist and neo-Marxist frameworks have been instrumental in demonstrating *how* the prison reproduces such forms of social order, not least through forms of conjunctural analysis associated most clearly with the work of Stuart Hall. Hall and Massey described the conjuncture as the 'period during which the different social, political, economic and ideological contradictions that are at work in society come together to give it a specific and distinctive shape' (Hall and Massey, 2010: 57). By developing conjunctural analyses which cut 'across political, economic, social and ideological level' (Danewid, 2022: 26), this in turn situates the particularities of the present 'within the antagonisms and ruptures of the historical longue durée' (Danewid, 2022: 26). In this regard, Marxist penal abolitionists – or those speaking to Marxist analyses of criminalization and punishment – have situated the prison materially, symbolically and instrumentally. For example, analyses have emphasized how the utilization of incarcerated people's labour power – fundamental to the origins of the prison – has largely been abandoned in the neoliberal conjuncture, where a core function of the prison has been to warehouse people, not least the swelling ranks of contemporary surplussed populations (see, for example, Wacquant, 2012). However, more recent analyses indicate that this could be elaborated further still, for a resurgent commitment to utilizing work in prisons (and also in immigration detention) does not contradict this notion of warehousing so much as develop understandings of it. Work roles in large part operate as mechanisms for constructing order *within* carceral institutions. While in some cases (in prisons) opened up to broader labour markets, work roles are utilized more frequently (and in conjunction) as mechanisms of social control within carceral sites. Here, work demands to be understood in terms of broader labour market functions, but also beyond them: by way of labour processes and what might be described as forms of pacification (see Burnett, 2022). Yet, in doing so, this further demands analysis of the ideological functions and rationalizations of carceral spaces; for work, in certain sites in particular, is held up as central to *market-led* notions of 'rehabilitation' and, in the process, rationalizes the continued growth of the prison itself.

For instance, the symbiotic relationship between liberal notions of reform and authoritarian ideals of punishment and control intersect spatially and materially at points where prison expansion is underpinned by claims of getting 'prisoners skilled up, and getting them into work' (Raab, 2022) and providing 'thousands of jobs for local communities, boosting economies' (Ministry of Justice, 2022). Judah Schept (2015) has documented extensively how liberalism is central to carceral reshaping and expansion, making absolutely clear how notions of reform and of 'progressive' punishment can exist symbiotically with punishing, punitive policies and practices to buttress carceral states. His work – on things like the euphemistically named 'Justice Campuses' in the United States – clearly shows how liberal ideals or perspectives operate seductively through reformist rationalizations for expansions of state power, while in turn, he foregrounds the importance of analyses of place and of space, which cannot be differentiated from such broader ideological positioning. Indeed, as his and other Marxist geographical analysis has demonstrated, at local levels carceral power is shaped materially, embedded within urban restructuring, labour deregulation, gender governance, and broader economic and social relations (Story, 2019: 5). And it is within such contexts that Marxist abolitionist analyses can have significant purchase. For the labour market functions of carceral logics do need foregrounding, but in terms of the *real* as opposed to the *imagined* social order (see Pearce, 1976). As has been demonstrated elsewhere, prisons 'drain resources from other areas of social life, such as hospitals, schools, housing or social services' (Drake and Scott, 2017). As 'fixes' for crises of land, capital and state capacity (see Wilson-Gilmore, 2007), they operate as 'warehouses of suffering and death', according to Scott (2017), and as they absorb people, he continues, it is imperative to foreground that they are, at heart, 'designed to inflict pain and suffering' (Scott, 2018: 207).

Conclusion

Ultimately, then, Marxist frameworks have provided and continue to provide 'ways of seeing' (to use Berger's [2008 (1972)] terminology) which are integral for abolitionist praxis. Underpinning a range of activist interventions and organizing, these frameworks have emphasized the ways in which the prison operates as one part of a 'mutually reinforcing web of social relationships' (Hart and Schlembach, 2015: 291) reproducing and shaping dominant forms of capitalist social relations. They have documented the ways in which the prison operates as one part of a broader form of 'revanchist common sense' (Camp, 2016: 9), legitimizing and naturalizing state power in the face of threat or revolt. In doing so, such frameworks have necessarily been attuned to continuities and discontinuities in penal policies and the broader social relations they reproduce, for 'having a longer historical perspective suggests some very different strategy interventions and policy conclusions compared with an analysis which focusses on relatively short-term historical trends' (Sim, 2020: 25). Indeed, what is distinctive about Marxist abolitionism in this regard is its ability to forge conjunctural analyses connecting contemporary and historical struggles dialectically and waging them organically.

For example, in their landmark neo-Marxist *British Prisons* (first published in 1979), Fitzgerald and Sim made it absolutely clear that 'to understand the role that imprisonment plays, prisons must be seen within the wider social, political and economic system in which they have been developed' (Fitzgerald and Sim, 1982: 23). Continuing, they demonstrated how imprisonment serves a 'class-based legal system': reinforcing it, legitimizing it and reproducing it symbiotically, all at once. Discussing the notion of a 'prison crisis' at that particular conjuncture, Fitzgerald and Sim (1982: 165) drew on Marxist conceptual frameworks to show how in contrast to the analyses of a range of political figures and liberal prison reform groups, 'the crisis in British prisons ... is the crisis of reform'. In other words, the contemporary prison system '*is the reformed prison system*', they argued, and, as such, the seeds of this crisis of reform were sown 'in the early nineteenth century as part of the wider struggle to impose new forms of class domination'. It is against such backdrops that Marxist frameworks have been integral to building the conceptual tools necessary to build, dialectically, the nonreformist reforms which foreground the primacy of human need while simultaneously delegitimizing carceral sites and logics.

Indeed, these are among the lessons and tools taken up either implicitly or explicitly by abolitionist campaigns and activist movements today. Foregrounding the ways in which racialization, bordering and the reproduction of violent social relations have been integral to the formation of carceral states, Marxist frameworks have been and are vital in struggles to 'meet human need and valorise the right to life for all' (Scott, 2020: 227). Providing materialist analysis of carcerality itself, neo-Marxist analyses such as those of Mathiesen (1974) and Fitzgerald and Sim (1982) speak directly to contemporary abolitionist voices while dialectically revealing how Marxism itself must incorporate an abolitionist imagination in order for it to be emancipatory. At the current conjuncture – marked by murderous inequality, multiple intersecting oppressions and repressive state violence bound up directly with dominant forms of accumulation – these lessons have a particular, profound urgency. But within Marxist abolitionist praxis, there are conceptual tools which contribute to ensuring that this is an urgency that can be met. For there can be no abolition within capitalism.

References

Aviram, H. (2015) *Cheap on Crime: Recession-Era Politics and the Transformation of American Punishment*, Berkeley: University of California Press.

Bailey, V. (2019) *The Rise and Fall of the Rehabilitative Ideal, 1895–1970*, Abingdon: Routledge.

Barlow, H.D. and Kauzlarich, D. (2010) *Explaining Crime: A Primer in Criminological Theory*, Lanham, MD: Rowman & Littlefield.

Bensaïd, D. (2021) *The Dispossessed: Karl Marx's Debates on Wood Theft and the Right of The Poor*, R. Nicols (trans.). Minneapolis: University of Minnesota Press.

Berger, J. (2008 [1972]) *Ways of Seeing*, London: Penguin.

Birmingham, L. (2003) 'The mental health of prisoners', *Advances in Psychiatric Treatment*, 9(3): 191–99.

Bogg, A. (2016) 'Beyond neo-liberalism: the Trade Union Act 2016 and the authoritarian state', *Industrial Law Journal*, 45(3): 299–336.

Bowling, B. and Westenra, S. (2020) '"A really hostile environment": adiaphorization, global policing and the crimmigration control system', *Theoretical Criminology*, 24(2): 163–183.

Box, S. (1981) *Deviance, Reality and Society* (2nd edn), London: Rinehart & Winston.

Burnett, J. (2015) 'The war on welfare and the war on asylum', *Race & Class*, 57(2): 96–100.

Burnett, J. (2022) *Work and the Carceral State*, London: Pluto Press.

Camp, J.T. (2016) *Incarcerating the Crisis: Freedom Struggles and the Rise of the Neoliberal State*, Berkeley: University of California Press.

Chiricos, T. and Delone, M. (1992) 'Labor surplus and punishment: a review and assessment of theory and evidence', *Social Problems*, 39(4): 421–446.

Danewid, I. (2022) 'Policing the (migrant) crisis: Stuart Hall and the defence of whiteness', *Security Dialogue*, 53(1): 21–37.

D'Atri, A. (2021) *Bread and Roses: Gender and Class under Capitalism*, London: Pluto Press.

De Giorgi, A. (2007) 'Rethinking the political economy of punishment', *Criminal Justice Matters*, 70: 17–18.

De Giorgi, A. (2018) 'Punishment, Marxism and political economy', in *The Oxford Research Encyclopaedia of Criminology*, Oxford: Oxford University Press, pp 1–28.

Drake, D. and Scott, D. (2017) 'Build communities, not prisons', *Centre for Crime and Justice Studies* (10 August). Available from: https://www.crimeandjustice.org.uk/resources/build-communities-not-prisons-0 [Accessed 15 September 2024].

Draper, H. (2011 [1977]) *Karl Marx's Theory of Revolution Volume 1: State and Bureaucracy*, Delhi: Aaker Books.

Engels, F. (2009 [1845]) *The Condition of the Working Class in England*, Oxford: Oxford University Press.

Engels, F. (1969 [1884]) 'The origins of the family, private property, and the state', in *Marx-Engels Selected Works*, vol. 3, London: Lawrence & Wishart, pp 377–428.

Fitzgerald, M. and Sim, J. (1982) *British Prisons* (2nd edn), Oxford: Oxford University Press.

Garland, D. (1990) *Punishment and Modern Society: A Study in Social Theory*, Oxford: Oxford University Press.

Hall, S. and Massey, D. (2010) 'Interpreting the crisis', *Soundings*, 44: 57–71.

Haiven, M. (2020) *Revenge Capitalism: The ghosts of Empire, the Demons of Capital, and the Settling of Unpayable Debts*, London: Pluto Press.

Hart, E. and Schlembach, R. (2015) 'The Wrexham Titan prison and the case against prison expansion', *Critical and Radical Social Work*, 3(2): 289–294.

Heidt, J.M. and Wheeldon, J.P. (2014) *Introducing Criminological Thinking: Maps, Theories and Understanding*, London: Sage.

Howe, A. (1994) *Punish and Critique: Towards a Feminist Analysis of Penality*, London: Routledge.

Kale, S. (2022) '"I'd never seen people treated with such contempt": Grenfell survivors speak out five years on', *The Guardian* (14 June). Available from: https://www.theguardian.com/uk-news/2022/jun/14/grenfell-fire-survivors-five-years-anniversary [Accessed 15 September 2024].

Kundnani, A. (2021) 'The racial constitution of neoliberalism', *Race & Class*, 63(1): 51–69.

Lamble, S. (2013) 'Queer necropolitics and the expanding carceral state: interrogating sexual investments in punishment', *Law and Critique*, 24(3): 229–253.

Linebaugh, P. (1976) 'Karl Marx, the theft of wood, and working class composition: a contribution to the current debate', *Crime and Social Justice*, 6: 5–16.

Mathiesen, T. (1974) *The Politics of Abolition: Essays in Political Action Theory*, London: Martin Robertson.
Mathiesen, T. (2006) *Prison on Trial* (3rd edn), Winchester: Waterside Press.
Mathiesen, T. (2015 [1974]) *The Politics of Abolition Revisited*, Abingdon: Routledge.
Marx, K. (1904 [1859]) *A Contribution of the Critique of Political Economy*, Chicago: Charles Kerr.
Marx, K. (1973) *Grundrisse: Foundations of the Critique of Political Economy (Rough Draft)*, London: Penguin in association with *New Left Review*.
Marx, K. (2013 [1867]) *Capital Volumes 1 and 2: A Critical Analysis of Capitalist Production*, London: Wordsworth.
Melossi, D. (1976) 'The penal question in capital', *Crime and Social Justice*, 5: 26–33.
Melossi, D. (2008) *Controlling Crime, Controlling Society: Thinking about Crime in Europe and America*, Cambridge: Polity Press.
Melossi, D. and Pavarini, M. (1981) *The Prison and the Factory: Origins of the Penitentiary System*, London: Macmillan.
Mills, C. (2019) 'Strengthening borders and toughening up on welfare: deaths by suicide in the UK's hostile environment', in M.E. Button and I. Marsh (eds) *Suicide and Social Justice: New Perspectives on the Politics of Suicide Prevention*, Abingdon: Routledge, pp 71–86.
Ministry of Justice (2022) 'Thousands of new prison places to rehabilitate offenders and cut crime'. *Ministry of Justice* (18 February). Available from: https://www.gov.uk/government/news/thousands-of-new-prison-places-to-rehabilitate-offenders-and-cut-crime [Accessed 15 September 2024].
Pashukanis, E.V. (1989 [1929]) *Law & Marxism: A General Theory*, London: Pluto Press.
Pearce, F. (1976) *Crimes of the Powerful: Marxism, Crime and Deviance*, London: Pluto Press.
Peck, J. (2001) *Workfare States*, New York: Guilford Press.
Prison Reform Trust (2016) *Bromley Briefing*, London: Prison Reform Trust.
Prison Reform Trust (2021) *Bromley Briefing*, London: Prison Reform Trust.
Raab, D. (2022) 'Dominic Raab speaks to officers at the Prison Officers' Association conference', *Speech to the Prison Officers' Association* (17 May). Available from: https://www.gov.uk/government/speeches/dominic-raab-speaks-to-officers-at-the-prison-officers-association-conference [Accessed 15 September 2024].
Reiman, J. (1979/2004) *The Rich Get Richer and the Poor Get Prison: Ideology, Class, and Criminal Justice* (7th edn), Boston: Pearson.
Rusche, G. (1978 [1933]) 'Labour market and penal sanction: thoughts on the sociology of criminal justice', *Social Justice*, 10: 2–8.

Rusche, G. and Kirchheimer, O. (2008 [1939]) *Punishment and Social Structure*, New York: Columbia University Press.

Ryan, F. (2019) *Crippled: Austerity and the Demonization of Disabled People*, London: Verso.

Sanders, H. (2009) 'Prussian censorship and Karl Marx's brief career as editor for the *Rheinische Zeitung*', *International Institute of Social History* (3 April). Available from: http://www.iisg.nl/collections/rheinischezeitung/history.php [Accessed 15 September 2024].

Schept, J. (2015) *Progressive Punishment: Job Loss, Jail Growth, and the Neoliberal Logic of Carceral Expansion*, New York: New York University Press.

Scott, D. (2017) 'Building warehouses of suffering and death: the case against the new prison in Wellinborough', *Community Action on Prison Expansion* (24 January). Available from: http://www.cape-campaign.org/building-warehouses-of-suffering-and-death [Accessed 15 September 2024].

Scott, D. (2018) 'Saying NO to the mega prison', *Justice, Power and Resistance*, 2(1): 204–221.

Scott, D. (2020) *For Abolition: Essays on Prisons and Socialist Ethics*, Hook: Waterside Press.

Scott, D, (2022) 'Escaping the logic of crime', in J. Piche (ed. and trans.) *Pain in Vain*, Toronto: Red Quill Books.

Scott, D. and Codd, H. (2010) *Controversial Issues in Prisons*, Maidenhead: Open University Press.

Sim, J. (2009) *Punishment and Prisons: Power and the Carceral State*, London: Sage.

Sim, J. (2017) 'Criminalisation and injustice: double standards which target the poor', *Centre for the Study of Crime, Criminalisation and Social Exclusion* (16 October). Available from: https://ccseljmu.wordpress.com/2017/10/16/criminalisation-and-injustice-double-standards-which-target-the-poor/ [Accessed 15 September 2024].

Sim, J. (2020) 'The modern prison in a "fear-haunted world"', *Prison Service Journal*, 250: 20–27.

Spitzer, S. (1975) 'Towards a Marxian theory of deviance', *Social Problems*, 22(5): 638–651.

Story, B. (2019) *Prison Land: Mapping Carceral Power across Neoliberal America*, Minneapolis: University of Minnesota Press.

Tombs, T. (2015) *Social Protection after the Crisis: Regulation without Enforcement*, Abingdon: Routledge.

Tombs, S. (2016) *'Better Regulation': Better for Whom?*, London: Centre for Crime and Justice Studies.

Tombs, S. (2020) 'Home as a site of state-corporate violence: Grenfell Tower, aetiologies and aftermaths', *Howard Journal of Crime and Justice*, 59(2): 120–142.

Wacquant, L. (2012) 'The prison is an outlaw institution', *Howard Journal of Crime and Justice*, 51(1): 1–15.

Weis, V.V. (2017) *Marxism and Criminology: A History of Criminal Selectivity*, Chicago: Haymarket Books.

Williams, P. and Clarke, B. (2016) *Dangerous Associations: Joint Enterprise, Gangs and Racism*, London: Centre for Crime and Justice Studies.

Williams, K., Poyser, J. and Hopkins, K. (2012) *Accommodation, Homelessness and Reoffending of Prisoners: Results from the Surveying Prisoner Crime Reduction (SPCR) Survey, Research Summary 3/12*, London: Ministry of Justice.

Wilson Gilmore, R. (2007) *Golden Gulag: Prisons, Surplus, Crisis, and Opposition in Globalizing California*, Berkeley: University of California Press.

Wyld, G., Lomax, P. and Collinge, T. (2018) *Understanding Women's Pathways through the Criminal Justice System*, London: NPC.

8

Foucault and Prison Abolition

Chloë Taylor

Introduction: Foucault's genealogy of the prison

In *Discipline and Punish* (1977), Foucault does not so much argue that incarceration produces recidivism as point out that this fact has been known since the birth of the prison (Foucault, 1977: 252–253, 265, 270–272, 276–284). We have long known that punishment does not deter and prisons do not rehabilitate. On the contrary, prisons produce criminals and thus more crime. Incarceration leads to situations of isolation from society and feelings of anti-sociality in those incarcerated, and simultaneously socializes offenders into a criminal milieu. Moreover, prisons deprive families and communities of parents and wage earners, leading to more crimes arising from poverty and familial and community dysfunction. Contemporary critical prison studies scholars such as Michelle Alexander (2011) have demonstrated that the manners in which offenders continue to be punished, restricted and regulated post-incarceration in countries such as the US leaves many former prisoners with few options other than to return to prison. Foucault offers more theoretical variations on these critiques of the prison, observing that the introduction of the discourses and activities of the psychological sciences into the criminal trial and the prison provided an opportunity not simply to punish a prisoner's body, but also to categorize, observe and refashion their soul. Prisoners are constructed as objects of knowledge for criminology, psychiatry and psychology, which predict their likelihood to reoffend and suggest further disciplinary measures based on this prediction, such as extended or reduced periods of incarceration and various forms of probation and post-incarceration surveillance. For Foucault, the production of 'objective' knowledge about criminals objectifies these human beings, producing the very objects and realities that are then known and acted upon. For all these reasons, prisons are not merely ineffective at preventing crime but also counterproductive, to the extent that it would be better for crime prevention to have no criminal justice system at all than to perpetuate the system we have (Davis, 2003: 105). As legal scholar Nicola Lacey puts it, the uselessness of prisons as a means of crime control is a 'frequently rediscovered insight' (Lacey, 2011: 18).

The subtitle of *Discipline and Punish* is 'birth of the prison', but to what prison does Foucault refer? On the one hand, clearly he is providing a genealogy of the prison in the sense of physical institutions of confinement. At the same time, *Discipline and Punish* provides a genealogy of the modern soul – the disciplined soul, which, he argues, is another kind of prison, or another way in which bodies are kept docile. Foucault (1977) thus shows that the prison both monitors and produces souls, but it does not produce the penitent souls that were anticipated by the original advocates of penitentiaries; rather, it produces *delinquent* souls that almost inevitably lead these bodies back to prison. So, as Foucault makes clear, the prison fails spectacularly at rehabilitating prisoners and thus prison is 'dangerous when it is not useless' (Foucault, 1977: 232). Although the failure of prisons to rehabilitate is important to note, Foucault insists that we must move beyond such naïve reiterations of familiar criminological facts and ask what prisons are doing well, such that biopolitical states do not dream of doing without them. For him, it cannot be the case that the failure of the prison to deter crime or to rehabilitate prisoners simply has not yet registered with the powers that be, or that we merely need to demonstrate these facts again. Such demonstrations have been ineffective for 200 years for a reason: the prison must in fact be effectively serving purposes that make it indispensable to the biopolitical state.

In order to explain what the prison is doing well, it is necessary to understand the ways in which sovereign power was failing in the punitive realm, such that a disciplinary response to crime – embodied by the birth of the prison – was appealing in the first place. Foucault (1977) argues that under sovereign power, crimes were viewed as offences against the sovereign rather than against their immediate crime victims. Punishment was conceived as the reassertion of the sovereign's power rather than the repaying of a debt to one's victim or to society. The people were not seen as the ones on whose behalf punishment took place, but as compulsory spectators of the bloody rites through which the sovereign reasserted his power. The population was not meant to feel vindicated or protected by the punishment of lawbreakers, but rather awed by the display of the sovereign's might. The result of this approach to punishment was that people often felt sympathy for the condemned and outrage at the excesses of the sovereign's violence. In contrast, disciplinary power is more likely to be supported by the population because it is packaged as the paying of a debt to and protection of society, and we are more likely to support an effort made on our own behalf than one aimed at terrorizing or subduing us. Thus, while the punitive spectacles of sovereign power frequently backfired by giving rise to revolt, popular manifestations of resistance have been relatively rare since the rise of the prison.

Beyond this, sovereign power was ineffective because it punished relatively few bodies. Disciplinary power, in contrast, targets all bodies and, more importantly, all souls. Significantly, we are less likely to resist a form of power that has already constituted who we are. The effectiveness of discipline lies in the fact that we are unlikely to recognize our self-formations and intuitions as the products of power. We thus accept contingent norms that are the product of disciplinary normalization as both universal and common sense. For example, although *what* is considered a crime as well as *how* criminals are perceived is contingent and socially constructed, we have internalized a pathologizing and fearful understanding of criminals, most of whom are not violent or dangerous, but the victims of poverty and racial profiling, whose acts may not have been criminal in another time and place. However, the idea that crime entails violence and wrongdoing, and thus that criminals should be feared and mistrusted, is normative today, and we do not usually resist what we have internalized as a norm. In short, even if disciplinary power – exemplified by the prison – fails to deter crime or to protect society, it remains desirable to the biopolitical state because it produces a population that is extraordinarily submissive to the criminal punishment system.

Foucault (1977) also notes that because the punishments were so extreme in the law codes under sovereign power, judges were not willing to enforce the laws consistently. Thus, justice could also be irregular because the judges themselves were not willing to be consistent, and therefore the punishments and laws of sovereign power were not enforced. All this made the exercise of sovereign power highly sporadic: sometimes it was applied according to the letter of the law and then people might revolt in sympathy for those being mutilated or killed for petty crimes such as larceny, while in other cases the law was not enforced because it was too severe and thus there was no certainty of punishment. In contrast, with disciplinary power, punishments are lighter and therefore judges are consistently willing to enforce them. Foucault writes that penal and legislative reform aimed 'to make of the punishment or repression of illegalities a regular function … Not to punish less but to punish better; to punish with an attenuated severity perhaps, but in order to punish with more universality and necessity' (Foucault, 1977: 82). Although popular resistance occurs far less often under disciplinary power than under sovereign power, when people *do* revolt, resist and riot in the streets against the exercise of the state's power to punish today, it is largely in cases where capital punishment (a remnant of sovereign power) still exists or is exercised by the police and in instances where punishment is applied inconsistently and thus unjustly. So, in the US, there are protests when people are about to be legally executed, when police execute unarmed Black people and when high-profile court decisions are blatantly racist. Thus, resurgences of sovereign power, seen in irregular, severe and biased punishments, still give rise to rebellion in a way that routine prison sentences typically do not.

Foucault observes in *Discipline and Punish* that penal reformers in the late 18th and early 19th centuries suggested a variety of approaches to punishment other than prison. For instance, one proposal was that punishments should match crimes: a thief would lose his hand; a poisoner would be scalded with boiling liquid; and a murderer would be executed. The only criminals who would be punished by being put into prison would be those who had deprived someone else of their liberty, such as kidnappers. Yet these ideas for penal reform never had traction, whereas the prison soon came to seem 'self-evident' and even 'natural'. Although the problems with the prison were quickly recognized, the 'self-evident' aspect of prisons remained. As Foucault (1977: 232) writes: 'It is the detestable solution, which one seems unable to do without.' But why can we not imagine doing without the prison? Why does it seem self-evident when we know that it is but a 200-year-old invention?

First and foremost, Foucault (1977) thinks that the prison seems self-evident to us today because it is an extension of the pervasive structure of society. We live in a disciplinary, carceral society and the prison is simply a more extreme disciplinary and carceral space than those of our regular lives. The prison thus seems natural to us because it is a mere intensification of what we have been habituated to in all the other institutions in which we are formed and trained (Foucault, 1977: 233). Thus, in the final chapter of *Discipline and Punish*, Foucault asks why we accept being punished, and being punished for such minor offences. In response, he suggests that we do so because we are habituated to disciplinary power as it extends from gentle to draconian forms, from parental discipline through schools, hospitals, workplaces, the army and on to prisons.

Beyond this, prisons seem self-evident because, compared to other punishments, they are perceived as egalitarian and democratic. Moreover, prisons are understood as economic and moral; prison terms are a means of 'paying one's debt to society', and the debt is calculated in terms of time served. This economic approach to punishment seems fair and consonant within a capitalist worldview. Finally, prisons were at least originally conceived as therapeutic and thus penal reformers could assure themselves that their punishments reflected a civilized and humane society in which we do not hurt wrongdoers, but merely deprive them of their liberty in order to help them to help themselves. However readily we may contest each of these perceptions of the prison, carceral institutions have proved palatable because they conform not only to capitalist values, but also to our self-perception in Western democracies as egalitarian, civilized and humane.

Foucault (1977) discusses another reason why prisons have come to seem inevitable. This is that prisons are sites of knowledge production. As Foucault argues in works such as *The Order of Things* and *The History of Sexuality*, modernity is characterized by the invention of human sciences and the desire to know ourselves. The French title of Foucault's *The History of Sexuality* is *La volonté de savoir: The Will to Know*. Modernity is unique in this desire to know the knower, especially in its 'problematic' forms. Foucault's 'will to know' is a play on Nietzsche's 'will to power', and the will to know about 'problematic' human kinds is caught up in a will to power insofar as we want to know about these human kinds to control or transform them. In the case of criminality, a great deal of knowledge is now considered necessary not only about crimes but also, more importantly, about criminals, as is most evident in the 19th-century invention of criminology. According to Foucault (1977), criminological knowledge is considered necessary today both to judge and to punish lawbreakers. The prison is in some ways the ideal place for deriving knowledge about criminals, both as individuals and as types. Carceral institutions are panoptic, providing the perfect opportunity for total observation of the human kinds housed there.

However. the idea that prisons, and other panopticons, give us objective knowledge about human kinds must be qualified in a significant way. For Foucault (1977), what is observed in prison is the 'delinquent', which is different from the agent of a crime. Agents are understood as having free will or autonomy, as having *chosen* to act as they did. Delinquents, on the other hand, are approached more in the way that zoologists study nonhuman animals: in terms of drives or tendencies that determine how they will behave. Foucault (1977: 253) thus refers to the production of knowledge in prisons as 'a zoology of social sub-species'. Unfortunately, criminologists have the same problems that zoologists have when they observe animals in captivity: the animals frequently self-mutilate, self-starve or otherwise harm themselves, each other and their keepers, go mad or die from broken hearts, stress and despair in their cages (Jamieson, 2002). Zoos are not actually good sites for zoological observation because the animals do not generally survive as well as they do in the wild and they do not behave 'naturally'; zoos, like laboratory cages, make captive animals go insane. Thus, one does not learn much about animal behaviour when one puts animals in a setting of captivity that is traumatizing, unnatural and depressing to them. In the same way, social and 'psy' scientists do not learn much about the human animals they observe in prisons other than how captivity crushes and deranges them.

It is in the chapter entitled 'Illegalities and Delinquencies' that we see that Foucault (1977) is a prison abolitionist, even though he never clearly described himself as such. The chapter's title suggests a shift from illegal acts to a kind of identity: the identity of the delinquent, a being for whom criminality is a way of being. Such a subject is nearly bound to reoffend in virtue of who they have been constructed to be. Prisons, in producing delinquents, result not in safer communities, but in more crime. Yet, as Foucault argues, the proposed solution to this glaring problem with prisons has never been to do away with these institutions, but has always been more prison. Foucault describes a kind of cycle in which the failure of the prison always leads to extensions of the prison, with the prison always 'offered as its own remedy' (Foucault, 1977: 268). In contrast, for Foucault the solution to prison is not prison reform. If prison is the problem, then more prison is never going to be the solution. In rejecting prison reform, Foucault is taking an abolitionist stance.

What, though, does Foucault think would be a better way of responding to crime? Although Foucault never spells out an answer to this question, in *Discipline and Punish* he does make it clear that the actual cause of what gets socially constructed as crime is usually poverty (Foucault, 1977: 276). Thus, it would follow for him that if we *really* wanted to fight 'crime' effectively, we would strive for a more egalitarian society. He would thus have advocated for redistributive responses to social harms. Instead, however, we continue to pour resources into policing and prisons in the full knowledge that this merely leads to more poverty and thus more crime.

It is remarkable to Foucault that, having long been aware that the prison and its disciplinary practices fail in their proclaimed goal of rehabilitating criminals, we have never seriously considered abolishing the prison. Rather, critiques of the prison lead only to prison reform and to an extension of the logic of the prison; the antidote to the problems of the prison has always been more prison. Indeed, since Foucault wrote *Discipline and Punish*, the prison has not only seen a colossal expansion, particularly in the US, but many of these disciplinary practices of the penal system have been intensified. This is most obvious in strategies of community notification, police registration, and periods of probation and parole involving scheduled and unscheduled visits from surveillance officers and parole officers as well as mandated 'therapeutic' treatments. The irony for Foucault is that these disciplinary measures do not so much fashion the subject away from their crime as constitute them in terms of it.

Since it has been known all along that prisons produce rather than rehabilitate delinquents, yet we continue to build and fill more prisons, Foucault thinks we must return to the question that has structured critical prison studies since *Discipline and Punish* was first published in French in 1975: what are the true functions of the prison such that it is in fact not a failure but a success? What is *really* at stake in the prison such that, despite its well-known recidivist-producing effect, it maintains its apparently unquestionable appeal? What is the prison doing *well* such that it is indispensable to the biopolitical state?

Foucault provides a series of answers to these questions, suggesting that the production of delinquents serves the political and economic interests of the middle and upper classes at the expense of the poor, who are those overwhelmingly incarcerated. In the contemporary context, Ruth Wilson Gilmore (2007) has described the ways in which the prison system serves as a capitalist response to surplus labour. The prison industry has vested financial interests in the construction of delinquency. Many rural communities near to which prisons have been built are now dependent on staffing and supplying prisons for their existence (Davis, 2003; Kutchins and Galloway, 2007). As Gottshalk writes, 'prison guards' unions, state departments of corrections, law enforcement groups, the private corrections industry and the financial firms that devise bonds and other mechanisms to fund the carceral state are all politically committed to the prison's perpetuation (Gottshalk, 2015: 14). For example, the largest and most powerful prison guard union, the California Correctional Peace Officers Association, has 'repeatedly stymied sensible proposals to modestly reduce California's prison population. It also has aggressively challenged public officials and political candidates who have sought to reduce the incarceration rate and to prosecute guards who abuse prisoners' (Gottshalk, 2015: 160). Economic interests in the perpetuation of the carceral state are not an inconsiderable factor, given that today Correctional Services is the third-largest employer in the US, outnumbered only by Manpower Incorporated and Walmart, and ahead of General Motors (Wacquant, 2009: 157).

Beyond this, Foucault (1977) argues that taking an unruly population of occasional lawbreakers and turning them into recidivist, pathologized offenders has depoliticized crime. The rationale behind prisons has made crime a psychiatric and sociological issue rather than a political issue related to poverty. For Foucault, the real function of the prison has thus been to transform politicized offenders into psychiatrized and stigmatized delinquents, people viewed as social problems or enemies of society. Importantly, depoliticizing crime in this way has driven a wedge between the poor and criminals. Thus, although criminals are still overwhelmingly poor people, there is often hostility towards criminals on the part of the poor. The dissolution of solidarity between the poor and the criminalized results in shame and secrecy on the part of the criminalized class and prevents the kind of spontaneous political uprisings around issues of penality and poverty that existed prior to disciplinary transformations in punishment. Thus, a significant consequence of the transformation of the lawbreaker into a delinquent is that the poor have largely ceased to identify and empathize with those subjected to the criminal punishment system. Crime is no longer understood as a normal response to conditions of poverty, distress and oppression, but is perceived to arise from a pathologized identity from which all who can dissociate themselves. The shame around criminalization results in silence on the part of those who most directly experience the injustices of incarceration, who are disproportionately people of colour. It is this consequence of the production of delinquency that has allowed for the astounding expansion of the prison across the Western world in recent decades, which has unfolded with little dissent and indeed with widespread public approval. For Foucault, therefore, the purpose and function of the prison is *not* to rehabilitate offenders, despite our continual rhetoric to this effect, but to discipline offenders into delinquents: manageable objects of knowledge cut off from the rest of the population, or contained criminal cases rather than political threats. In all these ways, although it does not prevent crime, rehabilitate criminals or make the population safer, the prison is instrumental to the interests of the capitalist, biopolitical and racist state.

Foucault's influence on prison abolition scholarship and activism

Prisons are functioning exactly as they are supposed to

Foucault's argument about the political instrumentality of prisons has been central to the critical prison studies scholarship and activism that has emerged in the 50 years since *Discipline and Punish* was published, to the extent that versions of this argument are frequently made both with and without reference to Foucault. In particular, critical race and decolonial scholars have adapted Foucault's argument to address the racist and colonial functions of prisons in North American contexts. In *Are Prisons Obsolete?*, Angela Davis (2003) situates prisons in the history of anti-Black racism in the US. As she notes, when slavery was theoretically abolished after the American Civil War, it was with one significant exception: involuntary servitude was still permissible 'as a punishment for crime, whereof the party shall have been duly convicted' (cited in Davis, 2003: 28). Thus, slavery was still perfectly legal in the form of the hard labour to which prisoners could be condemned as part of their punishment. As Davis observes, White people in the American South were quick to take advantage of this legal loophole to begin mass incarcerating Black people in order to put them back to work at the hard and unpaid labour they had been obliged to do as slaves. In this way, she argues, the criminal punishment system in the US 'recapitulated and further extended the regimes of slavery' (Davis, 2003: 33). In *Punishing the Poor*, Wacquant (2009) argues that the racialized ghetto emerged in the US as a means of containing African Americans following the elimination of Jim Crow Laws. When the urban ghetto was rendered partially obsolete by Black protests and race riots, the prison, with its 'slaughterhouse approach to justice' (Wacquant, 2009: 23), underwent a 'grotesque' expansion in order to function as a 'surrogate ghetto' (Wacquant, 2009: 196). In 'Life Behind Bars: The Eugenic Structure of Mass Incarceration', Lisa

Guenther (2016) argues that prisons perpetuate eugenics in both the US and Canadian contexts. As she demonstrates, not only do nonconsensual eugenic sterilizations continue to be practised by prison doctors, but the sex-segregated nature of prisons, in which racialized, poor and disabled people are separated from their children and are frequently detained for all or many of their childbearing years, prevents both the biological and social reproduction of biopolitically devalued populations. In 'The colonialism of incarceration', Robert Nichols (2014) examines the hyperincarceration of Indigenous people in the Canadian context and the ways in which the prison functions as a tool of ongoing colonial control. As Nichols argues, the incarceration of Indigenous people substituted for the use of residential schools when the latter were eliminated, and Indigenous people are discriminated against at every level of the criminal punishment system, from policing to trials to the security level of the prisons in which they are placed. Still other critical prison scholars have observed that one of the most significant functions of the prison today is to control immigration, with increasing numbers of both documented and undocumented immigrants being held in detention centres (Gottshalk, 2015; Walia, 2013).

Critical disability studies and Mad studies scholars observe that the prison has taken over the role of psychiatric asylums and residential homes for the intellectually disabled, with prison expansion occurring in the wake of the deinstitutionalization of these populations (Ben-Moshe, 2014). In the wake of so-called 'de-institutionalization', we have seen a criminalization of mental illness. As Michael Rembis has argued, there are 'important relationships among the rise of the prison industrial complex and the increasing psychiatrization of both socially "deviant" behavior and incarcerated populations, as well as the psychic trauma associated with incarceration' (Rembis, 2014: 139).

Feminist and queer critical prison scholars have demonstrated the instrumentality of the prison in the biopolitical objectives of policing gender (Mogul, Ritchie and Whitlock, 2012; Lydon, 2016). Penitentiaries were originally established in 18th-century England to house 'penitent' sex workers, punishing and reforming their aberrant gender and sexuality (Mogul, Ritchie and Whitlock, 2012: 94). 'Fallen women' were made to do domestic work in penitentiaries in training for the gendered roles of wives and domestic servants upon their release (Davis, 2003). According to queer theorist Gayle Rubin (2011), there have also been ulterior motives for the criminalization of aberrant sex acts, which have had less to do with protecting women, children or society than with fortifying the patriarchal, heteronormative family and its values. Mogul, Ritchie and Whitlock (2012) report the ways in which gender nonconforming people incarcerated in women's prisons are taunted and harassed by guards, referred to as 'little boys', and separated from the general population to be housed in a 'butch wing', 'little boys' wing' or 'studs' wing' (Mogul et al, 2012: 109). Gay and bisexual prisoners who can pass as straight often do so to avoid violence, administrative segregation and ridiculing by homophobic guards (Kunzel, 2008: 2, 8–9). Trans prisoners are often denied the gender-affirming medical care that they need, as well as gender-affirming clothing and cosmetics. Their gender is also routinely denied by placing them in sex-segregated prisons based on the gender they were assigned at birth, where they are at great risk of sexual violence (Spade, 2011; Lydon, 2016). Needless to say, all of these factors incentivize normative gender performance and normative sexuality with life-and-death stakes. In his 2011 book *Normal Life: Administrative Violence, Critical Trans Politics, and the Limits of Law*, prison abolitionist and critical trans legal theorist Dean Spade takes up Foucault's theories of power to argue that the oppression of trans people occurs largely at the level of administrative violence: everyday administrative decisions that are products of social norms and curtail the life chances of trans people. For these reasons, he argues that trans oppression is not effectively addressed by legalistic responses to discrimination and harm that rely on a racist, xenophobic, colonial, sexist, homophobic, transphobic and ableist juridical-legal system.

Therefore, even if the prison fails to prevent crime or rehabilitate prisoners, it is deeply embedded in the contemporary economy and has proved remarkably successful as a multi-purpose tool of capitalist, White supremacist, xenophobic, ableist, saneist, gender normative and heterosexist social control. Critical prison studies scholars working in the Foucauldian tradition have persuasively argued that this is what explains the prison's ongoing existence.

Prison reform extends the power of the prison

Foucault's argument that prison reform merely extends the power of the prison has also been central to prison abolition activism. Davis (2004) reiterates Foucault's point when she observes that there is a 'seemingly unbreakable link between prison reform and prison development' which 'has created a situation in which progress in prison reform has tended to render the prison more impermeable to change and has resulted in bigger, and what are considered "better", prisons' (Davis and Rodriguez, 2004). Two examples will be discussed here.

Nineteenth-century women reformers protested the incarceration of women in the same brutal institutions as men and their activism resulted in the construction of separate prisons for women (Smith, 2010: 266). However, in these new institutions women were often incarcerated for longer than they had been in men's prisons and the construction of special institutions for women enabled the incarceration of more women than before. Feminist prison reform again led to a growth in women's incarceration in the late 20th century in Canada. Until the 1990s, the situation of federally sentenced women in Canada was the subject of frequent political critique. There existed only one prison for such women in the country – the infamous Prison for Women in Kingston – which meant that most federally sentenced women were incarcerated far from their communities in an institution deemed 'unfit for bears, much less women' (Hayman, 2006: 19). Feminist prison reforms resulted in the building of numerous new prisons for women across the country: prisons whose design was informed by consultations with members of the Elizabeth Fry Society and Indigenous people, including formerly incarcerated Indigenous women. These prisons were built with the genuine intention of empowering women prisoners as well as to situate them closer to their families, and even included a 'Healing Lodge' for Indigenous women prisoners. The new prisons were initially characterized by cottage-style housing, an absence of conspicuous fencing and bars, and female staff who were trained to be closer to therapists and friends than correctional officers. However, in a matter of years, the new prisons reverted to the carceral models, logics and practices of the institution they had replaced. As a result, Canada now has vastly more beds for federally sentenced women than before, which it has been quick to fill (Hannah-Moffat and Shaw, 2000; Hayman, 2006; Montford, 2015).

Turning to a second example, legislation aimed at addressing the problem of prison rape in the US resulted in the 2003 Prison Rape Elimination Act (PREA). This Act has provided prisoners with little protection from rape and few legal resources in the aftermath of rape, but has resulted in more intense conditions of confinement (solitary confinement) for those whom guards deem at risk of sexual assault (often LGBTQ inmates) or of committing sexual assault (often racialized prisoners) (Arkles, 2014, 2015). The PREA has also led to extensions of prison sentences for those whom guards deem guilty of sexual misconduct, although this misconduct often involves consensual sexual contact between prisoners or transgressive gender expression (Arkles, 2014, 2015). LGBTQ prisoners are at particular risk of receiving PREA violations for consensual sexual activities. There is no indication that the PREA has reduced incidents of sexual assault, but there is considerable evidence that it has been used by prison staff to increase control of sexual and gender expression in prisons. The PREA has earmarked no money for survivors of sexual violence, yet millions of PREA dollars have flowed into funding 'personnel, training, technical assistance, data collection, and equipment to prevent and prosecute prisoner rape' (Arkles, 2015: 105). As Jason Lydon (2016: 64) writes: 'This well-intentioned reform effort by progressives has been turned into a tool of increased control of sex and sexuality in prison with little evidence that any of the PREA mandates actually reduce incidents of sexual harm.'

Because, as in these examples, prison reform consistently serves to expand and reinforce the power and logics of the carceral state, Gilmore (2015) has argued that the only kinds of reforms that prison abolitionists should strive for are 'non-reformist reforms'. These are reforms that address the abuses of the prison without allocating any new funds, resources or personnel to prisons and without building any new institutions. Examples of nonreformist reforms are decriminalizing sex work and drug possession; getting better food, a mail service, weekend passes and conjugal visits for prisoners, and compassionate release for ill, elderly and dying prisoners. None of these measures abolishes or even fundamentally challenges the prison, but they either reduce its use or improve the welfare of those who are currently in prisons without extending carceral power or logics. By engaging only in nonreformist reforms, activists strive to help some people avoid prison and to improve the conditions of those who are currently in prisons without reinforcing an institution that, ultimately, they hope to eliminate.

Abolishing prisons alone is ineffective

A final way in which Foucault's thought has influenced or been taken up by prison abolition activists is the recognition that abolishing prisons alone is an inadequate and ineffective goal, as prisons are just one part of a disciplinary network of power. We see this point in Foucault's 1972 response to the question of whether he knew of a model prison. He replied:

> The problem is not a model prison or the abolition of prisons. Currently, in our system, marginalization is effected by prisons. This marginalization will not automatically disappear by abolishing the prison. Society would quite simply institute another means. The problem is the following: to offer a critique of the system that explains the process by which contemporary society pushes a portion of the population to the margins. (Voilà, cited in Dillon, 2016: 259)

Foucault is arguing in this interview that we could do away with the prison and yet not resolve the underlying oppression, as other types of disciplinary institutions, for instance psychiatric institutions, would simply expand to absorb the surplus. As Stephen Dillon has written in response to this passage:

> the prison is more than an institution composed of cages, corridors, and guard towers; it is also a system of affects, desires, discourses, and ideas that make the prison possible. Thus, the prison captures not just bodies, but also feelings, desires, and forms of knowledge. The prison could disappear tomorrow and the types of power that give rise to its reign could live on in other forms such as the regimes we call freedom, rights, and the state or structures like settler-colonialism, heteropatriarchy, and white supremacy. (Dillon, 2016: 259)

As Foucault realized, prison abolitionism must be about much more than simply eliminating a single type of institution. Rather, it requires resisting a panoply of norms and disciplinary practices that are diffused throughout society and that characterize many types of institutions in more or less intense and pure forms.

Limitations

Despite these ways in which Foucault's arguments remain relevant to and have been taken up and extended within prison abolition scholarship and activism, scholars and activists have also observed the limitations of Foucault's analysis in the contemporary carceral context. First and foremost, Foucault has been reproached for his failure to consider race in his writings on prisons (James, 1996; Davis, 2005). Moreover, critical prison studies scholars have noted the ways in which the prison has changed in respects that were unanticipated by Foucault and that render some aspects of his study antiquated. For instance, studying prisons in the 1970s, Foucault did not foresee the massive prison expansion that was about to occur; on the contrary, he predicted the prison's demise. One effect of the unanticipated and nearly unfathomable expansion of the prison in countries such as the US since the 1970s is that the criminal punishment system no longer has the capacity to provide the attention to the soul that Foucault describes. This lack of interest in the defendant's soul extends from the trial – which is now better described as a plea bargain system – into the prison, where, as Guenther (2013) has argued, we have passed from the kind of carceral institutions Foucault describes to 'control prisons' in which no attempt is made to rehabilitate souls. Guenther describes three 'waves' of carceral regimes (Guenther, 2013: xv–xvii). The first was spearheaded by religious reformers in the 1850s and was grounded in the belief that the solitude of prison provided prisoners with a transformative opportunity for reflection and penitence. The second, which began in the 1960s and 1970s, was led by behavioural scientists and aimed not to rehabilitate criminals, but to recondition them to be 'productive members of society' (Guenther, 2013: xvi). These are the philosophies of prison that Foucault analysed in the 1970s. However, what he could not have described is the third 'wave' of carceral isolation, which:

> began in the 1980s and was led by prison administrators who sought less to redeem or rehabilitate criminal subjects than to isolate and control prison populations in ways that best suited the needs of wardens, prison staff, legislators, planners, and other stakeholders in the political economy of crime and incarceration ... We are living in the era of the control prison, where the immobilization of inmates has become an end in itself rather than a way of breaking through to the inwardness

of criminals' souls or even the outwardness of their abnormal behavior. (Guenther, 2013: xvi)

According to Kunzel, the control prison – which she calls the 'violent prison' – arose as a carceral response to the prisoners' rights movements and riots of the 1970s (Kunzel, 2008: 165). With the emergence of the control prison, there is now little pretence that carceral practices have a penitential or curative effect, or that this is even their purpose. 'Tough on crime' political discourses are purely retributive and eliminative, and prisons have become warehouses for biopolitically devalued bodies, or, in Sasha Abramsky's (2007: 129) words, 'storehouses of the living dead'. Lacey thus writes of 'a new, "post-disciplinary" practice of punishment peculiar to the circumstances of a post-Fordist, post-Keynesian world' (Lacey, 2011: 49) and writes that: 'These have rendered inappropriate the techniques of Foucauldian disciplinary "normalization" characteristic of the modern prison system, with its emphasis on socializing the deviant as "docile bodies" and conforming souls ready to be reinserted into the regular social economy' (Lacey, 2011: 50). Thus, Foucault's descriptions of the criminal punishment system are today far removed from many prisoners' actual experiences of top-down corporeal violence and complete disregard for the soul.

Conclusions

While this chapter has shown that Foucault's *Discipline and Punish* continues to offer insights into prisons and prison abolition that remain strategically useful today, the lacunas in his work and the ways in which carceral practices have changed since 1975 makes it clear that any reading of Foucault must be supplemented by attention to contemporary voices of people with lived experience of incarceration. Given his work with the Groupe d'information sur les prisons (Zurn and Dilts, 2016; Foucault, 2021), whose primary goal was to 'give prisoners the floor' or to make their voices heard, this is a point with which Foucault would have completely agreed.

References

Abramsky, S. (2007) *American Furies: Crime, Punishment and Vengeance in the Age of Mass Imprisonment*, Boston: Beacon Press.

Alexander, M. (2011) 'The new Jim Crow', *Ohio State Journal of Criminal Law*, 9(1): 7–26.

Arkles, G. (2014) 'Prison Rape Elimination Act litigation and the perpetuation of sexual harm', *Legislation and Public Policy*, 17(4): 801–834.

Arkles, G. (2015) 'Regulating prison sexual violence', *Northeastern Public Law and Theory Faculty Research Papers Series*, no. 233. Paper 19. Available from: http://lsr.nellco.org/nusl_faculty/19 [Accessed 15 September 2024].

Ben Moshe, L. (2014) 'Alternatives to (disability) incarceration', in L. Ben-Moshe, C. Chapman and A. Carey (eds) *Disability Incarcerated: Imprisonment and Disability in the United States and Canada*, Basingstoke: Palgrave Macmillan, pp 255–272.

Davis, A. (2003) *Are Prisons Obsolete?*, New York: Seven Stories Press.

Davis, A. (2005) 'Racialized punishment and prison abolition', in T.L. Lott and J.P. Pittman (eds) *A Companion to African American Philosophy*, Chichester: Blackwell, pp 360–371.

Davis, A. and Rodriguez, D. (2004) 'The challenge of prison abolition: a conversation'. Available from: http://www.historyisaweapon.com/defcon1/davisinterview.html [Accessed 15 September 2024].

Dillon, S. (2016) '"Can they ever escape?" Foucault, Black feminism, and the intimacy of abolition', in P. Zurn and A. Dilts (eds) *Active Intolerance Michel Foucault, the Prisons Information Group, and the Future of Abolition*, London: Palgrave Macmillan, pp 259–276.

Foucault, M. (1977) *Discipline and Punish: The Birth of the Prison*, New York: Vintage.

Foucault, M. and Prisons Information Group (2021) *Intolerable: Writings from Michel Foucault and the Prisons Information Group*, K. Thompson and P. Zurn (eds), P. Zurn and E. Beranek (trans.), Minneapolis: Minnesota University Press.

Gilmore, R.W. (2007) *Golden Gulag: Prisons, Surplus, Crisis, and Opposition in Globalizing California*, Oakland: University of California Press.

Gilmore, R.W. (2015) '"The economy of incarceration" interview on the Laura Flanders Show'. Available from: https://www.youtube.com/watch?v=39Axc3FIu9A [Accessed 15 September 2024].

Gottschalk, M. (2015) *Caught: The Prison State and the Lockdown of American Politics*, Princeton: Princeton University Press.

Guenther, L. (2013) *Solitary Confinement: Social Death and Its Afterlives*, Minneapolis: University of Minnesota Press.

Guenther, L. (2016) 'Life behind bars: the eugenic structure of mass incarceration', in H. Sharp and C. Taylor (eds) *Feminist Philosophies of Life*, Montreal: McGill-Queen's University Press, pp 217–238.

Hannah-Moffat, K. and Shaw, M. (2000) 'Gender, diversity and risk assessment in Canadian corrections', *Probation Journal*, 47(3): 163–172.

Hayman, S. (2006) *Imprisoning Our Sisters: The New Federal Women's Prison in Canada*, Montreal: McGill-Queens University Press.

James, J. (1996) 'Erasing the spectacle of racialized state violence', in J. James (ed.) *Resisting State Violence: Radicalism, Gender, and Race in U.S. Culture*, Minneapolis: University of Minnesota Press, pp 24–43.

Jamieson, D. (2002) 'Against zoos', in D. Jamieson (ed.) *Morality's Progress: Essays on Humans, Other Animals, and the Rest of Nature*, Oxford: Oxford University Press, pp 166–175.

Kunzel, R. (2008) *Criminal Intimacy: Prison and the Uneven History of Modern American Sexuality*, Chicago: University of Chicago Press.

Kutchins, P. and Galloway, K. (2007) *Prison Town USA*. Hybrid Films.

Lacey, N. (2011) *The Prisoner's Dilemma*, Cambridge: Cambridge University Press.

Lydon, J. (2016) 'Once there was no prison rape: ending sexual violence as strategy for prison abolitionism', *philoSOPHIA: A Journal of Continental Feminism*, 6(1): 61–71.

Mogul, J. Ritchie, A. and Whitlock, K. (2012) *Queer (In)Justice: The Criminalization of LGBT People in the United States*, Boston: Beacon Press.

Montford, K.S. (2015) 'Transforming choices: the marginalization of gender-specific policy making in Canadian approaches to women's federal imprisonment', *Canadian Journal of Women and the Law/Revue Femmes et Droit*, 27(2): 284–310.

Nichols, R. (2014) 'The colonialism of incarceration', *Radical Philosophy Review*, 17(2): 435–455.

Rembis, M. (2014) 'The new asylums: madness and mass incarceration in the neoliberal era', in L. Ben-Moshe, C. Chapman and A.C. Carey (eds) *Disability Incarcerated: Imprisonment and Disability in the United States and Canada*, New York: Palgrave Macmillan, pp 139–159.

Rubin, G. (2011) 'Blood under the bridge: reflections on "thinking sex"', in *Deviations: A Gayle Rubin Reader*, Durham, NC: Duke University Press, pp 195–223.

Smith, A. (2010) 'Beyond restorative justice: radical organizing against violence', in J. Ptacek (ed.) *Restorative Justice and Violence sgainst Women*, Oxford: Oxford University Press, pp 255–278.

Spade, D. (2011) *Normal Life: Administrative Violence, Critical Trans Politics, and the Limits of Law*, Durham, NC: Duke University Press.

Wacquant, L. (2009) *Punishing the Poor: The Neoliberal Government of Social Insecurity*, Durham, NC: Duke University Press.

Walia, H. (2013) *Undoing Border Imperialism*, Oakland: AK Press.

Zurn, P. and Dilts, A. (eds) (2016) *Active Intolerance Michel Foucault, the Prisons Information Group, and the Future of Abolition*, London: Palgrave Macmillan.

PART III

The Scope of Oppression

9

The Slavery Industrial Complex

Viviane Saleh-Hanna

Introduction

While studying and reassessing the shadowed and annexed histories of chattel slavery in Canada and western Europe, a ghosted entity revealed itself through repeating patterns and extensions of colonial enslavement: expanding and extending into contemporary carceral logics (Lamble, 2011) are the ghosts of northern hemispheric systems of African enslavement rooting and upholding the global slavery industrial complex. The slavery industrial complex is a colonizing ancestor and founding body that reproduces many prison industrial complexes. It is a system of colonial power composed of chattel slavery's historic cultures and economies enforcing and repeating renditions of colonialism. The haunting structures and enduring tentacles of the slavery industrial complex pave carceral pathways enabling the emergence of many colonizing industrial complexes through which imprisonment grows literally, figuratively and culturally to confine oppressed peoples in as many ways as white supremacy can create. Imprisonment these days occurs within penitentiaries, prisons, detention centres, jails, courtrooms and handcuffs; bodies and homes bound by electronic anklets and electric fences, entire neighbourhoods held behind surveillance cameras, and entire nations cut up and bound within man-made[1] colonial borders enforced by man-made walls and motion sensor-equipped machine guns. Racism is narrated by Euro-created cultures of violence imprisoning colonized peoples within white imaginations, creating larger-than-life and many-forms-of-death pathways into criminalization. These pathways serve as rerouting tools back into established forms of European colonialism and enslavement. That is the origin story of the slavery industrial complex. In sum, it is an interlocking, structurally abusive, colonizing system of land, human, and cultural enslavements and imprisonments holding a foundational role in the establishment and continued sustenance of white settler nation statehoods.

In western[2] academic discourse, the study of historic abolitionist movements often references the fall of empires (usually Rome), the end of specific carceral policies (usually the death penalty) and the abolition of chattel slavery (this is contested in the US, though it should be contested everywhere that criminal legal systems exist) as a few examples of the liberatory possibilities accomplished by abolitionist movements (see Scheerer, 1986; Mathiesen, 1997). In this chapter I provide a history and context that challenges these narratives while strengthening contemporary abolitionist voices and movements through a more expansive understanding of the global slavery industrial complex and its foundational role in the enforcement and extension of white settler nationhood. I explain why unearthing the slavery industrial complex and its founding role in the establishment of many prison and carceral industrial complexes allows for a more comprehensive understanding of how criminal legal systems are the fuel required to operationalize and extend white settler statehood. In practice, white settler statehoods institutionalize colonial conquest. Their very existence necessitates an expanding enforcement of Euro-supremacist carceral control to continue established land and human exploitations. A journey into these histories and their ghosted entities requires entry into the treacherous, gaslighting and haunted terrains of Canadian and western European colonialism and enslavement – manifested and manifesting along the shadowed edges of historic plantations – hidden and hiding within imagined northward freedom trails – spreading the mythologized and dangerous lie of 'western democracy' as synonymous with freedom for all.

In this chapter, I introduce global systems of chattel slavery within and beyond the lands we have been trained to see them. Generous westernized eyes may see plantations throughout the southern hemisphere on the western side of the globe; most will minimize chattel slavery's plantations to parts of the Caribbean, limited portions of South America (usually Brazil but not Ecuador, for example), and southern Turtle Island lands occupied by the United States. Contradicting these sweeping minimizations, I locate and map the slavery industrial complex within Canada's historic eastern maritime fishing industries and fur trades, New England's cotton mills in the northeastern US, and Portugal's local economies and mercantile functions. I also reintroduce the history of enslaved African labour within western Europe alongside a critical re-reading of Britain's 1833 Act (a performance and dramatization that never intended) to Abolish Slavery. Centring these shadowed histories allows for us to understand how chattel slavery fuelled the rise of imperial industrial revolutions by funding and incentivizing the entrenchment of white settler nation sates upon Indigenous lands around the world. Through this re-reading of colonialism's power, we can begin to locate chattel slavery within nations and economies we have been trained to read as unattached from Europe's bloody histories of African enslavement. This allows us to see the tightly bound structural relationships that exist between racial capitalism's global economies and systems of imprisonment enacted for colonial gain through slavery, through policing and imprisonment, and within colonial nation state borders that enforce Indigenous land control.

Recognizing that northern colonial histories perform and dramatize distance from chattel slavery in public narrations, I reconceptualize them as existing on the edges of southern plantations in matters akin to the multibillion-dollar industries that exist along the edges of the prison to feed and form many prison industrial complexes around the world (Sudbury, 2005; Evans and Goldberg, 2009). I explain how similarly, the slavery industrial complex is composed of carceral industries that fed into and grew through plantation labour, fuelling and building white settler nation states within and beyond western Europe. I introduce a critical analysis of Britain's Abolition Act of 1833 and the ways in which this law, as an extension of the slavery industrial complex, funded and expanded carceral white power around the globe. I end with an emphasis on the urgency of anti-colonial freedom struggles in this day and age. As colonial carceral power grows through intensified surveillance and warfare technology (Cuneen, 2023) abolitionist, freedom-driven movements face expanding forms of co-optation, criminalization and a widening array of threats waged against anti-colonial, freedom-driven thoughts, actions, and social movements (Rodríguez, 2020). Abolition Now, Abolition Everywhere has never been more urgent.

Chattel slavery in Canada

Chattel slavery was a global force enforced by western Europe's imperialist invasions and colonial conquests. Yet global imaginations continue to perpetuate the myth of enslaved African labour as limited to southern and western hemisphere plantations. Countering such lies, Whitfield (2018: 1) documents Europe's enforcement of chattel slavery 'throughout the New World, from Chile to Argentina in the south to Nova Scotia in the north'. Writing on Canada from the early 1600s to 1820, Whitfield (2018) reports that thousands of Africans enslaved by British and French colonizers were forced to live and work throughout the Maritimes, Quebec, and Ontario. In Canadian archives, Winks (1997) found evidence of Africans enslaved in Canada as early as 1628. Summarizing letters and documents by colonizers Winks (1997: 4) reveals how slavery was viewed by colonizers as 'one means of increasing manpower ... the fisheries, the mines, the agriculture all offered potential wealth too great for only nine thousand colonists to tap'.

This teaches us that the structural relationship between colonial land occupation and chattel slavery cannot be ignored or minimized.

Donovan's (1995) research on French Canadian slavers found that 90 per cent of enslaved Africans were forcibly migrated into Canada from French plantations in the Caribbean, resulting in more than 4,000 Africans enslaved in Canada by French colonizers between the late 1600s and early 1800s. Many enslaved Africans were also forcibly migrated to Prince Edward Island from Ouida in west Africa while Benin was under French occupation (Whitfield and Cahill, 2009).

Thousands of enslaved Africans were forced to work for the British military throughout north America during the Seven Years' War (1756–1763) with records indicating a significant use of enslaved African labour at Louisburg to aid the British Army and New England's militia during that worldwide war. One quarter of the money due to white soldiers was given to enslaved Africans, while three quarters was paid to slavers who made the ultimate decision to send enslaved Africans to war (Donovan, 1995: 24–25). When Britain won the Seven Years War, its conquests grew from northeastern US territories into Canada. As British colonizers moved north, they brought enslaved Africans with them creating one of the largest forced Black migrations in Canadian history (Cooper, 2006). From within these details of land and human conquest it is impossible to divorce slavery from colonialism. One co-created the other, and vice versa.

Cooper (2006) notes that under French occupation, the economic structures being established in Ontario, Quebec and the Maritimes were not initially openly dependent on enslaved labour. Early on, enslaved Africans were used as visible markers of status, and over time came to form an 'intrinsic part of the social and economic ladder' by being forced to labour in arenas that sustained Canada's white settler economy. These included:

> the back-breaking work of rowing golden-laden canoes upstream to meeting the unrelenting demands of mistresses and masters. The tasks that slaves performed freed up their owners to engage in economic pursuits: their free labour subsidized the colonial economy, making them an economic as well as social necessity. (Cooper, 2006: 127–128)

Donovan's research on Île Royale highlights how significant enslaved African labour was in establishing and growing Canada's early colonial economies:

> The women among them performed a wide range of duties, from looking after children to cleaning clothes, scrubbing floors, preparing meals and washing dishes. The men ... performed outdoor functions. They tended gardens, fed animals, cleaned stables, carried water and cut firewood ... on Île Royale they became servants, gardeners, bakers, tavern keepers, stone masons, musicians, laundry works, soldiers, sailors, fisherman, hospital workers, ferry men, executioners and nursemaids. (Donovan, 1995: 4)

Whitfield (2016: 55–56) also widens our vision of where and how enslaved African labour was enforced in Canada when she documents the following:

in towns such as Shelburne [Ontario], they cleared streets, built wharfs, dug cellars for houses, loaded and unloaded vessels, sawed boards, and split cordwood ... [in addition to domestic labour] the majority of their town labour included running errands, carrying baked items, shovelling snow, and clearing roads ... levelling the ground in front of the chapel. (Whitfield, 2016: 55–56)

Whitfield (2016: 55–56) also found evidence of enslaved African hard labour enforced within Canada's early timber shipping industries and records of specialized enslaved African labour in 'tailoring, blacksmithing, coppering', as well as inside grain mills and distilleries. Historical evidence clearly indicates that enslaved African labour was enforced widely in Canada, spanning across many industries to exploit skills and labour in as many ways as European colonists could imagine and enforce.

These histories of Canadian chattel slavery are hidden in plain sight behind Canada's more public presentation of itself as a freedom site at the end of the northbound Underground Railroad. While enslaved Africans in the US did escape north under the gradual abolition laws to gain freedom, in reality, enslaved Africans in Canada escaped south because gradual abolition laws only applied to those arriving from other locations and not to those enslaved within the territories passing these laws (Cooper, 2006). Further, those Africans who did arrive in Canada through the Underground Railroad faced the wrath of white Canadian racism both then and forward into present times (Maynard, 2017).

Systemic racism in Canada is clearly mapped through the structural violence slavers and colonizers committed against Canada's oldest established Black community. Dating back to the mid-1700s, Africville was founded by enslaved, free and fugitive Africans. It was also a brief home to marooned Africans deported from Jamaica to Canada (National Library of Jamaica, 1988) after the British took Jamaica from Spanish occupation after the Seven Years' War. In 1967, the city of Halifax demolished Africville after centuries of dumping toxins and sewage upon it, forcing industrial land use on its residents (including a cotton factory) and building a railroad through the middle of the community. A prison and an infectious diseases hospital were also built in Africville in the mid-1800s, and starting in the mid-1960s, the city of Halifax systematically tore down homes and community infrastructures that had survived previous attempts of removal. The largest loss occurred in 1967 when the city destroyed Africville's Black church in the middle of the night (Clairmont and Magill, 1999; Carvey, 2008; Saleh-Hanna, 2023).

Chattel slavery in western Europe

Afua Cooper (2006) documents the historic life and death of Angélique, and in so doing traces the histories of chattel slavery within Canada and western Europe. Angélique was an African woman born round 1705 to an enslaved African mother in Portugal. She was sold to white slavers, who extended her enslavement into the Flemish territories (now Belgium), where she was sold into British captivity and subsequently taken to the US. She was likely enslaved in New England and New York before being sold into French Canadian enslavement. She arrived in Montreal around the age of 22 in 1725 (Cooper, 2006: 23). The forced trajectories of Angélique's life and death document and unearth the transnational genealogies of chattel slavery in the northern hemisphere (Saleh-Hanna, 2023).

In the case of western Europe, a widely understudied and unacknowledged fact of this past is the capture and transport of 'considerable numbers of enslaved ... Africans into Europe in the hundred and fifty years succeeding the so-called voyages of discovery' (Lowe, 2005: 1). Addressing the invisibility of these histories, Lowe (2005: 3) explains:

> The reasons for this are manifold, but an absence of material is not one of them. Far from being genuinely invisible, the traces of these fifteenth and sixteenth century black Africans can be found in almost every type of record: documentary, textual and visual; secular and ecclesiastical; Northern and Southern European; factual and fictional.

Revealing the logistics of enforced silence, Lowe (2005) documents how Portuguese slavers baptized enslaved Africans into Catholicism, gave them Christian first names while denying them access to a surname, thus dissolving their inclusion in formal records. Nonetheless, the facts of their existence are archived and accessible to those who seek them (Saleh-Hanna, 2023).

Further exposing the details of this history, Lowe reveals a deportation order recorded in Queen Elizabeth I's archives: '[A] letter and warrant of July 1596 and her proclamation of January 10 ordering the expulsion of all black Africans ... from England, and the introduction of the concept of 'purity of blood' (*limpieza de sangre*) that took hold on the Iberian Peninsula in the sixteenth century' (Lowe, 2005: 9–10). In this warrant are recorded the facts of Black life (enslaved and free) in western Europe during those times. This archive also serves as record of 16th-century eugenics practised through the carceral logics of a mass deportation order determined by race and is traceable to the nature and function of so many colonial borders and deportation policies and rhetoric today.

As early as the 15th century, on 8 August 1444, the Portuguese royal chronicler Gomes Eanes de Zurara documented the spectacle of chattel slavery in Europe's public landscapes, including his own eyewitness accounts and 'amalgam of a lost narrative of Afonso Creveira' (Lowe, 2005: 10) about the day that 250 enslaved Africans were forced out of a slave ship into

Portugal. Lowe provides the following English translation and summary from de Zurara's Portuguese documents:

> local inhabitants were given a holiday from work and encouraged to play their part in the spectacle by being an awed audience. The captive, conquered [B]lack Africans were virtually or completely naked, and in chains. The free, triumphant white Portuguese separated their human booty into five equal groups, in the process dividing family units, whereupon the Africans began to scream and cry, and some began an African chant. Zurara and the audience of the day supposedly were moved by the Africans' suffering (although Zurara analysed it in terms of fate), but the behavior of … the commander of the slave raid and royal tax-collector … was reinforced when Prince Henrique spontaneously knighted him on the field where the scene had unfolded. The message could not have been clearer: it was not only permissible but right for Europeans to capture and enslave black Africans, and to treat them in an inhuman way; it was also financially rewarding and led directly to royal favours. (Lowe, 2005: 10–11)

Writing on Portuguese laws and the institutionalization of chattel slavery in Portugal, Saunders (1982: 113) found that 'the development and refinement of Portuguese slave law during the period under study was partly due to the general preoccupation with codifying Portuguese law but was mainly a response to the problems created by the massive influx of black slaves from western Africa'.

Saunders explains that some forms of servitude already existed in Portugal prior to the rise of chattel slavery, noting that the aristocracy assumed this would facilitate a seamless institutionalization of chattel slavery into Portuguese society. They were wrong. Royal laws through canon and Roman law were introduced alongside local customs, but the peculiar nature of chattel slavery did not translate into already-existing systems of servitude: 'The whole corpus … proved inadequate to cope with all the problems created by the advent of black slaves … the servile population had not been very large in the later Middle Ages', and enslaved Africans, having been forcibly removed from their homelands and denied access to family and identity, faced unprecedented circumstances, had more to fight against and proved more difficult to suppress than anticipated (Saunders, 1982: 113–114). These distinctions between chattel slavery and already-existing systems of enslavement and servitude are well documented in Orlando Patterson's (1982) comprehensive research and comparative global study of various forms of slavery and systems of servitude.

Patterson (1982) found that the peculiar nature of chattel slavery distinguishes it from indentured servitude and other systems of enslavement in many ways. A key distinction included the legal transformation of enslaved Africans into carceral property which extended slavery's economic tentacles in unprecedented ways, opening pathways into exploitation not yet imagined within already-existing systems of enslavement and indentured servitude (Saleh-Hanna, 2024). For example, in Portugal, 'as objects, [African] slaves could be left as securities for a debt, or in time of war, for ransom. They could also be pawned to raise money' redeemable at a later date (Saunders, 1982: 115). Any money made by the pawnbroker during the time they had ownership over an enslaved person's labour could be deducted from the sum owned by a slaver, who in this arrangement 'assumed responsibility' for their human property should the enslaved person escape or die (Saunders, 1982: 115). These forms of exploitation did not exist in other systems of servitude and enslavement, they are peculiar to chattel slavery's exploitation of Africans (Patterson, 1982). It was through these peculiar distinctions that the slavery industrial complex began to take form and shape its cultural and economic extensions into contemporary systems of colonial carceral power.

Writing specifically on the criminal legal system's role in chattel slavery Saunders (1982: 117) found that enslaved Africans were deemed legally responsible for their actions and could be tried in criminal courts: 'If convicted, the slave was punished by public officers or else a pardon could be bought for him, should the master deem himself served better in this way. At all stages of the proceedings, every effort was made to safeguard the master's interests in his slave.' Bearing similarities to documents of trials throughout north America (Cooper, 2006; Hine et al, 2013; Saleh-Hanna, 2015), Portugal's 'slave trials were usually heard very rapidly in order that the master might not lose his slave's labour for an appreciable length of time. Delays could occur in the higher, royal courts when a slave was being tried for a serious offence, but even here the crown attempted to act with all due speed' (Saunders, 1982: 117).

Archival records also indicate that if the courts deemed European slavers had not punished enslaved persons appropriately, the criminal legal system could step in. For instance, there are archived instances of municipal representatives complaining that enslaved Africans who stole fruit and vegetables from their vineyards and gardens were not punished severely enough by slavers. These municipal agents lobbied their King to enforce a 'standardization of punishment: all slaves who stole produce should be whipped at the post (*picota*) in public by royal officers of justice, because only then would the slaves be "ashamed" of their misdeed' (Saunders, 1982: 117–118). King Manuel I responded by establishing a 'formal scale of punishment for criminals' placing enslaved Africans 'in much the same category as free servants and labourers' and establishing a different scale for 'people of quality' or the upper class (Saunders, 1982: 118). These scales ensured that 'no person of quality could suffer a "degrading punishment" for a crime', but instead would be exiled to Portugal's occupied territories in South America to become slavers and white settler-colonizers in Brazil (Saunders, 1982: 118). The foundation of classical criminology's penal codes and the truly colonial nature of contemporary criminal legal systems is well preserved in these histories of time and labour extraction through chattel slavery (Saleh-Hanna, 2024).

Degrading punishments reserved for enslaved Africans and working-class Europeans included whipping at the post (20 lashes were standard) and being forced to wear a noose around your neck at the time of public sentencing. Lower-class persons could also be sentenced into exile, though this was not an option for enslaved Africans as their removal jeopardized white slaver wealth. If the sentence for the crime was a fine, slavers could decide to pay it or have the enslaved person whipped instead. In these archives we locate the slavery industrial complex's interlocking layers of carceral violence enforced through chattel slavery in western Europe, while also uncovering evidence of the fact that this is not an obscure history that took place in the corners of Portuguese society – chattel slavery was widespread and occurred in full public view. Foucault was wrong: the public spectacle did not disappear with the building of prison walls. The public spectacles of punishment remained well within public view for enslaved Africans within the US (James, 1996), and beyond.

Evidence of Africans enslaved within western Europe is also archived at the International Slavery Museum (2019) in Liverpool, England. Under the heading 'Black People in Europe', we find the following:

> A few Africans had visited and lived in Europe, including Britain, since Roman times. From the 1450s the Portuguese transported thousands of enslaved Africans to Spain, Portugal and Italy to work as *servants* or in the fields. Lisbon, for instance, had a significant African population from the 16th century.
>
> As the transatlantic trade developed, ships' captains and plantation owners brought Africans back to the countries of Northern Europe. They sold them to work, mainly as domestic *servants*. Many were children. (Italics added to disrupt colonizer narratives)

For many reasons, it is both incorrect and problematic to refer to enslaved Africans as 'servants' because the term 'servants' within systems of servitude is not synonymous with slavery within chattel enslavement (Patterson, 1982). Such misuse of language obscures the facts of these systems and these times. The museum's website does provide facts and figures worth noting: mid-18th-century London was home to approximately 10,000 Black people, including 'free and enslaved people, as well as many runaways ... there were Black people in many other towns, such as Liverpool, Bristol, Bath and

Lancaster. Smaller numbers of Black people were also found in rural areas throughout the country' (International Slavery Museum, 2019). Western Europe's false image of itself as a pristine white landscape thriving through a white Renaissance with an established geographical distance from chattel slavery's immediate bloodshed, slave ports and whipping posts quickly disintegrates if we begin to look just beneath the surface of this myth.

Within western Europe, enslaved African labour was used in a wide array of economies and industries, including but not limited to work 'as nurses, servants, and maids in hospitals. In fact, during periods of infection and plague, they were placed on the frontlines' (Cooper, 2006: 36). The history of enslaved Black labour forced into the frontlines during Europe's infections plagues rang through time as we witnessed the racialized use of frontline and essential labour during the onset and height of the COVID-19 pandemic in 2020 and 2021 (see Rogers et al [2020] for the US; Khare et al [2020] for Canada; and Pearce et al [2021] for the UK). This was also mirrored and repeated in the placement of an infectious diseases hospital staffed by Black workers in Africville in Canada in the 1800s, not to mention the irony and the salt in the wound of a cotton factory in Africville in the 1960s (Saleh-Hanna, 2023). These histories and legacies of enslaved and exploited Black labour across time and place, during pandemics and plagues, and through overlapping imperial industrial pursuits represent a few pathways among many that create the varied, enduring and deadly trajectories of the slavery industrial complex.

The slavery industrial complex

Contrary to dominant colonial mythologies, western Europeans enforced chattel slavery to extort labour and resources throughout the world. It is true that a huge percentage of white imperial profits reside within the raw materials and stolen territories they were grown in. Europe's industrial revolutions were created because slave-grown raw materials necessitated a rapid growth of factories in western Europe, and eventually northern US territories after the revolutionary war. Carceral chattel slavery and European colonialism *together* fuelled and made possible the industrial revolutions that established global economic dominance for western Europe and her settler colonies (Canada and the US) in north America (Williams, 1944).

The clearest path to uncovering the enduring powers of the slavery industrial complex is through the study of its closest structural kin, the prison industrial complex [PIC]. Stormy Ogden (2005: 63) defined the PIC as having a 'two-fold purpose: social control and profit. Like the military-industrial complex, the prison-industrial complex interweaves government agencies with business interests that seek to make a profit from imprisoning the poor and people of color'. Ogden identifies the prison economy as an industry like any other seeking raw materials to process for profit, concluding that 'in this case the raw materials are people – prisoners. Prisons generate profits for the companies that build prisons and house prisoners. They also generate profits by providing cheap, plentiful, and easily controlled workforce' (Ogden, 2005: 63).

Research and writing on the PIC have been key to abolitionist understandings of how the transformation of imprisoned bodies into commodities echoed and prolonged chattel slavery throughout the US. These writings are largely limited to discourse on the US and are obscured in liberal settings that uphold the assumption that carceral violence is problematic because it is expensive. This argument fails to recognize that PIC 'expenses' remain circulating within the same pot of power – their expansive nature is not problematic for systems that profit from carceral violence. Further, focusing on how expensive prisons and policing are insinuates (openly or in what is left unsaid) that carceral violence is problematic because it is expensive *compared to* 'rehabilitation' or 'more state-sponsored schooling' instead of centring the fact that regardless of monetary cost, carceral violence is immoral, is always exploitative and therefore should not be reformed into another form of social control. The *actual* problem is not 'profit' – yes, profit fuels and expands these systems – but the sanctioning and establishment of state violence, regardless of profit and economy; even if they found ways to enforce imprisonment and policing without profit, it would still be immoral.

The violent core of contemporary carcerality becomes clearer when we turn to the past. The slavery industrial complex produced carceral economies, yes, but the obvious problem (for slavery, but not yet obvious for policing, courts, colonial borders and prisons) is the undisputed violence of enslavement and the many possibilities it creates for colonizers and slavers to imagine and enforce their exploitative missions in the past and present, while continuing to rob us of our futures.

Indigenous beaver fur: African sweat, blood and tears

Canadian archives contain a 1689 memorandum written by New France's governor and Attorney General to the King of France. In this memo, colonizers claim that 'slavery would be profitable for New France, since even the expense of clothing the slaves might be turned to advantage: the Negroes could, as the Algonquins did, wear dry beaver skins, which, through use, would become *castor gras* or doubled value' (Winks, 1997: 5). Details on the felting process can help us better understand the depraved calculations colonizers present in their letter to their King:

> There were two types of beaver pelts: castor gras and castor sec. The term 'castor gras' designates pelts taken by the Indians when prime,

trimmed into rectangular shape ... and worn with the fur next to the body for 12 to 18 months. Constant friction of the fur reversed against the skin gradually loosened the outer guard hairs and sweat added a glossy sheen. As such, the skin became well greased, pliable and yellow in colour. Castor gras was seen as the most valuable because the long hair had already fallen and the felt had been enriched and thickened through contact with human skin. ('The Beaver and Other Pelts', 2001)

In this 1689 memo we find a literal plan to extract African sweat for profit, while at the same time flagging the interlocking nature of colonialism's exploitation of Black unfreedom and exploited labour with the theft and exploitation of Indigenous knowledges, lands and resources. The depths of depravity forming the slavery industrial complex's morally bankrupt tenacity for profit are immense. In the case of industrializing beaver fur through Canada's colonial-chattel slavery, the following is also significant for mapping the militarized and destructive core of the slavery industrial complex:

Until the 1650s, the fur trade in Canada remained a subsidiary activity, carried on by fisherman, whalers and explorers. But, at the end of sixteenth century, a change in European fashion created a rage for the broad-brimmed beaver hat. The fashion for felt hats came to be inspired by the hats worn by the Swedish soldiers during the Thirty Years' War (1618–48). As fashion changed and the Russian and Baltic beaver became extinct, people turned toward North America. The hat makers of Europe soon learned that the North American beaver under-fur could form good felt. Marten, fox, otter and mink were also bartered but beaver became the main staple of the fur trade. ('The Beaver and Other Pelts', 2001)

In this history of colonial industries merging to form the slavery industrial complex, we see a truly gruesome larger picture that captures the carceral legacy of slavery's ongoing colonial economies. A decades-long war in Europe inspired a fashion trend reliant upon hats, made by the furs of extinct Russian and Baltic beavers, inspiring French colonists in Canada to calculate into their request for enslaved African labour a felting process stolen from Indigenous Algonquin traditions: the sweat and friction of African bodies performing enslaved labour upon stolen lands would produce 'more expensive' renditions of non-European beaver fur to be marketed for fashions rooted in a celebration of Europe's growing militarization and war.[3] In this peculiar praxis of the slavery industrial complex, we locate *the literal manifestation of African blood, sweat and tears* embossed within Indigenous furs and processes for Europeans to literally place upon their heads in the form of military hats turned fashionable. This and many more historic antecedents to the prison industrial complex demand that we consider and archive carceralism's marketing of state violence as fashionable, entertaining and profitable – these are all renditions of historical colonial power extending and strengthening white power today. Some formations of these are mapped and archived through research on penal and prison tourism (Wilson et al, 2017). Other formations I continue to archive through @black_feminist_hauntology[4] on Instagram through the hashtag #carceralism.

Fishing industries in Canada: feeding enslaved Africans in the Caribbean for profit

Fishing was the main industry in Canada's occupied maritime territories, and enslaved African labour was crucial to this industry's success. Enslaved Africans were fishing cod and processing and preparing it for export throughout the world. This included the large-scale and profitable export of salted dried cod to French slavers in the Caribbean who bought it to feed enslaved Africans held captive and forced to labour there: 'By the 1740s, Île Royale was selling up to 40,000 quintals of cod per year in the West Indies' (Donovan, 1995: 8).[5] Île Royale colonizers and slavers also established unethical markets for products produced by enslaved Africans in the Caribbean: 'Shiploads of sugar, molasses and rum were brought to Île Royal and immediately re-exported to the British American Colonies. So extensive was the trade in rum and molasses that, by the 1750s, the value of Île Royale sugar products rivalled the value of the colony's codfish production' (Donovan, 1995: 8).

The same morally bankrupt tactics were used by British slavers and colonists. In *Capitalism and Slavery*, Eric Williams specifically addresses Britain's colonizing slaver industries in both Canada and England, allowing us to see how much they mirror and further institutionalized Île Royale's French colonizing slaver templates:

> Most important of all the food supplies was fish, an article dear to the heart of every mercantilist, because it provided employment for ships and training for seamen. Laws were passed in England to encourage the consumption of fish. Friday and Saturday were set apart as fish days. Fish was an important item of the diet of slaves on the plantations, and the English herring trade found its chief market in the sugar plantations. The [Canadian] Newfoundland fishery [heavily tied to Liverpool] depended to a considerable extent on the annual export of dried fish to the West Indies, the refuse or 'poor John' fish, 'fit for no other consumption'. (Williams, 1944: 59)

Throughout these networks of stolen wealth and white imperial industry, we see the immediately obvious and rippling structures of the prison industrial complex's vast profit-making schemes to 'feed, clothe, and house' prisoners through prison construction and monopolies on necessary access to food and other life-sustaining resources (Eisen, 2018). Global PIC economies are not only rooted in carceral power but are also an expansion of white settler state power and are preceded by and reproduced out of the slavery industrial complex.

Textile mills in Rhode Island

In Rhode Island, New England's colonists heavily invested in textile mills, producing 'negro cloth' or 'kensey' worn by enslaved Africans in southern US plantations (Clark-Pujara, 2016). Shaw (2012) explains that enslaved Africans on southern plantations 'raised, harvested, ginned, and baled raw cotton to send to local, northern [US], and European spinning, knitting, and weaving mills. They then received back the finished cloth and clothing that marked them as slaves'. Bailey (1994) provides a strong record of how deeply interlocked chattel slavery was with the expansion and dominance of industrial economies in the Britain and the US.

Further, when British defectors in the US broke ties with the British Empire through the Revolutionary War in the US, they were able to reproduce the cross-Atlantic slave trade's blueprint (of using raw materials from southern plantations to fuel northern factories to grow white settler economies) within the US by building factories along northeastern coastlines. This cut out time and costs associated with travelling back across the Atlantic with raw materials to manufacture within European factories. This shrinking and magnifying of the triangular slave trade within the stolen borders of the US paved the path for US colonial-slave economies to grow faster than Europe's empires, all of which were embroiled in the expensive and vicious task of waging and sustaining colonial wars around the planet. The US economy continues to be among the world's wealthiest. This is a direct result of the histories and systems of chattel slavery and white settler colonialism and a testament to the endurance and founding blueprints of the slavery industrial complex.

Slavery Abolition Act of 1833: an *act* indeed

The Act for the Abolition of Slavery (1833) is composed of 66 dizzying scenes full of provisions protecting the wealth and property of British slavers, particularly slavers in the Caribbean where the Act mandated compensation per 'legally purchased and owned slave' throughout England's 19 colonies in the sea. The Act reads like a British theatrical performance with dangerous liberal renditions of abolition written into scenes (called sections) comprising a theatrical rise to climax in its rewriting of villains (slavers) into victims of abolition (oppressed by the abolition of slavery), while reframing enslaved Africans as beneficiaries and 'employees' or 'apprentices' to be trained (as an apprenticeship would imply) by their captors. It is telling that those already *doing the work* would be framed as in need of 'training' by those profiting from said work. It is also telling that actual profits were never on the table for transfer to the workers and victims/survivors of chattel slavery. The carceral economic logics of white supremacy clearly structure these laws and 'reforms', and should serve as flags for white power for all contemporary abolitionist movements.

Scene 29 in the 1833 Act is dedicated solely to 'Monies raised to be paid to an Account at the Bank, called the West India Compensation Account' legislating the payment of Twenty Million Sterling Pounds, the equivalent of 17 Billion Pounds Sterling today, to slavers in the Caribbean. This stolen wealth was divided between 3,000 British slavers (and their descendants who inherited slavery's power) with zero compensation going to Africa or Africans as restitution for the exploitative and impoverishing harms and abuses of chattel slavery (Manning, 2013; Hall et al, 2014; Barragan, 2015).

It would take British taxpayers 132 years to pay back this billion-dollar 'debt to slavers'. In 2015, the same year that British taxpayers paid off this billion-dollar loan (Brown, 2020) the British Prime Minister David Cameron visited Jamaica, 'the brightest jewel in the British Crown' and caused controversy when he responded to a question about reparations to Jamaicans for British slavery by promising to use British funds to build a new prison on the island (Barragan, 2015).

Cameron's response was amplified by the fact that he is named in the Legacies of British Slave-Ownership project (2019) as a direct, patrilineal descendant of a colonizer-slaver who enslaved Africans in Jamaica: 'Sir James, who was the son of one of Mr. Cameron's great-grand-uncle's, the second Earl of Fife, was awarded £4,101, equal to more than £3m today, to compensate him for the 202 slaves he *forfeited* on the Grange Sugar Estate in Jamaica' (Manning, 2013). The facts of slavery's blood, in wealth and in lineage, are alive within Cameron's rise to power. In his trajectory we see that Scene 29 from the British Act to Abolish Slavery has not ended. The year 2024 marked its 141st year in production, with stories continuing to be documented in the Legacies of the British Slave-Ownership Project (2019). In practice, the 1833 Act embodies a hopelessly long list of villainous characters with wide-reaching powers in the same places across time and kin.

Cameron's response to the question of reparations was not only absurd and offensive, it was also abusive (Saleh-Hanna, 2017) and full of gaslighting diversions and manipulations. He directly asked the descendants of enslaved Africans to get over a past that extends into the present, to overlook England's own crimes, and to stop knowing that slavery is the actual backdrop and reason for England's current power and wealth, and by extension, Jamaica's current oppression and impoverishment. Cameron also expected Jamaicans to accept reparations in the form of a British-funded prison in Jamaica, perfectly personifying the absurd hypocrisy and central role criminal legal systems hold in the extension of slavery's power into contemporary colonial repressions. Cameron's response is a clear and perfected sighting of the ghost of the slavery industrial complex. It is the embodiment of #carceralism and the haunting nature of carceral violence. It is at the core of the question of 'why abolition'? The answer: because it is time to be free. Enough is enough.

Stepping back in time to locate the context of Cameron's absurd statement, we find the 1833 Act is racist and fuelled by the gaslighting he employed that day. First, although the Act is popularly referred to as the 'The Slavery Abolition Act of 1833', the law did not require British colonists and slavers make any changes until 1834. A year is a long time in anyone's life, particularly a life spent in captivity after centuries of stolen time within intergenerational enslavement. Placing 1833 in the popular title (then and now) while making it enforceable in August (near the end) of 1834 is structural gaslighting personifying the discrepancies of the Act – this pretending and performance dance repeatedly promises and withholds freedom at the same time, within the same sentence, inside or beside the same section.

Second, the Act did not legally emancipate enslaved Africans from slavery's captivity until 'up to 7 years later' through its required 'apprenticeship clause' defined in scene 20. Part II of scene 20 made it clear that slavers would be 'entitled to Services' of the same persons they enslaved through chattel slavery 'as an apprenticed Labourer.' This guaranteed that white slaver-colonists would continue to hold power and extract further profit from the same Africans they enslaved alongside the Act's 'reasonable compensation ... to the Persons hitherto entitled to the Services [enslaved labour] of such Slaves for the Loss which they [the slavers] will incur by being deprived of their Right to such services [a racist entitlement to enslave Africans]'. That 'reasonable' compensation defined in this Act is the absurd equivalent of £17 billion today (Brown, 2020). Another glaring point was the reference to enslavement, a mass violation and crime against humanity as a 'service' to which white slaver-colonizers were entitled and, therefore, the reframing of the abolition of slavery as a violation of white men's rights. This is only legible through the context of penal laws and European systems of governance that continue to hold on to the right to imprison (own) and punish (exploit) those they deem 'guilty' within white systems of law. Outside these colonial systems and 'codes', all of it is unimaginable. Penal abolitionist thinking must work hard to wrap its mind around the deeply pathological nature of penal codes and European systems of law in order to fully grasp the entirety and depravity of that which we seek to abolish.

Third, *the* 1833 *Act* is often referred to in shorthand as the 'The Slavery Abolition Act of 1833'when in *actuality* it is titled 'An Act for the Abolition of Slavery throughout the British Colonies; for **promoting the Industry** of manumitted **Slaves**; and for compensating the Persons hitherto **entitled to the Services** of such **Slaves**'. Bold emphasis has been added to highlight structural gaslighting in the use of: 'slave' instead of enslaved. Enslavement is enforced, it is a verb. Slave is descriptive, it has been used as an adjective or noun suggesting it exists in isolation of external actors and actions. The use of 'promoting the industry' instead of further oppressing enslaved workers is also dubious. And finally, the reference to enslaved labour as 'a service' (as if it is offered willingly to customers and consumers) as opposed to a militarily enforced carceral condition of confinement and exploitation is widely inappropriate and untruthful. And yet the Act's performance was legitimized and upheld with a straight face both then and now because it is performed through the pretentious enslaving legalities and culturally carceral industrial complexes of British colonialism.

Fourth, this Act provided, for the white children of colonizer-slavers, an inheritance as large as 40 per cent of the entire Treasury's spending, to be distributed between 3,000 white slavers occupying 19 islands in the Caribbean – while declaring African babies through to five years of age 'free' or, technically, as free as their parent's enslavement under apprenticeship would allow – all the while requiring all African children aged six and older to work 40.5 hours a week in order to be able to 'earn' room and board from their captors (Manning, 2013). As such, across time and place, the roots and extensions of slavery's stolen wealth and power were *not* redistributed by this British Act to abolish slavery; instead, they were further entrenched and extended by it. The Act is full of warnings, tones and rhetorical moves which contemporary abolitionists must not repeat (see also discussion of British abolitionists in Scott, Chapter 1 in this volume). The current push to invest in 'social work and behavioural health' in response to the push to divest from policing is the first marker of the start of a new cycle within the same old systems of repression (Ware, Ruzsa and Dias, 2014; Piepzna-Samarasinha, 2018; Nwadiogo and Ware, 2019; Ben-Moshe, 2020). Abolitionists must recognize that oppressed people do not need 'rehabilitation' or apprenticeships of any kind – what is needed is freedom and space to create collective self-determination.

And finally, the 'Slavery Abolition' Act of 1833 did no such thing. Instead of abolishing slavery by ending it and compensating its victims to disallow continued exploitation by white predators and their systems, the Act forced 'formerly' enslaved Africans into an almost decade-long 'apprenticeship' under their captors, thereby extending white power and slavery's stolen wealth: both in time and access to enslaved African labour through the seven years written into law and in the immense monetary funds paid out to slavers, allowing them to further extended white power to affect global policies and access to resources for generations and into contemporary times. In hindsight we can read the 1833 Act not as an abolitionist process, but instead as a process of transition through reform: a time where the slavery industrial complex laid stronger foundations and dug deeper roots so that newer, more established carceral regimes can rise.

That (now former) British prime minister who visited Jamaica in 2015 was one of many inheritors of slavery's blood money and white power, one of many legacies and extensions made possible by the slavery industrial complex. He represents one of many European slaver individuals and nations who continue to keep these histories alive through continued investments in colonialism's militarized carceral power. Cameron stood on one island among many that continue to struggle against the exploitative institutions of carceral enslavement and European colonialism – and he responded to the question of African reparations with a promise and commitment to build a British prison in Jamaica. The history of abolition from within Europe and its expanding white settler nations – 'abolition' via colonizer systems, laws, cultures and assumptions – has always been a history and process of white conquest. Contemporary abolitionists should never forget that and must work to undo these tendencies and defaults within freedom-driven movements today.

Conclusion: Abolitionist voices and carceral logics today

We live within the shadows of the slavery industrial complex. Enslaved Africans were forced to work on stolen Indigenous lands throughout the world. Black and Indigenous lives and deaths have been forced to carry and produce the largest expansions to global white power through colonial systems of conquest (Saleh-Hanna, 2008). In addition to death-making work on southern US and southern hemisphere plantations, enslaved Africans were forced to work inside homes and upon the battlefields of their captors, tending after the kin of colonizer-slavers and their accomplices throughout Europe, and within Europe's white settler nation states around the world. In addition, enslaved African labourers were forced to sustain local infrastructures and to establish and sustain white settler cities and towns immediately surrounding southern plantations, and beyond into northern territories and throughout all lands that Europeans (and their descendants) continue to occupy, colonize and exploit. And we should never forget nor overlook the fact that enslaved Africans were forced to look after ailing white people within Europe and white settler colonies during their most contagious plagues; and their descendants were forced to have direct contact with infectious diseases when Black and colonized people became the majority in essential frontline work forces during the COVID-19 global pandemic. The enormity and severity of repeating carceral histories demands ripple effects analysis. The slavery industrial complex is not limited in time to the past and cannot be minimized to geographical locations that serve and fuel false white power narratives and racist imaginations today.

Abolitionists today must begin to see and name carceral power as implicitly racializing-gendering-ableist and impoverishing. Carceral power is always tied to global systems of colonialism/enslavement/imprisonment/border making. Colonial carceral power is a manifestation of global systems of land-theft necessitating land occupations. We must work harder to draw clearer lines connecting what we know to be violent (the prison and all entities associated with all forms of imprisonment) and what we are trying to envision as 'needing' abolition: colonialism, enslavement, white power, heteropatriarchy, genderism, imperialism, ablism, ageism, western capitalism *and* western communism, the militarized takeover of life-sustaining and earth-destroying resources, and the removal of consent from decisions related to our bodies (from arrest/imprisonment, to access to safe abortions, to access to harm-free healthcare and educational settings). What we know from white abolitionist predecessors is that they refused to see the bigger picture, remained rooted within European bias and white supremacy, and therefore advocated the abolition of slavery in ways that expanded reliance upon criminal legal systems of punishment for social control (Saleh-Hanna, 2008, 2015; see also Scott, Chapter 1 in this volume). The histories shared in this chapter are meant to sound the alarm, to wake more of us up to the depths of this system's reaches, so that we can begin to map a more comprehensive and final exit from all of it.

When we place abolitionist histories within the larger context of European colonialism and chattel enslavement, we locate the essential role that abolitionist histories offer in their ability to rebuild and rebrand the public faces of white power. In Canada, the Underground Railroad – a distinctly Black freedom history – was consumed, repurposed and tokenized into Canada's one and only history of slavery. Due to its more obvious participation and investments in chattel slavery, western Europe could not invoke such a comprehensive annexation of its past. Instead, Europe's dominant culture and institutions have been able to construct a 'safe distance' between themselves and their descendants in the US by minimizing and ghosting the facts of enslaved labour in western Europe. They did so by curating public discourse on slavery into an unfortunate past that occurred in faraway places. At the same time, England's abolition of the cross-Atlantic slave trade is publicly celebrated in ways that repurpose Europe's white saviour narratives into a spectrum of 'white civility' that casts western Europe as the mother of all nations, as supreme, and its little offspring white settler nation states (particularly the US) as young and misbehaved, and its 'colony nations' as criminal and rogue. And Canada, as usual, flies under the radar, participating in a version of each (US and western European revisionist histories) to curate its own distance and false narratives of slavery's history in creating Canada.

Within the essence of such narratives on global white civility and white power, chattel slavery and colonization's land thefts/occupations/genocides are reframed as the unfortunate but necessary temper tantrums of a child – after all, acting out is a natural part of growing up and colonization is so often cast as that 'growing into civility' process by white colonizers. A clearer articulation of the calculated and interlocking symbiosis of the slavery industrial complex disallows such mythologies and undoes the distance that has been constructed between Europe's brutal global past and its enduring global powers today. At the same time, the history of slavery's 'abolition' is a key marker along the way, full of lessons to learn and traps to map, but most importantly reminding us that absolute freedom from white power can never emerge from within the reformed clutches of Europe's enslaving, colonizing institutions.

We cannot allow our freedom to continue to be driven from one colonial-enslaving institution into the next. While penal abolitionists do embody a wider view of abolition than most, we need to reorient ourselves to enable a wholistic recognition of colonialism's beast in all its formations and manifestations. Colonization's ways and methods of arrest and imprisonment continue to grow and exploit entire peoples, communities, lands and ways of life. Through slaver technologies and colonization's seemingly unending investment in land-theft and mass human exploitation, colonial systems of control consistently and collectively move colonized (and therefore imprisoned in one way or another) peoples towards less access to: land (including life-sustaining resources); freedom (anchored within collective self-determination); and life (requiring liberated futures). During these days of intensified colonial surveillance, arrest, imprisonment and death, it is urgent for abolitionist movements to amplify the importance of history. It is crucial to create and demand a contextualized and wholistic understanding of global and systemic structures that continue to keep a few nations and peoples in power while the majority are forced to endure the miserable and growing carceral conditions of colonial exploitation, confinement, hunger, scarcity and so many more forms of death consuming these days and times.

Notes

[1] Though 'man' has historically been used synonymously with 'human' in white colonial patriarchal cultures, in this instance 'man-made' is not referring to all humans, but intentionally referencing colonizers who created and enforced toxic masculinity and the systems of exploitation that institutionalize extractive forms of violence.

[2] I have started to use small case letters for directions (north African, western Europe and so on) to centre land and decentre the geopolitics of colonialism. I also use small case w for western because as a geopolitical entity the term is incorrect and offensive: 'western' is often used as a stand-alone entity not tied to specific lands, when in practice it references western Europe (not western hemispheric) systems and forms of thought. The reference to Canada and the United States as 'westernized' nations is absurd, for the lands literally exist in the western hemisphere, yet 'western' in this context does not mean direction or location on a global stage, but instead, the realities of conquests that extend western European systems of power beyond western Europe. My small case use of colonialism's geopolitical directions is meant to cause pause re-center the land, and allow space for reconsideration and critical thinking.

[3] Nazis in Germany's Third Reich identified their loss in the Thirty Years' War (1618–1648) as the fall of the First Reich (Ingaro, 2013). The first German holocaust in Namibia (the settler-colony named 'German South Africa') documents the rise and establishment of

Germany's Second Reich and the onset of Europe's Holocaust and genocide (Olusoga and Erichsen, 2011).

4   I am archiving some through the hashtag #carceralism within my @black_feminist_hauntology archives on Instagram.

5   I am archiving these through the hashtag #carceralism within my @black_feminist_hauntology archives on Instagram by documenting images representing cultural and digital apparitions of historic slavery and colonialism as they extend into modern-day culture and entertainment/media industries abundantly, not by accident or conspiracy, but due to the enduring facts and legacies of the slavery industrial complex.

References

Bailey, R. (1994) 'The other side of slavery: Black labor, cotton, and textile industrialization in Great Britain and the United States', *Agricultural History*, 68(2): 35–50.

Barragan, Y. (2015) 'Moving on: the logic of slavery in the reparations debate', *Truthout.org*. Available from: https://truthout.org/articles/moving-on-the-logic-of-slavery-in-the-reparations-debate/ [Accessed 15 September 2024].

'The Beaver and Other Pelts' (2001) Montreal, Quebec: McGill University copyright. Available from: http://digital.library.mcgill.ca/nwc/history/01.htm [Accessed 15 September 2024].

Ben-Moshe, L. (2020) *Decarcerating Disability: Deinstitutionalization and Prison Abolition*, Minneapolis: University of Minnesota Press.

Brown, M. (2020) 'Fact check: United Kingdom finished paying off debts to slave-owning families in 2015', *USA Today* (30 June). Available from: https://www.usatoday.com/story/news/factcheck/2020/06/30/fact-check-u-k-paid-off-debts-slave-owning-families-2015/3283908001/ [Accessed 20 June 2021].

Carvey, I. (2008) 'A community displaced', *Archived: Under a Northern Star, Library and Archives of Canada*. Available from: https://www.collectionscanada.gc.ca/northern-star/033005-2601-e.html [Accessed 15 September 2024].

Clairmont, D.H. and Magill, D.W. (1999) *Africville: The Life and Death of a Canadian Black Community* (3rd edn), Toronto: Canadian Scholars' Press.

Clark-Pujara, C. (2016) *Dark Work: The Business of Slavery in Rhode Island*, New York: New York University Press.

Cooper, A. (2006) *The Hanging of Angélique: The Untold Story of Canadian Slavery and the Burning of Old Montréal*, Athens, GA: University of Georgia Press.

Cuneen, C. (2023) *Defund the Police: An International Insurrection*. Bristol: Policy Press.

Donovan, K. (1995) 'Slaves and their owners in Île Royale, 1713–1760', *Acadiensis*, 25(1): 3–32.

Eisen, L.-B. (2018) *Inside Private Prisons: An American Dilemma inside Mass Incarceration*, New York: Columbia University Press.

Evans, L. and Goldberg, E. (2009). *The Prison Industrial Complex and the Global Economy* New York: PM Press.

Hall, C., McClelland, K., Draper, N., Donington, K. and Lang, R. (2014) *Legacies of British Slave-Ownership: Colonial Slavery and the Formation of Victorian Britain*, Cambridge: Cambridge University Press.

Hine, D.C., Bellinger, N.R., Cousins, O., LaRoche, C.J., Mazloomi, C., McDaniels-Wilson, C., Roma, C., Seif, H., Sharp, S.P., de Souza, R.L. and Smith, J. (2013) *Gendered Resistance: Women, Slavery, and the Legacy of Margaret Garner*, Urbana: University of Illinois Press.

Ingaro, C. (2013). *Believe and Destroy: Intellectuals in the SS War Machine*, A. Brown (trans.). Cambridge: Polity Press.

International Slavery Museum (2019) 'Black people in Europe'. Available from: http://www.liverpoolmuseums.org.uk/ism/slavery/europe/black_people.aspx [Accessed 15 September 2024].

James, J. (1996) *Resisting State Violence: Radicalism, Gender and Race in US Culture*, Minneapolis: University of Minnesota Press.

Khare, N., Farah S., Blessing N. and Baijayanta M. (2020) 'Reimagining safety in a pandemic: the imperative to dismantle structural oppression in Canada', *Canadian Medical Association Journal*, 192(41): E1218–E1220.

Lamble, S. (2011) 'Transforming carceral logics: 10 reasons to dismantle the prison industrial complex using a queer/trans analysis', in N. Smith and E.A. Stanley (eds) *Captive Genders: Trans Embodiment and the Prison Industrial Complex*. Oakland: AK Press, pp 235–266.

Legacies of British Slave-Ownership (2019) 'Center for the Study of Legacies of British Slave-Ownership,' *University College London Department of History*. Available from: https://www.ucl.ac.uk/lbs [Accessed 15 September 2024].

Lowe, K. (2005) 'Introduction: the Black African presence in Renaissance Europe', in T.F. Earle and K.J.P. Lowe (eds) *Black Africans in Renaissance Europe*, Cambridge: Cambridge University Press, pp 1–14.

Manning, S. (2013) 'Britain's colonial shame: slave-owners given huge payouts after abolition', *The Independent* (24 February). Available from: https://www.independent.co.uk/news/uk/home-news/britains-colonial-shame-slave-owners-given-huge-payouts-after-abolition-8508358.html [Accessed 15 September 2024].

Mathiesen, T. (1997) 'Towards the 21st century: abolition, an impossible dream?' Paper presented at the Eight International Conference on Penal Abolition, Auckland.

Maynard, R. (2017) *Policing Black Lives: State Violence in Canada from Slavery to the Present*, Blackpoint, Nova Scotia: Fernwood Publishing.

National Library of Jamaica, 'The Jamaican maroons'. Available from: http://www.nlj.gov.jm/history-notes/The%20Maroons%20edited%20final.htm [Accessed 15 September 2024]. Excerpted from Campbell, M.C. (1988) 'The Maroons of Jamaica, 1655–1796: a history of resistance, collaboration & betrayal', Granby, MA: Bergin & Garvey Inc.

Nwadiogo, E. and Ware S.M. (2019) 'Calling a shrimp a shrimp: a Black queer intervention in disability studies', in J. Haritaworn et al (eds) *Queering Urban Justice*, Toronto: University of Toronto Press, pp 121–137.

Ogden, S. (2005) 'The prison industrial complex in Indigenous California', in J.O. Chinyere (ed.) *Global Lockdown: Race, Gender, and the Prison-Industrial-Complex*, New York: Routledge, pp 57–65.

Olusoga, D. and Erichsen, C.W. (2011) *The Kaiser's Holocaust: Germany's Forgotten Genocide and the Colonial Roots of Nazism*, London: Faber & Faber.

Patterson, O. (1982) *Slavery and Social Death: A Comparative Study*, Cambridge, MA: Harvard University Press.

Pearce, N., Rhodes, S., Stocking, K., Pembrey, L., van Veldhoven, K., Brickley, E.B., Robertson, S., Davoren, D., Nafilyan, B., Windsor-Shellard, B., Fletcher, T. and van Tongeren, M. (2021) 'Occupational differences in COVID-19 incidence, severity, and mortality in the United Kingdom: available data and framework for analyses', *National Library of Medicine in Welcome Open Research*, 6: 102. DOI: 10.12688/wellcomeopenres.16729.

Piepzna-Samarasinha L.L. (2018) *Care Work: Dreaming Disability Justice*, Vancouver: Arsenal Pulp Press.

Rodríguez, D. (2020) *White Reconstruction: Domestic Warfare and the Logics of Genocide*, New York: Fordham University Press.

Rogers, T.N., Rogers, C.R., VanSant-Webb, E., Gu, L.Y., Yan, B. and Qeadan, F. (2020) 'Racial disparities in COVID-19 mortality among essential workers in the United States', *World Medical & Health Policy*, 12(3): 311–327.

Saleh-Hanna, V. (2008) *Colonial Systems of Control: Criminal Justice in Nigeria*. Ottawa: University of Ottawa Press.

Saleh-Hanna, V. (2015) 'Black feminist hauntology: rememory the ghosts of abolition?', *Champ pénal/Penal Field 12*. Available from: http://journals.openedition.org/champpenal/9168 [Accessed 15 September 2024].

Saleh-Hanna, V. (2017) 'An abolitionist theory on crime: ending the abusive relationship with racist-imperialist-patriarchy [R.I.P.]', *Contemporary Justice Review*, 20(4): 419–441.

Saleh-Hanna, V. (2023) 'Memoryscapes: Canadian chattel slavery, gaslighting, and carceral phantom pain', in V. Chartrand and J. Savarese (eds) *Unsettling Colonialism in the Canadian Criminal Justice System*, Athabasca, Alberta: Athabasca University Press, pp 21–43.

Saleh-Hanna, V. (2024) 'The history of criminology is a history of white supremacy', in V. Saleh-Hanna, J. Williams and M. Coyle (eds) *Abolish Criminology*, New York: Routledge, pp 36–51.

Saleh-Hanna, V. (2024) 'black_feminist_hauntology', *Instagram*.. Available from: https://www.instagram.com/black_feminist_hauntology/ [Accessed 15 September 2024].

Saunders, A.C. de C.M. (1982) *A Social History of Black Slaves and Freedmen in Portugal, 1441–1555*, Cambridge: Cambridge University Press.

Scheerer, S. (1986) 'Towards abolitionism', *Contemporary Crises*, 10: 5–20.

Shaw, M. (2012) 'Slave cloth and clothing slaves: craftsmanship, commerce, and industry', *Journal of Early and Southern Decorative Arts*, 33. Available from: http://www.mesdajournal.org/2012/slave-cloth-clothing-slaves-craftsmanship-commerce-industry/ [Accessed 15 September 2024].

Sudbury, J. (2005) 'Ceiling Black bodies: Black women in the global prison industrial complex', *Feminist Review*, 80: 162–179.

Ware, S.M., Ruzsa, J. and Dias. G. (2014) 'It can't be fixed because it's not broken: racism and disability in the prison industrial complex', in L. Ben-Moshe, C. Chapman and A.C. Carey (eds) *Disability Incarcerated*, New York: Palgrave Macmillan, pp 163–184.

Whitfield, H.A. (2016) *North to Bondage: Loyalist Slavery in the Maritimes*, Vancouver, British Columbia: University of British Columbia Press.

Whitfield, H.A. (ed.) (2018) *Black Slavery in the Maritimes: A History in Documents*, Peterborough, Ontario: Broadview Canada.

Whitfield, H.A. and Cahill, B. (2009) 'Slave life and slave law in colonial Prince Edward Island, 1769–1825', *Acadiensis*, 38(2): 29–51.

Williams, E. (1944) *Capitalism and Slavery*, Chapel Hill: University of North Carolina Press.

Winks, W.R. (1997) *The Blacks in Canada: A History* (2nd edn), Montreal: McGill-Queens Press.

Wilson, J.Z., Hodgkinson, S., Piché, J. and Walby, K. (2017). *The Palgrave Handbook of Prison Tourism,* London: Palgrave Macmillan.

10

Abolition and the Colonial Carceral Archipelago

Thalia Anthony and Harry Blagg

Introduction

This chapter focuses on prison abolition as it relates to the Australian colony where issues of justice, law and penalty are inextricably interwoven with colonial violence and the unceded sovereignty of First Nations people. It discusses issues related to the land known as Australia, although they also resonate with colonial harms in North America and Aotearoa/New Zealand. Across these colonies, First Nations people are hyperincarcerated more than any other population in the world (see Anthony, 2017). We critique the notion that prison represents a unique form of 'social death' (Price, 2015). Instead, we position the prison within a colonial constellation of intersecting carceral 'camps' (Agamben, 1998). The notion that prisons administer a 'social death' on people in prison is ubiquitous in the penological literature. Treating prisoners as dead is achieved through a range of degradation ceremonies and routinized processes of shaming and dehumanization. The 'social death' marks the excision of the subject from the civil world of rights and entitlements, which may be returned to him or her on completion of his or her sentence. The pains of confinement include not just physical and psychic violence but also the loss of a social self and self-esteem.

However, the notion of 'social death' is challenged by First Nations peoples' 'refusal' (Simpson, 2014) to be eliminated by colonizers. This includes a refusal to appropriate colonial inscriptions of First Nations people as criminals, prisoners and lawless (Fanon, 1986: 95; Watego, 2021). Instead, First Nations people, including those in prison, continue to express their radical resistance through connections to one another, culture and law (Anthony, Sentance and Behrendt, 2021). In research with Aboriginal women in New South Wales prisons, identity was expressed in the following terms: 'We are strong independent black women'; 'I'm the fighter of the family. So ... when it comes to my family I'm a big protector' (Anthony, Sentance and Behrendt, 2021: 8, 10). Aboriginal women's sense of self and sovereignty is not usurped by a 'social death' in prison.

We draw on Mbembé's (2003) notion of colonialism as 'necropower'. This focuses attention on the role of the state in subjugating First Nations people to discipline and death. This encapsulates the state harms of incarceration and how it looms large in the 'everyday colony' (see Watego, 2021). Both inside and outside prison, First Nations people are excluded from the network of positive rights enjoyed by the upholders of settler law and instead are subjected to racism, trauma and death at the hands of the colonial state.

Penal abolition in settler colonies must centre white colonization as its defining problematic and work to decolonize relationships between colonizer and colonized if it is to imagine a society without prisons. Penal abolitionism, which provides a structural critique of penal systems, resonates profusely with the hyperincarceration of First Nations people in settler colonies. Yet, to fulfil its promise in settler colonial societies, it must extend to all other colonial carceral sites – such as child protection and forced resettlement from Indigenous Country – that are designed to socially control First Nations people to enforce 'white possessiveness', to use the phrase of Goenpul woman and professor Aileen Moreton-Robinson (2015). A principal task of settler colonial states – where British governance structures, laws, traditions and people seek dominance – is to dispossess the First Nations population and hasten the exploitation of their lands and resources.

While penological literature on incarceration draws heavily upon a rich Euro-American literature from the 'birth' of the penitentiary through to mass or hyperincarceration, we suggest that an alternative, or 'contrapuntal' (Said, 1993), reading of incarceration under conditions of settler colonialism yields a landscape cross-hatched by multiple sites of enforced enclosure: prisons certainly, but also asylums, lock-up hospitals, missions, orphanages, police cells, farms and cattle stations all formed part of an interlocking system designed not just to create passive subjects (in the Foucauldian sense) but also to strip First Nations people of agency exploit their labour and reduce them to a bare life existence. 'Bare life', to use the language of Agamben (1998), is enforced existence as expendable human beings without legal or moral rights who can be killed with impunity. We have embraced decolonial theory that emerged during struggles for decolonization in the Global South and focuses on the colonial state's continuity of purpose over time (for example, Fanon 1986, 1991) rather than 'ruptures', 'breaks' or 'cultural shifts' that shapes influential theories in the Global North.

We maintain that the movement to abolish the prison (see Blagg and Anthony, 2019: 13, 42), must progress in lockstep with the abolition of what Anibal Quijano (2007) and Walter Mignolo (2007: 156) refer to as the 'colonial matrix of power'. This is otherwise known as the 'coloniality of power' and describes a matrix that connects various forms of hegemonic control over First Nations governance processes, labour, sexuality and subjectivity. Under conditions of settler colonialism, this matrix incorporates a panoply of institutions that have sought to erase First Nations laws and cultures, steal First Nations lands and children, enslave First Nations people, impose Western ideals of sexuality, patriarchy and family, control fertility and assimilate First Nations peoples into Western ways of knowing, being and doing. Accordingly, recent roundtables on 'anti-colonial penal abolition' at the North American and Indigenous Studies Association (NAISA) Conference (2021) and published in a special edition of *Journal of Prisoners on Prisons* (see, for example, Pranteau et al, 2022) have highlighted the need for abolition to address demands of First Nations sovereignty and land reclamation.

The colonial matrix of power is buttressed by a range of correctional, policing, medical, welfare and other structures, which, taken together, constitute a concatenated chain, or archipelago, of colonial prisons. Colonialism inscribed a white European imaginary into First Nations space, displacing, but not eradicating, First Nations sovereignty. This has created a 'binary' within settler colonial societies between a hegemonic white state and a First Nations population that still claims sovereign rights, particularly to land (Behrendt and Watson, 2007: 102). Seeking to eradicate First Nations sovereignty rather than simply disciplining and controlling bodies has been the lynchpin of colonial intervention in the lives of First Nations people. This has required a particularized range of social policies, laws, practices and forms of governmentality designed to unmake First Nation's communities and reconstitute them in the image of white society, although without the requisite rights ('never quite white').

First Nations societies have not capitulated in the face of colonization, but have risen up in spite of the state. First Peoples' self-determination and sovereignty, according to Eualeyai/Kamillaroi scholar Larissa Behrendt (2002: 45), garners strength at a 'grassroots level' to give power to First Peoples. For Tanganekald, Meintangk and Boandik woman and law professor Irene Watson (2016: 33), the ongoing 'political and territorial integrity of First Nations' sustains First Nations societies outside of the nation state. Audra Simpson (2014) maintains that First Nations people have worked to sustain a sovereign order 'nested' within the dominant white order that refuses to accept the realities imposed upon it: refusal, resistance and cultural resurgence have formed the basis for a new First Nations politics. It is the 'modalities of Indigenous land-connected practices' (Coulthard, 2014: 139) that shape First Nations movements to challenge colonial relationships. These perspectives constitute the language and practice that counters the colonial carceral archipelago in all its forms.

The state of exception: exclusion of First Nations people from legal rights

The colonial carceral archipelago exists outside of the rule of law by design. Massacres in the colony, the exclusion and segregation of Aboriginal people in the name of protectionism, and the recent Commonwealth government intervention to deprive the rights of remote Aboriginal communities in the Northern Territory all occurred outside of legal norms that applied to non-Indigenous people. The hegemonic power of the Western state relies on its capacity to suspend the rule of law, at certain times, in certain places (and for certain people) (Arendt, 1966). This is nowhere more evident than in its pursuit of 'structured dispossession' of First Peoples (Coulthard, 2014: 7). First Peoples are suspended in a 'state of exception' (Schmitt, 2005: 5) in which systemic incarceration and rule by martial law characterize their interaction with the legal order. In this respect, colonial rule is 'Janus faced', displaying one set of characteristics to the hegemonic white majority (human rights, citizenship) and another to the displaced minority (bare life, carceralism).

The exclusion from rights occurs 'more nakedly and clearly than anywhere else' in the operations of the police, who are not merely an administrative function of law enforcement; rather, the police are constitutive of the exchange between violence and right that characterizes the figure of the sovereign (Agamben, 1998: 3). The police are authorized to use lethal violence in the state of legal exception, which is justified by perceived threat or danger of the 'Other'. Because First Nations lives are already constituted as a form of bare life, encounters with police are governed by the state of emergency rather than law and unlawful killings are judged acceptable, even necessary. As we have argued elsewhere (Blagg and Anthony, 2019), the police control the thresholds to numerous institutions of bare life, where First Nations are in constant danger of death.

Colonization has so consistently enforced the state of exception on First Nations people that it appears normal to the legal and penal system. Agamben (1998) writes that the camp exists in a state of exception, where inmates become *homo sacer*, quite literally capable of being killed with impunity. Legal restraints and protection are constantly 'paused' in order to deal with a presumed state of emergency. For First Nations peoples, the 'pause' has been become an incessant and institutionalized reality, and they have been detained and moved around under a permanent state of emergency.

Archipelago of colonial carceral camps

Anglocentric histories and theories of the prison as the pivotal site of exclusion and harm fail to grasp the significance of a ubiquitous system of 'camps', as articulated by Agamben (1998), where First Nations people are subject to colonial subjugation and segregation. For Agamben, the enduring legacy of Euro-modernity is its bestowal of camps – places in which there are no moral or legal rights – on people deemed to be outside of its legal order as its enduring legacy. The integrity of the Western rule of law depends on who is cast outside of the law. For First Nations people, exclusion from rights in the legal system is not an unfortunate product of being designated to the camp; it is the very foundation of the legal system. This exists not only behind prison walls, but also in the personal spaces of family life, the professional spaces of work life, the public spaces of the consumer and civic participant, and the therapeutic and care spaces of health, education and housing. First Nations peoples' exclusion from basic rights pervades the colonial order. The colonial settler state is incapable of providing anything more than 'bare life' to First Nations people, on either the 'inside' or the 'outside' of prison, because its logic is eliminatory and dispossessory (Wolfe, 2006; Coulthard, 2014).

Eurocentric binaries of 'inside' and 'outside' prison obscure the ways in which First Nations peoples are 'moved about in a zone of indistinction between the outside and the inside, the exception and the rule' (Agamben, 2000: 40). In the settler colonial context, oppression 'inside' prison is a continuum of systemic racism 'outside' prison, both of which are constitutive of the colonial prison that entraps First Nations peoples in its structured dispossession. Colonial carceralism manifests in displacement from land and forced resettlement, forced removal to child 'welfare' facilities and foster families, mandatory placement in psychiatric institutions and 'lock' hospitals, forced unpaid labour relations *and* in police stations, youth detention centres and prisons. For prison abolition to be relevant to anti-colonial struggles, it must engage with all these carceral islands in the colonial archipelago.

Our research with First Nations organizations in the Northern Territory, which involved a critical analysis of how the criminal system affects Aboriginal people, resulted in broader critique of the colonial system. First Nations people on the ground reveal how prison intersects with state controls and harms in the community (see Anthony and Blagg, 2013; Anthony and Sherwood, 2018). Our work with Tangentyere Council and the North Australian Aboriginal Justice Agency identified not only discriminatory policing against Aboriginal people, but also the broader impacts of the Northern Territory Intervention (2007–2022), which was racially targeted at removing Aboriginal people from their homelands, controlling social security income, bureaucratic management of Aboriginal families and children, and displacing Aboriginal community governance structures (see Gibson, 2012). For First Nations people and organizations in the Northern Territory, the law enforcement response was part of the broader government attack on First Nations communities. Police were sent into Aboriginal communities in 2007 alongside white government business managers, social security and child welfare bureaucrats and nongovernmental organizations (NGOs) contracted by the government. The result was a rapid rise in imprisonment and Aboriginal child removals from families as well as a loss of rights to governance, self-management and homelands. Tangentyere Council Chief Executive Officer (CEO) Walter Shaw (2012) said that the Northern Territory Intervention is 'paternalism at its worst' and that Aboriginal people in Central Australia 'are at breaking point'. North Australia Aboriginal Justice Agency (NAAJA) Chairman Norman George commented:

> Many fundamental aspects of Aboriginal people's lives changed in the last 2 years [since the Northern Territory Intervention] including their employment arrangements, welfare payments, the status of the Aboriginal land on which they live, how they are policed and what is prohibited. Furthermore, Aboriginal people in the prescribed areas have had to comprehend that they now live under different legislation and have different rules apply to them. (George, 2009: 2)

In terms of Aboriginal imprisonment, there were 'huge increases' arising from the Northern Territory Intervention, according to NAAJA's Principal Legal Officer Glen Dooley (NAAJA, 2009: 12). Simultaneously, the Northern Territory government committed unprecedented funding for a new prison in Darwin, Northern Territory – a facility built to house Aboriginal people who comprise 90 per cent of the prison population. The rise in Aboriginal imprisonment was fuelled by the establishment of 18 new police stations and 60 new police officers that 'hyperpolice' Aboriginal people. Dooley observed the injustice that 'massive expenditure on police' under the Northern Territory Intervention went hand in hand with the denial of 'basic housing, education and health support' to Aboriginal people in the Northern Territory (NAAJA, 2009: 12). These colonial interventions reveal the everyday racism in the life of the colony that dispossesses and harms First Nations people; as Munanjahi and South Sea Islander activist Professor Chelsea Watego (2021), describes it, 'another day in the colony'.

Bare life emerges in the racism of everyday life; the lack of humane housing; the denial of a living income and valued employment; the fear and reality of the state stealing children; and their pervasive policing is an indictment on the so-called freedom that the state confers outside of prison. Darumbal/South Sea Islander journalist, scholar and activist Dr Amy McQuire (2016) observes 'even if you aren't confined by physical walls, sometimes the reality of being Aboriginal in this country can feel like a prison in itself'. Therefore, control in the contemporary settler colony can be regarded as an archipelago of intersecting camps founded on what Sylvester (2006: 66) calls 'bare life biopolitics'. The camp, not the penitentiary, serves as the template for multiple, interconnecting forms of institutional control over the Indigenous people. What ties these dispersed sites together is what Diken and Laustsen (2002: 291) refer to as the 'logic of camp', as the 'zone of indistinction', where 'notions of inside and outside ... tend to disappear'. In settler colonies, it is not the materiality of prison bars that makes a prison, but the structures of oppression that enable carceralism across a range of institutional and dispossession sites.

Abolitionists need to confront the colonial landscape in which prison is set, where numerous institutions act to constrain First Nations sovereignty and control First Nations lives. This is a truism not only in the colonies, but also for the Global North that continues to benefit from stolen First Nations land and the displacement of First Nations peoples. The language of abolishing the colony – which has been garnered by First Nations incarceration survivors in the colonies of Australia, Canada, New Zealand/Aotearoa (see generally the special edition 'Anti-colonial Approach to Abolition' of *Journal of Prisoners on Prisons* [2022]) – accounts for the totality of oppressions on the colony that includes but is not limited to the prison. Abolitionist Debbie Kilroy, founder of *Sisters Inside*, and Gunditjmara activist Tabitha Lean reflect on the deep colonizing role of the nation:

> In the making and sustaining of a nation, colonization must abuse Blak minds, Blak bodies, Blak lands, and Blak waters. It must lock Blak fullas out of housing markets, job markets and labour markets. If it did not, Australia – as the illegitimate nation state that it is – would cease to exist. This brand of colonialism, and indeed racial capitalism, requires police and prisons, judges and lawyers, teachers, and child 'protection' workers. They are a very deliberate part of the arsenal of the settler colonial war machine, whereby the criminal punishment system contributes in a real way to maintaining the economic and social hierarchy in this country. They all form a crucial element to progressing and maintaining the colonial project through the consistent and persistent subjugation of Aboriginal people. (Kilroy and Lean, 2022: 94)

The structure of colonization means that its force is everywhere – in out-of-home care for stolen First Nations children, overcrowded, dilapidated public housing and on the overpoliced streets and public transport – and not simply contained within prison walls. It is the reality described by Yorta Yorta activist Tanya Day, whose mother died in police custody after being arrested while sleeping on a train, of the law being applied differently to her mother than 'a white Australian grandmother, drunk and asleep on a train, on her way to Melbourne to visit her daughter' (Day, 2020). Keenan Mundine, Biripi and Wakka Wakka man and co-founder of Deadly

Connections Community and Justice Services in New South Wales, explains how Aboriginal children are segregated in prisons and then thrown out in the community with no support and to face the same injustice, usually in the child protection system: 'society thinks the way to address problems facing children is to chase young children and arrest them, and put them in a cell with no support, no understanding, no access to opportunities. When they come out, they just open the gate and put them back in their community' (Mundine, 2022: 39).

The archipelago of colonial camps is bedded in the settler colonial psyche, practices, laws and institutions. Abolition discourses in colonies need to contend with the far-reaching carceral prisons that currently exist and the enduring harms from historical prisons across ration depots, white settlements, Christian missions, government reserves, massacre sites, cattle stations, white homesteads and children's homes. As with abolitionist movements in North America, abolition is more than about dismantling; it is also about building community (Davis, 2003; Wilson Gilmore, 2020; Kaba, 2021). The late Moana Jackson (2017a), a trailblazing Maori scholar for justice, believed that 'Criminology for Indigenous people must be based on an Indigenous intellectual tradition' and in turn abolition for Indigenous people must be imagined in terms of engaging Indigenous justice traditions. Sheri Pranteau, a First Nations woman born in Winnipeg, Manitoba, who advocates for abolition after 19 years of imprisonment, describes abolition as entitlement to governance and basic rights denied in colonial society:

> I think about abolition in terms of the government sitting at the table with us and honouring the land and treaties that they have signed – that they would invest in the communities and clean water, access to housing, and programs, rather than millions upon millions of dollars to lock us away. (Pranteau et al, 2022: 79)

From paternal to penal hyperincarceration

First Nations people have expressed how the 'colonial imperative and the carceral imperative are so entwined' that there needs to be a retracing of 'state, colonial, neocolonial, legislative, structural, political, economic, cultural, institutional, religious and collective forms of violence' (Moana Jackson and Tracey McIntosh, quoted in Pranteau et al, 2022: 82). The history and contemporaneity of colonization in the territory known as Australia is evidenced in the various forms of carceralism since colonial settler invasion.

Segregation of First Nations people took root in the early days of colonization, originally on Gadigal land in 1788, and has continued unabated since. This paternalist imprisonment sought to soften the dying pillow of First Nations people in the eyes of the missionaries and Aboriginal 'protectors'. Across the British colonies, Britain formally unleashed a policy of *protectionism*, following its endorsement by the 1837 British Parliamentary Select Committee on Aboriginal Tribes. In Australia and Canada, the legislative inception of protectionism imposed a series of protectorates on First Nations people in which 'protectors' had legislative powers to police and manage all aspects of First Nations lives, including their movement, associations, marriages, clothing, food, income and work. It sought to instil non-First Nations values and routines on First Nations people through forced work and instruction. This was consistent with the colonizing task of civilizing First Nations people (British Parliamentary Select Committee, 1837).

In Australia, protectionism was enacted through what became known as the 'Aboriginal Protection Acts' or simply 'Aboriginal Acts', which continued well into the 20th century.[1] These placed Aboriginal people in an official state of legal 'exceptionalism' where they were rendered outside of the rule of law (Agamben, 1998). A key feature of the Aboriginal Acts was the forced placement of Aboriginal people in confinement, including in government settlements, reserves, church missions, cattle stations (for forced labour) and other institutions. Paul Havemann (2005), employing Agambian terminology, describes the legal exclusion and segregation of Aboriginal people in the following terms:

> In the colonies Indigenous people ... have been the paradigm non-people, non-citizens, *homines sacri*. If not, at worst, exterminated with legal impunity, they have been excluded and condemned to placelessness in 'zones of exception' such as reserves, mission schools or camps and other forms of segregation under the regime of the sovereign's draconian 'protection'. (Havemann, 2005: 59)

In this historical context, the carceral webs that capture First Nations peoples are not a recent or ad hoc construct, but a design of the colonial system (see Roach, 2022). They are perpetuated through the current hyperincarceration of First Nations people in youth and adult prisons. In the late 20th century, the policy of assimilation made it no longer necessary, or desirable, for governments to segregate First Nations people in church missions, government settlements or cattle stations and homesteads under the explicitly discriminatory legislation of the Aboriginal Protection Acts. Rather, First Nations people would be managed through mainstream policies and institutions, albeit with differential impacts that would see their rights restricted. From the 1960s onwards, there were sharp increases in both First Nations imprisonment and child removals by the state under ostensibly neutral criminal and welfare laws respectively. Arguably, this was Australia's 'New Jim Crow' (Alexander, 2020) moment – when the ascendancy in civil rights for First Nations people dovetailed with the ascendancy of punitive controls. This coheres with Guha's (1997) observation of the colonial impulse to exclude the colonized even when imposing an inclusive hegemony.

Today, over 30 per cent of the incarcerated populations are First Nations – a rate of 15 times that of the non-First Nations population. First Nations Australians are the most incarcerated people in the world (Anthony, 2017). They are trailed by First Nations people in prisons in Aotearoa/New Zealand and Canada, which reflects similar settler colonial practises of penalty. Unlike the criminological notion of 'mass incarceration' popularized in the work of David Garland (2001: 2), the notion of 'hyperincarceration' is more useful in the settler colonial context. Mass imprisonment captures 'systematic imprisonment of whole groups of the population'. However, in colonies it is the imprisonment of First Nations people, and not the masses, who are entangled in the carceral mesh. In Australia, rates of *non*-First Nations imprisonment have remained relatively stable over recent years. Indeed, in youth detention settings *non*-First Nations rates have declined over the past decade, while the proportion of First Nations children has steadily increased. The term 'hyperincarceration', coined by Wacquant (2014: 41–42), identifies the targeted nature of incarceration towards specific racialized and class demographics in contrast to '*mass* incarceration [that] suggests that confinement concerns large swaths of the citizenry' (see also Cunneen et al, 2013).

First Nations people have borne the brunt of law and order politics as an extension of the colonial carceral logics. Wiradjuri woman Professor Juanita Sherwood articulates that the drive to fill prisons with First Nations people is a governance strategy to 'perpetrate ongoing colonial power' (Foreword to Blagg and Anthony, 2019: ix). Following paternalist segregation, street police became the arbiters of responsibilization and civilization in the criminal sphere, whereas welfare authorities were the arbiters in the child removal realm. These arbiters did not 'simply impose the law, they imposed the law of an alien [colonial] culture' (Blagg, 2008: 131). Public spaces saw the inscription of colonizing worldviews, systems, rules, regulations and practices (Spivak, 1996). This translated in targeted control of First Nations people in public in the form of criminalizing minor 'offences' such as offensive language, public drunkenness, breach of move-on orders, public nuisance and breaching traffic rules (Eggleston, 1976: 176; O'Shane, 1992: 5; Anthony and Blagg, 2013). Like protectionism, these new penal strategies were designed to move First Nations people into various places of confinement and 'away from the wider/whiter community' (Tedmanson, 2008: 149).

Colonial prisons, panopticons and necropower

Early colonial prisons for First Nations people, such as Roebourne and Rottnest Island in Western Australia, exhibited the features of Bentham's panopticon, with its architecture that facilitated internalized surveillance. However, colonial authorities were not satisfied with confining First Nations people; they also brutalized their bodies. Roebourne Prison in the remote northwest of Australia, which opened in 1886, was of an octagonal design with a central 'inspection house' and inmates stationed around the perimeter. However, the design ultimately gave way to a colonial hierarchy in which white prisoners lived in one section in relative comfort while First Nations prisoners were kept chained up to 24 hours a day in a separate long section of their own. First Nations people were also neck chained by police, who transported them hundreds of kilometres from their homelands and forced them to undertake heavy work developing the colonial infrastructures.

Similarly on Rottnest Island, a penal island off Western Australia established as a prison in 1838, First Nations people were imprisoned thousands of kilometres from their homelands in the Kimberley region. There, a ruthless regime of hard labour served to reinforce the domination embedded in panopticon architecture through 'flogging and chaining to a wheelbarrow'. Parliamentarians in 1895 believed that this punishment would 'reduce the incidence of spearing of cattle' (quoted in Finnane and McGuire, 2001: 284). Between 1838 and 1931, some 369 First Nations prisoners died on Rottnest Island (Green, 1998).

The necropower of prisons continues in contemporary custodial settings where more than 600 First Nations people have died since 1980 (Royal Commission into Aboriginal Deaths in Custody, 1991; Allam, 2021). This evidences the genocidal tendencies of this punitive regime. Although Foucault (1977) described imprisonment as punishing the soul rather than the body, and in this sense a more refined form of disciplinary power, the imprisonment of First Nations people manifests in systemic, and at times unfettered, violence. Achile Mbembé (2003) refers to biopower that authorizes death as 'necropower' – meaning technologies of control and discipline through which life is strategically subjugated to the power of death while enabling power to live. It finds its extreme manifestation in colonial power, here 'sovereignty consists fundamentally in the exercise of a power outside the law ... and where "peace" is more likely to take on the face of a "war without end"' (Mbembé, 2003: 13).

At the same time, it is not always within the prison walls that the racist violence of law enforcement is inflicted; it is also in vans, police cells, homes and hospitals. Anywhere is a prison and place of punishment for First Nations people, whether in the form of massacres, mass poisoning, rapes, deracination, criminalization and occupation. This embodies the state of exception – where controls and violence are 'deemed to operate in the service of "civilization"' across the 'camp' and only for First Nations people (Mbembé, 2003: 41). First Nations deaths in custody demonstrate how the camp and its manufacture of bare life carcerality is endemic to the colonial penal system.

Some recent examples of First Nations deaths in custody outside of the prison setting reveal necrocolonial power in its deliberate and reckless dispensations. The killing of Ngaanyatjarra Elder Mr Ward from the remote community of Warburton demonstrates how white law enforcement encroaches on Aboriginal land to assert authority and designate First Nations people to bare life. Mr Ward was arrested by police on what police maintained was a 'sealed' road outside the town of Laverton. Conversely, the Aboriginal Legal Service of Western Australia, based on evidence from the car's passenger, argued that it was on a dirt track that was understood to be outside the white legal domain. Mr Ward was detained in custody, denied bail and confined in the back of a G46 security vehicle for the 352-kilometre trip to prison in Kalgoorlie. He literally boiled to death in the back of a prison van with faulty air conditioning. The two white contractors did not check on him once during the journey (Western Australian Coroner's Court, 2009: 83–84). For them, Mr Ward did not qualify for empathy, nor did he deserve a duty of care. The corrections vehicle was a mobile 'camp' for an Aboriginal man worthy only of bare life – he was *homo sacer* because none of those involved in the process of his dehumanization were brought to account.

The killing of 19-year-old Warlpiri man Kumanajayi Walker in the remote Warlpiri community of Yuendumu, Central Australia occurred while he was at his family's home on the evening of 9 November 2019. The Immediate Response Team (a specialized police unit with military weapons and paramilitary uniforms) invaded Walker's home and police officer Zachary Rolfe shot him three times (Anthony and Cubillo, 2020). Walker died soon after the shooting, while his family was denied the opportunity to comfort him. The shooting prompted the aggrieved Yuendumu community to call for the disarming of police in their community. The calls to reform the penal system were part of a broader and long-time call to abolish the racist policies of the aforementioned Northern Territory Intervention. Senior Warlpiri Elder Harry Jakamarra Nelson condemned the Northern Territory Intervention, which he labelled as an 'occupation' of our lands due to its control of welfare payments and compulsory leasing of lands. He identified the expenditure on police and prisons as well as the stealing of Warlpiri children, the disempowerment of their local council and their lack of housing as all linked to the killing of Kumunjayi Walker:

> The biggest lot of money ever spent on Yuendumu was more than 7 million dollars to build a new police station …
>
> We have more police than ever, and more people in jail than ever. The welfare mob keep taking children away and don't respect our extended families.

We want our local council back, we want our houses back, we want police to respect us and stop wearing guns. (Quoted in Hocking and Bhole, 2020)

The demands of Jakamarra and the Warlpiri community at Yuendumu reveal that abolishing one carceral site is not enough for First Nations sovereignty or even human rights. The entire fabric of the colonial system needs to be unweaved for there to be peace, justice and sovereignty.

Abolition as sovereignty enactment

In order for abolition to challenge the colonial carceral system, it must do more than abolish the prison. Prison is the extension of several centuries of policies, laws and practices designed to complete the dispossession of sovereign First Nations. It is entwined with systems of land occupation, enforced child removals, enslaved labour and lethal policing of First Nations. Abolition must seek to dismantle processes of 'structured dispossession' that give 'ongoing state access to the land and resources' and buttress 'colonial state-formation, settlement, and capitalist development' (Coulthard, 2014: 6–7). As evident from Yellowknives Dene scholar Glen Coulthard's characterization of structured dispossession, imprisonment is only one aspect of a broader agenda of colonial state formation and land invasion. The prison provides one avenue for settler colonialism's persistent tendency, as Wolfe (2013) explains, to drive out First Nations people.

It is also not enough to focus on dismantling the nonpenal aspects of colonialism in the hope that the hyperincarceration of First Nations people will be in turn remedied. The disproportionate incarceration of First Nations peoples is not a product of a 'malfunctioning' system that can be cured by addressing 'underlying' problems. The system is not 'broken'; it is doing what it is designed for – fulfilling the role set out for it under colonialism (Roach, 2022). Hyperincarceration is an outcome of deliberate intervention by the colonial state and it therefore is nonsensical that there can be some 'normal' level of involvement in this alien white settler justice system which has been imposed from outside, without First Nations consent, and despite the fact that First Nations people were already regulated by existing laws: *their own* (Blagg, 2016). As Seth Adema (2016: 13) states, the incarceration of First Nations people 'is not a symptom of colonialism, it is colonialism'. For this reason, Palawa woman Professor Maggie Walter (2016: 89–90) remarks that studies in criminology need to be couched in past and ongoing struggles for land and sovereignty.

The belief that criminal 'justice' systems urgently need to be transformed and decolonized, rather than simply reformed or democratized, has become a critical demand of First Nations anti-prison advocates across the colonies of Australia, Canada and Aotearoa/New Zealand (Jackson 2017a; O'Brien, 2017; Canning, 2022; Mundine, 2022; Pranteau et al, 2022). While other approaches to abolition are based on the axes of race and class and challenging structural discrimination and organized abandonment (Wilson Gilmore, 2020), First Nations voices also emphasize that abolition is also about harnessing connections to Country and First Nations laws, cultures and relationships. Tracey McIntosh, a Ngā i Tū hoe mother and grandmother and Professor of Indigenous Studies, points to anti-colonial abolition as Indigenous empowerment and sovereignty:

> Abolition is about what it is to be human and what our responsibilities are to each other. That is a really important element of abolition, particularly anti-colonial abolition, that allows us to really think much more closely and much more strongly about our relationships with each other, with our lands, with our waters and with our people – people that we love, people that we protect, and those people who have been harmed and who have gone on and harmed others. An important element of abolition is thinking about ways of creating a space where everyone can flourish. Abolition sits in a space, that does not ignore harm, but recognizes what produces and reproduces harm. Abolition is an emancipatory project. (Quoted in Pranteau et al, 2022: 78–79)

Abolish the colonial carceral system and not just the prison

Abolition provides an important language in framing the dismantling of carceral sites. In colonial societies, emancipation requires the colonial camps to release their clutches on First Nations lives. It means transferring power to sovereign holders and, in the words of Alfred (2005: 131), 'resurgence' of First Nations '*spirit* and *consciousness*', '*contention* with the very foundations of colonialism'. Anything less than a paradigm shift will simply perpetuate the dominance of the colonial realm and white possession (Coulthard, 2014; Moreton-Robinson, 2015).

Criminology's tendency to fetishize the prison as the master form of incarceration elides the diversity of colonial camps intended to eradicate First Nations sovereignty and maintain settler colonial power. It also had a proclivity to only seeing the institutions and overlooking First Nations societies, organizations and families that both have and are the solutions. Turning to First Nations penal abolitionists, as discussed in this chapter, we can see their radical challenge to carceral capitalism is embedded in resistance to colonial relations and practices in all their manifestations. Equally, abolitionist imagining needs to apply to the entire colonial carceral archipelago, including its penal prison, its welfare prison, its psychiatric prison and its racialized capitalist prison.

Māori change maker and scholar Moana Jackson (2017b) reminds us that colonial practices of domination and control, including prisons, are foreign concepts to First Nations people. They are antithetical to First Nations ontologies, epistemologies and methodologies. Abolishing the colonial matrix of power requires disrupting all its carceral sites and shifting the focus to First Nations sovereignty. This is not a pipe dream as First Nations peoples' refusal of the colonial hegemony already diminishes colonial attempts to render First Nations lives *homo sacer*. Abolitionists should honour First Nations calls for sovereignty, land reclamation and the strengthening of First Nations governance and law. It is First Nations ways of knowing, doing and being that provide learnings for abolitionists to imagine a community without prisons.

Note

[1] See, for example, Aborigines Protection Act 1886 (WA); Aboriginal Protection Act and Restriction of the Sale of Opium Act 1897 (Qld); Aborigines Protection Act 1909 (NSW); Aborigines Act 1911 (SA); Aboriginals Ordinance 1911 (NT); and Aboriginals Ordinance 1918 (Cth).

References

Adema, S. (2016) 'More than stone and iron: Indigenous history and incarceration in Canada, 1834–1996', doctoral thesis, Wilfrid Laurier University.

Agamben, G. (1998) *Homo Sacer: Sovereign Power and Bare Life*, D. Heller-Roazen (trans.), Stanford: Stanford University Press.

Agamben, G. (2000) *Means without Ends: Notes on Politics*, V. Binetti and C. Casarino (trans.), Minneapolis: University of Minnesota Press.

Alexander, M. (2020) *The New Jim Crow: Mass Incarceration in the Age of Colorblindness*, New York: New Press.

Alfred, T. (2005) *Wasáse: Indigenous Pathways of Action and Freedom*, Toronto: University of Toronto Press.

Allam, L. (2021) '"Beyond heartbreaking": 500 Indigenous deaths in custody since 1991 Royal Commission', *The Guardian* (6 December). Available from: https://www.theguardian.com/australia-news/2021/dec/06/beyond-heartbreaking-500-indigenous-deaths-in-custody-since-1991-royal-commission [Accessed 15 September 2024].

Anthony, T. (2017) 'Are First Australians the most imprisoned people on Earth?', *The Conversation* (6 June). Available from: https://theconversation.com/factcheck-are-first-australians-the-most-imprisoned-people-on-earth-78528 [Accessed 15 September 2024].

Anthony, T. and Blagg, H. (2013) 'STOP in the name of who's law? Driving and the regulation of contested space in Central Australia', *Social & Legal Studies*, 22(1): 43–66.

Anthony, T. and Cubillo, E. (2020) 'Kumanjayi Walker murder trial will be a first in NT for an Indigenous death in custody', *The Conversation* (28 October). Available from: https://theconversation.com/kumanjayi-walker-murder-trial-will-be-a-first-in-nt-for-an-indigenous-death-in-custody-why-has-it-taken-so-long-148922 [Accessed 15 September 2024].

Anthony, T. and Sherwood, J. (2018) 'Post-disciplinary responses to positivism's punitiveness', *Journal of Global Indigeneity*, 3(1): 1–33.

Anthony, T., Sentance, G. and Behrendt, L. (2021) '"We're not being treated like mothers": listening to the stories of First Nations mothers in prison', *Laws*, 10(3): 1–18.

Arendt, H. (1966) *The Origins of Totalitarianism*, New York: Harvest Books.

Behrendt, L. (2002) 'Self-determination and Indigenous policy: the rights framework and practical outcomes', *Journal of Indigenous Policy*, 1: 43–58.

Behrendt, L. and Watson, N. (2007) 'Shifting ground: why land rights and native title have not delivered social justice', *Journal of Indigenous Policy*, 8: 94–102.

Blagg, H. (2008) 'Colonial critique and critical criminology: issues in Aboriginal law and Aboriginal violence', in T. Anthony and C. Cunneen (eds) *The Critical Criminology Companion*, Sydney: Hawkins Press, pp 129–143.

Blagg, H. (2016) *Crime, Aboriginality and the Decolonisation of Justice* (2nd edn), Sydney: Hawkins Press.

Blagg, H. and Anthony, T. (2019) *Decolonising Criminology: Imagining Justice in a Postcolonial World*, London: Palgrave Macmillan.

British Parliamentary Select Committee (1837) *Aboriginal Tribes (British Settlements)*, London: Aborigines Protection Society. Available from: http://apo.org.au/system/files/61306/apo-nid61306-14546.pdf [Accessed 15 September 2024].

Canning, K. (2022) 'A cacophony of mayhem: colonialist prisons', *Journal of Prisoners on Prisons*, 30: 504–515.

Coulthard, G. (2014) *Red Skin, White Masks: Rejecting the Colonial Politics of Recognition*, Minneapolis: University of Minnesota Press.

Cunneen, C., Baldry, E., Brown, D., Brown, Schwartz, M., and Steel, A. (2013) *Penal Culture and Hyperincarceration: The Revival of the Prison*, Farnham: Ashgate.

Davis, A. (2003) *Abolition Democracy: Beyond Prison, Torture and Empire*, New York: Seven Stories Press.

Day, A. (2020) 'Without accountability there is no justice for my mother's death in Australian police custody', *The Guardian* (3 September). Available from: https://www.theguardian.com/commentisfree/2020/sep/03/without-accountability-there-is-no-justice-for-my-mothers-death-in-australian-police-custody [Accessed 15 September 2024].

Diken, B. and Laustsen, C.B. (2002) 'Zones of indistinction: security, terror, and bare life', *Space and Culture*, 5(3): 290–307.

Eggleston, E. (1976) *Fear, Favour or Affection: Aborigines and the Criminal Law in Victoria, South Australia and Western Australia*, Canberra: Australian National University Press.

Fanon, F. (1986) *Black Skin, White Masks*, London: Pluto Press.

Fanon, F. (1991) *The Wretched of the Earth*, New York: Grove Weidenfled.

Foucault M. (1977) *Discipline and Punish: The Birth of the Prison*, A.M. Sheridan Smith (trans.), London: Penguin.

Garland, D. (2001) *The Culture of Control: Crime and Social Order in Contemporary Society*, Oxford: Oxford University Press.

George, N. (2009) *Chairpersons Report. North Australian Aboriginal Justice Agency Annual Report*. Available from www.naaja.org.au/wp-content/uploads/2014/05/Annual-Report-2009.pdf [Accessed 15 September 2024].

Gibson, P. (2012) 'Return to the ration days: the Northern Territory intervention – grassroots experience and resistance', *Ngiya: Talk the Law*, 3: 58–107.

Green, N. (1998) *Far from Home: Aboriginal Prisoners of Rottnest Island 1838– 1931*, Perth: University of Western Australia Press.

Guha, R. (1997) *Dominance without Hegemony: History and Power in Colonial India*, Cambridge, MA: Harvard University Press.

Havemann, P. (2005) 'Denial, modernity and exclusion: Indigenous placelessness in Australia', *Macquarie Law Journal*, 5: 57–80.

Hocking, R. and Bhole, A. (2020) '"Guns is not our law, it is not our culture": calls for systemic change as Kumanjayi Walker matter back in court', *NITV News* (25 June). Available from: https://www.sbs.com.au/nitv/article/2020/06/25/guns-not-our-law-it-not-our-culture-calls-systemic-change-kumanjayi-walker-matter [Accessed 15 September 2024].

Jackson, M. (2017a) 'FIRE presentation 2016'. Available from: https://www.youtube.com/watch?v=mPnf0cbFIuo&t=39s [Accessed 15 September 2024].

Jackson, M. (2017b) 'Prison should never be the only answer', *E-Tangata* (14 October). Available from: https://e-tangata.co.nz/comment-and-analysis/moana-jackson-prison-should-never-be-the-only-answer/ [Accessed 15 September 2024].

Kaba, M. (2021) *We Do This 'Til We Free Us: Abolitionist Organizing and Transforming Justice*, Chicago: Haymarket Books.

Kilroy, D. and Lean, T. (2022) 'The not so easy, simple solution', *Journal of Prisoners on Prisons*, 30(2): 91–95.

Mbembé, J.A. (2003) 'Necropolitics', *Public Culture*, 15(1): 11–40.

McQuire, A. (2016) 'The indignities that killed Ms Dhu are the same indignities hurting her family', *Medium* (28 September). Available from: https://medium.com/@amymcquire/the-indignities-that-killed-ms-dhu-are-the-same-indignities-hurting-her-family-5320278fd433 [Accessed 15 September 2024].

Mignolo, W.D. (2007) 'Introduction: coloniality of power and de-colonial thinking', *Cultural Studies*, 21(2–3): 155–167.

Moreton-Robinson, A. (2015) *White Possessive*, Minneapolis: University of Minnesota Press.

Mundine, K. (2022) 'Anti-carceral and anti-colonial work on the ground', *Journal of Prisoners on Prisons*, 30: 26–27.

O'Brien, E. (2017) 'Beyond prison', *Overland* (16 May). Available from: https://overland.org.au/2017/05/beyond-prison [Accessed 15 September 2024].

O'Shane, P. (1992) 'Aborigines and the criminal justice system', in C. Cunneen (ed.) *Aboriginal Perspectives on Criminal Justice*, Sydney: Institute of Criminology, University of Sydney, pp 3–6.

Pranteau, S., McIntosh, T., Anthony T. and Chartrand, V. (2022) 'Anti-colonial abolition: international context', *Journal of Prisoners on Prisons*, 30: 26–27.

Price, J. (2015) *Prison and Social Death*, New Brunswick, NJ: Rutgers University Press.

Quijano, A. (2007) 'Coloniality and modernity/rationality', *Cultural Studies*, 21(2–3): 168–178.

Roach, V. (2022) 'The system is not failing, it is working to harm First Nations people', *Journal of Prisoners on Prisons*, 30: 54–56.

Royal Commission into Aboriginal Deaths in Custody (1991) *National Report*, Canberra: Australian Government Publishing Service.

Said, E. (1993) *Culture and Imperialism*, London: Vintage.

Schmitt, C. (2005) *Political Theology: Four Chapters on the Concept of Sovereignty*, G.D. Schwab (trans.), Chicago: University of Chicago Press.

Shaw, W. (2012) 'Tangentyere CEO calls for help from "fair-minded" Australians', press release (4 June), Tangentere Council Inc., Alice Springs, Northern Territory. Available from: http://concernedaustralians.com.au/media/stronger_futures_yolngu/Tangentyere_Council.pdf [Accessed 15 September 2024].

Simpson, A. (2014) *Mohawk Interruptus: Political Life across the Borders of Settler States*, Durham, NC: Duke University Press.

Spivak, G.C. (1996) *The Spivak Reader: Selected Works of Gayatri Chakravorty Spivak*. D. Landry and G. Maclaen (eds), London: Routledge.

Sylvester, C. (2006) 'Bare life as a development/postcolonial problematic', *Geographical Journal*, 172(1): 66–77.

Tedmanson, D. (2008) 'Isle of exception: sovereign power and Palm Island', *Critical Perspectives on International Business*, 4(2–3): 142–165.

Wacquant, L. (2014) 'Class, race & hyperincarceration in revanchist America', *Socialism and Democracy*, 28(3): 35–56.

Walter, M. (2016) 'Indigenous peoples, research and ethics', in M. Adorjan and R. Ricciardelli (eds) *Engaging with Ethics in International Criminological Research*, Abingdon: Routledge, pp 87–105.

Watego, C. (2021) *Another Day in the Colony*, Brisbane: University of Queensland Press.

Watson, I. (2016) 'First Nations and the colonial project', *Inter Gentes*, 1(1): 30–39.

Western Australian Coroner's Court (2009) *Inquest into Death of Ian Ward, Record of Investigation into Death, Western Australian State Coroner*, Ref. 9/09.

Wolfe, P. (2006) 'Settler colonialism and the elimination of the native', *Journal of Genocide Research*, 8(4): 387–409.

Wolfe, P. (2013) 'Comparing colonial and racial regimes', *CASAR Lecture*, American University of Beirut. Available from: https://www.youtube.com/watch?v=xwj5bcLG8ic&t=2058s [Accessed 15 September 2024].

Wilson Gilmore, R. (2020) 'Geographies of racial capitalism with Ruth Wilson Gilmore', *Antipode Online*. Available from: https://antipodeonline.org/geographies-of-racial-capitalism [Accessed 15 September 2024].

11

Southerning Nonpunitive and Abolitionist Feminism

Valeria Vegh Weis

Introduction

The criminal justice system is not only old-fashioned and patriarchal but is also part of a centuries-long history of resolving criminal conflicts through punishment and humiliation under the false guise of resocialization and prevention. Criminology and the criminal justice system have been privileged architects of this punitive quagmire. To confront these historical shortcomings, women, queer collectives and scholars from the margins have come forward to show that another world is possible.

While the first feminist waves were focused on the Global North – to be introduced in the following section – the current fourth wave is heavily influenced by insights from the Global South. Moreover, this fourth wave does not just represent a geographical expansion of the movement but also entails a transformation of the whole feminist framework. Building from the Black abolitionist tradition from the US and the UK, this wave expands the discussion on anti-punitive and criminal justice system abolitionist ideas that reject the criminal justice system as the unique response to female oppression and gender-based violence.

Within this framework, the Argentinian feminist movement has been at the forefront of radical changes over the last decade. In general terms, changes that resulted from this bottom-up/top-down dialogues included the legalization of the equal right to marriage,[1] the right to abortion,[2] the enforcement of quotas to include trans people in the public administration,[3] the development of a pension system that recognizes housework and childrearing as labour[4] and the emergence of the right to identify as nonbinary on the national identity card[5] (see more in Ministerio de las Mujeres, Géneros y Diversidad, 2021a).

A further outcome is the Ministry of Women, Genders, and Diversity,[6] first led by Elizabeth Gómez Alcorta, a longstanding human rights activist with an excellent track record (*Revista Anfibia*, 2021).

Particularly connected to the abolitionist claims, one of the feminist movement's main demands is to obtain broader responses to address gender violence together with the passing of a feminist judicial reform that responds to various challenges in law and justice, particularly to crime and punishment. In numbers, 48 per cent of Argentinians distrust the judiciary, nine out of every ten do not have confidence in the impartiality of the judges, and 227 femicides happened in the period from January to October 2021 alone (equivalent to one every 23 hours). Furthermore, 12 per cent of them were perpetrated by police officers (*Resumen Latinoamericano*, 2021). This delayed reform is still pending.

Based on this framework, this study will explore the legacies of feminist abolitionism from the Global North, particularly through the first three feminist waves, to later focus on the nonpunitive responses developed in the Global South within the ongoing fourth feminist wave. It will provide an overview of the situation of gender-based violence in Argentina followed by the anti-punitive and abolitionist initiatives developed within the feminist movement, academia and the state as part of a confrontation with carceral feminism. This includes the identification of the three fallacies of the punitive discourse as well as three nonpunitive approaches that are currently being developed to tackle gender-based violence without resorting to the criminal justice system. Overall, by exploring the case of Argentina, the chapter aims to explore lessons and challenges within Southern abolitionist criminology.

Abolitionist feminist thoughts in the Global North

Feminist history is often narrated through waves. The first feminist wave (in the 18th and 19th centuries) was marked by retributive works such as Olympe de Gouges's demand for equality in civil and political rights, mainly women's right to education and the right to vote. 'Liberal feminism' led the second wave, which showed how women are socialized into specific roles with a certain status and power that perpetuate inequality between genders (Chesney-Lind, 2006).

With the third wave, it soon became clear that mainstream (malestream) criminology had not recognized existing inequalities – including gender disparities – and that even critical criminology, which did study the impact of class in crime and punishment, had not paid enough attention to gender issues. As criminology faced these shortcomings, publications on gender and crime with a critical perspective on incarceration and punishment were generated, including abolitionist perspectives. These included 'Prison for Women' (Heidensohn, 1969), *Any Woman's Blues: A Critical Overview of*

Women, Crime and the Criminal Justice System (Klein and Kress, 1976), *Women, Crime and Criminology: A Feminist Critique* (Smart, 1977a), 'Criminological theory: its ideology and implications concerning women' (Smart, 1977b) and *Women's Imprisonment: A Study in Social Control* (Carlen, 1983).

Furthermore, within this third wave, Black radical feminism advanced the debate with a masterful critique of essentialism: no one woman can speak for all, but rather women (in plural). The big shortcoming, they proclaimed, was that, just as criminology had long claimed to speak for humanity when it had only focused on (already prisonalized) men, feminism was claiming to speak for all women when it spoke only for white, bourgeois women. Particularly, building upon slavery abolitionist Sojourner Truth, who posed the famous question 'Ain't I a woman?', bell hooks (1987) criticised how, up to that moment, feminists had focused on the discrimination of women under patriarchy while struggles against racism were only concerned with Black men. Are there only white women and Black men? What about those who suffer double oppression, that of race and gender? If I am Black, bell hooks (1987) asked, am I not also a woman? Since then, research on gender and race has elucidated relevant discrepancies in criminalization and victimization (Bernard, 2012; Koons-Witt and Schram, 2016; Potter, 2016; Pérez, 2017).

This third wave also opened the discussion about the futility and iatrogenic features of prison and the criminal justice system, even when dealing with gender-based violence. These 'anti-punitive feminists', 'anti-carceral feminists' or even 'feminism abolitionists', located mainly in the US and the UK, confronted the so-called 'carceral feminism'. While carceral feminism argues that the penal system is a way of curbing gender violence and it therefore embraces demands for the creation of new criminal offences and harsher punishments, the abolitionist perspectives stated that the criminal justice system has never solved social problems, let alone structural violence linked to capitalism and patriarchy, which is, in fact, a function of penal control. In this vein, from an abolitionist perspective, it has been argued that it is not enough to have a 'better' or 'more human' criminal justice system. It is not 'reform' but the 'abolition' of the criminal justice system that is at stake. In other words, while carceral feminism insists on the criminalization of stalking, more punishment for gender-related crimes and the prohibition of restorative justice mechanisms and early release, critical abolition activists have been warning of the risks of punitive solutions and imprisonment (Cole and Phillips, 2008; Balfour, 2021). Even more broadly, feminist abolitionism involves a critical stand based on calling for the dismantling of all the apparatuses of oppression, including carceral institutions, and challenging racial capitalism (Davis et al, 2022).

The pamphlet *Alternatives to Holloway* (1972) created by Radical Alternatives to Prison and written in part by Carol Smart protested against the rebuilding of the women's prison in North London, while the 1970s Santa Cruz Women's Prison

Project involved different activities of mobilization against prisons and provided support for the prisoner movement.[7] Similarly, *Instead of Prison: A Handbook for Abolitionists*, inspired by the Quaker feminist work of Faye Honey Knopp, gathered nine perspectives from prison abolitionists that set a clear agenda for change (see Morris, 1976).[8] Likewise, in the UK in 1983, Chris Tchialovsky and Pat Carlen set up the abolitionist pressure group *Women in Prison*, which continues today.[9] In continuation of these efforts, the national organization *Critical Resistance* in the US was created in 1998 (see James, Chapter 3 in this volume) centring its work on the prison industrial complex – defined as 'the overlapping interests of government and industry that use surveillance, policing, and imprisonment as solutions to economic, social and political problems' – but its agenda also chimed with feminist concerns (Davis et al, 2022).

Furthermore, feminist abolitionism emerging during the third wave was not about delegitimizing the criminal justice system alone, but about building alternatives and life-affirming institutions (Gilmore, 2019). In this direction, the 1998 conference on the prison industrial complex began a new phase of anti-prison activism in the US with demands such as 'schools not jails' and 'education not incarceration' (for discussion of this and other related conferences at the time, see James, Chapter 3 in this volume). The presenters at the conference also argued for an abolitionist perspective that includes working critically through the language (for example, it is not about 'criminals', but about 'criminalized people'); considering intersectionality as a core aspect of the criminalization process; and acknowledging that people in prison are 'subjects capable of understanding and transforming their own conditions' (Davis et al, 2022: 54). Concrete proposals included preventative community-based responses aimed at reducing the incidence of gender and sexual violence and addressing harm without calling the police. The 21st century would see a reinvigoration of this movement with a strong impetus from the Global South within the so-called fourth wave.

The fourth wave: nonpunitive feminism and the Global South

The fourth feminist wave brought with it a broader understanding of intersectionality. It is not only about 'race' and gender; rather, more interweaving factors multiply (or not) the situation of a vulnerability to violence, including glocalization. Thus, patterns of criminalization and victimization have a stronger impact on women and queer peoples located in or coming from the Global South. Following this stand, the fourth feminist wave, with a strong impulse from the South, brought the concepts of diversity, gender identity,[10] sisterhood, sexual rights (particularly the right to abortion) and gender violence, but also colonialism and neocolonialism. Indeed, decolonial feminism argues that gender as an organizing principle of society only appeared in Latin America after colonization. Indigenous communities granted equal access to public and symbolic power to women, their languages and kinship systems did not subordinate women to men and there was no sexual division of labour (Mendoza, 2010).

To dig into the Southern influence in the fourth wave, with these components of radical intersectionality, along with neoliberal and anti-colonial critique, the following will look at the anti-carceral contributions within the Argentina feminist movement.

Gender-based violence in Argentina

In 2010, Wanda Taddei was burnt alive by her partner, a musician of the rock band Callejeros. This triggered a 'contagious effect', with 136 cases of women burnt alive by their partners between 2010 and 2012 (Carabajal, 2014). In 2012, as a result of the public effect of the femicides and following the logic of carceral feminism, Argentina passed a specific criminal statute increasing the punishment for homicides against a woman when she is killed because of her gender.[11] The law did not stop the death count.

In May 2015, the body of Chiara Páez, a 14-year-old girl from Santa Fe, was found buried in her boyfriend's backyard. Chiara was pregnant at the time. This was the breaking point for the emergence of the so-called 'Not One More!' movement to stop femicides in the country for real. More than 300,000 people gathered at Congress Square (de los Santos, 2016). Notably, the 'Not Even One Less' claim was made by a Mexican and feminist poet, Susana Chavez, killed in Ciudad Juarez in 2011: 'Not even one woman less, not even one more dead woman' was her usual statement in the demonstrations (Chávez, 2015). The movement in Argentina has been growing since then, gathering demands for gender equality, legal abortion and the end of femicides, without necessarily relying on criminalization (de Gomes, 2021). In its platform, the *Ni una menos* movement explicitly described itself as 'anti-punitive' and claims:

> Women who work in the informal economy are persecuted, sex workers criminalised, activists prosecuted, and feminist demonstrations and activism are subjected to repression ... the enactment of laws that exacerbate the humanitarian crisis in prisons and the proposal of tougher sentences aggravate our situation because they do not only evade comprehensive public policies aimed at prevention, care and accompaniment, but on top, this demagogic discourse only appears when we [the victims] are already dead. (Ni una menos, 2023)

The femicides and gender-based violence did not stop in the meantime. In terms of judgments made, one of the most outrageous cases was the trial for the 2016 femicide of Lucía Pérez, when three male judges, instead of focusing on the young woman's murder, inquired into the victim's private life and sexual choices (Sanchez, 2018). This case was no exception: sentencing often ends up being a moral judgement on how the victims lived; how they exercised their motherhood; how they bonded with other people; and even on whether and how they dedicated themselves to housework or the care of their bodies.

A striking case in this regard was that of María Ovando: she was the mother of 12 children, yet did not have the means to take care of all of them. Instead of blaming the state for failing to provide social welfare, the courts sentenced her twice: once when one of her daughters died of malnutrition and on a second occasion for not protecting one of her daughters and one of her granddaughters from sexual assault. Ovando was sentenced to 20 years' imprisonment in 2020, while the men who perpetrated the sexual assault received a less severe sentence (*Cosecha Roja*, 2020; Hayes, 2021).

Aligned with the statements of Northern abolitionist feminism, this structural injustice may be associated with women being absent from the three branches of the state and particularly from the justice system. In Argentina, only 30 per cent of decision-making positions at the federal level are held by women, and the heads of the Public Prosecutor's Office in all 23 provinces and the autonomous city of Buenos Aires are men. Furthermore, even when 61 per cent of the personnel are women, these employees are limited to lower or intermediate-level positions (Corte Suprema de Justicia de la Nación, 2019). If we go further and take up the concept of intersectionality, observing any court building in Argentina provides enough information to show that the white, upper-class men who lead the judiciary hardly represent the diverse national population in terms of gender, skin colour or social class (Corte Suprema de Justicia de la Nación, 2019). The challenge is how to confront systemic gender-based violence and a faulted justice system without resorting to more punishment.

A nonpunitive paradigm to confront gender-based violence in Argentina

Building on the abolitionist experience of the Global North, many critical feminist voices in the Global South within the fourth feminist wave have embraced a nonpunitive perspective, while adding further arguments connected with structural selectivity, neoliberalism, global inequalities and neocolonialism. Moreover, even the state and particularly the Head of the Ministry of Women, Genders and Diversity (created in 2019), Eli Gomez Alcorta, who came from the feminist grassroots movement to be later appointed as a state representative, has embraced this growing anti-punitive approach. The Ministry has avoided resorting to further criminalization and, instead, has been fostering holistic mechanisms to prevent, assist and eradicate gender-based violence and gender inequality.

The fallacies of the punitive response

The lack of creativity and epistemological confinement

The first critique raised by the Southern feminist critical movement is that punitive approaches seem to propose solid solutions, but this is just a fallacy that masks a lack of creativity and epistemological confinement. This is because they are presented as the only option, when in truth there are multiple ways to address violence, which remain invisible because of the penal system's monopolistic response. Perez and Huarte (2020), two Argentinian researchers who specialized in gender, clarify the matter: 'Punitivity is an epistemic prison, in that it creates the illusion that we are freely choosing from a wide range of options, when in fact we are moving within a very limited space' (Pérez and Huarte, 2020).

Luciana Sánchez (2006), a queer feminist Argentinian attorney, reflects that when women are victimized, they are pushed to file criminal proceedings and no other option to claim their rights is presented to them. There is a lack of alternative solutions: the system only makes one option available to women to deal with violence. Nuñes Rebolledo (2019), a critical feminist criminologist from Mexico, adds: 'The overestimation of criminal law as a symbolic means of prevention ... has led to the concealment of the structural and material factors that sustain gender violence, especially against women' (Rebolledo, 2019: 72).

On the contrary, when it is possible to articulate that the penal solution is one option among many, other paths appear (community, restorative and civil) that are focused on the victim's wellbeing and the broken social relationships underlying the conflict. Such comprehensive approaches seek to address the economic, social, educational and legal causes and consequences of violence instead of focusing solely on the specific act of physical or verbal violence. Usually embraced through interdisciplinarity, these approaches also make it clear that complex phenomena, such as gender-based violence, can hardly be solved via a legal mechanism alone. Finally, empowering solutions change the power relationship between victim and perpetrator, making space for long-term transformative processes.

The individualist and ex post features

Southern voices have also called attention to the fact that punitive responses arguably tackle the cause of the problem as soon as possible, but this is, again, a fallacy. When looking at the real functioning of the criminal justice systems, it becomes clear that they reduce the complex problem of gender-based violence to an individual phenomenon and that they only intervene when it is already too late.

In terms of the individual nature of the criminal justice system, it only pursues behaviours considered harmful to a specific person (for example, Peter sexually abused Maria). This means that they are abstracted from the system of gender inequality and oppression against women, which frames the conflict (that is, the fact that Peter and Maria are part of a much broader and complex network of unequal power relations). Therefore, when confronting gender violence through criminal law, the best-case scenario is the conviction of an individual perpetrator, that is, a person isolated from the society in which we live and from the other factors that promote and induce inequality and discrimination more broadly. This reduces the horizon of action to individualized responses in the form of criminal punishment.

In this vein, Ileana Arduino, a feminist researcher and attorney from Argentina, claims that if the feminist movement is trying to change the structural nature of violence and demand radical transformations, it cannot do so through punitive solutions that are only individually based, enhance violence and do not question the system as a whole (Arduino, 2017). Instead, from an anti-punitive perspective, violence is perceived as structural violence: 'As we become conscious of the abuses, subjugation, and violence we feel urged to take action ... Now, we are all collectively challenging these situations, renaming formerly naturalised practices as violence legitimised by the patriarchal culture and pointing out the existing gender hierarchy' (Arduino, 2018, np).

As mentioned earlier, these added punitive reactions are not only individual-based, but also leave only one temporal possibility open: the *ex post* solution, that is, a reaction that can only come after the violence has already taken place. The police, the courts and the prisons only intervene when the harmful act has already been committed and the woman is already suffering the consequences of the violence. This approach therefore removes the possibility of focusing on preventive solutions to ensure that violence does not take place. Thus, as a privileged option, criminalization involves assuming that gender violence will never end, that there is no possible preventive function and that the most we can do is something after it occurs and on an individual basis alone. In sum, the penal solution is defeatist and it has no confidence that an end to violence is an achievable aim.

The selectivity of the criminal justice system

Even when the punitive solution is arguably applicable to all, this is also a fallacy. Southern and particularly Latin American criminologists have been calling attention to the selective features of the criminal justice systems throughout history, with gender being no exception. While the criminal justice system is slow, inefficient and iatrogenic when dealing with gender-based violence, it is straightforward when dealing with women who escape the socially imposed roles of submission.

In this vein, Raúl Zaffaroni, a leading scholar in the continent, has identified the book *The Cautio Criminalis* written by Friedrich Spee – which portrayed 'witches' (rebellious women) as the most dangerous criminals of the time – the first criminological (and misogynistic) analysis in history in the 16th century (Zaffaroni, 2011). As further clarified by Vegh Weis (2017), in this context, witches were a kind of marginalized category that threatened the social ideal of a docile workforce. Witchcraft and Poor Laws worked together to ensure the necessary conditions for the foundation of capitalism. Thus, the original overcriminalization of women served to break cultural patterns and create new social bases outside the matriarchal tradition, which was exercising a function of resistance against the new relations of domination.

In turn, Gago (2013), a leader of the *Ni una menos* movement, specifically connects this original persecution of witches with colonization. She states that the accusations of witchcraft were a way of criminalizing precolonial beliefs. In her words: 'The persecution, criminalisation and massacre under the accusation of witchcraft experienced in Europe is transferred to the colonies, expanding the map of the war against women beyond Europe, towards Africa and India, and beyond women, towards Indigenous Peoples and slaves' (Gago, 2013: 92).

Since then and until today, the accusation of being a 'bad mom' has also enhanced the selective deployment of the criminal justice system against (mostly marginalized) women through the enforcement of the criminal offences of abortion and infanticide (di Corleto, 2018). Moreover, criminalization goes hand in hand with 'pathologisation': it is common for criminalized women to be labelled as 'wild', 'crazy', 'hysterical' and 'abnormal', as opposed to being socially legitimized and 'normal' women and mothers (Bassotti, 2021, np).

As intersectionality points out, criminalization on these grounds is even stronger when the women are poor and/or trans. In terms of poverty and prior victimization, 60 per cent of incarcerated women in Argentina are charged with drug-related offences, while criminal cases based on these offences grew by 271 per cent between 1989 and 2008. A gender-based vulnerability underpins these changes (di Marco and Evans, 2020). In a similar line with US patterns (Becker and Mccorkel, 2011), female incarceration in Argentina also often involves a male co-offender. To give the numbers, 47 per cent of incarcerated women have a partner who is also in prison, while only 5 per cent of men are in the same situation. This seems to indicate that women often commit crimes that support or are supported by their companions. Moreover, 39 per cent of women reported having experienced partner abuse before the arrest, and 13.6 per cent were raped at least once.

In other words, the overcriminalization of women neglects the underlying gender-based violence, and it is a symptom of a broader flaw in a justice system that is unresponsive to female victimization.

Concerning trans women, in the Province of Buenos Aires, the most populated one in Argentina, the incarceration rate for this group is 1 in 73, which means that one trans or trans person is almost 7.3 times more likely to be incarcerated than a cisgender person. In 90 per cent of the cases, the accusation is drug trafficking, even if in a significant number of situations, the only evidence is a police statement, some money and a small dose of drugs, which is not for sale.[12]

To this is added that selectivity comes from not only the formal criminal justice system but also from other social control mechanisms, particularly the media. In Latin America, the media is owned by a handful of influential actors that have the power of creating common sense by repeating specific messages in different outlets day after day. María Florencia Actis (2021), an Argentinian researcher specializing in gender, explains how sexual and gender identities are forged and regulated in the media, reinvigorating the symbolic and material roles of inclusion/exclusion and the selective enforcement of social, sexual and institutional means of control. Actis (2021) shows how the terms 'woman' and 'crime' are always presented as exotic, reinforcing an idea of alienation between cis-women and these roles. This is done, for example, by assigning nicknames to female offenders, such as 'The Queen of Fuerte Apache', linking them with ideas of excess, ambition and despotism. When referring to women and crime, the media also includes information about their private lives and the arguably 'passionate' motives of their criminal behaviour in a specific situation. In contrast, Actis (2021) argues that trans women are presented as intrinsically criminals, regardless of the context.

The broad range of possibilities within nonpunitive responses to gender-based violence

Like abolitionism, Southern and decolonial perspectives also propose alternative ways of thinking through which reality can be explained, understood and transformed. On this basis, a broad range of nonpunitive responses to gender-based violence has been articulated by the Argentinian feminist social movement and scholarship as well as from the state.

Empowered local actors

The strong feminist movement in the country and the broad range of social organizations working locally means that the most relevant approaches to tackling gender-based violence have been articulated from the bottom up (even if some have been more recently institutionalized through the newly created Ministry). This happens not only in relation to gender-based violence but also when looking at preventive mechanisms to avoid the criminalization for abortion. For example, the network Socorristas en Red[13] is one of the main actors that has been granting access to safe and discreet abortion practices before legalization, which was, in turn, promoted by another grassroots network, the Campaña por el Aborto Legal, Seguro y Gratuito (Campaign for Legal, Safe and Free Abortion).

Acknowledging this background, the newly created Ministry set its agenda based on promoting social engagement with local actors. This included the creation of the Registry of Promoters of Gender Violence and Diversity,[14] which in the first ten days collected 14,000 applications for registration from people who are already working in social organizations, neighbourhood networks, political parties and local government structures. In the words of Gómez Alcorta, 'the central idea of this registry and of this network of promoters is to generate an articulation between the Ministry and the territories' (Fundación para el Estudio e Investigación de la Mujer, 2023). Following the same logic, even with limited success, the Ministry launched the Red Masks programme to encourage victims of gender-based violence to use this reference to get help from local pharmacists during the COVID-19 pandemic.

When looking at strategies to tackle the collateral consequences of punishment affecting particularly women and queer communities, there are also local actors taking the lead. Following the lessons from US Black abolitionism, women and queer people who experienced imprisonment themselves are the most well equipped to change the conditions that can lead to a cycle of incarceration (Davis et al, 2022). Among the many groups working on this area, the Yo No Fui (I Was Not/I Did Not Do It)[15] network has been operating since 2002 and defines itself as a transfeminist-anti-prison collective made up of women and LGBT+ who are going through or went through contexts of confinement in federal and provincial prisons in Buenos Aires and La Pampa. In these establishments, as well as in their headquarters, they provide arts, crafts and communication workshops that collaborate with the social and labour reintegration of those who participate. In this way, they constitute themselves as a reference in the collective of liberated. Currently, around 200 people are part of the six productive units of the cooperative: textile, bookbinding, screen printing and engraving, digital tools, audiovisual and editorial.

Achieving more rights

Tamar Pitch (2003) states that criminalization not only adds more criminal offences to the legislation but also changes the cognitive framework we use to approach social problems. She argues that, in contrast, achieving more rights for marginalized groups helps raise awareness about situations that were taken as natural and that can now be seen as problematic without resorting to criminal law.

Following this logic, the trans collectives in Argentina have been demanding a labour quota rather than criminalizing sex work, which is often the only income alternative for this group. In response to these demands, in 2021 Argentina approved Act 27.636 that guarantees access to the labour market for trans people. The law was named after two leading trans activists, Diana Sacayan and Lohana Berkins, and establishes that a minimum of 1 per cent of the governmental positions must be filled by trans people.[16]

Following all these inputs of focusing on expanding access to rights rather than enhancing criminalization, the Ministry of Women, Genders and Diversities also created the Producir (To Produce) programme devoted to providing economic and technical support to women and LGBT+ people so that they can create and strengthen community-based entrepreneurship projects. Again, in line with the aim to limit social control, these projects do not need to be legally registered.[17] Likewise, the Acercar Derechos (Bringing Rights Closer) programme provides legal, psychological and welfare assistance to people suffering gender-based violence, and to their families and communities to promote and facilitate access to and enforcement of their rights.[18]

Further policies include support for community projects already working on gender-based violence,[19] economic reparations for children of victims of femicide[20] and integral assistance to other relatives of victims of femicide.[21] In turn, the Acompañar (Accompany) programme provided a minimum wage for six months as well as psychosocial support to women and LGBT+ people who are at risk of gender-based violence and need economic assistance. Interestingly, in terms of the abolitionist perspective, the programme does not require a complaint to be presented before the police; instead, the testimony of the victim is sufficient to provide access.[22]

Comprehensive and preventive strategies

Against dark figures excluded from the criminal justice system, a first step to building comprehensive and preventive strategies specifically aimed at tackling gender-based violence has focused on gathering reliable data. Following this goal, the first self-managed and public register of patriarchal violence against cis and trans women was created within the grassroots movement. According to the Observatorio Lucía Perez, generated by the *La Vaca* magazine, there were 315 femicides in 2022 and 375 demonstrations against patriarchal violence.[23]

In terms of gender training, a specific programme aimed at tackling gender-based violence through nonpunitive prevention strategies was established through the Micaela Act 37499, which was passed in 2018 in honour of a victim of femicide. Interestingly, Micaela's parents were the ones who rejected punitive responses to address the killing of their daughter and pushed for this educational reform, aiming at gender training for all those working in the state (Figueroa, 2021). However, the law does not impose compulsory training and it has been implemented unevenly. This pending task is part of the overall feminist judicial reform that has been discussed in recent years, but is still waiting to be agreed upon and implemented.

Concerning nonpunitive comprehensive and early interventions to prevent gender-based violence, the Ministry of Women, Genders and Diversities relied on the collected data that states that almost 80 per cent of the femicides are perpetrated by someone close to the victim. In the words of the first woman to lead the Ministry of Women, Genders and Diversity, Eli Gómez Alcorta: 'There is a bond, a relationship, [the perpetrator is] the partner, the former partner, or a family member. It is not someone who meets you in the street, which would be more difficult to prevent ... [thus] it is possible to intervene based on early warnings ... information is key' (Fundación para el Estudio e Investigación de la Mujer, 2023).

Under this logic, the first legislation that set the basis of the Ministry's work was Act No. 26,485 on the Comprehensive Protection of Women, which introduced a nonpunitive and holistic paradigm. The Act refers not only to domestic violence but also to the different types and modalities of gender violence in the public space against women and people from the LGBT+ community. As the report of the Ministry explicitly highlights:

> When we talk about a comprehensive approach to gender-based violence, we say that we change the existing paradigm, going from the individual approach to the construction of the subjective and material conditions that can allow people suffering situations of gender-based violence to strengthen their independence. In other words, our interventions are not focused exclusively on the emergency, but on modifying the structural conditions that sustain situations of gender-based violence. (Ministerio de las Mujeres, Géneros y Diversidad, 2021a, np)

This comprehensive approach includes designing and implementing policies for the prevention, assistance, protection and strengthening of access to justice; modifying the cultural and structural patterns that sustain gender-based inequalities, including a diversity perspective as a cross-cutting approach to all existing state policies; engaging in evidence-based decision making; mainstreaming prevention and protection policies throughout all the state agencies and jurisdictions; territorially developing policies for the prevention of, assistance with and protection against gender violence; and working in networks with grassroots social and community organizations (Ministerio de las Mujeres, Géneros y Diversidad, 2021a).

The approach also includes preventing victimization and revictimization in state interventions by focusing on the aggressors rather than only on the victims. The assumption is that when seeking to build new gender-equal paradigms within the justice system, the crucial lesson is that gender is not something limited to women and queer collectives; instead, it also includes the male gender and masculinities, which should be conceived as another variable rather than the norm. Based on these convictions, the Ministry developed the National Plan of Action against Gender-Based Violence 2020–2022, which was designed on a participatory, interministerial, community-based and federal platform. The focus of the National Plan is on seeking to modify the subjective and material conditions of people suffering gender-based violence rather than only addressing the emergency; promoting their economic independence, through access to formal work, education and housing, while also providing comprehensive physical and mental health care; and incorporating the rights of the LGBT+ community (Ministerio de las Mujeres, Géneros y Diversidad, 2020, 2021b).[24]

Some of the implemented policies include the creation of a phone line (#144) that can also be accessed via WhatsApp to give more possibilities to get in touch with those victims cohabitating with their aggressor. In this way, women and LGBT+ as well as their family members and members of their community can receive support and counselling without necessarily relying on the criminal justice system. The staff who answer the phone calls and messages are lawyers, psychologists and social workers trained in gender-based violence.[25]

Particularly in terms of alternatives to incarceration (although not always outside the penal system) when the perpetrator has already committed the crime, proposals are discussed, ranging from victim-oriented policies such as anti-panic buttons, shelters and 24-hour hotlines, to policies involving the perpetrator such as through the use of electronic bracelets (attached to the perpetrator and victim) and disqualification from renting a house or carrying weapons (INECIP, 2022). However, more radical positions reject the role of the state as a potential saviour and rely on community support under the slogan 'The police do not take care of me, my friends do' (García, 2021).

Conclusion: Hearing Southern abolitionist feminist voices

This chapter has looked at the legacies of abolitionist feminist thoughts in the Global North, identifying the main ideas, assumptions, arguments and claims that travelled to the Global South. It has then proceeded to shed light on the fresh and more recent contributions that, in turn, have been developed in the

Global South within the fourth feminist wave. Throughout, a revitalization of the tensions between 'carceral feminism' and 'abolitionist/anti-punitive perspectives' has been matured and nourished with the discussions in the Global South.

In particular, the chapter has looked at the case of Argentina and has shed light on how nonpunitive Southern abolitionist feminist voices have identified three key fallacies within the supposedly miraculous punitive response to violence proposed by carceral feminism:

1. the promise of solid solutions, which is denounced as a mask that hides a lack creativity and an epistemological confinement;
2. the arguably punitive concern with the causes of gender-based violence, when indeed crime control is only addressing the problem on an individual and *ex post facto* basis; and
3. the punitive penal solution as arguably applicable to all, when the selective features of the criminal justice systems have been a common feature throughout history, with gender being no exception.

Faced with these various limitations of the penal approach, Argentinian nonpunitive feminist voices has warned that the gender perspective as a tool of analysis must be separated from the creation of new criminal offences, stricter punishments or more police. A nonpunitive approach instead invites us to move from the individual to the collective; from criminal justice to social justice; from the written record to careful dialogue; from copying and pasting precedents to a case-by-case approach; from the victim–victimizer opposition to the network of violence in which these two people are embedded; from punishment to reparation, and from late intervention to prevention. In concrete terms, the chapter has highlighted how the nonpunitive approach to gender-based violence has been moved forward by social movements, academia and the state. In particular, comprehensive and preventive strategies, empowering local social actors and achieving more rights have been the nonpunitive leading approach.

Under this framework and even though gender-based violence continues to be a major social problem with femicides continuously on the rise, Argentina has been at the forefront of the feminist movement in the fourth wave and today is implementing groundbreaking changes from below and from the top down without relying on more criminalization. The major pending challenge is carrying out a feminist judicial reform. Lessons from feminist abolitionists from the North and the South shed light on the fact that this reform needs to avoid more punishment, include gender equality on an intersectional basis, provide gender-sensitive training, overcome the bureaucratization and automatism of the justice system through reorganizing the courts in a way that ensures personal accountability, and embraces interdisciplinarity, including the democratization of the antique legal language and communication channels when speaking to the population.

Today, in the fourth wave and even with vital challenges still pending, the Southern feminist movement and the voices within it reverberate with critical ideas and projects led by all kinds of 'modern witches' ready to change everything that needs to be changed.

Notes

1. Act 26.618, https://identidadydiversidad.adc.org.ar/normativa/ley-26-618-matrimonio-igualitario-2010/
2. Act 27.610, https://www.argentina.gob.ar/noticias/ley-no-27610-acceso-la-interrupcion-voluntaria-del-embarazo-ive-obligatoriedad-de-brindar
3. Executive Order 721/2020, https://www.argentina.gob.ar/justicia/derechofacil/leysimple/cupo-laboral-personas-travestis-transexuales-transgenero
4. Act 24.476, https://tramitejubilacion.com.ar/tipos/ama-de-casa/#:~:text=Jubilacion%20para%20Amas%20de%20Casa,por%20el%20%C3%ADndice%20de%20movilidad
5. Executive Order 476/2021, https://www.argentina.gob.ar/justicia/derechofacil/leysimple/identidad-de-genero
6. Executive Order 7/2019, https://www.boletinoficial.gob.ar/detalleAviso/primera/232653/20200728
7. Santa Cruz Women's Prison Project Collection, https://freedomarchives.org/santa-cruz-womens-prison-project-collection/
8. This was the tone of the American Friends Service Committee's publication *Struggle for Justice: A Report on Crime and Punishment in America*, which argued against the construction of more prisons as a suitable response to overcrowded institutions. Instead, it stated: 'If prisons are overcrowded, ways should be found to cut back the mass of criminal laws and the types of enforcement that send so many people to prison' (American Friends Service Committee Working Party, 1971).
9. https://womeninprison.org.uk/about/our-story
10. Even when not homogeneous, the fourth wave generally embraces transfeminism or queer feminism. With this, the concept of woman moves further away from essentialism to embrace its conceptualization as a social construction and individual decision: I am a woman because I choose to be one. In criminology, this involves including under-researched topics such as the criminalization of homosexuality, which is still in force in 72 countries that prohibit same-sex relations, 13 under penalty of death. Notably, these laws not only affect LGBT+ people but also generate gender expectations in which all those who do not conform to the stereotype may face consequences within the criminal justice system.
11. Act 26.791, http://servicios.infoleg.gob.ar/infolegInternet/anexos/205000-209999/206018/norma.htm
12. http://otransargentina.com.ar/
13. https://socorristasenred.org/
14. https://www.argentina.gob.ar/generos/registro-nacional-de-promotorxs
15. https://yonofui.org.ar/
16. https://www.argentina.gob.ar/generos/cupo-laboral-travesti-trans
17. https://www.argentina.gob.ar/generos/plan_nacional_de_accion_contra_las_violencias_por_motivos_de_genero/programa-producir
18. Ehttps://www.argentina.gob.ar/generos/programa-acercar-derechos

[19] https://www.argentina.gob.ar/generos/plan_nacional_de_ action_against_gender-based_violence/prog-strengthening_for-personal-protection-territory-disp-territor
[20] https://www.anses.gob.ar/regimen-de-reparacion-economica-para-las-ninas-ninos-y-adolescentes-ley-27452=
[21] https://www.argentina.gob.ar/generos/plan_nacional_de_ action_against_gender-based_violence/program-for-urgent-support-and-immediate-integrated-assistance
[22] https://www.argentina.gob.ar/generos/plan_nacional_ de_accion_contra_las_violencias_por_motivos_de_genero/programa-acompanar
[23] http://observatorioluciaperez.org/
[24] https://www.argentina.gob.ar/generos/plan_
[25] https://www.argentina.gob.ar/aplicaciones/ line-144-women-and-LGBTI-care

References

Actis, M.F. (2021) 'La construcción de la delincuencia femenina en las tramas de la criminología mediática', *Investigaciones Feministas*, 12(2): 639–652.

Alternatives to Holloway (1972) Available from: https://abolitionistfutures.com/latest-news/alternatives-to-holloway [Accessed 15 September 2024].

American Friends Service Committee Working Party (1971) *Struggle for Justice: A Report on Crime and Punishment in America,* https://www.ojp.gov/ncjrs/virtual-library/abstracts/struggle-justice-report-crime-and-punishment-america-prepared [Accessed 30 September 2024].

Arduino, I. (2017) 'A Cordera ni probation, a las mujeres ni justicia', *Cosecha Roja*. Available from: https://www.cosecharoja.org/cordera-ni-probation-las-mujeres-ni-justicia/ [Accessed 15 September 2024].

Arduino, I. (2018) 'No nos callamos más: ¿y después?', *Cosecha Roja*. Available from: https://www.cosecharoja.org/no-nos-callamos-mas-y-despues/ [Accessed 15 September 2024].

Balfour, G. (2021) 'Decriminalizing domestic violence and fighting prostitution abolition: lessons learned from Canada's anti-carceral feminist struggles', *International Journal for Crime, Justice and Social Democracy*, 10(4): 66–77.

Bassotti, M.E. (2021) 'Mujeres que delinquen: la otra cara de la femineidad', *Revista Pensamiento Penal*. Available from: www.pensamientopenal.com.ar [Accessed 15 September 2024].

Becker, S. and Mccorkel, J.A. (2011) 'The gender of criminal opportunity: the impact of male co-offenders on women's crime', *Feminist Criminology*, 6(2): 79–110.

Bernard, A. (2012) 'The intersectional alternative: explaining female criminality', *Feminist Criminology*, 8(1): 3–19.

Carabajal, M. (2014) 'Otra víctima del fuego y el machismo', *Página/12*. Available from: https://www.pagina12.com.ar/diario/sociedad/3-236949-2014-01-03.html [Accessed 15 September 2024].

Carlen, P. (1983) *Women's Imprisonment: A Study in Social Control*. Routledge.

Chávez, S. (2015) 'Ni una muerta más', *Página/12*. Available from: https://www.pagina12.com.ar/diario/suplementos/las12/13-9703-2015-05-15.html [Accessed 15 September 2024].

Chesney-Lind, M. (2006) 'Patriarchy, crime, and justice: feminist criminology in an era of backlash', *Feminist Criminology*, 1(1): 6–26.

Cole, S. and Phillips, L. (2008) 'The violence against women campaigns in Latin America new feminist alliances', *Feminist Criminology*, 3: 145–168.

Corte Suprema de Justicia de la Nación (2019) *Mapa de Género de la Justicia Argentina*. Available from: https://www.cij.gov.ar/nota-36835-La-Corte-Suprema-public--la-actualizaci-n-del-Mapa-de-G-nero-de-la-Justicia. Argentina.html [Accessed 15 September 2024].

Cosecha Roja (2020) 'A María Ovando la juzgan por "mala madre"'. Available from: https://www.cosecharoja.org/maria-ovando-la-juzgan-por-mala-madre/ [Accessed 15 September 2024].

Davis, A., Dent, G., Meiners, E.R. and Richie, B. (2022) *Abolition. Feminism. Now.* Chicago: Haymarket Books.

De Gomes Magalhães, C. (2021) 'Notes on gender, race and punishment from a decolonial perspective to a southern criminology agenda', *International Journal for Crime, Justice and Social Democracy*, 10(4): 90–101.

De los Santos, G. (2016) 'Chiara Páez, el crimen de la adolescente que disparó las marchas de Ni una menos', *La Nación*. Available from: https://www.lanacion.com.ar/seguridad/rufino-chiara-nid1905389/ [Accessed 15 September 2024].

Di Corleto, J. (2018) *Malas madres Aborto e infanticidio en perspectiva histórica*, Buenos Aires: Didot.

Di Marco, M.H. and Evans, D.P. (2020) 'Society, her or me? An explanatory model of intimate femicide among male perpetrators in Buenos Aires, Argentina', *Feminist Criminology*, 16(5): 607–630.

Figueroa, J. (2021) 'Padre de Micaela García: "Transitamos el dolor reivindicando el nombre de Mica"', *Agencia Paco Urondo*. Available from: https://www.agenciapacourondo.com.ar/generos/padre-de-micaela-garcia-transitamos-el-dolor-reivindicando-el-nombre-de-mica [Accessed 15 September 2024].

Fundación para el Estudio e Investigación de la Mujer (2023) 'Elizabeth Gómez Alcorta: "Nosotras ponemos el centro de la política en la vida"'. Available from: http://feim.org.ar/2020/07/08/elizabeth-gomez-alcorta-nosotras-ponemos-el-centro-de-la-politica-en-la-vida/ [Accessed 27 December 2022].

Gago, V. (2013) 'La vida de las mujeres infames', *Derecho Penal y Criminología*, 3(7): 89–96.

García, K. (2021) 'La policía no me cuida, me cuidan mis amigas', *Revista La Brújula*. Available from: https://revistalabrujula.com/2021/06/03/la-policia-no-me-cuida-me-cuidan-mis-amigas-por-katherine-garcia/ [Accessed 15 September 2024].

Hayes, I. (2021) 'Mala madres: un esigma pesado como las rejas ¿Por qué encarcelaron por tercera vez a María Ovando?' *Pagina/12*. Available from: https://www.pagina12.com.ar/330049-por-que-encarcelaron-por-tercera-vez-a-maria-ovando [Accessed 15 September 2024].

Heidensohn, F. (1969) 'Prison for women', *Howard Journal of Criminal Justice*, 12(4): 281–288.

hooks, b. (1987) *Ain't I a Woman*, London: Pluto Press.

INECIP (2022) *Feminismos y política criminal*, Buenos Aires: INECIP. Available from: https://inecip.org/publicaciones/feminismos-y-politica-criminal-una-agenda-feminista-para-la-justicia/ [Accessed 20 September 2024].

Klein, D. and Kress, J. (1976) 'Any woman's blues: a critical overview of women, crime and the criminal justice system', *Crime and Social Justice*, 5(1): 34–49.

Koons-Witt, B.A. and Schram, P.J. (2016) 'Does race matter? Examining the relationship between co-offending and victim characteristics for violent incidents involving female offenders', *Feminist Criminology*, 1(2): 125–146.

Mendoza, B. (2010) 'La epistemología del sur, la colonialidad del género y el feminismo latinoamericano', in Y. Espinosa Miñoso (ed.) *Aproximaciones críticas a las prácticas teórico-políticas del feminismo latinoamericano*, Buenos Aires: En la Frontera, pp 19–36.

Ministerio de las Mujeres, Géneros y Diversidad (2020) *Plan Nacional de Acción contra las violencias por motivos de género-Resumen ejecutivo*.

Ministerio de las Mujeres, Géneros y Diversidad (2021a) *Violencias por motivos de género*.

Ministerio de las Mujeres, Géneros y Diversidad (2021b) *Argentina Unida contra las Violencias de Género: la justicia social como horizonte y el compromiso con la igualdad Informe de avance del Plan Nacional de Acción contra las Violencias por Motivos de Genero*.

Morris, M. (ed.) (1976) *Instead of Prison: A Handbook for Abolitionists*, Prison Research Education Action Project. Available from: https://www.ojp.gov/ncjrs/virtual-library/abstracts/instead-prison-handbook-abolitionists [Accessed 15 September 2024].

Ni una menos (2023) Available from: http://niunamenos.org.ar/quienes-somos/carta-organica/ [Accessed 15 September 2024].

Pérez, A.R. (2017) 'The experiences of Black and Colombian female offenders with the police in Ecuador: understanding minorities' intersecting identities', *Feminist Criminology*, 14(3): 330–348.

Pérez, M. and Huarte, G. (2020) 'Entrevista: "Reflexiones en torno a la razón punitiva"', *Enfant Terrible*. Available from: https://www.aacademica.org/moira.perez/72 [Accessed 20 September 2024].

Pitch, T. (2003) *Responsabilidades limitadas: actores, conflictos y justicia penal*, Buenos Aires: Ad. Hoc.

Potter, H. (2016) 'An argument for Black feminist criminology: understanding African American women's experiences with intimate partner abuse using an integrated approach', *Feminist Criminology*, 1(2): 106–124.

Rebolledo, L.N. (2019) 'El giro punitivo, neoliberalismo, feminismos y violencia de género', *Política y Cultura*, 51: 55–81.

Resumen Latinoamericano (2021) 'Argentina, 227 femicidios y 10 trans/travesticidios'. Available from: https://www.resumenlatinoamericano.org/2021/11/04/argentina-227-femicidios-y-10-trans-travesticidios/ [Accessed 15 September 2024].

Revista Anfibia (2021). 'Eli Gómez Alcorta'. Available from: https://www.revistaanfibia.com/autor/eli-gomez-alcorta/ [Accessed 15 September 2024].

Sánchez, L. (2006) 'Feminismo legal y abolicionismo: el cocinero, el ladrón, su mujer y su amante', *Revista Pensamiento Penal*. Available from: https://www.pensamientopenal.com.ar/doctrina/30752-feminismo-legal-y-abolicionismo-cocinero-ladron-su-mujer-y-su-amante [Accessed 15 September 2024].

Sanchez, R.R. (2018) 'Lucia Perez Montero's murder inspired Black Wednesday; now her rapists have been let off', *Feminist Current*. Available from: https://www.feministcurrent.com/2018/12/05/lucia-perez-monteros-murder-inspired-black-wednesday-now-rapists-let-off/ [Accessed 15 September 2024].

Smart, C. (1977a) *Women, Crime, and Criminology: A Feminist Critique*, London: Routledge.

Smart, C. (1977b) 'Criminological theory: its ideology and implications concerning women', *British Journal of Sociology*, 28(1): 89–100.

Vegh Weis, V. (2017) *Marxism and Criminology: A History of Criminal Selectivity*, Chicago: Haymarket Books.

Wilson Gilmore, R. (2019) *Making and Unmaking Mass Incarceration Conference*. Available from: https://mumiconference.com/wp-content/uploads/2019/12/MUMI-Program.pdf [Accessed 15 September 2024].

Zaffaroni, R. (2011) *La Cuestión Criminal*, Buenos Aires: Planeta.

PART IV

Struggles for Liberation and Justice

12

Eco-Abolition: Policing Environmental Injustice

Nathan Stephens-Griffin and Andrea Brock

Introduction

The 2020s have seen an unprecedented rise in academic and activist critiques of carcerality – prisons, policing, schools and psychiatry – as well as ecological degradation and climate catastrophe. While some activists have been stressing the connectivity between ecological and carceral harms for decades – Black radical thinkers have long emphasized the links between 'prisons, police, and pollution' (Braz and Gilmore, 2006) and the *Fight Toxic Prisons* movement has criticized the environmental injustices of prisons in the US – the relationship between abolition and ecological liberation is rarely explicitly problematized (Brock and Stephens-Griffin, 2021; Stephens-Griffin, 2022). This chapter argues that carceral and ecological harms are entangled in many different and complex ways, and these two struggles should be considered as different sides of the same coin.

This entanglement is well documented: from the murder and brutalization of land defenders resisting extractivism globally (Rossi, 2021; Global Witness, 2023; Stop Cop City, 2023), to the environmentally disastrous 'boot print' of contemporary police and military expansionism (Selwyn, 2022), to the greenwashing of new private mega-prison projects (Jewkes and Moran, 2015) and the traumatizing, sexual coercion of environmental activists by undercover police in the UK (Stephens-Griffin, 2020; Alison et al, 2022). Hence, it is vital that we understand struggles for ecological justice and liberation as deeply entwined with abolitionist causes (Brock and Stephens-Griffin, 2021). In this chapter our aim is to work towards underlining those connections through an exploration of eco-abolitionist thought.

To do this, we first briefly examine historical entanglements of policing and environmental injustice in order to better contextualize eco-abolitionist struggles today, acknowledging colonial, capitalist and state continuities. We then explore some contemporary cases which serve to underline these connections (specifically, the Stop Cop City campaign, the spycops case and the murder of Isac Tembé). Finally, we discuss the total liberation perspective which commits itself to acknowledging and revealing the interrelationships between diverse and seemingly distinct forms of oppression and exploitation, and works towards a unified goal of human, nonhuman and earth liberation (Pellow, 2014). We argue that total liberation represents a vital means of coalescing what have often been distinct struggles under one diverse struggle for social ecological justice and that by acknowledging and foregrounding the ecological dynamics of carcerality, and the carceral underpinnings of ecocide, we create a more solid foundation from which emancipatory struggle can be achieved.

Before delving into a historical discussion, we first introduce and briefly explain the way we will be using the concepts of 'policing' and of 'abolition'.[1] We adopt a definition of policing which develops from that of abolitionist organization Critical Resistance (2023: para 1), which states that 'policing is a social relationship made up of a set of practices that are empowered by the state to enforce law and social control through the use of force'. Accepting this premise, and following on from Neocleous' (2021) work, in this chapter the term 'policing' will be used to refer to diverse forms of population management (often by the state or state-aligned corporate actors), which seek to maintain and preserve a specific social order. This is not limited to work done by formal/state institutions of 'the police', and can include diverse forms of control and containment, as well as through surveillance and intelligence gathering. It can also be enacted indirectly through legal and bureaucratic means; by state (uniformed or undercover) police/military actors, corporate/private contractors, militias/paramilitary organizations, institutions of the welfare state, nongovernmental organizations and movements, and people themselves. That's why we emphasize the importance of policing as relational practice rather than a single focus on policing *actors*.

We use the term 'abolitionism' to refer to radical anti-carceral movements primarily organized against prisons and policing, recognizing that these struggles are historically entwined with resistance to colonialism and slavery (Duff, 2021; Elliott-Cooper, 2021). 'Abolition' therefore requires us to imagine a society without incarceration and policing, and to work for a world without (the need for) those things. Coyle and Nagel (2021) define abolition in opposition to 'carceral logics' – ways of organizing society based on assumptions about the necessity of control, criminalization and punishment that are frequently rooted in colonial, white supremacist and racial capitalist modes of thinking. As Critical Resistance (2008: xii) puts it, 'we are not only struggling to tear down the cages of the Prison-Industrial Complex (PIC), but also to abolish the actions of policing, surveillance, and imprisonment that give the PIC its power'. As a radical concept vulnerable to watering down, Maher (2021: 151) clarifies what abolition is *not*:

> Abolition isn't reform, it isn't social policy, lobbying, progressive think tanks, or progressive legislation to cushion the blows of a violent status quo. Abolition isn't mandatory diversity training, new university hiring lines or harm reduction – no matter how necessary or welcome these may be. It's a horizon for the total rebuilding of society from the bottom up: a society with no police or prisons, because there's nothing that needs policing and no one who needs to be in prison. Abolition means dismantling all systems of inequality, oppression and institutional inhumanity at the same time that we build new, more emancipatory alternatives, that put the power directly in the hands of poor communities.

Scholars have delineated different perspectives within abolition, for example, 'penal abolition' which is sometimes considered as focusing primarily on the abolition of prisons, and 'carceral abolition', which expands much further into wider forms of punitive control, punishment and detention (Carrier and Piche, 2015). This chapter sits within the latter tendency, expanding beyond the prison estate. It is also important that contemporary abolitionist struggle be viewed in terms of its continuity with historical struggles to abolish slavery (McDowell and Fernandez, 2018; Elliott-Cooper, 2021). As Maher suggests, abolition is an inherently practical and prefigurative struggle, as much about building the new, as it is about tearing down the old; about dreaming of and creating radical possibilities (Davis, 2003; McDowell and Fernandez, 2018). Kaba (2021: 2–3) argues that 'abolition is a positive project that focuses, in part, on building a society where it is possible to address harm without relying on structural forms of oppression or the violent systems that increase it'. Having very briefly given an idea of the aims and focus of the chapter, we will now discuss some historical context.

Contextualizing policing and environmental injustice

It is widely recognized that globally, poorer people, Indigenous communities, people of colour and women, especially those in the Global South, bear the brunt of environmental harms (Shiva, 2008; Pulido and de Lara, 2018; Pellow, 2021). These contemporary inequalities, harms and injustices, some specific instances of which will be cited later on, are rooted in colonialism, extractivism and racial capitalism. Policing, along with the carceral systems it supports, has always been central to these dynamics. Policing has always helped facilitate 'forms of industrial development and globalisation that are environmentally unjust and inherently harmful to nature and human society' (Brock and Stephens-Griffin, 2021: 2). Policing has always been central to colonialism, counterinsurgency efforts and imperial conquest.²

Turning our focus to ecological concerns, we must first acknowledge that 'environmental problems are fundamentally social and political in nature and are rooted in the historical legacies of domination and social hierarchy' (Tokar, 2018: 170), as Murray Bookchin and others have long argued. Colonialism was at its core extractive and about controlling humans, animals, land and ecosystems for exploitation. British imperialism, for instance, involved various forms of policing to repress resistance and ensure the security of the extractive industries it was establishing in colonized nations as it expanded its bloody empire (Verweijen and Dunlap, 2021). These industries relied on the extraction of natural resources, and in doing so established the foundations for contemporary fossil capitalist climate crises we face today. As Dunlap and Brock (2022: 8) note: 'Modernist development came at an extraordinary socio-ecological cost to habitats and Indigenous cultures North and South of the globe – now extending to the entire biosphere, as the planet is heating, species are dying at unprecedented rates, and many people are suffering radical insecurity from climate catastrophe.'

Linked to this, Ferdinand (2022) argues against conventional wisdom that traces the genus of present-day environmental problems back to the Industrial Revolutions of the 18th and 19th centuries. He argues that while these changes did accelerate environmental destruction, the real roots of contemporary ecological crisis go back to the birth of colonialism, and the 15th century specifically. This is where a certain way of inhabiting the earth ('colonial inhabitation') became entrenched (Ferdinand, 2022). This way of living is inherently violent and rests on the assumption that lands, humans and nonhumans should be subjugated to the desires of colonizers – rooted in white supremacist ideas about land and people. Policing, as coercive population management, has been central to these processes. As Pulido and De Lara (2018: 78) have argued, 'capitalism and modernity are unviable systems', rooted in the impossible aim of infinite economic growth on a finite planet.

Anthropocentric command over nature, and particularly over nonhuman animals, has provided extremely effective means of aiding and abetting forms of colonization, violence and control. In North America, for instance, the mass slaughter of the buffalo and bison was used to control and contribute to the elimination of Indigenous people and their ways of living (Isenberg, 2000; Moloney and Chambliss, 2014). As Nibert (2017: xiii) describes it:

> The European invasion of much of the world was violent and genocidal, driven by a quest for economic gain and enabled by the

ongoing oppression of other animals as instruments of war, laborers, and rations. While colonizers certainly sought gold and silver, much wealth was obtained through what came to be a never-ending war on other animals.

Cohen (2017: 268) also argued that this can be seen in the way in which domesticated farmed animals were instrumentalized to enclose and colonize landscapes (a process she calls 'animal colonialism'). Studying the ecological dimensions of colonial history provides vital ways of resisting colonial continuities today. While we have barely dipped a toe into the water of these extremely important historical dynamics, we must now shift the focus on to contemporary eco-abolitionist literature, as a means of understanding and resisting environmental injustice today.

Eco-abolitionist scholarship

Ruth Wilson Gilmore (a co-founder of *Critical Resistance*) is perhaps the most prominent abolitionist scholar with an ecological and spatial focus. Her 2007 book *Golden Gulag* was extremely influential in terms of its critical analysis of political, economic and geographical dynamics of the expansion of California's prison population. Gilmore (2007: 5) argues that the 'phenomenal growth of California's state prison system since 1982' is not a reflection of priorities around crime, security or justice, but is in fact deeply embedded in political economic and spatial-geographical factors. Specifically, she identifies 'four surpluses' that drove this expansion: surpluses of 'finance capital, land, labour, and state capacity' (Gilmore, 2007: 57). Prison expansion at this time was therefore understood as a response to crises *of* and *under* capitalism. Of particular interest is the relationship between land and prison expansion – specifically the impact that environmental issues such as droughts and severe winters had in the 20th century, leading to declining cotton industry in California, with knock-on economic impacts on populations and towns. This is also mirrored in declining industry resulting in surplus labour within racialized communities. Building new prisons provided a solution to these problems: investment, employment, as well as inhabitants for the prisons themselves. It provided one carceral solution to all the surpluses she identified. Gilmore's work is extremely insightful in helping cultivate a spatial and ecological lens when examining carcerality and pushing thinking towards meaningful alternatives.

Turning to political ecology, the connections between policing and ecology are increasingly being acknowledged. In their edited volume *Enforcing Ecocide*, Dunlap and Brock (2022) explore the relationship between policing and ecological crises, examining the ways in which police, security, and military forces intersect with, facilitate and reinforce ecological and climate catastrophe. Building on this, we argue that struggles against police violence and for environmental justice should be understood as one and the same – each representing vital elements of a global movement for total liberation under an ecocidal, racial capitalist patriarchy; a struggle to save the planet, and for the justice, dignity and survival of all life on it (Brock and Stephens-Griffin, forthcoming).

'Abolition ecology' as an approach emerged from political ecology scholarship, and draws upon abolitionist theory and practice, as well as work on environmental racism, and on the historical and contemporary connection between racial and ecological forms of injustice (Heynen, 2018; Pellow, 2021). Heynen (2018: 244) states that abolition ecology aims to challenge and resist the 'continued existence of white supremacist logics that continue to produce uneven racial development within land and property relations'. It draws and aims to build directly on historical abolitionist struggle against slavery, drawing parallels between campaigns and direct action against enslavement in the past, and present-day struggles against policing and prisons (Heynen, 2018).

Abolition ecology therefore works to reveal and foreground the role that white supremacy plays in shaping relations between nature and society (Heynen and Ybarra, 2021) as well as working to locate, name and actively resist harms to ecosystems, acknowledging the ways in which these are produced, aggravated or intensified by white supremacist penal and carceral systems, and in so doing strives to envision and produce alternative ways of doing things (Stephens-Griffin, 2022). It sees the exploitation of people and nature as being fundamentally connected. Adopting such a critical lens necessitates an examination of colonial continuities today, including the role that policing plays in protecting and helping expand ecologically destructive enterprises and megaprojects – such as infrastructure projects or prisons – and the repression of those who seek to defend their ecosystems (Brock and Stephens-Griffin, 2021).

Abolition ecology begs the question how the ideas and ideals of abolitionist thought and activism can help to inform struggles for ecological justice, whether that be pollution of water, air or soil, or issues around shelter and food insecurity, all of which disproportionately impact poorer racialized communities (Heynen, 2018). A diverse range of research and scholarship has sought to examine these issues in recent years (for example, Ranganathan, 2016; Kimari and Parish, 2020; Hardy, Bailey and Heynen, 2022; Ybarra, 2021). Recent work has also examined the links between green criminology and abolition ecology, asking how the subdiscipline of green criminology might meaningfully contribute to abolition ecology (Stephens-Griffin, 2022). This chapter seeks to build on such foundations in its exploration of eco-abolitionism.

Contemporary cases

In this section, we discuss three cases which provide snapshot illustrations of the connections between struggles for ecological justice and against policing: the 'Stop Cop City' case in Atlanta, Georgia, US, the 'spycops' case in the UK and the murder of Indigenous activist Isac Tembé in Brazil. We hope that these three cases help make visible the ecological dynamics of carcerality.

Stop Cop City

Such is the extent of police violence in the US that it has been described by a leading UK medical journal as a 'public health crisis' (*The Lancet*, 2021). In a study of fatal police violence between 1980 and 2018, it was found that around 55 per cent of deaths resulting from police violence were misclassified or unreported. In other words, over 17,000 people killed by police were not properly counted as such. Within those statistics, Black Americans were found to be 3.5 times more likely to be killed by police than white Americans (*The Lancet*, 2021). While there is not the space to expand on the dire situation of racist policing in the US here, it is vital to analyse the 'Stop Cop City' campaign against this backdrop of racial capitalism and ecological harm.

'Stop Cop City' (SCC) is the name used by a decentralized movement of land defenders and campaigners resisting a new $90 million policing academy, presently under construction near Atlanta, Georgia (Bethea, 2022). The facility will reportedly include multiple shooting ranges, dedicated space for weapons and explosions testing and burning buildings tests, a mock-city for urban warfare training, as well as a military helicopter landing pad. The policing academy/cop city project has come under fierce opposition from environmentalists, anti-racist activists and abolitionists alike, presenting, as it does, a very instructive illustration of the overlaps between ecological and carceral harms in the contemporary US. As Kwame Olufemi puts it, 'cop city is not just a controversial training centre. It is a war base where police will learn military-like manoeuvres to kill black people and control our bodies and movements' (Stop Cop City, 2023: para 2).

The ecological dimensions of this project are self-evident: its construction necessitates the demolition of hundreds of acres of the ancient Weelaunee forest (also known as South River Forest), and in both construction and operation will be massively environmentally destructive, given the loss of habitat and impact on biodiversity to name just two negative dimensions of forest demolition plans. In wider terms, the relationship between policing, militarism and ecological harm is well evidenced (Dunlap and Brock, 2022; Selwyn, 2022). As Dunlap (2022: 153–154) argues, 'the military and police are intimately related to ecological and climate catastrophe. Not only do repressive forces facilitate land grabbing, mining and establishing toxic industries, but they also necessitate these activities for their own equipment, vehicles, and, weapons, which damage ecosystems and socio-ecological relationships across the world'. Notwithstanding the wider issues around racist police violence in the US and the rapidly accelerating militarization of policing that the facility is reflective of, the placement of the facility has significance in relation to the colonial past and present of the US, located, as it is, in an area with a predominantly poor, Black population subject to disproportionate police violence today, and on land formerly inhabited by the Muskogee Indigenous community until their displacement by settler colonists. The location of the proposed facility is also close to where police murdered Rayshard Brooks, a significant event in the Black Lives Matter uprisings of 2020. The entire project is unavoidably steeped in the history of racial settler colonial violence in the US.

Resistance to the project abounds. As campaigners themselves argue 'basically, no one wants cop city … Except the investors, contractors and politicians driving this project' (Stop Cop City Solidarity, 2023: para 1). Opposition has existed since plans were shared, but since the winter of 2021, land defenders have been occupying the forest, barricading the area and constructing 'tree-sits' to prevent the cutting of trees. Forest defenders have used sabotage tactics, destroying equipment being used for forest demolition, on- and off-site, with companies implicated in the cop city development also being targeted. The state and police response has naturally been violent and repressive. A raid in late 2022 saw five land defenders arrested and charged as 'domestic terrorists' (a common tactic used to weaken movements and challenge their legitimacy on erroneous grounds).

In January 2023 another police raid resulted in the murder of Indigenous forest defender Manuel Esteban Paez Terán, known as 'Tortuguita' or 'Tort'. Police claim that during the raid, Tort had shot an officer in the leg without warning and that they had shot and killed him because they came under fire. Forest defenders challenge this narrative strenuously, arguing that the officer was shot in friendly fire and pointing out the lack of body cam footage which has been produced by police to support the narrative that Tort had fired first. Police ballistic tests predictably found that the bullet that struck the officer had come from a gun legally owned by Tort. Results of an independent autopsy found no gunpowder residue on Tort's hands, and that Tort had been shot fourteen times while sitting cross-legged on the floor with his hands raised in the air (Owen, 2023).

The Stop Cop City campaign is significant because it is a contemporary example of eco-abolitionist organizing in practice, which articulates its criticisms in both anti-carceral and ecological terms, bringing together critiques of police expansion and militarization, and ecological and social harm to local ecosystems and communities. The forest defenders in Weelaunee seek to defend these historic lands where Muscogee people lived for centuries before US colonization. An eco-abolitionist lens allows us to understand the demolition of this forest, both as ecologically harmful, but also in service of a racial capitalist status quo, in which violent militarized policing continues to persist, disproportionately harming racialized communities. We need only look to the ample extant literature on environmental racism to see that ecological harms disproportionately impact communities of colour (for example, Bullard, 2000). In this context, Stop Cop City provides a vital contemporary instance of eco-abolitionist struggle, epitomizing the ecological dynamics of carcerality.

Spycops

To say that British policing is in a tumultuous period is an understatement. From the 2023 Casey Report which found the Metropolitan Police to be institutionally, racist, misogynistic and homophobic (Dodd, 2023), to the Daniel Morgan Independent Panel report which found that same force to be institutionally corrupt (Dodd and Sabagh, 2021), evidence of a malaise abounds. Sarah Everard's rape and murder by serving police officer Wayne Cousins in 2021 brought issues of institutional sexism in policing to the national fore (Dodd and Siddique, 2021), and public fears were not allayed by the brutal repression with which the police responded to a nonviolent vigil held in Everard's memory (Lowerson, 2022), or the revelations that Cousin's fellow officers regularly shared misogynistic and racist messages with one another in private (Dodd, 2022). Data from the National Police Chief's Council suggest that these problems are not isolated, with more than 1,500 UK police officers accused of violence against women and girls between October 2021 and April 2022, of whom just 1 per cent were sacked (Hall, 2023). But for the victims of intimate-state surveillance (also known as 'the spycops case'), these are not new issues or debates (Alison et al, 2022, Evans, 2023).

The 'spycops' case refers to the large-scale undercover policing and intimate-state surveillance of activists in Britain. The case presents an illustration of the ways in which the harms of policing and state surveillance are entangled with harms to ecosystems and nonhuman animals, as well as highlighting the ways in which ecological campaigns are inevitably connected with campaigns for gender and racial justice in terms of state responses. It is now known that over 130 undercover police officers have infiltrated and spied on over 1,000 groups in the UK since 1968, the vast majority of them left-wing groups. Unlike typical undercover deployments which seek convictions against so-called 'perpetrators of crime', these deployments appear to have been about simply disrupting protest. The initial revelations followed the investigations of a group of activists, who in 2010 discovered that a core figure in their activist movement and social lives, 'Mark Stone', was in reality a police spy called Mark Kennedy, who had at that point been infiltrating the environmentalist movement for seven years. Kennedy's use of sexual coercion of activists, tricking them into romantic and sexual relationships, was particularly shocking. We now know that this was common among undercover officers who would frequently use their assumed identities to start relationships with activists (often while also having a wife and children elsewhere). Activists who were subject to this disgraceful practice have described it as like having been 'raped by the state' (Lewis, Evans and Pollak, 2013).

It is now believed that at least four children have been born as a result of such relationships between activists and undercover police (Evans, 2021; Evans, 2023), including, notably, a child born from a relationship between an activist and Bob Lambert, a senior figure within British undercover policing. Undercover officers engaged in a range of other unethical practices while undercover, using the identities of dead children without permission, encouraging and engaging in criminal activity, appearing in court under their assumed identities and spying on schoolchildren, among other practices. The ongoing Undercover Policing Inquiry (UCPI) was set up to investigate the spycops scandal in depth, but has been fiercely criticized by activists as a whitewash, lacking transparency and providing unnecessary protection and cover for undercover officers. And while the gendered and structurally misogynist dynamics of the case are very clear, with a predominantly male police force utilizing sexual coercion against female activist targets, the spycops case also illustrates the shocking institutional racism and other forms of prejudice within the Metropolitan Police, who targeted anti-racist organizers, including Stephen Lawrence's family, as well as targeting other marginalized groups in their campaigns for social change, such as LGBTQ+, disabled and working-class activists. Well-known collaboration between police and employers in the illegal and shameful blacklisting trade union activists (Smith and Chamberlayne, 2015) illustrate the latter.

The spycops case is useful to illustrate the harms of policing and the abject myth of 'policing by consent' (Woodman, 2020). The state can and will do everything within its power to suppress and marginalize activists and to protect corporate and state interests. This is particularly notable in the repeated targeting of ecological and animal rights groups who campaign for environmental and species justice. The police consistently prioritize the interests of those wrecking the environment, over the rights and dignity of those struggling to defend the planet and its inhabitants.

An eco-abolitionist lens reveals the extent to which the state does not simply protect polluters and climate wreckers, but in fact acts as a driver of gendered and racialized ecological harms (Brock and Stephens-Griffin, 2021, forthcoming; Dunlap and Brock, 2022), actively stopping ecological defence while itself relying on policing and militaristic technologies that cause immense ecological harm, resource extraction and carbon emissions (Dunlap, 2022). Therefore, the case for social and ecological justice and liberation must be, by necessity, an abolitionist one. As Gilmore and Gilmore (2023: 390) argue, 'thinking about state violence, and especially racist state violence, as an aberration to be reformed away misses the way that states work and the work that states do'. We cannot 'reform' these tendencies away because the harms policing of this kind engenders are deeply rooted in its very foundations. The spycops case shatters the myth of 'policing by consent', demonstrating that policing exists not for the safety or security of the public, but for the maintenance of an existing social and ecological order which is killing the planet and which in turn disproportionately harms women/nonbinary/trans people, people of colour and the poor.

The murder of Isac Tembé

Brazil presents another context from which to explore the relationship between policing and ecological harm. In 2022, United Nations (UN) experts issued a public statement calling on the Brazilian government to radically reform its policing practices, because of shocking police violence and killings which disproportionately impact racialized communities in Brazil (United Nations, 2022). They called for the government to demilitarize all law enforcement agencies and vigorously address systemic racism and racial discrimination. Placing this in the context of ongoing environmental conflicts in the region helps us to further understand the ways in which police violence intersects with the slow violence of ecological destruction that is disproportionately experienced by people in the Global South (Nixon, 2011).

These global conflicts are keenly felt by Indigenous communities, particularly in Brazil, one of the deadliest countries in the world for land and environmental defenders according to human rights organization Global Witness (2022). Indigenous territories within Brazil face near-constant attacks from illegal loggers and farmers who wish to occupy land through cattle ranching and other forms of profit-seeking business. The murder of Brazilian Indigenous activist and teacher Isac Tembé is not unique – hundreds of land defenders are killed in environmental conflicts across the world every year[3] (Global Witness, 2022). To draw out one particular death is not intended to suggest that this is an uncommon occurrence; rather, it aims to account for the specificity of each of these tragic cases and the way in which an abolition ecology lens can expand our thinking when viewing such cases, helping us draw the connections between state violence and ecological harm.

In February 2021, 24-year-old Indigenous leader Isac Tembé was travelling across the Alto Rio Guama Indigenous Territory when he was stopped and shot at point-blank range in the chest by a member of Brazil's military police, killing him (Amazon Watch, 2021). Tembé was a leader of the Tembe-Tenetehara people, who are actively struggling against the illegal encroachment and occupation by farmers and ranchers onto Indigenous territories, which became more acute under the then premiership of Jair Bolsonaro. Tembé's death devastated his community, who see Brazil's military police essentially serving as private militias defending the interests of Brazil's agribusiness industry (Global Witness, 2022). Military police tried to suggest that Tembé had been killed for his involvement in vaguely defined 'criminal activity', but as his community argued in a statement issued following his murder, his death must be understood within the context of the ongoing war on Indigenous people and forms of knowledge in Brazil. As this public statement issued by the Tembé-Theneteraha people (2021, cited in Rossi, 2021: para 11) states:

> The hearts of the Tembé-Tenetehara people bleed with the brutal murder of our young warrior Isac Tembé. The bullet that took his life, at only 24 years old, hit everyone who has lived in this land since time immemorial. We are permanently defending the forest and our traditional knowledge ... The Military Police twice murdered Isac Tembé: they killed his body and try to kill his memory when they attacked the nature of our young warrior and exemplary leadership.

The case presents a very clear instance of state-sanctioned violence against Indigenous people which must be understood as part of wider conflicts over land, resources and sovereignty. Rossi (2021: para 3), who advocates for rainforest protection and Indigenous peoples' rights in the Amazon basin, argued that the case:

> reveals a tragic reality faced by Indigenous land defenders in the Brazilian Amazon, whose lands and lives are increasingly targeted by a range of criminal actors with implicit support from the federal government ... Spurred by Bolsonaro's violent and racist discourse and policies, land invaders have acted with impunity, brazenly expropriating Indigenous lands, razing protected forests, and parcelling lots for land speculation. These practices are being aggressively consolidated across the Amazon, causing immeasurable destruction.

The war on Indigenous communities and ecosystems is made possible by police and other security forces that are 'enforcing ecocide' (Dunlap and

Brock, 2022) and illustrates too well the connection between the violence against humans and ecologies. Applying an eco-abolitionist lens allows us to 'engage with the ways that white supremacy shapes human relationships with land through entangled processes of settler colonialism, empire and racial capitalism' (Heynen and Ybarra, 2021: 21). We therefore immediately move away from the idea that this case can be understood as an isolated or localized incident, and instead view this case within the long and bloody history of colonialism both in Brazil and globally. This sort of violence against Indigenous people in South America dates back at least to the 1500s, when Europeans first began to colonize the region. Within about 100 years of Pedro Alvar Cabral's genocidal violence and colonial expansion, less than 10 per cent of Brazil's 2.5 million Indigenous inhabitants survived (Churchill, 1999). Adopting an eco-abolitionist lens first ensures we are placing this current tragedy in the context of an ongoing and centuries-long process of depopulation of Indigenous people.

An eco-abolitionist lens allows acknowledgement of the ways that this racialized carceral violence from military police is deeply entwined with ecological harms, and the ways that the two dynamics mutually reproduce one another – for example, the harsh policing and repression of land defenders struggling against extractivism and neocolonialism today (Acosta, 2013).

Total liberation

Having discussed these three cases, which provide insights into the varied entanglements of policing, carcerality and ecological harm, we now turn to the concept of total liberation (Pellow, 2014) as a unifying principle for eco-abolitionist thought and action. A total liberation approach commits itself to acknowledging and revealing the interrelationships between diverse and seemingly distinct forms of oppression and exploitation, and works towards a unified goal of human, nonhuman and earth liberation. As Pellow (2014: 9) puts it:

> Whether the example is a slaughterhouse, a petrochemical facility, industrial agriculture, a hydroelectric dam, or a mining operation, each reveals the ways in which humans exploit and produce harm among other humans, nonhuman animals, and ecosystems. While these forms of hierarchy and violence are uniquely experienced across species and space, they are inseparable and interrelated.

Pellow (2014: 5–6) argues that a total liberation approach comprises four key pillars: '(1) an ethic of justice and anti-oppression inclusive of humans, nonhuman animals, and ecosystems; (2) anarchism; (3) anti-capitalism; and (4) an embrace of direct-action tactics'. We suggest that the four pillars of total liberation are useful to understanding and resisting the social and ecological harms of policing. Committing to these pillars, we believe, can help better position our scholarship and action towards the goals of justice and liberation. In practical terms, this means acknowledging the nonhuman (be that ecosystems or animals) in our work as critical scholars. All too often nonhuman animals and ecosystems have been excluded from conceptions of the social or the criminological (Peggs, 2013; Bierne, 2018; Taylor and Fitzgerald, 2018), including in political ecology and environmental justice scholarship, but a total liberation framework provides a means of including them within our analysis. In this sense, the struggle over Cop City, Indigenous land in Brazil or even the animals liberated by activists targeted by spycops can be understood in broader terms of liberation.

Coupled with this, there are strong ecological cases for the embrace of nonhierarchical modes of thought (which might be described as anarchist). Unpicking and resisting hierarchy itself as a structuring force which contributes to social and ecological harm is fundamental to abolitionist goals of realizing a society where it is possible to address harm without relying on structural forms of oppression. Illustrating this, Bookchin (1986: 155) argues that 'there are no hierarchies in nature other than those imposed by hierarchical modes of human thought, but rather differences merely in function between and within living things'. A critical analysis of difference as nonhierarchical can help expand our thinking and do away with the idea that hierarchical thinking is normal or necessary, where in fact it is often antithetical to ecological health. Linked to this is of course a critique of capitalism and growthism (Hickel, 2020), and an explicitly anti-capitalist approach to contemporary social and ecological problems, which appreciates capitalism as a key driver of ecological problems, both historically and today (Nibert, 2017).

This approach also necessitates a vociferous support for direct action, self-defence and the kinds of community organizing that help protect communities and ecosystems alike. In the context of abolition, Maher (2021) explores myriad examples of abolitionist style social organizing in practice, from armed community organizing to drive out drug dealers and police (working with the drug gangs) in Caracas, Venezuela in the 1980s, for instance, to the Black Panthers community organizing in the US, to the Zapatista rebellion in Chiapas, Mexico, to the autonomous region of Rojava in Kurdistan, where communities were built from the ground up, with citizens trained in self-defence. It calls on academics to get out of the ivory tower and organize in their communities, be 'accomplices not allies' (Indigenous Action Media, 2014), and support prisoners and live in solidarity with communities and individuals who are being repressed and policed, including those who might not fall under liberal conceptualizations of nonviolent environmental defenders and who are forced to resort to more combative methods and tactics.

We support calls for total liberation that are grounded in abolitionism, rather than 'just' environmental justice, because we want an end to ecological social harm instead of producing a 'just distribution' of environmental 'goods' and 'bads', enforced through more or less authoritarian ways, including through state structures and their carceral institutions. Despite its radical roots in the Black civil rights movements and the Black Panther Party, championed by Black people, Latinx, Indigenous peoples and Asian Americans (Perkins, 2021), much environmental justice scholarship still reflects a liberal Western focus on a more equal distribution of harms rather than challenging the underlying systems of exploitation these harms rest upon (Álvarez and Coolsaet, 2020). And while some environmental justice activists have long worked with abolitionists in their communities, critiquing the ways in which policing, prisons and pollution are entangled and racially constituted (Braz and Gilmore, 2006), environmental justice does not go far enough in critiquing how ecological harm and exploitation are inherent to the hierarchical social ecological ordering that is secured and enforced through policing, and is enforced through carcerality. All too often (though not always!), environmental justice campaigns tend towards liberal reformism (Dunlap, 2021). Total liberation, on the other hand, calls for an end of the carcerality and logics of control that are part of state power, capitalism and extractivism. This helps us understand the way the state itself is an institutionalization of hierarchy and social ecological harm (Gorz, 1980). A total liberationist orientation provides a blueprint for building a radically transformed future, with a foundation of justice and equality.

The statist social ecological order cannot, by definition, allow for the autonomy and human/nonhuman freedom that we desire, and the creativity and beauty that allows us to live in different non-extractivist relationships to each other and our ecosystems, grounded in ideas of mutual aid and solidarity, not punitive responses, competition and control (see also Scott, Chapter 1 in this volume). Prisons and policing serve 'to attack anyone the state deems a threat to its sovereignty, or anyone who it would be beneficial to the state's image (and thus a crucial aspect of the maintenance of its sovereignty) to bring the might of the criminalization system down upon' (Shevek, 2022, para 6) – and that is tied to ecology and the ecological social order we live under (Brock and Stephens-Griffin, forthcoming).

Conclusion

The aim of this chapter has been to work towards underlining connections between carceral and ecological harms as interlocking and mutually generative through an exploration of eco-abolitionist thinking as well as examining three contemporary case studies. Carceral logics are not only integral in terms of enforcing and defending ecological degradation and injustice, but carcerality itself causes ecological hazards, as the *Fight Toxic Prisons* campaign in the US has long shown: forcing people to live near or on top of toxic waste sites and other health hazards, where prisons are often built; facilitating toxic conditions inside prisons (such as polluted water and air), preventing the movement of people to escape and adapt to heatwaves and other effects of climate catastrophe, and severely limiting access to healthy food.[4]

We have argued that in acknowledging and making visible the ecological dynamics of carcerality, we build more solid foundations for emancipation in the future, particularly through the embrace of a total liberation ethic grounded in justice and anti-oppression, anarchism, anti-capitalism and an embrace of direct action (Pellow, 2014). Fundamentally, we need to be able to look beyond the existing and imagine alternatives rather than just relying on the same old responses. Our response to environmental problems must not be limited to existing carceral responses which, as this edited collection shows, continue to reproduce the same inequalities, harms and injustices. As David Scott (2022) has argued, we need to look beyond legal reforms, which are by their nature likely to stop short of what is truly necessary to solve these problems, and which will reproduce ecologically damaging carceral responses to social and ecological problems. Instead, Scott (2022: para 24) argues that we must 'work collectively for a radical and progressive transformation of our social, economic, and political system that places ecological sustainability at its centre. It is perhaps our only hope'. Fundamentally, we must think beyond the limits of our current imaginations and entertain the possibility that things could be different – societies can exist in ecologically healthy ways and can respond to social problems without relying on oppressive hierarchies and carceral thinking, the kind of which seldom solves but instead frequently exacerbates social and ecological harms. The problems we face are monumental, but we can overcome them. Things can be different, things can be better: we just have to have the courage to imagine alternatives, and work to build a new ecologically just world – a world within which many worlds fit, as the Zapatista movement tells us – in the here and now.

Notes

[1] Both terms have had many and varied uses historically and academically, but brevity precludes a very in-depth discussion of this.

[2] Again, space constraints mean we cannot delve too deeply into the historical connectivity between policing, criminal justice and colonialism, but there is ample extant literature exploring this (for example, Agozino, 2004; Sinclair and Williams, 2007; Abrahamsen and Williams, 2011; Woodman, 2020; Elliott-Cooper, 2021; Go, 2024).

3   The number would be much higher if it were to also include those killed in armed struggles against ecological or colonial violence, but which are deemed insufficiently peaceful to be counted in such statistics (Gelderloos, 2022).
4   https://fighttoxicprisons.wordpress.com/

References

Abrahamsen, R. and Williams, M.C. (2011) *Security beyond the State: Private Security in International Politics*, Cambridge: Cambridge University Press.

Acosta, A. (2013) 'Extractivism and neoextractivism: two sides of the same curse', in M. Lang and D. Mokrani (eds) *Beyond Development: Alternative Visions from Latin America*, S. Shields and R. Underhay (trans.), Quito and Amsterdam: Fundación Rosa Luxemburg and Transnational Institute, pp 61–86.

Agozino, B. (2004) 'Imperialism, crime and criminology: towards the decolonisation of criminology', *Crime, Law and Social Change*, 41(4): 343–358.

Alison, Belinda, Steel, Helen, Lisa and Naomi (2022) *Deep Deception: The Story of the Spycops Network by the Women Who Uncovered the Shocking Truth*, London: Ebury Spotlight.

Álvarez, L. and Coolsaet, B. (2018) 'Decolonizing environmental justice studies: a Latin American perspective', *Capitalism Nature Socialism*, 31(2): 50–69.

Beirne, P. (2018) *Murdering Animals: Writings on Theriocide, Homicide and Non-Speciesist Criminology*, London: Palgrave Macmillan.

Bethea, C. (2022) 'The new fight over an old forest in Atlanta', *New Yorker* (3 August). Available from: https://www.newyorker.com/news/letter-from-the-south/the-new-fight-over-an-old-forest-in-atlanta [Accessed 15 May 2023].

Bookchin, M. (1986) *Post-scarcity Anarchism,* Anarchist Library. Available from: https://theanarchistlibrary.org/library/murray-bookchin-post-scarcity-anarchism-book.pdf [Accessed 24 May 2023].

Braz, R. and Gilmore, C. (2006) 'Joining forces: prisons and environmental justice in recent California organizing', *Radical History Review*, 96: 95–111.

Brock, A. and Stephens-Griffin, N. (2021) 'Policing environmental injustice', *IDS Bulletin*. https://doi.org/10.19088/1968-2021.130.

Brock, A. and Stephens-Griffin, N. (Forthcoming) *Policing Ecocide: Abolition for Total Liberation.*

Bullard, R. D. (2000) *Dumping in Dixie: Race, Class, and Environmental Quality*, Abingdon-on-Thames: Routledge.

Carrier, N. and Piché, J. (2015) 'Blind spots of abolitionist thought in academia', *Champ pénal/Penal field* [En ligne], XII. DOI: 10.4000/champpenal.9162.

Churchill, W. (1999) 'Genocide of native populations in South America', in I.W. Charny (ed.) *The Encyclopaedia of Genocide Volume 1*, Santa Barbara: ABC-CLIO, pp 433–434.

Cohen, M. (2017) 'Animal colonialism: the case of milk', *AJIL Unbound*, 111: 267–271. DOI: 10.1017/aju.2017.66.

Coyle, M.J. and Nagel, M. (eds) (2021) *Contesting Carceral Logic: Towards Abolitionist Futures*, Abingdon: Routledge.

Critical Resistance (2008) *Abolition Now! Ten Years of Strategy and Struggle against the Prison Industrial Complex*, Oakland, CA: AK Press.

Critical Resistance (2023) 'Critical Resistance's definition of policing'. Available from: https://criticalresistance.org/abolish-policing/#:~:text=Critical%20Resistance's%20Definition%20of%20Policing,through%20the%20use%20of%20force. [Accessed 11 May 2023].

Davis, A.Y. (2003) *Are Prisons Obsolete?* New York: Seven Stories Press.

Dodd, V. (2022) 'Met officers charged over Wayne Couzens WhatsApp group named', *The Guardian* (21 February). Available from: https://www.theguardian.com/uk-news/2022/feb/21/met-officers-charged-over-wayne-couzens-whatsapp-group-named [Accessed 18 May 2023].

Dodd, V. (2023) 'Met Police found to be institutionally racist, misogynistic and homophobic', *The Guardian* (21 March). Available from: https://www.theguardian.com/uk-news/2023/mar/21/metropolitan-police-institutionally-racist-misogynistic-homophobic-louise-casey-report [Accessed 18 May 2023].

Dodd, V. and Sabbagh, D. (2021) 'Daniel Morgan murder: inquiry brands Met Police "institutionally corrupt"', *The Guardian* (15 June). Available from: https://www.theguardian.com/uk-news/2021/jun/15/daniel-morgan-met-chief-censured-for-hampering-corruption-inquiry [Accessed 18 May 2023].

Dodd, V. and Siddique, H. (2021) 'Sarah Everard murder: Wayne Couzens given whole-life sentence', *The Guardian* (30 September). Available from: https://www.theguardian.com/uk-news/2021/sep/30/sarah-everard-murder-wayne-couzens-whole-life-sentence [Accessed 18 May 2023].

Duff, K. (ed.) (2021) *Abolishing the Police*, London: Dog Section Press.

Dunlap, A. (2021) 'Toward an anarchist decolonization: a few notes', *Capitalism Nature Socialism*, 32(4): 62–72.

Dunlap, A. and Brock, A. (eds) (2022) *Enforcing Ecocide*, Cham: Palgrave Macmillan.

Elliott-Cooper, A. (2021) *Black Resistance to British Policing*. Manchester: Manchester University Press.

Evans, R. (2021) 'Police spy admits women would not have agreed to sex if they knew his identity', *The Guardian* (11 May). Available from: https://www.theguardian.com/uk- news/2021/may/11/police-spy-admits-women-would-not-have-agreed-to-sex-if-they-knew- his-identity [Accessed 14 October 2021].

Evans, R. (2023) '"Endemic" sexism in Met Police led to undercover deception, inquiry told', *The Guardian* (21 February). Available from: https://www.theguardian.com/uk-news/2023/feb/21/endemic-sexism-in-met-police-led-to-undercover-deception-inquiry-told [Accessed 16 May 2023].

Ferdinand, M. (2022) *Decolonial Ecology: Thinking from the Caribbean World*, A.P. Smith (trans.), Cambridge: Polity Press.

Gelderloos, P. (2022) 'Ecological terror and pacification: counterinsurgency for the climate crisis', in A. Dunlap and A. Brock (eds) *Enforcing Ecocide*, Cham: Palgrave Macmillan, pp 269–305.

Gilmore, R.W. (2007) *Golden Gulag: Prison, Surplus, Crisis and Opposition in Globalizing California*, Berkeley: University of California Press.

Gilmore, R.W. and Gilmore, C. (2023) 'Restating the obvious', in R.W. Gilmore (ed.) *Abolition Geography: Essays towards Liberation*, London: Verso, pp 352–392.

Global Witness (2022) 'Decade of defiance'. Available from: https://www.globalwitness.org/en/campaigns/environmental-activists/decade-defiance/ [Accessed 27 June 2023].

Global Witness (2023) 'Almost 2,000 land and environmental defenders killed between 2012 and 2022 for protecting the planet', *Global Witness* (13 September). Available from: https://www.globalwitness.org/en/press-releases/almost-2000-land-and-environmental-defenders-killed-between-2012-and-2022-protecting-planet/ [Accessed 8 January 2024].

Go, J. (2024) *Policing Empires: Militarization, Race, and the Imperial Boomerang in Britain and the US*, Oxford: Oxford University Press.

Gorz, A. (1980) *Ecology as Politics*, Boston, MA: South End Press.

Hall, R. (2023) 'More than 1,500 UK police officers accused of violence against women in six months', *The Guardian* (14 March) Available from: https://www.theguardian.com/uk-news/2023/mar/14/more-than-1500-uk-police-officers-accused-of-violence-against-women-in-six-months [Accessed 18 May 2023].

Hardy, D., Bailey, M. and Heynen, N. (2022) '"We're still here": an abolition ecology blockade of double dispossession of Gullah/Geechee land', *Annals of the American Association of Geographers*, 112(3): 867–876.

Heynen, N. (2018) 'Toward an abolition ecology'. *Abolition: A Journal of Insurgent Politics*, 1(1): 240–247.

Heynen, N. and Ybarra, M. (2021) 'On abolition ecologies and making "freedom as a place"', *Antipode*, 53: 21–35. DOI: 10.1111/anti.12666.

Hickel, J (2020) *Less is More: How Degrowth Will Save the World*, London: Penguin.

Indigenous Action Media (2014) 'Accomplices not allies: abolishing the ally industrial complex, an Indigenous perspective', version 2. Available from: https://www.indigenousaction.org/accomplices-not-allies-abolishing-the-ally-industrial-complex/ [Accessed 27 June 2023].

Isenberg, A.C. (2000) *The Destruction of the Bison: An Environmental History, 1750–1920*, Cambridge: Cambridge University Press.

Jewkes, Y. and Moran, D. (2015) 'The paradox of the "green" prison: sustaining the environment or sustaining the penal complex?' *Theoretical Criminology*, 19(4): 451–469.

Kaba, M. (2021) *We Do This 'Til We Free Us: Abolitionist Organizing and Transforming Justice*, Chicago: Haymarket Books.

Kimari, W. and Parish, J. (2020) 'What is a river? A transnational meditation on the colonial city, abolition ecologies and the future of geography', *Urban Geography*, 41(5): 643–656. DOI: 10.1080/02723638.2020.1743089.

Lancet, The (2021) 'Fatal police violence by race and state in the USA, 1980–2019: a network meta-regression'. Available from: https://www.thelancet.com/journals/lancet/article/PIIS0140-6736(21)01609-3/fulltext [Accessed 27 June 2023].

Lewis, P., Evans, R. and Pollak, S. (2013) 'Trauma of spy's girlfriend: "like being raped by the state"', *The Guardian* (24 June). Available from: https://www.theguardian.com/uk/2013/jun/24/undercover- police-spy-girlfriend-child [Accessed 27 June 2023].

Lowerson, A.J. (2022) 'Proportionate? The Metropolitan Police Service response to the Sarah Everard vigil: *Leigh v Commissioner of Police of the Metropolis* [2022] EWHC 527 (Admin)', *Journal of Criminal Law*, 86(4). DOI: 10.1177/00220183221101957.

Maher, G. (2021) *A World without Police: How Strong Communities Make Cops Obsolete*, London: Verso.

McDowell, M.G. and Fernandez, L.A. (2018) '"Disband, disempower, and disarm": amplifying the theory and practice of police abolition', *Critical Criminology*, 26: 373–391. DOI: 10.1007/s10612-018-9400-4.

Moloney, C.J. and Chambliss, W.J. (2014) 'Slaughtering the bison, controlling Native Americans: a state crime and green criminology synthesis', *Critical Criminology*, 22: 319–338. DOI: 10.1007/s10612-013-9220-5.

Owen, T. (2023) 'Police shot "Stop Cop City" activist 14 times with their hands up, independent autopsy shows', *Vice News* (13 March). Available from: https://www.vice.com/en/article/pkae48/cop-city-activist-shot-hands-up-tortuguita-death [Accessed 6 June 2023].

Pulido, L (2017) 'Geographies of race and ethnicity ii: environmental racism, racial capitalism and state-sanctioned violence', *Progress in Human Geography*, 41(4): 524–533. DOI: 10.1177/ 03091 32516 646495.

Neocleous, M. (2021) *A Critical Theory of Police Power: The Fabrication of the Social Order*, London: Verso.

Nibert, D. (2017) *Animal Oppression and Capitalism, vol. 1*, Santa Barbara, CA: ABC-CLIO.

Nixon, R. (2011) *Slow Violence and the Environmentalism of the Poor*, Cambridge, MA: Harvard University Press.

Peggs, K. (2013) 'The "animal-advocacy agenda": exploring sociology for non-human animals', *Sociological Review*, 61: 591–606.

Pellow, D.N. (2014) *Total Liberation: The Power and Promise of Animal Rights and the Radical Earth Movement*, Minneapolis: University of Minnesota Press.

Pellow, D.N. (2021) 'Struggles for environmental justice in US prisons and jails', *Antipode*, 53: 56–73. DOI: 10.1111/anti.12569.

Perkins, T. (2021) 'The multiple people of color origins of the US Environmental Justice Movement: social movement spillover and regional racial projects in California', *Environmental Sociology*, 7.2: 147–59, DOI: 10.1080/23251042.2020.1848502.

Pulido, L. and De Lara, J. (2018) 'Reimagining "justice" in environmental justice: radical ecologies, decolonial thought, and the Black Radical Tradition', *Environment and Planning E: Nature and Space*, 1(1–2): 76–98. DOI: 10.1177/2514848618770363.

Ranganathan, M. (2016) 'Thinking with flint: racial liberalism and the roots of an American water tragedy', *Capitalism Nature Socialism*, 27(3): 17–33. DOI: 10.1080/10455752.2016.1206583.

Rossi, C. (2021) 'Justice for Isac Tembé!', *Amazon Watch* (19 February). Available from: https://amazonwatch.org/news/2021/0219-justice-for-isac-tembe [Accessed 2 May 2023].

Scott, D. (2022) 'Stopping ecocide and climate catastrophe: a critique of the criminal law', *Open University: Harm and Evidence Research Collaborative Blog*. Available from: https://www.open.ac.uk/researchcentres/herc/blog/stopping-ecocide-and-climate-catastrophe-critique-criminal-law [Accessed 12 April 2023].

Selwyn, D. (2022) 'Global Britain and London's mega-mining corporations: colonial ecocide, extractive zones and frontiers of martial mining', in A. Dunlap and A. Brock (eds) *Enforcing Ecocide*, Cham: Palgrave Macmillan, pp 125–152.

Shevek, L. (2022) 'Against a liberal abolitionism', *Medium*. Available from: https://butchanarchy.medium.com/against-a-liberal-abolitionism-762e1d98f5d9 [Accessed 27 June 2023].

Shiva, V. (2008) *Soil Not Oil: Environmental Justice in a Time of Climate Crisis*, Boston, MA: South End Press.

Sinclair, G. and Williams, C.A. (2007) '"Home and away": the cross-fertilisation between "colonial" and "British" policing, 1921–85', *Journal of Imperial and Commonwealth History*, 35(2): 221–238.

Smith, D. & Chamberlain, P. (2015) *Blacklisted: The Secret War between Big Business and Union Activists*, Oxford: New Internationalist.

Stephens-Griffin, N. (2020) '"Everyone was questioning everything": understanding the derailing impact of undercover policing on the lives of UK environmentalists', *Social Movement Studies*, 20(4): 459–477. DOI: 10.1080/14742837.2020.1770073.

Stephens-Griffin, N. (2022) 'Embracing abolition ecology: a green criminological rejoinder', *Critical Criminology*. DOI: 10.1007/s10612-022-09672-7.

Stop Cop City (2023) 'What is Cop City?'. Available from: https://stopcop.city/what-is-cop-city/ [Accessed 15 May 2023].

Stop Cop City Solidarity (2023) 'Take action'. Available from: https://www.stopcopcitysolidarity.org/takeaction [Accessed 18 May 2023].

Taylor, N. and Fitzgerald, A. (2018) 'Understanding animal (ab)use: green criminological contributions, missed opportunities and a way forward', *Theoretical Criminology*, 22(3): 402–425.

Tokar, B. (2018) 'On social ecology and the movement for climate justice', in S.G. Jacobsen (ed.) *Climate Justice and the Economy*, London: Routledge, pp 168–187.

United Nations (2022) 'Brazil: UN experts decry acts of racialised police brutality', press release (6 July). Available from: www.ohchr.org/en/press-releases/2022/07/brazil-un-experts-decry-acts-racialised-police-brutality [Accessed 27 June 2023].

Verweijen, J. and A. Dunlap (2021) 'The evolving techniques of the social engineering of extraction: Introducing political (re)actions "from above" in large-scale mining and energy projects', *Political Geography*, 88: 102342.

Woodman, C. (2020) 'How British police and intelligence are a product of the imperial boomerang effect', *Verso Blog*, 10 June. Available from: https://www.versobooks.com/en-gb/blogs/news/4390-how-british-police-and-intelligence-are-a-product-of-the-imperial-boomerang-effect#:~:text=British%20police%20and%20intelligence%20services,collection%20by%20metropolitan%20security%20services [Accessed 3 May 2023].

Ybarra, M. (2021) 'Site fight! Toward the abolition of immigrant detention on Tacoma's tar pits (and everywhere else)', *Antipode*, 53(1): 36–55.

13

Abolitionist Activism in Post-Mass-Media Societies: Moral Panic and the Amplification of Abolitionist Voices

Michael Dellwing

How can we ensure that the voice of abolitionist and other grassroots activists are heard in societies where mainstream mass media constantly touts excessively punitive responses for those to whom the criminal label has been successfully applied? What are the potentials and pitfalls in attempting to amplify penal abolitionist voices, ideas and associated radical worldviews in post mass-media societies? The focus of this chapter is on how a relatively recent shift in media economies has impacted upon the analyses of penal abolitionism and the subsequent hearing of progressive activist voices. Counterhegemonic activism, including that aspiring for penal abolition, has rarely been as strong as it is today. This strength, however, has brought with it concerted institutional efforts to defend centralized forms of meaning making, forms which are referred to here as the state and corporate media, known as 'mass media'. This defence of the mass media has been underscored by a series of major moral panics dismissing the counterhegemonic claims and content of radical activists as 'misinformation'. This way, only the state-corporate media is painted as the conveyor of truth.

While the media debate on 'fake news', and with it much of the more shallow academic debate, hinges on debates on whether or not something is true in some abstract sense, the sociologically much more interesting question is who gets to label something as 'true', in what power structures this label occurs and against whom it is utilized. The unleashing of moral panics around 'fake news' of activists and the unreliability of the knowledge – for example, claims and evidence of radical voices from below – has been part of an orchestrated attempt to hinder and denounce the credibility of leftist activism and their associated counterhegemonic struggles. This chapter argues that it is essential that the resistance and revolutionary struggle of such progressive activists does not fall victim to this kind of moral panic, lest it risk hurting its own chances of success. It is especially decentralized media (that is, media not produced by corporate or state entities) where penal abolitionist narratives have thrived in recent years. In fact, the destabilization of mass-media structures of dominant discourses gives even greater hope to the spread of counterhegemonic and countercolonial positions by penal abolitionist activists and others directly engaged in the struggle for liberation.

In recent years we have witnessed a strong increase in the prevalence of moral panics focusing on the need to combat a rise in 'misinformation', an epithet usually used by state actors and their synergetic corporate media in the Global North against state actors in conflict with the imperial hegemony of the US and Europe. This 'misinformation' is claimed to originate and be disseminated through decentralized news content not controlled by corporate or state actors in these imperial contexts. Rather than threats to 'liberal democracy' or 'a well-informed public' (or 'public health'), 'misinformation' and 'disinformation' or 'fake news' are better understood as labels given to counterhegemonic information to limit the spread of resistance against corporate and state-managed information distribution (Dellwing, 2022). As labels, they are key weapons in the battles to resist against the loss of power of state- and corporate-owned and managed media. This mislabelling of knowledge, claims and evidence generated from below is a general issue for activists and rebels, and is not unique to those advocating penal abolitionism. This chapter therefore discusses this state-corporate orchestrated moral panic in general terms, referring to penal abolitionist activist voices as one illustrative example among others. The point being that the disavowal of radical voices through this 'anti-misinformation moral panic' has detrimental impacts on amplifying the voices of all progressive activists engaging in liberative struggles for justice irrespective of specific focus.

Further, it is impossible in practice to disentangle abolitionist activism from wider calls for emancipation. There is undoubtedly considerable overlap between those activists involved in the struggle against Palestinian genocide, climate catastrophe, imperialism (whether in Ukraine, the Middle East or elsewhere) and/or the harms and exploitation of rampant neoliberal capitalism, especially among penal abolitionists inspired by communists and socialists (see Scott, Chapter 14 in this volume). This chapter therefore brings the readers' attention to pluralized and decentralized media that is grounded in an emancipatory logic, and these examples are especially helpful when exploring the potential to amplify activist voices where no specific penal abolitionist platform currently exists. Finally, such reflections like those on the harms of power are also a central aspect of abolitionist strategy in exposing how the criminal law is only focused on the 'harms' of the powerless.

Strategically, such 'anti-misinformation' moral panics first, and very prominently in the mass media, target content labelled as 'right-wing', openly racist or oppressive speech. However, this focus is nothing but an insidious smokescreen. The 'anti-misinformation moral panic' is first used to empower states and corporations to easily ban such speech. However, it also creates a mechanism which can then be easily used against any kind of speech to remove actors from distribution networks or to moderate and censor content. Quickly, and initially less publicly, this censorship extends to anti-imperialist, anti-colonialist and anti-capitalist speech in online contexts. Significantly for this chapter, it can also be used to censor abolitionist voices.

While the strategic first step of targeting the right often manages to convince progressives to nod along and join into a chorus demanding state and corporate control, it is imperative to understand this movement of control as an attack on *all* forms of resistance, especially on the forms of resistance most dangerous to existing state structures: anti-imperialist and anti-capitalist speech. Therefore, it is in the interests of counterhegemonic actors, including penal abolitionists, to defend the integrity of citizen-distributed information against corporate capture, centralized control and algorithmic moderation. Penal abolitionist activists, as fellow counterhegemonic actors, must also join the fight against such moral panics that introduce mechanisms control over what and how news can be distributed as a solution 'misinformation' and 'fake news'.

Ending the 20th-century exception

Although not always explicitly acknowledged, contemporary studies of penal abolition rely heavily on the sociology of labelling and critical sociology, which expanded and deepened significantly in the postwar era (Cohen, 1988). They are related to the study of social problems, which has asked how *ideas* of social problems become successful and widespread enough to gain traction and effect policy change. To answer this question, the classical studies in labelling theory and associated sociological analysis have studied the paths definitions of problems take (Becker, 1963). From the ground up, they can rise in media pyramids where interested actors 'conquer' newspapers and TV news, from where they are passed on to state apparatuses. Top-down, they can originate within the state to then be propagandized through the mass media. Often, the latter disguises itself as the former, as is the case in the now paradigmatic 'colour revolutions' the US curated in countries resistant to US policy demands. These present themselves as grassroots movements which are orchestrated by US institutions and aided by US corporate media and social network algorithms. Punitivity measures, mass incarcerations, wars on crime and drugs (and actual, US colonial wars against Middle Eastern countries, Central and South American coups, and so on) often take this route. Activism has relied, and has to rely, on the conquering of narrative and its successful dissemination, thus facing a steep uphill battle in environments dominated by state and corporate media. Corporate mass media economies are, at best, interested in activism-as-spectacle, but usually have no interest in aiding the advance of real critical challenges to existing structures of power. This of course also includes activist voices calling for penal abolition.

The sociology of social problems and moral panics has focused on this battle to achieve recognition in media pyramids. However, this is not endemic to labelling perspectives and the sociology of social problems; it is merely a result of the structures of power and the technical structure of media distribution in postwar capitalism. Postwar mass media was centralized from the start and there was little technical chance for the emergence and development of a decentralized television network given the nature of broadcast technology in the postwar era. Corporate mass audiovisual media started out centred on just a few actors: originally, three networks served countries of millions. Cable television brought a large expansion of channels, but not of sources: within late-stage corporate capitalism, seven corporations controlled the thousands of channels that cable television made possible. At the same time, corporate consolidations had also significantly streamlined newspaper production and distribution. This is where the 'bottleneck', or pyramid, of social problems sociology originates, and with it its 'conquest model' of the media to effect change through amplifying the knowledge, claims and evidence of progressive activism. This is the same structure in which penal abolitionisms, and their 'social problem' definition about the harms of state institutional violence, have had to operate. Yet abolitionist voices have largely not succeeded in their attempts to 'conquer' state-corporate media and consequently have in the past often failed to be heard.

This postwar mass media offers narrow pathways for what is reported as 'settled truth' on the evening TV news. This 'settled truth' has 'a bias towards the status quo and a deference to authority' (Viner, 2016), as 'the story of journalism, on a day-to-day basis, is the story of the interaction of reporters and officials' (Schudson, 1989: 272), including of course officials representing prisons and other state punishments. This one-way, centralized, silo structure of the mass media in the 20th century also made it 'prohibitively difficult for ordinary people to challenge the power of the press' (Viner, 2016). Thus, '[w]hile news may be viewed as a window on the world through which Americans learn of their institutions and their leaders, it is a window that reflects largely the media's own construction of reality' (Turk, 1985: 34) which, far from being a simple representation of reality, reproduces 'the practices of those who have the power to determine the experience of others'(Molotch and Lester, 1974: 54) to 'make newspaper ideals and practices consonant with the culture of dominant social classes' (Conboy, 2017: 1267), reproducing 'hegemonic morality' (Stehr, 1998).

Famous studies of the 1970s, 1980s and 1990s showed how the mass (or now legacy) media was structured toward the top-down model of problems construction, to emotionalize moral panics into 'manufacturing consent' (Herman and Chomsky, 1988) for surveillance and control policies, and for war. The success of many of these strategies depended on there being no counternarrative widely available outside of very specialized existing social resistance groups. Not only organized labour, Marxists, anarchists, abolitionists and other leftist interest and identity groups, but also churches and conservative groups could disseminate information that refuted corporate propaganda. Marginalized groups could use their internal channels to fight moral panic narratives that targeted them, from fans of role-playing games in the case of the 'Dungeons and Dragons' panics (Laycock, 2015) and organized secular Satanists against Satanic moral panics (Victor, 1993) to LGBTQ networks against sexual moral panics (Herdt, 2009). Resistance and the voices of counterhegemonic actors, where they existed, remained localized and had little chance of being amplified beyond these local networks, as the means of widespread amplification remained in the hands of corporate and state actors. These actors not only had no interest in amplifying resistance, but were also central in disseminating the very propaganda that these resistance movements aimed to counteract. The same is also true in the context of penal abolition.

Resistance content and the propagation of subversive knowledge is thus not new to the social media age. It is the era of institutional control over media that is the historical exception. The nationally unified media world, one under nation states and transnational capital, is a relatively new development. Newspapers were historically partisan and a divergent means of in-group communication in localized areas. They only became national later. Emancipatory knowledge was widely available in the pre-mass-media newspaper age, often through labour unions, communist and socialist parties and internal-facing newsletters of activist groups. For a long time, decentralized and pluralized forms of meaning making were the historical *norm*, and only the mass-media culture of the short[1] 20th century disrupted it, as an island of exception.

The corporate centralization of the media, along with the systematic dismantling of communist parties and labour unions in the Anglo-Saxon world and their integration into and conquest by capitalist political structures in the European part of empire, have erased much emancipatory content from the 20th-century media. At the same time, right-wing content, often with a punitive ideology at its core, thrived, with corporate support, in niches such as talk radio, the wider circles of the corporate newspaper press and in corporate news channels. The internet age broke the chains of all-out, direct commercial editorial control and brought about wider recognition for emancipatory content. This change creates enormous opportunities for abolitionists.

The internet has massively decentralized the creation and distribution of information. Contemporary media worlds are multipolar, with a strong popular-participatory drive. It has introduced a post-mass-media form of communication that has eroded old structures of power over meaning making and shifts the paths of social discourses. Even though the production and posting of content has become decentralized, corporate control over internet content has slowly and quietly been re-established – where five mass-media corporations editorially control television and four internet corporations control much of social media content distribution (Facebook, Google, Amazon, and X) – and have siloed and monetized this citizen-centred production. The system monetizes content made and posted by everyone, without editors which prescreen content (yet),[2] without news anchors paid by centralized corporations. However, these systems do censor and block after the fact, when this decentralized content is deemed objectionable for whatever reason, where 'after the fact' is often milliseconds after the fact as algorithmic moderation blocks content. This happens in cooperation with governments; especially with the US government, where these corporations are located, they have become the new social problem construction chokepoint (Pandey, 2022; Taibbi, 2022).

Resistant content

The decentralized, two-way communication street of the internet enables independent, citizen-centred communication away from the immediate control by editors of state- and corporate-owned media entities. Online decentralized spaces are now again full of critical, leftist, anti-imperialist, abolitionism-friendly channels and content, much of which had lived a sequestered life before. In what is at least formally the 'decentralized' communication system of the internet, nonhegemonic narratives that are not scripted after dominant narratives still have a much larger reach; whereas before they could only spread within the limits of informal or counterstructural networks, they now have a potentially global reach. While there are only limited examples directly focused on penal abolition, important wider examples include daily news like *Counterpunch*, anti-imperialist journalism like *The Gray Zone, Code Pink, The Socialist Correspondent*, the *World Tonight*,[3] *Status Coup, Mango Press, Workers Today*, Richard Medhurst and also a large number of socialist and communist channels offering social science education like *The Socialist Program, Proletarian TV*,[4] *Red Menace, RevLeft, Second Thought*[5] and *Leftist Reading*. Penal abolitionists could take inspiration from these examples.

These kinds of interventions provide a significant opportunity for the amplification of critical voices with regard to both abolishing prisons and the police in the service of empire. For example, in decentralized media, police violence in the US has been exposed as a routine occurrence rather than the 'deplorable exception' as portrayed by the mainstream media in the event that it became public, which was itself unlikely in the age of controlled mass media. Images like those of the killing of George Floyd now go around the world in an instant. The same is true of police killings in European countries that have liked to portray their police as friendly assistants rather than US-type stormtroopers (a very popular image with German law enforcement[6]).[7] Police and military violence against protesters in Peru[8] can be related to US support of Peru's coup regime, and its likely role in instigating the coup,[9] after Pedro Castillo, the elected President, planned to nationalize natural resource incomes, not to speak of a genocide in Gaza that is happening in real time on smartphones all over the world since 7 October 2023, where the images of devastation that would in the past have been hidden are now inescapable and force their way into mainstream media because they already have been made public in telegram channels and cannot be as easily ignored as before.

State and corporate propaganda has a long tradition. In the past, official propaganda about the Vietnam or Iraq Wars, about the US Civil Rights movement, about the context of rebellion against racial discrimination and so on and so forth was often uncovered by historians and political scientists, though usually years and sometimes decades later. Today, the resistance against state and corporate media propaganda is immediate and often quite impactful. In the official playbook, this challenge against propaganda is then (in turn and quite ironically) labelled 'misinformation', 'conspiracy theory' (on the social use of the label, see Anton and Schetsche [2013]) or 'foreign propaganda'; many of the aforementioned resistance narratives will have sparked an immediate reaction of this kind in the reader, which only goes to show how deeply successful this 'anti-misinformation moral panic' has been. However, the reader is invited to remember how propaganda about the Vietnam and Iraq Wars were not committed by foreign governments or citizen journalists, but by the US state, and how many of the stories first called 'fake' by official sources were often quietly acknowledged later. Those who do not have to be reminded have already entered into the new world of decentralized communication, where 'people distrust much of what is presented as fact' (Viner, 2016) by corporate media. Viner (2016) reinforces decades of moral panic and social problems research when he adds that such distrust in corporate media narratives is not at all misplaced. Thus, as Nagle (2017: 13) asserts, 'the media's mainstream hold over formal politics died' in the middle of the 2010s – and good riddance.

This has affected abolitionist content as well. Like other progressive content in the struggle for liberation, it does not need the internet to exist; it has existed outside corporate media for centuries, from anti-slavery abolitionist newspapers to prison newsletters and papers. In a chapter in the *International Handbook of Penal Abolition* (Coyle and Scott, 2021), abolitionist activists at Rustbelt Abolition Radio recount the history of Prison Radio in the 'golden age' of corporate media. This moment 'featured prerecorded dialogues with revolutionaries such as Leonard Peltier, Stanley 'Tookie' Williams ... and ... Mumia Abu Jamal', but its origins in the mass media age mean that it was hidden in local distribution, if it was accessible at all. Prison newspapers are a common occurrence, and Rustbelt Abolition Radio (2021) recalls newspapers founded in the 1970s in the US. Alongside this, there are examples in the UK, such as the prisoner-led publication *Inside Time*, and those in Germany.[10] While, as Rustbelt Abolition Radio (2021) notes, 'abolitionist media projects foster connections and help to build and sustain networks engaged in long-term struggles against state violence', they have only been able to do so within closed networks, often of the already convinced and those affected by personal relations. The end of the corporate and state oligopoly on information distribution has changed this. Rustbelt Abolition Radio (2021) specifically mentions podcasts as an avenue of wider distribution or emancipatory abolitionist knowledge, claims and evidence; indeed, podcasts are an island that is largely free from corporate content control.

As Phan (2021: 45) has noted, abolition has gained considerable traction in online spaces in the last few years. A sentiment analysis conducted on Twitter/X shows a steep rise of positive interaction with the idea of abolition in the last half century. Table 13.1 provides an overview of the findings of a #PrisonAbolition sentiment analysis using the azure machine learning tool from 2015 to 2020.

Not only have mentions of penal abolitionism skyrocketed, which would be a success no matter what kind of mentions the topic gathers, but they have also been positive by a wide margin. Notably, the gap between positive

Table 13.1: Abolitionist sentiments

Views	Year					
	2015	2016	2017	2018	2019	2020
Negative	38	62	75	117	211	252
Neutral	29	43	67	71	106	145
Positive	221	202	260	336	408	653
Total	**288**	**307**	**402**	**524**	**725**	**1,050**

and negative mentions has reduced, which is undoubtedly part of the controversy-inviting structure prevalent in for-profit social media, which monetizes attention, which largely means monetizing ideological battles and therefore hones algorithms to produce such battles. This rise in the popularity of penal abolitionism goes hand in hand with the rise of #BlackLivesMatter, together with #acab, #defundthepolice and #PrisonAbolition; more fodder for network attention battles and therefore more possible profit centres, where 'the hashtagging of these movements on Twitter [X] made them more accessible to a broader audience' (Phan, 2021: 43). This brings prison abolition into the same tent as wider decentralized movements that are critical of state power, especially state power as exercised through its plethora of monopoly of violence actors, bringing prison abolition together with movements to abolish the police and the immigration enforcement troops of Immigration and Customs Enforcement (ICE) (Phan, 2021: 48).

Content on both penal and prison abolition can be found on *Democracy Now*,[11] Haymarket Books[12] and the independent channels Critical Resistance,[13] Red May[14] and AfroMarxist.[15] All these platforms can perform a valuable service in amplifying abolitionist activist voices. Futher, the educational Center for Contemporary Critical Thought publishes seminars on abolitionism,[16] as does the New School[17] and the German Rosa Luxemburg Stiftung, which is associated with the German party Die Linke.[18] Foreign news organizations like Al Jazeera[19] also take up the subject, as has the UK-based BBC Ideas website.[20]

Chris Hedges, one of the most well-known alternative media actors in the abolitionist space, regularly teaches English to incarcerated people through a Rutgers-affiliated programme and has produced academic work that is critical of the prison system (Hedges, 2021). In past years, his journalism was published exclusively in alternative written media venues (Hedges, 2011: 2014), but mostly in video formats through alternative outlets such as *Democracy Now*,[21] *Democracy at Work* (a socialist activism and news site),[22] the 'alternative radio' show on the *Prison Plantation System*,[23] activist channel act. tv,[24] *Media Sanctuary*[25] and through many activism organizations and academic institutions.[26] However, the main outlet for Hedges' anti-imperialism, anti-war and social criticism was a regular show on *Russia Today*, titled *On Contact*. This TV show ran for six years and included interviews with Hugh Hamilton,[27] Walter Fortson and Boris Franklin,[28] and Mumia Abdul-Jamal,[29] as well as large amounts of content on Julian Assange.[30] In the wake of both anti-Russian censorship on social media and the global confrontation that the US is currently seeking with its geopolitical rivals, the entire archive of this show was deleted by YouTube. Despite the fact that it consisted exclusively of anti-imperialist, anti-war and social activism content and hosted no content on the Russian government, the war in Ukraine, or related subjects, it still fell victim to a wholesale purge of everything Russian.[31]

The preceding cases are examples of the kind of sources that were not widely available outside of academia and closed groups 20 years ago. In the time before the internet, such subversive knowledge (see Scott, Chapter 14 in this volume) required underground organizing to distribute. Yet such subversive knowledge, including that challenging the logic of punishment, has for a while now been available widely over text, video and podcasting platforms. Abolitionists and others working for emancipatory transformations should not lose sight of the opportunities that such platforms can bring about in terms of building movements and momentum for change. Interestingly, among counterhegemonic narratives in corporate-controlled decentralized spaces, penal abolitionism occupies a more tolerated position in contrast to other anti-imperialist content, such as reports from warzones from countries under Western attack like Yemen or Palestine. Conversely, countries under non-Western attack have a privileged position in the corporate-controlled online sphere.

Media diversity as a moral panic target

This post-mass-media narrative diversity and the dismantling of the singular pinnacle of information distribution have become the target of much vitriol in the last few years. The legacy media's reaction to its loss of importance has been to stigmatize online content as hate speech, misinformation, filter bubbles and fake news, with charges of 'post-truth societies' taking hold, which really means 'post-centralized information control societies'. This panic discourse attributes 'dysfunctionality' (Benkler, Faris and Roberts, 2018: 267) to media economies in which the concentrated mass media no longer commands the trust of citizens. Current debates bemoan '[e]cho chambers ringing with false news' and warn of 'ungovernable' (Benkler, et al, 2018: 5) Western democracies if the decentralization of the realm of information dismantles the 'simultaneity' (Anderson, 1991) on which the shared meaning of the nation state is built. In this 'anti-misinformation moral panic', diversity, resistance, criticism and challenges to mainstream news narratives are portrayed as corrosive not only to public discourse, but also to the entire constitution of the nation state, while trying, increasingly helplessly, to paint corporate and state media as the only source of 'reliable', 'true' information.[32]

In line with past moral panics, the problem narrative picks the most egregious elements as a *pars pro toto* example to portray the entire field through the lens of such egregious examples, a technique that is well examined in cases of discrimination against lower-status groups (Elias and Scotson, 1994). In the case of decentralized information, this role has run through a number of hand-picked absurdist stories, from 'pizzagate' in 2016 and 2017, 'the Clinton-is-running-a-pedophilia-ring-out-of-a-pizza-shop conspiracy' (Grim and Cherkis, 2017), to QAnon narratives since 2018, to less and less absurdist ones in the contemporary 'misinformation' circuit. These narratives have also been reduced to comically simplistic representations as supposed 'examples' of foolish online narratives and all have served to equate decentralized narratives with easily refuted 'crazy' fringe theories. From right-wing moral panics, through COVID-19 panics and finally, in the course of North Atlantic Treaty Organization (NATO)-imperial anti-Russian and anti-Chinese panics, catalysed official legitimacy for an increasing crackdown on noncorporate-friendly content through information filtering in social media, controls, moderation and deletion mechanisms that quickly targeted truly critical information rather than the absurdist content that was used to justify the control tools. The 'anti-misinformation moral panic' portrays it as if decentralized information distribution apart from corporate and state channels means a danger from absurd conspiracy narratives. Lately, however, the moral panic seems to have shifted focus to foreign actors and 'foreign propaganda' (a term tellingly not usually used in reference to narratives that support Western imperialist governments). It thus tars both the enemy within and the enemy at the gates.

By painting the newfound access of private persons to the distribution of meaning and the loss of control over this meaning by state and corporate actors as dangerous exactly when, and *only* when, it disagrees with dominant problem constructions it repaints centralized actors as trustworthy and truthful. This is something that ascriptions of the classical critique of punitive state power and punitive media narratives would quickly question, and have done so (Hall et al, 1978). It also indicates the virtually insurmountable challenge abolitionists face if they are to 'conquer' the legacy media and spread the subversive abolitionist message through such a medium.

While the role of media distribution as a target of problems construction is somewhat new, moral panic about new media technologies is, of course, not. New media technologies have regularly sparked moral panics, complete with ascriptions that the changes in media distribution would constitute a danger for society. For example, this happened with the printing press, the theatre, novels and television. In a sense, these fears were justified from the perspective of the established order, as these technologies did indeed help bring down established frames by reshuffling the structures of access to the public and thereby diversifying the positions that make up public debate. In many ways, the current 'fake news' and 'anti-misinformation moral panic' is a rerun of the panics the Catholic Church instigated against the printing press, where it also feared a loss of control over the distribution of information. Indeed, it did suffer such a loss of control and a subsequent crash of its power position.

Also, the distribution of decentralized narratives long pre-dates the internet. Even though Benedict Anderson puts the newspaper as the shared source of information, simultaneously consumed each morning (or as an evening edition) at the centre of national unification, newspapers were once very divisive and partisan institutions. An undercurrent of this partisanship has remained throughout the mass-media era. Schudson (1989: 4) notes that: 'Before the 1830s ... American newspapers were expected to present a partisan viewpoint, not a neutral one.' He pins the emergence of news to the emergence of a new 'middle class' and the formation of the Associated Press in 1848, which was carefully distant exactly because its member newspapers were all 'differently partisan' (Schudson 1989: 4). Although this is an idea that is sometimes credited with starting the dramatization of neutrality, it is in effect actually a dramatization that erases the particular socioeconomic interests embedded in dominant narratives of their time.

What is now decried as polarizing online information sharing also has its roots in mass media. Commercial talk radio of the 1980s and 1990s already carried right-wing 'challenges' to official narratives, and news channels picked up the strategy of polarizing content production to serve different niches of the political market and to create engagement in the form of outrage and passionate support (Dellwing, 2019). While sharp right-wing narratives were already common here, sharp left-wing narratives were not; conservative narratives are, in the end, not dangerous to the corporate order and hence are much easier to integrate into it, while its more absurdist arms serve as ready-made targets to advance media control panics while not actually threatening the corporate state. Online content like Alex Jones' *InfoWars*, for instance, fits into this talk-radio tradition and the polarizing setup that had been part of media economies for decades, if not centuries. Local radio 'phone-ins' are often grounded in penological illiteracy and emotive retributive content that targets progressive ideas on responding to crime. This regressive agenda is also something found in mainstream forums, including alleged 'high-brow' media content such as the BBC *Moral Maze*. Despite claims to impartiality, the *Moral Maze* is a gladiatorial-style battleground for liberal and right-wing panel members to 'cross-examine' 'witnesses'. For example, on the 2023 episode 'Do prisons do more harm than good?', a platform was given to both right-wing and leftist penal abolitionist voices. Yet the abolitionist voice was most likely present only to give a pretence of 'balance' to legitimate the focus on hegemonic ideas like liberal reform and retributivism.

Classical sociological approaches to information and news have long noted the structural pressures under which mass-media news is made and how these pressures support the reproduction of hegemonic power structures. Centralized channels of meaning making (that is, the mass media) are part of the institutional order in which they live and, as such, are always already infused with the interests of these institutions. That was the core argument in Herman and Chomsky's (1988) *Manufacturing Consent*, which analysed how the structures of mass media news are entangled and intertwined with the very institutions the media was, in the idealized narrative, supposed to act as a 'check' on and hold to account. Herman and Chomsky (1988) identify a series of filters through which media 'manufactures consent' for existing power structures and their actions. Different mechanisms of power are at play here: the structure of media ownership and its pressures; the fact that media financing means advertisements, which creates dependence on advertisers; a further dependence on official sources and the relationships with officials to get those sources makes it difficult to oppose them openly so as not to burn bridges; and ideological frameworks grip the personnel of media corporations before they are hired, making open coercion unnecessary. Finally, the authors identify 'flak', 'negative responses to a media statement' (Herman and Chomsky 1988: 26) that contradicts hegemonic narratives, as means to discredit challenges to these power structures. The labels 'fake news', 'disinformation' and finally 'conspiracy theory' (Anton, Schetsche and Walter, 2013) are, in that frame, flak.

Also, while the 'anti-misinformation moral panic' portrays decentralized communication as caught in filter bubbles, the opposite is the case. Cory Doctorow (2021) notes that the active mix of production and consumption in decentralized networks affords much wider, deeper, more plural and diverse meaning making than the oligopoly of corporate and state media ever could. Not only are online citizen-sourced narratives not 'filter bubbles', but '[t]he real 'bubble' wasn't choosing your own programming – it was everyone turning on their TV on Thursday nights to Friends, Seinfeld and The Simpsons', (Doctorow, 2021) or the evening news and the big newspapers. The reintroduction of the bubble happens at the level of corporate social networks that privilege mass media posts and derank rebellious, counterhegemonic content, including that focused on penal abolition. Just like the flak works in a negative sense of discrediting, the corporate filter bubble is also a significant strategy in the attempt at re-creating corporate mass media control.

Sociological analysis' baseline critical attitude to institutional meaning making allies it with these new pluralities much more than it puts them at odds with one another. This pluralization of meaning making allows a wide challenge of structures that reproduce bourgeois normality and the punitive mentality, in content as well as in style. When Becker (2018) recounts his colleague Alfred Lindesmith's visit from federal agents who told him that institutions were keeping an eye on him for challenging the official narratives of dangerous drugs – a visit the agencies later, of course, denied – this is not qualitatively different from mass media efforts to denigrate decentralized news for going against hegemonic narratives and hegemonic styles of argument and, in fact, from federal agents today visiting participants in decentralized media for their opposition to dominant narratives. The producers of the Marxist YouTube channel *Second Thought* were also indeed visited by Homeland Security Agents and questioned for 'anti-American content' online in 2020, as was the founder of Odysee in 2024, and also, a few weeks earlier, Scott Ritter. This form of intimidation is the tip of control. Below it, governments regularly instruct large media platforms to block and remove content for political reasons, under the institutional fiction that it is 'disinformation' or 'terrorist content'. At the beginning of 2024, when finalizing this chapter, a number of pro-Palestinian channels on X (formerly Twitter) were summarily banned, a practice Meta (Facebook) had been engaging in for years before the 2023 crisis; channels documenting life in occupied Palestine are regularly deleted from Facebook and YouTube.[33] This extends to many contexts. For instance, YouTube channels in support of the anti-imperialist Nicaraguan government were deleted in the runup to that country's 2021 presidential election.[34] While this deletion of channels in support of the enemy side in Western wars has gone on for years, it came to the forefront in the Ukraine war, where channels critical of the West and NATO, and those pointing out the long history of US intervention and regime change in Ukraine, indiscriminate NATO confrontation with Russia, Western sabotage of peace deals in the Ukrainian civil war and subsequently sabotage of peace deals in the Ukraine war were deleted in quick succession. However, as decentralized media channels can be formed anew in a decentralized system, this control is a practice of swatting ever-regenerating new channels. Though any channel that reaches a noticeable mass of subscribers is quickly doomed, it can be reborn through 'calling' subscribers through other channels.[35] The nature of the internet allows new platforms to take advantage of the gaps opened by platform censorship, and video platforms like Rumble and Odysee and platforms like Substack and Medium have gained much traction as users flee censored corporate systems. However, being corporate themselves, these newer platforms are vulnerable to state pressure and capture once they grow to larger user counts. Decentralized or federated platforms like Peertube, Mastodon or platforms operating on blockchain systems, like Nostr, are again harder to control, as they are not and indeed could not be incorporated in any specific state.

Of course, these noninstitutional, nonstate, noncorporate actors are not free from economic and ideological frameworks; however, they do not operate under the same pressures of access, advertisement and ownership that corporate and state media do. They are also more independent on the level of liability: 'Corporate media culture, being corporate and therefore funded, is always at risk of expensive legal challenges; hence, everything is potentially serious' (Dellwing, 2019). People in everyday life, talking to other individuals, have historically not been subject to such liabilities. While political actors often try to portray this as a 'lack of accountability', it is actually a lack of institutional frames of control that shape news narratives and make it unnecessary to openly censor mass media, as these pressures make it compliant before the fact; policies to silence private persons, non-disclosure 'agreements' (actually, orders within a power structure) and silence mandates are policies to make them compliant and scared. In the prison industry, the constant monitoring of all communication and the limitation of visits, as well as the difficult lines of access to prisoners, are parts that introduce such limits and fear. As Cory Doctorow (2021) has noted, we should keep an eye on the surveillance and control systems used in prisons, as the literally captive audience of prisons is often the testing ground for surveillance technology that is later applied to larger and larger parts of the population (see Taylor, Chapter 8 in this volume). Online pseudonymity, often portrayed as a 'hate speech danger', protects the speech of individuals by extending the informality that characterizes normal everyday interaction to online spaces and thus counters the straitjacket of anticipatory obedience to institutional pressure that the mass media flatters as 'accountability'. Sennett (1977: 311) already noted in the 1970s that 'people can be sociable only when they have some protection from each other'. This is increased by magnitudes for people being able to be critical. Communication in civil society has access to possibilities of critical communication that institutional actors cannot activate.

Destabilization as hope

So where does this leave us in terms of reflections on the amplification of abolitionist voices in post-mass-media societies? The contemporary 'anti-misinformation moral panic' over 'fake news' and the social distribution of information is therefore, more deeply, once again a question of the power over the distribution of hegemonic knowledge and a reaction to the loss of position suffered by legacy media. The 'misinformation' tag is only applied to content that resists hegemonic narratives; content that supports hegemonic narratives and content shared by Western imperialist governments, is immune from being attacked this way.[36] This can leave penal abolitionist advocates out in the cold.

It is no surprise that the internet has awoken hopes for democratization and decentralization of meaning making, which was most pronounced in the early days of the internet before the takeover by corporate silos. The destabilization of corporate and state monopoly over information distribution has allowed the broadcast of images of police violence against protesters and minorities that subvert the official stories and interpretations about these protests that otherwise make the news; have highlighted the plight and death of migrants that otherwise remain unseen; have documented pervasive normalized violence against women across the globe; and have uncovered the ongoing warmongering of imperialist countries around the US hegemon desperate to safeguard their neocolonial position in times of decline. This destabilization of the narrative offers hope for those engaged in abolitionist activism for finding new ways of shining a spotlight on the unnecessary and useless harms, suffering and injury systematically generated in prisons, and the immunity and impunity of these harms and suffering perpetrated by those in power (Scott and Sim, 2023).

Decentralized media, for the first time in history, offers a structural opportunity to deliver information worldwide without having to conquer the citadels of communication and without having to rely on building one's own translocal networks. Already we can see prison newspapers, prison radio and wider information about prison life and prison struggles distributed. We can see a widespread publication of state violence in policing and prisons take hold through the perseverance of social media posting and independent media reporting on these matters. In a certain way, this is similar to the movements within sociology in the 1950s and 1960s, but on a much larger scale. The late, great, labelling theorist Howard Becker credits his rise into sociological prominence and that of his contemporaries to the widening of opportunities within academia in that period, where many people from working-class backgrounds, and even many without degrees, became instructors at university following a severe shortage and an expansion of educational opportunities (Becker, 2018).

Decentralized communication expands the realm of discourse much more widely and does so without the institutional aid that allowed for the expansion of the 1950s and 1960s. Howard Becker noted that in the 1950s, resistance against hegemonic narratives entered academia when people participated who, from their everyday life experiences, knew the institutional façades to be frauds (Becker, 2018). Gramsci would have called them 'organic intellectuals', and though it is doubted that Becker read Gramsci, there are strong points of contact to be found here (see also the ideas in Becker, 1967). It was lifeworld knowledge and socialization into a background where persecution by police was common. State institutions were not seen as the servants that they are to the monied strata of society. This allowed Becker and his colleagues to strongly resist dominant narratives about marijuana as they arose in new reports and official papers, noting that it was clear to anyone who had taken part in drug subcultures that the substance was neither addictive nor degenerative, though this was news to anyone who got their information from newspapers. While in the 1960s, such resistance was limited to academic and insider circles, the online resistance against dominant narratives now has forced mass media to pick up at least the scraps of the discourses that have already disseminated online, to not openly look as if the media was ignoring these issues; still, in-depth, analytical, detailed information that, most importantly, gives people outside of corporate media a voice can be found in the decentralized content generation of the internet much more than on corporate news.

It is also no surprise that this hope has been severely dampened by the colonization of online discussion by corporate silos and the content controls implemented in them. These controls occur in symbiosis with the US government, which has an interest in maintaining large quasi-monopolistic platforms like YouTube, Twitter/X and Facebook, as the presence of only few points of control can be more easily deputized to control content (see for example the close relationship at the end of 2024 between Elon Musk and incoming US President Donald Trump). Yet, some of the hopes associated with decentralized communication have indeed come true. Digital cultures have normalized the critical stance towards institutional meaning making that was and remains central to sociological analysis and social criticism, at least where sociology has not become analysis in service of the state.

This shifts the 'career' of meaning making as well as the political possibilities that such analysis affords. Conquering the mass media remains an option for definitions of social problems, but the integration of mass media into corporate structures means that it is always already conquered by the interests of capital. Any discourse that challenges hegemonic narratives will be filtered and softened to fit that interest, included as a façade of progressive action or as a narrative to create controversy, only to introduce a 'real' (that is, compliant) expert to either counter or appropriate a softened-up version of it afterwards. In his study on Twitter/X sentiment on abolition, Phan (2021) calls upon the ideas of Foucault to note that it is 'secrecy [that] allows for the state to practice political violence onto the body without the concern of drawing public controversy and removes the criminal-justice system from the minds of average citizens' (Phan, 2021: 16; see also Taylor, Chapter 8 in this volume). It is therefore the implicit understanding that a news media that is intertwined with the dominant, hegemonic structures of power can be trusted not to dig too deeply into situations that would lead to citizens questioning these punitive state practices.

This is evidenced in the Black Lives Matter movement, which did not pick up a sudden onset of police violence that was non-existent in times of centralized mass media, but rather drew attention to events that had happened unseen, unreported and unscrutinized when the role of a 'check' on government power through the media was performed by state media or corporate media systems entangled in that power structure financially, structurally and through access requirements. It needed the addition of new structures apart from the centralized structures of state and corporate media to add this scrutiny. From here on, it could make its way into the corporate media. Though classical moral panic sociology might call this the path of 'conquering' mass media, although there exists ample reason to question this: the mass media, structurally embedded in power structures, can in its current form not be conquered unless the state also is. The Black Lives Matter movement and prison abolition have both seen exposure on mass corporate media. 'Abolitionist stars' such as Angela Davis are often booked on corporate media, and other leading academic activists such as Ruthie Wilson Gilmore, Justin Piche and David Scott have also made appearances on corporate and state media. However, that role is unthinkable for anti-imperialist voices such as Chris Hedges, who lost his position at the *New York Times* in 2003 after delivering a graduation speech severely criticizing the Iraq War (*Democracy Now*, 2003).

This points to the wider benefit of decentralized information for amplifying the voices of abolitionist and other dissident voices from below. Beyond police matters, decentralized sources show a flood of proof of the widespread use of Nazi symbolism in the Ukrainian army[37] and US regime change coups and year-long arming of Ukraine into Europe's largest military force (excluding Turkey) pointing Western arms at the Russian border.[38] Both are nowhere to be found in corporate and state media. Images that expose supposed 'Cuban anti-government protests' as staged influence campaigns hatched in the US,[39] as well as the mountains of proof that the alleged 'cultural genocide' of Uyghurs in China is a US (and German, as Adrian Zenz is German) invention aimed at destabilizing (and, in imperialist wet dreams, even breaking up) China by blocking, creating chaos and perhaps even removing a vital part of the Belt and Road Initiative transit territory as well as generally destabilizing a global competitor.[40]

Likewise, corporate news consumers know nothing about Pakistan, Yemen, Venezuela, Bolivia, Nicaragua, Mali, Burkina Faso and multiple other places in which the neoliberal world order is succumbing to anti-imperialist uprisings. There are many, many other bits of news that do not fit official narratives and therefore remain ignored on state and corporate news in the global northwest and are now labelled either 'misinformation', 'Russian propaganda' or both[41] when they do arise in public debate. The success of narratives critical of mass media coverage has made decentralized information sources a prime target of media moral panics. This also has consequences for penal abolition – this mystification of the harms of power gives greater legitimacy to the mainstream media focus on the harms of the powerless. Concealing state harms perpetuates the myth that the criminal (in)justice system really is dealing with the most harmful people in society (Scott and Sim, 2023). Breaking such an interpretive stranglehold is essential for abolitionist aspirations.

Contrary to classical models of social problems sociology, the increased attention this has received in legacy media is not due to a 'problem pressure' building in the public discourse; many other such problem pressures build with the legacy media actively ignoring or fighting them. The increased play that narratives critical of policing and prisons have received in the media can perhaps be understood as an attempt of legacy media to appear to represent fundamental opposition and criticism of state power in a field where they feel safe that nothing materially will change; a year of 'defund the police' activism with much legacy mass media attention has only resulted in increased policing budgets in the US, and increased numbers of police officers. We therefore have to ask the question as to whether such legacy attention in the end serves only to support the media façade of 'progressive' journalism and 'criticism' of government action – the 'fourth estate' role of a check on government that neither state nor corporate mass media can realistically play. Thus, social problems sociology should divorce itself from the idea of 'conquering' corporate media; actual criticism can only be absorbed and transformed into corporate-friendly narratives this way. Not only is independent media an irreplaceable tool to connect citizen action beyond corporate control, but it may also be the only avenue through which abolitionists and other progressive activism can achieve their aims. A critical analysis of decentralized media should therefore be wary of joining the 'anti-misinformation moral panic' against decentralized media and the social problem construction around 'fake news' used to delegitimize noncorporate media channels – quite the opposite. Moral panic and social problems sociology has long shown the politically servile nature of state and corporate media (Hall et al, 1978). The strength of decentralized information strips the mass media of their control over narratives.

Far from being a danger to critical discourses, it is decentralized, critical narratives that are able to question institutionalized, hegemonic structures of meaning making and establish a common discourse beyond that found in state- and corporate-centred media systems. The critical power of decentralized challenges could already be seen in lightly resistant social movements such as Occupy Wall Street, Black Lives Matter, Fridays for Future and various, stronger anti-imperialist war and conflict reporting on Palestine, Yemen, Colombia, Somalia, Syria and other conflicts. Success depends on decentralized media networking, distributing the message and organizing people for their respective struggles by sharing information and building communities that are not filtered through the editorial controls of the legacy mass media. Already in war reporting and Occupy Wall Street, these decentralized movements were often subverted and widely controlled through banning and filtering tools, often with the formal rules against 'hate speech' and 'misinformation' as justifications for bans – tools that were never used against legacy media even when there were concerted media efforts to manufacture narratives that legitimized the invasion of Iraq, the continued war against Syria or the media distribution of an equation of all Palestinians with terrorists, including infants. In this respect, the 'misinformation' and 'hate speech' narratives worked just like how the drug narratives were found to work in the moral panics on drugs: as vehicles that could be used to legally control unwanted populations (Gusfield, 1986), a narrative that legitimized the mass incarceration of minorities and one which abolitionists have long and actively fought. It is decentralized, independent media that interviews prisoners without framing them as dangers for the evening news; it is independent media that cooperates with prisoners to produce prison radio, prison newspapers and distribute their content, taking prisoners seriously as cooperators rather than treating them as predator figures; it is independent media that can advocate and advance activism that actively opposes the corporate interests that fund mass media as well as the imperialist state. 'Conquering' corporate media is not possible in its current structural frame, and nor is it realistic that corporate media would advance actual counterhegemonic messages. Decentralized information allows rebuttals of old hegemonic meaning that used to dominate the public sphere. This only works through the possibility for individuals to share and spread meaning making without corporate editors: videos of police violence against minorities and protesters that challenge official law-enforcement propaganda and dominant media narratives.

Videos and eyewitness reports from war zones that counter official government narratives and resistance narratives shared by members of this resistance themselves show that government and media meaning making is not only often contradicted by the meaning making that arises within the population, it is often easily falsifiable and easily deconstructed using the internal contradictions that are often inherent in official meaning making. This all opens up spaces for abolitionist critique of the selective application of the criminal label to the harms of the powerless rather than the harms of power (Scott and Sim, 2023).

Instead of the derogatory and propagandistic term of a 'post-truth era' – which, given the pervasive and systematic disinformation in the mass media over many decades regarding narcotic substances, minority crime, war justifications and so on, is more than ironic anyway – Pedro-Carañana, Broudy and Klaehn (2018: 167) speak here of a period of a '(quite understandable) general contempt for institutions'. Penal abolitionism and other counterhegemonic, counterimperialist discourse and activism are well served to join this contempt. While it is general knowledge that *FOX News*, *Sky News*, the *Daily Mail* and the *Washington Times*, *Bild* and *RTL* in Germany are not your friend, neither are CNN, MSNBC, the *New York Times*, the BBC or PBS or any other public or corporate broadcaster or newspaper.

Notes

1. Historians refer to the 'long' 19th century and the 'short' 20th century to denote that the tendencies of the 19th century continued into the world wars, whereafter the world shifted qualitatively.
2. Uploaded filters for platforms, introduced in the EU as part of copyright laws and anti-terrorist laws, would reinsert automated gatekeepers that again control discourse on large platforms like X, Facebook, Instagram and YouTube.
3. This is an excellent daily news podcast by the Communist Party of Great Britain, available at https://rumble.com/user/ARMC82
4. The excellent channel that miraculously still has its YouTube presence, probably because it is very academic.

5   In 2020, the Department of Homeland Security raided the homes of the producers of *Second Thought* for making Marxist content, charging them with 'anti-American activity'.
6   My old university had a cooperation agreement with a local police training school to provide classes. The quoted sentiment could often be heard cited by lecturers who took the exchange: when confronted with the brutality of US police, German policing students would pat themselves on the back for being 'the good ones', ignoring the widespread prevalence of police violence in Germany.
7   Collected, for instance, in the subreddit r/pozilei, which is a play on the Polizei, the German word for police, exchanging the letters 'z' and 'l'.
8   For example, https://www.youtube.com/watch?v=0ZW-H47ZORI, reporting by the activist group AmazonWatch (no relation to the corporation that uses the same name).
9   As reported, among many sources, by the socialist magazine *Monthly Review* (https://mronline.org/2022/12/18/peru-coup/) and the anti-imperialist source geopolitical economy (https://geopoliticaleconomy.com/2022/12/20/latin-america-rejects-coup-peru/).
10 See, for example, Aaron Bielejewski's current study of prison newspaper management in a German prison (Bielejewski, *ongoing research*).
11 For example, https://www.youtube.com/watch?v=1HWqYANmWLY on prison abolition and COVID-19, https://www.youtube.com/watch?v=aB-LsYyMFWI on prison abolition and the war on drugs, and https://www.youtube.com/watch?v=5aOKqbg4_Y4 on the construction of new prisons and the for-profit prison industry.
12 For example, https://www.youtube.com/watch?v=WLO0UuSnPzU
13 For example, https://www.youtube.com/watch?v=QIbccfycasA on prisons and COVID-19, and https://www.youtube.com/watch?v=TwBuA2ZKpSo on the prison industrial complex.
14 For example, https://www.youtube.com/watch?v=ik09tg3lA2w on carceral capitalism.
15 For example, https://www.youtube.com/watch?v=utKcnPqcTn4 with Angela Davis on prison abolition, and https://www.youtube.com/watch?v=gpFZxYU7hbw, again with Angela Davis.
16 For example, https://www.youtube.com/watch?v=Ew6PlZYhTa4
17 For example, https://www.youtube.com/watch?v=d4dpvLHyMg4 on abolitionist economics.
18 For example, https://www.youtube.com/watch?v=_Ap4DNoHdZI on the link between civil rights struggles and prison abolition.
19 For example, https://www.youtube.com/watch?v=cQzDmrIGTuE on prison conditions in Mississippi.
20 For example, https://www.bbc.co.uk/ideas/videos/viewpoint-what-would-a-world-without-prisons-be-li/p08nbj02 on the case for prison abolition.
21 https://www.linktv.org/shows/democracy-now/episodes/complicity-in-neoslavery-chris-hedges-calls-out-corporate-america-for-exploiting-prison-labor
22 https://www.democracyatwork.info/eu_chris_hedges_us_prisons
23 'Alternative Radio' is the title of the source, not my description: https://www.alternativeradio.org/products/hedc018/
24 https://www.youtube.com/watch?v=EPsTKHgpqMQ
25 https://www.youtube.com/watch?v=rlVPCK8lHCI
26 https://www.youtube.com/watch?v=kvqIaTnh23I
27 This can no longer be linked; reference at https://scheerpost.com/2021/10/19/hugh-hamilton-and-chris-hedges-on-trauma-transformation-in-an-american-prison%EF%BF%BC/
28 This can no longer be linked; reference at: https://www.truthdig.com/articles/on-contact-with-chris-hedges-the-big-business-of-keeping-people-in-cages/
29 https://www.prisonradio.org/commentary/on-contact-chris-hedges-interviews-mumia/

30. For example, https://scheerpost.com/2021/12/21/chris-hedges-on-the-persecution-of-julian-assange-video/
31. https://www.wsws.org/en/articles/2022/03/31/hedg-m31.html, https://www.democracynow.org/2022/4/1/on_contact_chris_hedges_youtube_russia and https://www.youtube.com/watch?v=mMHqwHJahzA. Josep Borrell, head of EU foreign policy, in Orwellian fashion, labelled this ban on Russian content a 'protection of freedom of speech'.
32. These silos are, again, US-dominated everywhere in the world, with the notable exception of China, though the worldwide social media censorship in the course of the Ukraine war by US corporations will likely boost the Chinese model of local social media independent of US control.
33. https://peoplesdispatch.org/2020/05/07/facebook-deletes-dozens-of-palestinian-activists-accounts/; https://www.aljazeera.com/opinions/2021/5/13/social-media-companies-are-trying-to-silence-palestinian-voices
34. https://www.zdnet.com/article/facebook-targets-nicaragua-government-for-alleged-troll-farm-campaign/
35. The socialist channel 'Red, for instance, was banned on Instagram, made a second Instagram account, and used its reach on telegram to re-invite old followers to the new channels, although this is a pattern that the algorithms of Meta will surely notice.
36. Again, this is true all over the world, with the exception of China, which, quite presciently, took control of its social media and systematically shuts out US corporate control. This is, itself, often the target of moral panics, such as when the Western media feigns outrage over China banning the gay dating app Grindr as homophobic discrimination. In fact, the Chinese market has its own gay dating app, and shutting out Grindr shuts out a monopolistic corporation that gathers sensitive data on Chinese citizens. The Chinese internet is open to viewing outside content through VPN, as is every closed internet; however, it is also difficult for outsiders to participate in Chinese social media. It is difficult for foreigners to create accounts on Chinese social media, which blocks Western astroturfing and informational warfare within China.
37. As reported early on by activists at CounterPunch, among many others: https://www.counterpunch.org/2022/02/11/the-resurgence-of-nazism-in-ukraine/ and https://twitter.com/BenjaminNorton/status/1526229689840328708. It is exceedingly difficult to prompt any Western search engine to show this rather than presenting page after page of obviously engineered whitewashing 'the symbols are out of context' apologia – try it.
38. https://towardfreedom.org/story/archives/europe/ukrainian-leftist-criticizes-western-war-drive-with-russia-united-states-using-ukraine-as-cannon-fodder/. In general: https://geopoliticaleconomy.com/tag/ukraine/
39. A collection of counterimperialist resistance against this campaign can be found at: https://cuba-solidarity.org.uk/news/article/4292/whats-going-on-in-cuba---alternative-media-archive
40. That is, notable independent journalist Kim Iverson's interview with Chinese-American Danny Haiphong, who is generally a good source on China outside the Western bubble: https://www.youtube.com/watch?v=p4s6QNjad7o
41. 'Propaganda', of course, does not mean 'incorrect'. Russia is able to use many of these narratives in propaganda, and can do so quite efficiently because there are mountains of evidence supporting their veracity, which usually cannot be said about US propaganda like 'Iraq has weapons of mass destruction' or 'Russia destroyed the Nord Stream pipelines', which lack any supporting evidence and remain unsubstantiated, and have since been retracted for complete lack of evidence and/or general common sense.

References

Anderson, B. (1991) *Imagined Communities: Reflections on the Origin and Spread of Nationalism*, London: Verso.

Anton, A., Schetsche, M. and Walter, M. (eds) (2013) *Konspiration: Soziologie des Verschwörungsdenkens*, Wiesbaden: Springer VS.

Becker, H. (1963) *Outsiders: Studies in the Sociology of Deviance*, New York: Free Press of Glencoe.

Becker, H. (1967) 'Whose side are we on?', *Social Problems*, 14(3): 239–253.

Becker, H. (2018) *Outsiders*, New York: Free Press.

Benkler, Y., Robert, F. and Roberts, H. (2018) *Network Propaganda: Manipulation, Disinformation, and Radicalization in American Politics*, Oxford: Oxford University Press.

Cohen, S. (1988) *Against Criminology*, Cambridge: Polity Press.

Conboy, M. (2017) 'Journalism and the democratic market society: decline and fall?', *Journalism Studies*, 18(10): 1263–176.

Coyle, M. and Scott, D. (eds) (2021 *International Handbook of Penal Abolition*, Abingdon: Routledge.

Dellwing, M. (2019) 'The digital backstage: entangled and disentangled online interaction', in V. Zydziunaite and J. Kasperiune (eds) *Professional Identity*, Pisa: Pisa University Press, pp 103–136.

Dellwing, M. (2022) 'Wandernde fake news', in M. Harbusch (ed.) *Wanderndes Wissen*, Frankfurt: Springer.

Democracy Now (2003) '*New York Times* reporter, Chris Hedges was booed off the stage and had his microphone cut twice as he delivered a graduation speech on war and empire at Rockford College in Illinois', *Democracy Now* (21 May). Available from: https://www.democracynow.org/2003/5/21/new_york_times_reporter_chris_hedges [Accessed 15 September 2024].

Doctorow, C. (2021) 'Recommendation engines and "lean-back" media', *Pluralistic* (5 June). Available from: https://pluralistic.net/2021/06/05/lean-back/#lean-forward [Accessed 15 September 2024].

Elias, N. and Scotson, J. (1994) *The Established and the Outsiders*, London: Sage.

Grim, R. and Cherkis, J. (2017) 'Bernie Sanders' campaign faced a fake news tsunami: where did it come from?', *Huffington Post* (13 March). Available from: https://www.huffingtonpost.co.uk/entry/bernie-sanders-fake-news-russia_n_58c34d97e4b0ed71826cdb36 [Accessed 15 September 2024].

Gusfield, J. (1986) *Symbolic Crusade*, Urbana: University of Illinois Press.

Hall, S. Jefferson, T., Clark, J., Critcher, C. and Roberts, B. (1978) *Policing the Crisis*, London: Macmillan.

Hedges, C. (2011) 'Recognizing the language of tyranny', *Common Dreams* (7 February). Available from: https://www.commondreams.org/views/2011/02/07/recognizing-language-tyranny [Accessed 15 September 2024].

Hedges, C. (2014) 'The prison state of America', *Truthdig* (29 December). Available from: https://www.truthdig.com/articles/the-prison-state-of-america [Accessed 15 September 2024].

Hedges, C. (2021) *Our Class: Trauma and Transformation in an American Prison*, New York: Simon & Schuster.

Herdt, G. (ed.) (2009) *Moral Panics, Sex Panics: Fear and the Fight over Sexual Rights*, New York: New York University Press.

Herman, E.S. and Chomsky, N. (1988) *Manufacturing Consent: The Political Economy of the Mass Media*, New York: Random House.

Laycock, J. (2015) *Dangerous Games*, Berkeley: University of California Press.

Molotch, H. and Lester, M. (1974) 'News as purposive behavior: on the strategic use of routine events, accidents, and scandals', *American Sociological Review*, 39: 101–112.

Nagle, A. (2017) *Kill All Normies: The Online Culture Wars from Tumblr and 4chan to the Alt-right and Trump*, London: Zero Books.

Pandey, N. (2022). 'Part 6 of the Twitter Files reveals FBI connections to the platform'. *ndtv* (18 December). Available from: https://www.ndtv.com/offbeat/twitter-files-elon-musk-matt-taibbi-part-6-of-the-twitter-files-reveals-fbi-connections-to-the-platform-3616467 [Accessed 15 September 2024].

Pedro-Carañana, J., Broudy, D. and Klaehn, J. (2018) *The Propaganda Model Today: Filtering Perception and Awareness (Critical Digital and Social Media Studies)*, London: University of Westminster Press.

Phan, T. (2021) 'It's #PrisonAbolition until the bad guys show up: conflicting discourses on Twitter about carceral networks in 2020'. Available from: https://digitalcommons.bowdoin.edu/cgi/viewcontent.cgi?article=1293&context=honorsprojects [Accessed 15 September 2024].

Rustbelt Abolition Radio (2021) 'Abolitionist media making', in M.J. Coyle and D. Scott, (eds) *The International Handbook of Penal Abolition*, London: Routledge. Available from: https://www.routledgehandbooks.com/citation?doi=10.4324/9780429425035-10 [Accessed 15 September 2024].

Schudson, M. (1989) 'The sociology of news production', *Media, Culture & Society*, 11(3): 263–282.

Scott, D. and Sim, J. (eds) (2023) *Demystifying Power, Crime and Social Harm* London: Palgrave Macmillan.

Sennet, R. (1977). *The Fall of Public Man.* New York: Alfred A. Knopf.

Stehr, J. (1998) *Sagenhafter Alltag: über die private Aneignung herrschender Moral*, Dordrecht: Springer.

Taibbi, Matt (2022). 'The Twitter files'. *Twitter* (3 December). Available from: https://twitter.com/mtaibbi/status/1598822959866683394?lang=en [Accessed 15 September 2024].

Turk, J. VanSlyke (1985) 'Subsidizing the news: public information officers and their impact on media coverage of state government', PhD dissertation, Syracuse University.

Victor, J.S. (1993) *Satanic Panic: The Creation of a Contemporary Legend*, Chicago: Open Court Press.

Viner, K. (2016) 'How technology disrupted the truth', *The Guardian* (12 July). Available from: https://www.theguardian.com/media/2016/jul/12/how-technology-disrupted-the-truth [Accessed 10 May 2018].

14

Libertarian Socialism and the Struggle for Liberative Justice

David Gordon Scott

Introduction

A central leitmotif of libertarian socialism is the liberation of people from oppression.[1] Libertarian socialism is a 'Socialism from Below' (see Feest in the Foreword to this volume) rooted in nonauthoritarian principles committed to emancipation and the valorization of life on planet earth. Drawing primarily upon Marxism, early socialism and anarchism,[2] libertarian socialism offers an anti-capitalist critique of current material inequities and the racialized, class-based, patriarchal power structures they reflect. Libertarian socialism is lived through participatory democracy, self-governance and direct resistance to the yoke of oppression, violence, domination and exploitation of carceral colonial capitalism. Emancipatory politics and praxis are part of the everyday struggle for liberation and, as such, there is constant engagement with both theory and practice (see the companion volume *Enivisoning Abolition* for further discussion).

Libertarian socialists eulogize the relational values of inclusion, love, solidarity, tolerance and the human vitality that arises through diversity. They promote socialist socioeconomic contexts based on an equitable distribution of the social product which meets human need, facilitates life and results in flourishing for all. Libertarian socialists highlight the importance of empathy and an ethics of care for others, and suggest noncoercive responses to conflicts, wrongdoing and social harms that respect human dignity (Scott, 2016c, 2020). This includes the promotion of ideas around repair, reparations, redress and healing (Bell and Scott, 2016). Such desires for liberation have been present in socialist-inspired abolitionism and visions of justice for centuries, and remain equally significant today (Bowman, Chapter 5 in this volume; Scott and Bell, 2025).

Libertarian socialism is *revolutionary* because it requires the subverting and overturning of existing social, economic and power relations, and the ending of institutions maintaining the existing exploitative and repressive social order. In so doing, libertarian socialism calls for the dissolution of the penal apparatus of the capitalist state and its replacement with *life* affirming alternatives. Power should be widely dispersed, hierarchies dissolved and decisions made through the collective will of the people in a participatory *democracy* which hears and ethically responds to all voices. Further, libertarian socialism recognizes that justice is only possible through socialist transformations (Dussel, 1987; Scott, 2020). But any such socialist interventions and aspirations should also be feasible and achievable – in other words, 'real utopian' (Wright, 2010; Scott, 2013a). The importance of real utopian interventions are reflected in the three key socialist principles advocated by the great Argentinian socialist Enrique Dussel (2013): the *material principle* challenging inequities; the *formal principle* promoting democracy; and the *feasibility principle* shaping what is to be done in the here and now. We will return in detail to these socialist principles later in the chapter with regard to the advocation of an abolitionist victim-centred approach.[3]

For libertarian socialists, justice necessitates the ending of unnecessary and useless suffering and the freeing of people from oppression, domination and exploitation. Justice requires all to have the capacity to live a dignified life and this in turn must entail an ethical critique of existing inequitable and unjust power relations. Dussel (1987: 65) argues that liberative justice 'does not give to each what is due within the law and the prevailing order but grants to all what they deserve in their dignity as others. Thus, liberative justice is not legal justice, whether distributive or commutative …'. Rather, 'real justice' is 'subversive' for its explicit aim is 'subverting the established unjust order'.

Liberative justice[4] finds its inspiration in liberation philosophy (Dussel, 1987, 2013) and the ethics of alterity (that is, our response-abilities for the powerless).[5] For Dussel (1987), liberative justice means respecting the intrinsic dignity of all and subverting – that is, *upending* – systems of exploitation and domination. *Real justice* can only arise through liberation and the ending of societal injustice. Punishment can never deliver *real justice* (Hudson, 1987; Scott, 2013b) and nor does the penal rationale effectively protect ordinary people from serious social harms. Rather, the penal apparatus of the capitalist state largely protects existing power relations and maintains systems of domination and exploitation, thus contravening libertarian socialist ethics (Scott, 2020). Those who most lack justice (and indeed also security) are the poor, powerless and disadvantaged. Too often their sufferings are neglected, ignored, or marginalized, too often their voice is delegitimated, and too often their dignity is violated or denied. There can be no *real justice* for the oppressed without their liberation.

The first section of this chapter argues that struggles for liberative justice are always unfinished. Freedom from oppression, domination and exploitation remains a constant and ongoing struggle. There can be no complacency and we should always remain vigilant of new hierarchies of power. The second section of the chapter explores how liberative justice must come from, and be led by, oppressed people themselves. This section highlights the importance of socialist response ethics, and in particular: a) ethically responding to the voice of victims,[6] defined here following Dussel (2013) as those 'akin to death'; and b) activist scholars bearing witness to injustice when contributing to revolutionary praxis.[7]

The focus in the third section is on promoting revolutionary praxis (that is, practice informed by theory and vice versa). Calls for penal abolition are at their strongest when they are part of ongoing struggles for liberative justice. Libertarian socialist activist scholars can enhance revolutionary praxis by engaging in 'subversive thinking' – that is, devising lines of thought that can be of assistance in the upending of the existing social order and visibilizing the hidden harms of power. In aid of penal abolition, subversive knowledge may entail challenging the language and assumptions of the penal order and reframing focus onto the social problems and serious harms derived from the exercise of power (Scott and Sim, 2023).

Over the last 200 years, abolitionists have worked tirelessly for justice, calling for the abolition of legal coercion, slavery and other forms of state repression, domination and violence (Scott and Bell, 2025; see also preceding chapters in this volume, especially in Part III). Yet it is important that abolitionist ideas are not defined out of the debates or perceived as irrelevant. They must both 'compete' yet at the same time also 'contradict' the oppressive social order (see Mathiesen, 1974; Scott, 2013a). Therefore, the fourth section returns to Dussel's (1987) three socialist principles – *material, formal, feasible* – and connects them to some abolitionist real utopian interventions that are historically immanent in the current conjuncture to illustrate how they can inform a strategy for emancipatory politics and praxis via a victim-centred response to harm (Scott, 2013a, 2016a). The fifth section argues that the aspiration to liberate oppressed peoples should be guided by *revolutionary love* and the chapter concludes by arguing that activist scholars should promote the agency of the oppressed and themselves directly engage in struggles for freedom.

The unfinished struggle

To talk of liberative justice is to bring emancipation, liberation and freedom to the forefront of our minds, for justice is only possible through liberation. To be liberated is to be free from oppression, domination and exploitation (and its associated suffering) and to have capacity to live a dignified life. Liberative justice is thus an aspiration for those rising up and directly engaging in struggles against their oppression; its meaning and content is shaped by oppressed peoples themselves through such struggles for freedom. This means that there can be no homogenized vision of justice – justice will be plurivocal and have different meanings to those engaged in different struggles for liberation. Yet, they are all united in their challenge of power and the desire for freedom and liberation.

The active struggle for liberative justice will always be without an end: unfinished. The concept of the 'unfinished', found in the work of Mathiesen, (1974) and Dussel (2013), is situated within a material context and ethical concern about the inherent abuse of power. The greatest social harms in society are perpetrated against, and not by, the most powerless people in society. Liberative justice thus requires a radical subversion and dispersal of power, and libertarian socialists should always remain conscious of the creation of new hierarchies of power that simply replace the old. There should be a constant interrogation of what liberation entails and this means going forward without a sense of closure – and hence dogmatism.

Liberative justice is an unfinished project because freedom requires openness to new ways of thinking and being-in-the-world, and renewal whenever social contexts and power relations change. As human conflicts are inevitable and there may never be a way of ensuring that decision making is always without fault, the work towards liberation and emancipation can never be entirely complete. Socialists cannot be solely guided by individual utopian blueprints or follow pre-planned routes to transformations; liberation evolves and takes shape *through struggles for freedom* generated by the oppressed from below. Further, there may be limits to the capacity of the oppressed to adhere the rules and requirements of dominant regimes of representation (Dussel, 2013; Dreher and Modal, 2018; Scott, 2020), and thus visions of liberative justice, and how it is to be achieved, must constantly remain open and subject to revision – in other words, unfinished. Liberative justice is then an aspiration which will always be just out of reach, a promise of something still to come – a freedom always on the horizon, but never quite within our grasp (Dussel, 1987; Hudson, 2003).

Libertarian socialist inspired penal abolitionism raises fundamental questions about not only the ethical and political justifications of the criminal laws but also the kind of unjust society within which they operate. There can be absolutely no doubt that the penal apparatus of a given state is intimately connected to socioeconomic structures and power relations. There can also be no doubt that any radical transformation of the penal field can only be successfully brought about in conjunction with a radical overturning and transformation of the current social system and its political economy (Scott and Sim, 2023; Burnett, Chapter 7 in this volume). Without radical social change, the struggle for *real justice* remains partial and unfinished. Critical analysis of the social and the penal should not be separated in the pursuit of liberative justice, as social and economic emancipations underscore the sustainability and full implementation of nonpenal alternatives.

Socialist response ethics

Liberative justice is grounded in an ethics of liberation (Dussel, 2013). It requires an ethical response to the voice of victims and their appeals for urgent assistance. Such injustice may have arisen through colonization, immigration, corporate or bureaucratic indifference, capitalist exploitation, state violence, patriarchies, white supremacy or other abuses of power (Scott and Sim, 2023; see also many of the preceding chapters). To hear and respond ethically means to fully acknowledge and engage with compassion and empathy to the cry of the oppressed in a meaningful way (for further discussion on hearing oppressed voices, see Scott, Chapter 1 in this volume; Guenther, Chapter 4 in this volume). For Dussel (2013), it is not enough to just acknowledge that the victim is close to death – that is, to see their starvation, pain, suffering or nearness to dying – but that we have an ethical obligation to understand the world from their perspective and subsequently join their struggle for liberation.

Dussel (1987) maintains that the basis of any ethical relationship – by which he means the relationship between ourselves and those less powerful than us, and thus to whom we owe ethical responsibilities – arises through seeing the face of another who is suffering. This seeing of 'face' is not necessarily literal and an encounter can be mediated by different forms of representation, such as through literature or the media, but undoubtedly our strongest emotional responses arise through close physical proximity with a person on the underside of power. This may be by seeing someone homeless near where we live; seeing the pains of imprisonment etched on the face of prisoners firsthand as a prison researcher; seeing the face of migrants and asylum seekers at an immigration detention centre; seeing the sadness and desperation on the faces of parents and children at a local foodbank; or seeing the anger and frustration in the eyes of those demanding their basic rights on a demonstration.

Seeing the world through the eyes of those on the underside of power is the basis of emancipatory knowledge. An ethical response requires us to engage with empathy, solidarity and love: we must be prepared to imagine ourselves in the place of the victim of social injustice. Seeing ethically requires a genuine openness to how we interpret and understand other people's lives (Dreher and Modal, 2018). We should learn to understand and engage alongside the oppressed in a nonhierarchal way so that everyone has an opportunity to share and express their vision of justice in a way that is received with openness, receptivity and attentiveness. Those of us in privileged positions must therefore be prepared to 'learn to learn' from the insights of the marginalized and powerless (Scott, 2016b).

So, what does this learning and ethical response-ability of the libertarian socialist activist-scholar entail? It is argued here that it means adhering to *socialist response ethics*. As indicated previously, socialist response ethics refer to our ability to empathetically respond to knowledge of profound injustices and our subsequent attempts to ameliorate the suffering of those who are less powerful than we are (Oliver, 2000; Cohen, 2000; Hudson, 2003; Dussel, 2013; Scott, 2016b). The greater the power we hold, the greater our responsibility to respond to the needs of the powerless. For socialists, this means direct engagement in the struggle for liberation alongside the oppressed and the realization of socialist-based transformations.

There are three steps in socialist response ethics: *hearing, seeing* and *revolutionary praxis*. The first step is *hearing* and undertaking an ethical interpretation of the oppressed voice, which, as indicated previously, means empathetically listening to the views of the most marginalized and excluded – the victim (Dussel, 2013; Scott, 2016b). The second step is acknowledging the voice of the victim, which means (selectively) adopting their struggle for liberative justice as one's own and *seeing* the world (again sometimes selectively) through their eyes (Scott, 2020). The third step is accepting our co-responsibility for calling into question the systemic causes of the victims suffering and attempting to generate, to the best of our ability, a new critical ethical consciousness of power through active engagement in *revolutionary praxis*. Such a questioning of power can only be done by taking the social and structural approach. Indeed, socialist response ethics require us to reimagine responsibility as an *ability to respond* (Oliver, 2000). Our response-ability for human suffering means including in our moral universe people we do not know or may not be similar in any way to us, and to engage in the struggle for continued life on planet earth of a good society focused on maximizing wellbeing and life (Cohen, 2000; Hudson, 2003).

Importantly, our response-ability also entails *bearing witness* to the injustices of power and is a key part of any engagement in revolutionary praxis. Oliver (2000) notes that there are two meanings to bearing witness. The first meaning is to testify as an eyewitness. Bearing witness in this sense is to give a truthful account of something that has happened – to speak truth (to power) through personal testimony. This is significant and is one of the reasons why a close and empathetic hearing of the voices of ordinary people who have suffered injustice is so important. We can learn by listening to such testimonies This means platforming not appropriating the abolitionist voices of others (see discussion by James, Chapter 3 in this volume). Survivors may also benefit from the knowledge that their voice has been heard and responded to appropriately, or at the very least avoid the harm of knowing that the voice remains unheard.

But there is also a second meaning to bearing witness. This is not about the words we speak, but by our everyday actions, sometimes by our very existence and survival in the face of great harm, injury and injustice. In this sense, bearing witness is shining a light on the very truth of humanity and what it means to be human itself (Oliver, 2000). We learn through witnessing the life struggles and actions of others – the overcoming of great tyranny and repression. Bearing witness, in this second sense, is a way of revealing a hidden truth through our life and actions. Our struggles against injustice in their own right are profoundly significant irrespective of whether they result in the desired transformations or not.

An individual's action of bearing witness through struggles against injustice may provide a sense of inspiration to others. Resisting power shows that acquiescence is not inevitable and that another way is possible. This resistance against penal expansion, fascist regimes, impending climate catastrophe, the afterlives of slavery, state violence, capitalist exploitation, white supremacy or colonial rule may in the long term prove to be of considerable importance (Scott and Sim, 2023). It demonstrates human agency in the face of structural oppression. Bearing witness then is not just about achieving certain outcomes in the here and now, but about *a way of being in the world* (Oliver, 2000).

An understanding of Olivers' (2000) second meaning of bearing witness is crucial in terms of comprehending the important contribution of penal abolitionist grassroots liberation movements and other forms of resistance to carceral colonial capitalism. Activism by ordinary rebels is not likely to be initially fully recognized by state power and may not change the law in and of itself, but the energy and engagement of activists, campaigners, ex-prisoners and their families and friends in such revolutionary praxis can be a platform for moving closer towards liberative justice. Direct activism holds liberation movements together and while this sense of simply *being present* may not always be a mechanism for penal or social transformation, many people can recognize the importance of what ordinary rebels are doing by resisting the penal state (see discussion of 'total liberation' by Stephens-Griffin and Brock, Chapter 12 in this volume).

The meaning of the struggle, activist self-confidence and belief, and the overall significance of their bearing of witness should not be based on recognition bestowed by others. Those engaging in struggles for liberative justice should be allowed to self-define their achievements and rationale for engagement. They are promoting a philosophy of hope in opposition to a philosophy of oppression, and this alone should be enough. Indeed, just the very existence of such activism and broader liberation movements visibilizes our shared humanity in the face of brutally violent repression. Contributing in a small way to a liberation movement may be all that any of us can ever achieve in our lifetimes. But everyone can have a part to play. Engaging in revolutionary praxis can bring people together to generate interventions that can rebuild world and help generate both resilience and change for those involved and other victims of injustice.

Revolutionary praxis

Liberative justice requires direct participation in struggle through revolutionary praxis. Struggles against oppression, domination and exploitation have emerged in human societies for thousands of years and have often focused on systemic forms of oppression and harms created through power structures. There can be no doubting that the strength and vitality of penal abolitionisms come from their incorporation into and association with a diverse range of historical liberation movements (Scott, Chapter 1 in this volume; see also several other contributions to this book for examples of the diversity of freedom movements inspiring calls for abolition). When we look back in history for examples of where abolitionist (and especially penal abolitionist) ideas have flourished, they are largely in times of a groundswell of support for certain liberation movements. Counterhegemonic struggles around class, 'race' and gender-based oppressions as well as wider struggles around identity politics, both in the past and today, have found their voice in direct struggles against state violence. But alongside questioning legal coercion and state punishments, libertarian socialists have also called for the abolition of more generic forms of domination and exploitation, including white privilege, heteronormativity and corporate and patriarchal power (Scott and Sim, 2023; Scott, Chapter 1 in this volume; Kinna, Chapter 2 in this volume; Burnett, Chapter 7 in this volume; Vegh Weis, Chapter 11 in this volume). The moral questioning of material inequities and the exercise of authoritarian power is thus central to the abolitionist rhizome. This has led to a constant renewal and refocusing of penal abolitionisms.

Today penal abolitionisms are much talked about precisely because of their connections to liberation movements – whether they be Indigenous movements struggling for freedom against colonization; anti-capitalist activists fighting against oppressive anti-protest laws and state-corporate power; Black Lives Matter and those fighting against cultural representations of Britain's brutal empire and the injustice of police killings and deaths in state custody; or climate activists and eco-abolitionists struggling to try and prevent the worst ravages of climate catastrophe before it is too late (see, for example, Saleh-Hanna, Chapter 9 in this volume; Anthony and Blagg, Chapter 10 in this volume; Stephens-Griffin and Brock, Chapter 12 in this volume). Liberation movements in the 2020s, especially those after the death of George Floyd in May 2020 and the global protests calling the abolition of policing and prisons (notably by Black Lives Matter), have significantly raised the awareness of penal abolitionist ideas in political, media, activist and academic circles (see Dellwing, Chapter 13 in this volume). High-profile demands for the defunding of the police in both the UK and the US have sat alongside calls for the reimagining of policing so that it focuses on peace, safety, protection and acknowledgement of community diversity rather than the maintaining of social divisions through use of deadly force. This making and remaking of penal abolitionism keeps it relevant and at the heart of public debate.

Libertarian socialists argue for both the transformation of state responses to human wrongdoing, harms and conflicts, and the creation of economic and social conditions within which life on earth can prosper. Revolutionary praxis requires a sustained challenge to material realities under carceral colonial capitalism and the already irreversible devastation of the earth's ecosystems inflicted by corporate power. It requires the cultivation and fostering of what Gramsci (1971) called 'good sense'. Good sense is created by ordinary people who have become newly self-aware of their subject position and collective power through engagement in organized struggles against oppression, injustice and exploitation. Libertarian socialist activist scholars should then use and orientate their academic work to help facilitate the generation of such good sense and ensure that the views and lived experiences and agency of victims are incorporated into demands for social change.

Those engaging in revolutionary praxis can bear witness to the failings of state mechanisms of coercion, control and domination, and help forge a new hegemonic consensus against oppression, domination and exploitation. It is then essential that activist-scholars directly *engage* with *liberation movements* and actively participate in grassroots struggle and take inspiration and strength from such emancipatory praxis (Scott, 2016a, 2018, 2020).

There are of course two interlocked aspects to praxis: direct action (practice) and subversive thinking (theory). The establishing and defending of penal abolitionist arguments and lines of reasoning through *theoretical* work can generate new concepts (or revive older of forgotten ones) to aid revolutionary praxis (see Brandão, Chapter 6 in this volume). The constant theoretical reinvigoration of the 'middle' of the abolitionist rhizome – the melting pot of ideas that allows insights from different traditions to meld together to strengthen the core arguments of penal abolition – can shine new light of perennial questions, such as why prisons continue to exist and expand despite the constant failure to meet its basic aims (see Scott, 2013c; Scott, Chapter 1 in this volume; Taylor, Chapter 8 in this volume; Bowman, Chapter 5 in this volume).

The emergence of 'academic abolitionism' in universities since the 1970s (initially in Europe through the scholarship of Thomas Mathiesen as well as by other pioneers around the world in the same decade) has undoubtedly strengthened theoretical credentials of penal abolitionism. While the promotion and development of abolitionist ideas in the academic arena has led to (sometimes overtly hostile) critique from liberal and right-wing scholars, what is most notable more than 50 years on is that penal abolitionist ideas are not just standing still; they are positively thriving (see Coyle and Scott, 2021). Indeed, libertarian socialist-activist scholars can continue to enhance the abolitionist cause and the struggle for liberative justice through theoretical innovations and the production of subversive knowledge (see Scott and Bell, 2025).

Liberative justice emerges through the subverting of power (Dussel, 1987). To subvert is to turn something upside down – to overthrow the oppressor and turn existing power relations on their head. To bring about liberation and freedom, it is essential to work against the interests of power. As highlighted earlier, one way of doing this is by changing the narrative of social problems by platforming the voice of those on the underside of power. Hearing the voice of the victim means rewriting the story from the perspective of the oppressed (Dussel, 2013; Scott, 2016b). This subversive knowledge can reveal the humanity and agency of the oppressed and raise new and powerful questions about their social conditions and the suitability of criminalization. This form of subversive theorizing has been central to libertarian socialism and abolitionist thought for centuries and is a good way of questioning the existing 'law and order' agenda of politicians and the mainstream media (Scott and Sim, 2023; Scott and Bell, 2025; Dellwing, Chapter 13 in this volume). It is a method of critique which problematizes the basic assumptions about 'crime' and the associated myths, mystifications, omissions and silences of the criminal process, laying bare the ineffectuality and counterproductiveness of the criminal process.

But we need to go further than this in the struggle for liberative justice. To avoid being silenced in contemporary political debates, it is essential that penal abolitionists go on the offensive and call out the harms of power – these are the most serious harms in society, but they are not necessarily the ones which are taken most seriously (Hudson, 1987) What is *defined* as a 'crime' is shaped by the social organization and the inequitable distribution of power and resources. Those making and upholding the law often share similar values, networks and assumptions about the social order, and have what can be considered as a collective mindset and way of seeing social reality. In other words, because of their homogeneous character, the ultimate loyalty of those creating laws lies with the protection of *their* shared values, resulting in both a coincidence of interests and a shared way of interpreting the world (Griffiths, 2010). The application of the criminal law serves this common interest as it individualizes, compartmentalizes specific aspects of illegality and responsibilizes the perpetrator, while at the same time removing broader social, economic and historical contexts and any collective dynamics behind such a breach of law (see also Dellwing, Chapter 13 in this volume).

There is then a need to liberate our imaginations and proffer new ways of constructing social problems, drawing upon new language and concepts that can visibilize the harms of power. Penal abolitionists such as Louk Hulsman (1986) and Willem de Haan (1990) some time ago called for the invention of a new language to understand both 'crime' and how we should ethically respond to it. Willem de Haan (1990) powerfully argued that we require a more rational basis for thinking about human conflicts, troubles, problems and harmful conduct, and if we did collectively adopt a more rational approach, then the criminal process would start to collapse like a house of cards.

It is just as important today to show how the limitations and closure to judgments in the criminal law and the broader ideological construction of 'crime' with its bias towards the illegalities of the poor is irreducibly flawed (Hulsman, 1986). Social problems, law breaking and individual and collective troubles are complex and often context-specific, and may be beyond the kind of closure that the language of 'crime' provides (see Kinna, Chapter 2 in this volume). They require completely new forms of valuation that are not based on notions of blame or blameworthiness (Brandão, Chapter 6 in this volume). Any destabilization of existing meanings and interpretations to allow for a rethinking of the current social order should be constantly open to new ways of thinking and an opportunity to reinterpret or reimagine the real. This itself may, as Gramsci (1971) hoped, provide an opportunity to foster a new form of radical consciousness facilitating alternative means of conceptualizing and responding to personal and collective injustice (see Burnett, Chapter 7 in this volume).

Thus, whereas reframing the illegalities of the powerless is well established in abolitionist thought (Hulsman, 1986; de Haan, 1990), the converse of shining the spotlight on the harms of power and the hurt, injury, suffering and death amassed through carceral colonial capitalism has been somewhat neglected by abolitionists (Scott and Sim, 2023). This has not though been the case with critical criminologies, especially in feminist, countercolonial and Marxist-inspired analysis of avoidable and premature deaths (Box, 1983; Scott and Sim, 2023; Anthony and Blagg, Chapter 10 in this volume; Vegh Weis, Chapter 11 in this volume). Nor is this the case for early socialist thinkers such as Friedrich Engels or those in the Chartist Movement in England in the late 1830s and early 1840s.

For example, in an article entitled 'Liberation of Political Victims' in the *English Chartist Circular*, questions were raised about the generation of avoidable deaths in prisons,[8] which were referred to in this article as 'legal murder' (cited in Godfrey, 1979: 218). English Chartists also questioned the role of state policies and capitalist working practices and 'the cruel and murderous effects produced ... upon the lives of the subjects of this realm' (Duncombe, 1842: 132) as ordinary people died of want due to the acts of omission by the emerging British state. These English Chartist claims formed the context and basis of the later concept of 'social murder' (Engels, 1999 [1845]), something which Engels fully acknowledged in his *Conditions of the English Working Class in England* 1844.[9]

It is essential that penal abolitionists attempt to make more visible the harms and injustice that are part and parcel of the application of the criminal law, as well as the wider harms and injuries of power as part of the struggle for liberative justice. Abolitionists should utilize an alternative language that demystifies and names what the penal apparatus of the state perpetrates daily – state violence – and to note that such violence not only fails to address but also escalates existing violence in society (Scott, 2015). The greater the exercise of powers through coercion and physical force, the weaker the likelihood of public compliance and cooperation, and the more likely the generation of more social problems, more public distrust and more contestation.

A victim-centred approach

Let us now turn to some of the affirmative policy interventions libertarian socialists can call for as part of the struggle for liberative justice in our politically regressive historical conjuncture. Dussel (1987, 2013) proposes three key ethical principles to guide our strategic responses to social and penal injustice: the *material principle*, focused on the paradigm of life; the *formal principle*, noting that decision making should be made via democratic process; and the *feasibility principle*, which indicates that socialist responses to death-creating institutions should be based on what is possible in the current historical conjuncture – in other words, a real utopian strategy. Let us briefly consider these three principles in the context of an abolitionist victim-centred response to harm.

The material principle

The material principle has a long history in socialist thought. In the work of Dussel (1987, 2013), it is closely associated with the 'paradigm of life' or the importance of society and its institutions being organized in a way that sustains life rather than generates death. This material principle connects strongly with the discussion at the end of the previous section about returning to some of the concepts from early socialist thought. Indeed, Dussel (2013) takes inspiration from Engel's (1999 [1845]) classic analysis in *The Conditions of the Working Class in England* and other concerns at the time (see the earlier discussion) that the social conditions of industrialized capitalism were curtailing rather than sustaining life. This phenomenon, referred to earlier as 'social murder', is, in certain ways, the opposite of the 'paradigm of life'. It is perhaps no surprise then that Dussel (2013) places such heavy emphasis on the need for liberative justice for those who cannot live – the victims of injustice – or those who are akin to death:

> In effect, in order for there to be justice, solidarity, and goodness in the face of the victims, it is necessary to 'criticize' the given order so

the impossibility of living for these victims is transformed into the possibility of living and of living better lives. But in order to accomplish this end it is necessary to 'transform' the prevailing order, to make it grow, to create a new one. (Dussel 2013: 289)

The material principle and *paradigm of life* promote socialist transformations of the existing social order to ensure that there continues to be sustainable life on planet earth. This means a society not just free of domination and exploitation, but also one where the social conditions of all in society can ensure a dignified life – in other words, 'justice for all' (Box, 1983; see also Scott and Sim, 2023). The production and reproduction of human life should also be in harmony with the sustainability of earth's ecosystems, something which is clearly threatened by carceral colonial capitalism and its drive for ecocide (Stephens-Griffin and Brock, Chapter 12 in this volume). The material principle thus implies a socialist conception of freedom – a freedom for sentient beings to live and not just survive a 'bare life' (Anthony and Blagg, Chapter 10 in this volume). Socialist freedom depends on the liberation of humans from the degrading, meaningless, alienating and environmentally destructive capitalist society, and other forms of domination and exploitation.

Building life-affirming institutions embedded in the material principle for all responses to social problems requires radical transformation, but the ethical demand on socialists also requires immediate intervention. The material principle then should be conceived as a real utopian intervention (Wright, 2010; Scott, 2013b). People cannot speak and we cannot hear their voice if they are not alive. The material principle demands the alleviation of the suffering and the ending of social/institutional conditions likely to generate death (or a bare life akin to death rather than a dignified life) in the here and now. Abolishing state institutions which systematically generate death – social death, civil death or literal corporeal death – such as prisons should be high on the socialist agenda, as should their replacement with institutions which can sustain a dignified life (Scott, 2018, 2020). Drawing on the insights of Dussel (2013) implies that subversive abolitionist knowledge should inform demands for the end of penalization and its replacement with policy interventions that meet the needs of victims (that is, those akin to death through social injustice).

It has long been noted in criminological literature that victims, even of the most seriously harmful acts, often call for three things in response: assurances and safeguards so that they are now safe; that what they experienced does not happen to someone else; and that the person/people/organization that hurt them explains why they abused their power over them (Renvoize, 1992). Victims demand answers, safety and protection. Although requiring a rethinking of victims – where victimhood incorporates victims of injustice as indicated by Dussel (2013) – penal abolition can be conceived as a victim-centred approach to social problems, harms and troublesome conduct (Scott, 2013a; Mathiesen and Hjemdal, 2016). Significantly, this involves seeing state harms, violence and oppression through the eyes of victims/survivors, undermining the hegemonic 'law and order' narrative (see the earlier discussion on this). Subversive thinking then means *turning the system on its head*. It is revolutionary praxis. This could involve promoting a victim-centred response to injustice focussed on repair, redress, restitution and reparation, and the fostering of an abolitionist imagination that can promote the introduction of nonpenal real utopian alternatives to the criminal process (Scott, 2013a, 2018, 2020). This can reaffirm the possibility of negotiation, compensation and speaking on one's own behalf. The new victim-centred response could focus on putting right what went wrong and allow for the creation of a new life-affirming relationship to the world for the person/people who sustained the initial injuries. Rather than a dehumanizing system of punishment, a victim-centred response could produce a form of justice no longer based on repression and one which could take different forms depending on the circumstances of the individual involved, but is one that facilitates the liberation of victims of injustice from oppression (see Vegh Weis, Chapter 11 in this volume).

The formal principle

The formal principle implies that the achievement of goals and aspirations of the material principle and the broader liberation of the oppressed ought to be pursued through democratic process (Dussel, 2013). This means that all parties who may be impacted by any decisions are included in the decision-making process. Democracy is a constant daily struggle. It is also something that is forever unfinished. It is also something we have to actively choose, which can be hard work and time-consuming. However, cutting corners will invariably lead to oppression and authoritarianism. A key element of democracy is that the people who make decisions should be fully answerable to others and this notion of answerability has clear resonance for a victim-centred response to harm. This requirement for answerability remains the case for all forms of democracy, including participatory democracy, although in a participatory democracy, answerability implies that decisions should only be made after informed deliberations have been conducted on the merits or otherwise of following a course of action (what is often referred to as deliberative democracy). Under the representative democracies of societies shaped by carceral colonial capitalism, answerability means focusing on the decision-making powers of the elite and ensuring that those who harm others (including the neoliberal state) are answerable to their victims. Libertarian socialists the world over have a mandate to reveal the hypocrisy and futility of the excessive focus on the punishment of the powerless, while at the same exposing those with social and economic power who undertake socially harmful actions with virtual immunity and impunity (Scott and Sim, 2023; see also Burnett, Chapter 7 in this volume).

Despite claims to the contrary, the criminal law is unable to effectively provide answerability: its recourse simply leads to more questions (rather than answers) about its harm-creating implications. Predicated upon notions of 'individual responsibility', categories of criminal harm wilfully fail to incorporate the harms of the powerful, such as by states and corporations. Furthermore, the underenforcement of laws, such as those relating to health and safety in the workplace, results in thousands of avoidable and premature deaths each year (Scott, 2020). A victim-centred approach to answerability cannot be facilitated through criminalization.

Answerability implies transparent decision making of those in power and the visibilizing of any harms of power, whether through acts of commission or omission (Engels, 1999 [1845]). Therefore, in the short term, what is required are real utopian interventions that can ensure that the capitalist state and corporate power are answerable to victims of harm/injustice and indeed all other people.

Answerability for victims of harm means ensuring that formal responses to harm hear the voices of victims and that those who are harmed are encouraged to provide full and honest answers. This implies the importance of mediation, dialogue and openness. It also implies that formal processes focused on truth and reconciliation (and also liberation from oppression and transformation for victims of injustice) sit at the centre of an abolitionist victim-centred response. However, the notion of answerability goes further than this. Answerability implies developing democratic interventions, including the following: greater control for workers in the workplace to help keep a check on corporate environmental irresponsibility and ensure that health and safety is placed above the accumulation of profits; the radical decentralization of power and creation of smaller organizations with decision-making powers, resulting in more local control and input on decision making; local participatory democracy – like an agora – where local people can ensure their surrounding areas are not laid to waste by environmental pollution or corporations relocating elsewhere to escalate profit margins; and local Indigenous and First Nations peoples being returned sovereignty and decision-making power over their ancestors lands, which could ensure a more environmentally sustainable use of the land (Bell and Scott, 2016; Scott, 2020; Burnett, Chapter 7 in this volume; Anthony and Blagg, Chapter 10 in this volume; Stephens-Griffin and Brock, Chapter 12 in this volume). All these interventions place democracy at their heart and can result in greater individual and collective forms of answerability.

The feasibility principle

The feasibility principle indicates that changes should be historically immanent and achievable in the current historical conjuncture (Dussel, 2013; Scott, 2013a). The struggle for liberative justice is inevitably underscored by a humanitarian impulse – the search for an ethical response to the pain and suffering of others, especially that of the excluded and oppressed. Yet this ethical response must be achieved in a way which is feasible in the here and now. Over 50 years ago, Mathiesen (1974) argued that penal abolitionism strategically must adhere to the 'competing contradiction'. To remain relevant in the present moment, abolitionists must offer alternatives to the penal apparatus of the capitalist state that not only can compete in the current political context, but which at the same time can also contradict the logic of the penal rationale.

Following Mathiesen (1974), this means strategically focusing attention on exploiting contradictions and advocating historically immanent alternatives (Scott, 2013a). As such, an abolitionist real utopian victim-centred response must ensure the safety of those who have been harmed and also look to prevent the future occurrence of such harms. A focus on keeping victims/survivors[10] safe would entail the promotion of health and safety regulations in the workplace; the appropriate funding of refuges and places of sanctuary for (mainly) women and children escaping domestic violence; and a focus on policing which places peace, protection and safety above the rigid enforcement of law (see also Vegh Weis, Chapter 11 in this volume). Preventing future harms would require the adoption of interventions that can genuinely result in answerability, which would imply working with those who have perpetrated serious interpersonal harms in nonpenal therapeutic settings and other kinds of intentional communities (Scott, 2013a; Bell and Scott, 2016; see also Brandão, Chapter 6 in this volume).

There is considerable evidence that a victim-centred approach can provide an opportunity to compete and contradict existing penal policies in the current historical conjuncture. It opens up a significant space to explore the victims of social injustice and other key abolitionist priorities in the mainstream. For example, in June 2024 the Labour Party (2024) published its election manifesto. While the 'taking back our streets' agenda is largely regressive and grounded in coercion, calling, for example, for 20,000 more prison places and thousands more neighbourhood police offices, some aspects of the Labour Party agenda do provide opportunities for abolitionists to engage in and possibly transform the agenda of the current British government. The Labour Party (2024) manifesto highlights failings around responses to women who have been victims of sexual violence (a problem which abolitionists in the UK have raised for decades; see also Vegh Weis, Chapter 11 in this volume), calls for a 'justice system that puts victims first' and highlights the importance of responding to historical injustices and the need for 'truth and justice': 'Labour will introduce a "Hillsborough Law" which will place a legal duty of candour on public servants and authorities, and provide legal aid for victims of disasters or state-related deaths.' The first legislative steps towards this began towards the end of 2024.

Highlighting these progressive proposals is certainly not, of course, to endorse the Labour Party agenda in its entirety. It remains hugely problematic. However, what this brief reflection does show are some 'ways in' for penal abolitionists in policy debates in the next few years following the landslide Labour Party election victory on 4 July 2024. It gives us an indication of the kind of arguments that abolitionists can *compete with* and also those aspects of the current debate that can be *contradicted,* subverted and reconceived with libertarian socialist and penal abolitionist meanings. It keeps abolitionism relevant. For abolitionists, using the language of 'victims' as advocated by Dussel (2013) is to disrupt, subvert and transform its current meanings in official discourse.

Feasible and historically immanent ways to reduce human suffering generated by state violence also include calling for a moratorium on prison buildings and the systematic dismantling of the penal apparatus of the capitalist state via a step-by-step process, perhaps starting by: 1) closing the most inhumane prisons; 2) abolishing certain laws or sentences, such as those around joint enterprise (where innocent people can be convicted of murder) and those still serving Indeterminate Public Protection (IPP) sentences, but are long over the original sentence tariff in the UK today; and 3) campaigning for the selective abolition of criminal law sanctions for certain categories of people, such as children under the age of 18 (see Scott, 2013a). Like the victim-centred approach discussed earlier, these three 'negative reforms', as Mathiesen (1974) put it, *contradict* the logic of the prison, but are also feasible suggestions in the present day as they can *compete* with contemporary suggestions for penal change.[11] The promotion of a victim-centred approach and the gradual dismantling of the penal apparatus of the capitalist state are only a starting point on the journey to liberation and justice, but we never get anywhere until we make a start. And we need to start now.

Conclusion: For the love of justice

The influential critical criminologist Stanley Cohen (1988) once wrote a fictional paper called 'the last seminar' in which he argued that academics should step outside of the classroom and become directly engaged in struggles for justice. Let us conclude on this very same point. Libertarian socialism and penal abolitionisms should not be confined to the seminar room. In my mind, it is the ethical response-ability of academics to bear witness *in service of liberation movements.* So, while the goals and aspirations of penal abolitionisms should be spearheaded by the voices and actions of the oppressed, the voices of activist-scholars and collective organic intellectuals are also key players in the continuing struggle for liberative justice. For me, this struggle should be grounded in an ethics of care, solidarity and revolutionary love.

The great Argentinian socialist Ernesto Guevara (1965) wrote in his short pamphlet *Socialism and Man in Cuba* under the subheading 'Love of living humanity':

> At the risk of seeming ridiculous, let me say that the true revolutionary is guided by a great feeling of love. It is impossible to think of a genuine revolutionary lacking this quality ... one must have a large dose of humanity, a large dose of a sense of justice and truth to avoid dogmatic extremes, cold scholasticism, or an isolation from the masses. We must strive every day so that this love of living humanity will be transformed into actual deeds, into acts that serve as examples, as a moving force.

The love of living humanity (or indeed a liveable planet earth) is revealed through a commitment and openness to the worldview of the victim of injustice and acknowledgement of their hurt and suffering (Dussel, 1987; hooks, 1994; Cohen, 2000; Oliver, 2000). It is through love – seeing victims with compassion in our eyes – that we can find the energy, motivation and willingness to fight for the paradigm of life (see also Kinna, Chapter 2 in this volume). A strong presence of what Guevara called the love of living humanity can promote repair, reconnection with the world, and the rebuilding of lives and human growth. It can lead to healing and hope. It can lead to an ethical response. Such an ethical response may well be difficult, requiring considerable emotional labour, but it is an important part of the struggle for liberative justice. Dussel's ethics are aimed at a *negation of the negation* of (human) life. His conception of liberative justice is motivated by a love of humanity and the desire to realize the material principle by bringing an end to systems of oppression and transforming the world through democratic means (see also the arguments made by James, in Chapter 2 in this volume, on the method of struggle for freedom).

Socialist response ethics entails engaging empathetically with victims of the harms of power, seeing through their eyes and coming together in solidarity with sufferers to help them rebuild their lives with confidence and a new sense of personal belief. Aspirations for liberative justice should be guided by love, and the ethic of love shaping our political engagements will always be unfinished.

Notes

[1] Libertarian socialism is a leftist and *socialist* approach that privileges socialist conceptions of liberty, autonomy and freedom. Alternative phrases, encapsulating many of the ideas advocated in this chapter, are 'non-authoritarian socialism' or, as Johannes Feest notes in the foreword to this book, a 'Socialism from Below'. This phrasing could certainly

be used when engaging with audiences unfamiliar with the term 'libertarian socialist' to express the intended socialist sentiments. However, the tradition of 'libertarian socialism' has a long history (see the collection of thinkers discussed in the companion volume *Envisioning Abolition* and also Scott [2016a]) and is still commonly used in leftist circles, at least in Europe today. My intended audiences, both here and elsewhere, when framing penal abolition through the lens of 'libertarian socialism' are primarily other socialists. By conceiving of penal abolition in this way, I hope common ground can be found between anarchists, autonomist Marxists, Gramscians, democratic socialists and various other socialist and Marxist-inspired credos. A libertarian socialist approach to penal abolitionism can help facilitate solidarity and perhaps a unified socialist 'abolitionism in red and black' agenda critiquing the coercive state (Bell and Scott, 2025).

2 Libertarian socialism also draws inspiration from the socialist ideas of G.D.H. Cole (2021) and other democratic socialists (see the discussion in Scott and Sim, [2023] and Scott and Bell [2025]). Cole wrote extensively and on several occasions across his oeuvre raised the tantalizing prospect of a noncoercive state. While his vision of a noncoercive state was not always fully refined, at the very least, the idea is strongly inferred in a number of his writings and his scepticism of the state is especially clear in his later writings (see, for example, the selection of essays in Cole [2021], the contents of which were originally devised in collaboration with an Italian anarchist). For Cole (2021: 117), concentrated state power was a problem, for 'a truly democratic socialist society should rest on the widest diffusion of power and responsibility among working people' (for similar discussion on diffusion of power, see Box [1983] and Scott and Sim [2023])). Yet while Cole (2021) strongly emphasizes self-governance and worker control, he did not envisage a society without some kind of state-based organization. A noncoercive form of collective organizing going beyond the pure voluntarism and spontaneousness of mutual aid seems important, for example, in ensuring long-term and sustainable welfare distribution and the abolition of poverty.

3 I refer to Dussel as a libertarian socialist in the broadest sense. However, it should be noted that he did have a rather limited and distorted understanding of 'anarchism'. This has led to some anarchists to question the influence he should have on contemporary penal abolitionism. It can be argued that despite some unfortunate comments by Dussel (2013) about anarchism, overall, his nonauthoritarian ethical and political commitments are clearly consistent with abolitionist aspirations to live in a world without legal coercion (for further critical discussion, see several chapters in Scott and Bell [2025]).

4 Liberative justice has many similarities with transformative justice (see Kaba, 2021; Coyle and Scott, 2025). Briefly, liberative justice is: (1) focused on systemic forms of oppression and harms created through existing power structures; (2) grounded in liberation movements and associated grassroots community organizing and collective political action against oppression; (3) dedicated to both the demand for the abolition of state-sanctioned punishments and for the promotion of radical nonpenal alternatives; (4) places emphasis on victims and hearing voice; (5) calls for interventions that remain part of the wider political dialogue; and (6) emphasizes the ongoing nature of the struggle for freedom inferring that no outcome/transformation, no matter how progressive, will ever be the end of the story. See Scott (2016a) for further discussion.

5 My understanding of liberative justice is inspired by the ideas of four key thinkers: Thomas Mathiesen (1974), Enrique Dussel (1987), Barbara Hudson (1987) and Kelly Oliver (2000).

6 It is important to note that my use of the term 'victim' is not referring to the restrictive meaning that is given the legal/victimology definitions. I draw upon, and subvert, the language of victim and victimization as part of the abolitionist strategy of a 'competing contradiction' that expands and stretches the currently dominant meaning of 'victim'. The language of victim/victimhood is a key part of the mainstream debates on harm and responses

to it. I espouse it through the interpretive lens and meanings detailed in the writings of Dussel (2013), where the victim is a victim not merely of a criminal harm but also of social harms and social injustice (Coyle and Scott, 2025). Engagement with debates around victimization (and who it currently includes and excludes in mainstream debates as a victim) not only make it unlikely that abolitionists will be 'ruled out' as irrelevant, but also has the potential to shine a spotlight on the victims of the harms of power, such as through state violence, institutional and structural violence, and what is referred to in this chapter as 'social murder' (see also note 9). Espousing a victim-centred approach is particularly important for penal abolitionists at risk of being defined out of debates in politically regressive political contexts.

[7] An ethical response to voice does not necessarily confer 'epistemic privilege' to the voice of the oppressed (it is still important to draw upon the normative framework of an 'abolitionist compass' when interpreting and sometimes criticizing voice; see Scott [2013a], [2016b]), but for liberative justice the cries of the oppressed should be heard, platformed and, if appropriate, incorporated into a libertarian socialist worldview and struggle for freedom. See also the discussion in Guenther, Chapter 4 in this volume.

[8] The Chartists also questioned the 'unconstitutional police force'. It was noted that: 'An unconstitutional police is distributed all over the country, at enormous cost, to prevent the due exercise of the peoples' rights. The Poor Law bastilles and the police stations, being co-existent, have originated from the same cause, viz, the increased desire on the part of the irresponsible few to oppress and starve the many' (Duncombe, 1842: 132). The English Chartists can thus be considered as a historical antecedent of the contemporary 'defund the police' movement. The prison was also referred to as a 'Bastille' in the 1800s.

[9] The concept of 'social murder' was first introduced by Engels in the German language and it was number of decades before its English translation. The application of the concept of social murder has had somewhat of a revival in the early 21st century (see Scott and Sim, 2023), shining an important spotlight on the avoidable harms and violence of the capitalist state.

[10] Following Dussel (2013), I use the term 'victims', but I also appreciate the importance of other terms, such as 'survivors', in the context of rape, sexual violence and other serious harms.

[11] Negative reforms (or 'non-reformist reforms') can be contrasted with 'reformist reforms', which are penal reforms that do not contradict carceral logic. I recognize the possible creative tension of promoting revolutionary love and praxis alongside those of 'negative reforms' within the context of a real utopian libertarian socialist agenda. It reflects the moral dilemma of holding revolutionary socialist desires and commitments while at the same time recognizing the pragmatic necessity to remain relevant in our politically regressive historical conjuncture. The reader may also find it helpful to refer to James, Chapter 3 in this volume, on this matter.

References

Bell, E. and Scott, D. (eds) (2016) *Non-penal Real Utopias: Justice, Power and Resistance*, Bristol: EG Press.

Bell, E. and Scott, D. (2025) 'Abolitionism in red and black' in D. Scott, and E. Bell (eds) *Envisioning Abolition*, Bristol: Bristol University Press.

Box, S. (1983) *Power, Crime and Mystification*, London: Routledge.

Cohen, S. (1988) *Against Criminology*, Cambridge: Polity Press.

Cohen, S. (2000) *States of Denial*, Cambridge: Polity Press.

Cole, G.D.H. (2021) *Towards a Libertarian Socialism*, Oakland: AK Press.

Coyle, M. and Scott, D. (2021) *International Handbook of Penal Abolition*, Abingdon: Routledge.

Coyle, M and Scott, D. (2025) 'Questioning the logic of criminalisation and penal policy: abolitionist aspirations and the search for transformative justice', in A. Corda (ed.) *Research Handbook on Penal Policy*, Cheltenham: Edward Elgar.

de Haan, W. (1990) *The Politics of Redress*, London: Unwin Hyman.

Dreher, T. and Modal, A. (eds) (2018) *Ethical Responsiveness and the Politics of Difference*, London: Palgrave Macmillan.

Duncombe, T. (1842) 'Second national petition of the Chartists', in M. Beer, *A History of British Socialism*, New York: Harcourt, Brace and Howe, pp 130–34.

Dussel, E. (1987) *Philosophy of Liberation*, Durham, NC: Duke University Press.

Dussel, E. (2013) *The Ethics of Liberation*, Durham, NC: Duke University Press.

Engels, F. (1999 [1845]) *The Conditions of the Working Class in England*, Oxford: Oxford University Press.

Gramsci, A. (1971) *Selections from the Prison Notebooks*, London: Lawrence & Wishart.

Griffiths, J.A.G. (2010) *The Politics of the Judiciary*, London: Fontana.

Godfrey, C. (1979) 'The Chartist prisoners, 1839–41', *International Review of Social History*, 24(2): 189–236.

Guevara, E. (1965) *Socialism and Man in Cuba*, London: Verso. [see also unpaginated version, https://www.marxists.org/archive/guevara/1965/03/man-socialism.htm]

hooks, b. (1994) *Outlaw Culture*, London: Routledge.

Hudson, B.A. (1987) *Justice through Punishment*, London: Macmillan.

Hudson, B.A. (2003) *Justice in the Risk Society*, London: Sage.

Hulsman, L. (1986) 'Critical criminology and the concept of crime', *Contemporary Crisis*, 10(1): 63–80.

Kaba, M. (2021) *We Do This to Free Us*, Chicago: Haymarket Books.

Labour Party (2024) *Change: Labour Party Manifesto 2024*, London: Labour Party.

Mathiesen, T. (1974) *The Politics of Abolition*, Oxford: Martin Robertson

Mathiesen, T. and Hjemdal, O.K. (2016) 'A new look at victim and offender: an abolitionist approach', in E. Bell and D. Scott (eds) *Non-penal Real Utopias: Justice, Power and Resistance*, Bristol: EG Press, pp 137–150.

Oliver, K. (2000) *Witnessing*, Minnesota: University of Minnesota Press.

Renvioze J. (1992) *Innocence Destroyed*, London: Routledge.

Scott, D. (2013a) 'Visualising an abolitionist real utopia', in M. Malloch and B. Munro (eds) *Crime, Critique and Utopia*, Basingstoke: Palgrave Macmillan, pp 90–113.

Scott, D. (2013b) 'Rehumanising the other and the meaning of justice', *European Group Newsletter* (2 November).

Scott, D. (ed.) (2013c) *Why Prison?*, Cambridge: Cambridge University Press.

Scott, D. (2015) 'Eating your insides out: physical, cultural and institutionally-structured violence', *Prison Service Journal*, 221: 58–62.

Scott D (2016a) *Emancipatory Politics and Praxis*, Bristol: EG Press.

Scott, D. (2016b) 'Hearing the voice of the estranged other', *Kriminologisches Journal*, 3: 184–201.

Scott, D. (2016c) 'Regarding rights for the other' in L. Weber, E. Fishwick and M. Marmo (eds) *The Routledge Handbook of Criminology and Human Rights*, Abingdon: Routledge, pp 46–57.

Scott, D. (2018) *Against Imprisonment*, Hook: Waterside Press.

Scott, D. (2020) *For Abolition*, Hook: Waterside Press.

Scott, D. and Bell, E. (eds) (2025) *Envisioning Abolition*, Bristol: Bristol University Press.

Scott, D. and Sim, J. (eds) (2023) *Demystifying Power, Crime and Social Harm*, London: Palgrave Macmillan.

Wright, E.O. (2010) *Envisioning Real Utopias*, London: Verso.

Index

References to tables appear in **bold** type; references to endnotes show both the page number and the note number (95n1).

Numbers

18th century penal reformers 141
19th century anarchists 37–38
19th century penal reformers 141
19th century women reformers 147

A

Abbott, Jack Henry 65–66
Abdul-Jamal, Mumia 253
abolishing slavery 38, 73, 145, 170–174
abolition
   Christian traditions 91, 96–97
   defining 76, 224–225
   discourses in colonies 188
   online mentions 252–253, **252**
   as *praxis* 77
   radical horizons 98
   sovereignty enactment 193–194
Abolition (Davis) 59
'abolition ecology' 18, 228
Abolition. Feminism. Now. (Davis, Dent, Meiners and Richie) 59–60
abolitionism
   confronting colonial landscapes 187
   lines of reasoning 1–2
   and the media 251–252
   and prison abolition 37–40
   radical anti-carceral movements 224
   struggles for freedom and dignified life 3–4
   struggles for justice 18–19
   and total liberation 237
abolitionist activism 246, 260
abolitionist histories 175
abolitionist ideas 2–3, 9–12, 272
abolitionist labour 58
abolitionist phenomenology 72, 76–77
abolitionist real utopian victim-centred responses 285
abolitionist rhizome xii, 278
abolition theology 10, 86, 88, 92, 94, 97–99

see also Christianity
Aboriginal children 188
Aboriginal Legal Service of Western Australia 192
Aboriginal people 185–189
Aboriginal women 181–182
abortion 210
Abramsky, Sasha 151
absurdist stories 254–255
Abu-Jamal, Mumia 49, 50, 51, 55
abuse of authority 30–31
#acab 253
'academic abolitionism' 278–279
academic-based abolition 47
Acercar Derechos programme 211
Acompañar programme 211
action function of prisons 128–129
Actis, María Florencia 209
activism 59, 248, 276
activists and undercover police 231–232
Adema, Seth 193
African Americans 145
Africa, Ramona 53
Africville, Halifax 161
AfroMarxist 253
'afterlife' of slavery 12
Agamben, G. 182, 184–185, 189
agents and delinquents 142
Alexander, Michelle 138
Algonquin people 167, 168
Al Jazeera 253
All Power to the People! (film) 50
Alternatives to Holloway (Smart) 202
Alto Rio Guama Indigenous Territory, Brazil 234
Alyokhina, Maria 26, 30
'ambassadors of reconciliation' 93
America 40, 87
   see also US
American Civil War 145

INDEX

American Friends Service Committee (AFSC) 85, 215n8
American Indian Movement (AIM) 46, 51
Amnesty International 52
anarchism 25, 38, 288n3
Anastácio, Lara 106
An Autobiography: Angela Y. Davis (Davis) 45
Anderson, Benedict 255–256
The Angela Y. Davis Reader (James) 53–54
Angelique (African slave) 162
'animal colonialism' (Cohen) 227
answerability 283–284
anthologies 53–55
anthropocentric command over nature 226–227
anti-American online content 258
'anti-carceral feminists' 202
anti-chattel slavery 1, 2, 12–13, 18
The Antichrist (Nietzsche) 104
anti-colonial freedom struggles 159
anti-imperialist and anti-capitalist speech 247
anti-imperialist journalism 250
anti-imperialist uprisings 262
anti-imperialist voices 262
'anti-misinformation moral panic' 246–247, 254–255, 257, 259, 263
 see also 'fake news'
anti-punitive perspectives 202, 207
anti-racist praxis 88
anti-Russian censorship 253
anti-slavery campaigns 38
anti-social behaviour 37
Aotearoa/New Zealand 181, 187, 190
apprenticeships 172, 173
Aptheker, Bettina 46
arbitrary authority 30–31
Arduino, Ileana 207
Arendt, Hannah 69
Are Prisons Obsolete? (Davis) 49, 145
Argentina 200–215
　Acercar Derechos programme 211
　Acompañar programme 211
　Act 26485 Comprehensive Protection of Women 212
　Act 27499 Micaela Act 212
　Act 27636 211
　decision-making positions 205
　female incarceration 208
　femicides 204–205
　feminist movement 200
　gender-based violence 204–206
　LGBTQIA+ people 211
　Ministry of Women, Genders and Diversity 201, 205–206, 210, 211, 212–213
　National Plan of Action against Gender-Based Violence 2020–2022 213
　nonpunitive feminist voices 205–206, 214
　Producir programme 211
　Registry of Promoters of Gender Violence and Diversity 210
　trans collectives 211
Arkles, G. 148
Aryan Brotherhood 66
Assange, Julian 253
Associated Press 256
Atlanta, Georgia 229
atonement theology 98
Australia 181–195
　Aboriginal Protection Acts 189
　colonial carceral system 184–188, 194–195
　colonial prisons 190–193
　hyperincarceration 188–190
　prison population 190
　see also First Nations people
autobiographies 6
Aviram, H. 126

B

Babylonian Exile 89
'bad apple' corporations 16–17
'bad mom' criminalization 208
Bailey, R. 170
Baliga, Sujatha 99n12
The Ballad of Reading Gaol (Wilde) 31
Banks, Dennis 53
baptizing enslaved Africans 162
'bare life' (Agamben) 182, 186, 282
'bare life biopolitics' (Sylvester) 186
Barker, Joanne 60
Bassotti, M.E. 208
Bavarian Criminal Code 1813 119n5
Baxter, C. 67
BBC 256
BBC Ideas website 253
bearing witness 275–276, 286–287
'The Beaver and Other Pelts' (McGill University) 167–168
beaver furs 167–168
Becker, Howard 257, 260
Behrendt, Larissa 183
Being-with Others (Heidegger) 70
Belgium 162
bell hooks (Gloria Jean Watkins) 202
Belt and Road Initiative, China 262
Bentham, Jeremy 13, 190–191
Berkins, Lohana 211
Berkman, Alexander 25
Bernard, Claude 106
Betts, Reginald Dwayne 65
Beyond Good and Evil (Nietzsche) 111
Bianchi, Herman ix, 3
Biblical references
　2 Corinthians 5:19 93
　Deuteronomy 15 88
　Deuteronomy 19:1–13 92
　Isaiah 61 89
　Leviticus 25 88

293

Luke 4:18–19 88, 89
Matthew 25 88
Numbers 35:6–28 92
'biological theory' (Kropotkin) 35
bisexual prisoners 147
Black Americans 229
Black and white, prisoner and 'human' oppositions 70–71
Black liberation 85, 86
Black Liberation Army (BLA) 46, 51, 53
Black liberation theology 87, 88
#BlackLivesMatter 253
Black Lives Matter 230, 261
Blackness 87–88
Black Panther Party (BPP) 45, 53, 237
  New York/Harlem 47, 50
  Oakland 43
  West Coast 46–47
'Black People in Europe' (International Slavery Museum) 165–166
Black Power movements 46
Black prisoners 7
Black radical feminism 202
Black radicals 8–9, 47
Blagg, Helen 38, 39
Blood in My Eye (G. Jackson) 45
Bodin, Jean 12
Bolsonaro, Jair 234
Bookchin, Murray 226, 236
'born criminal' physiological typology (Lombroso) 107
bourgeois societies 125
Box, Steven 126–127
Boycott, Divestment and Sanctions (BDS) movement 48
Brazil 233–235
Britain
  18th-century Black people 165–166
  chattel slavery 170
  colonialism 226
  colonizing slaver industries 169
  deregulation of corporate harms 129
  enslaved Africans' military work 160
  protectionism in colonies 189
  undercover policing 231–232
  women's prisons 38
  see also UK
British anti-chattel-slavery abolitionism 12–13, 17–18
British Prisons (Fitzgerald and Sim) 11, 132
Brock, A. 226, 227–228
Brooks, Rayshard 230
Broudy, D. 264
Brown Berets 46
Brown, Elaine 50, 51
Brown University 55
Buck, Richard 92
Buenos Aires 205, 209
buffalo and bison slaughter 226

Bukhari, Safiyah 50–51
bureaucratic and autocratic practices 30
Buxton, Thomas Fowell 13

C

cable television 248
Cabral, Pedro Alvar 235
Caleb Williams (Godwin) 33
California 144, 227
California Correctional Peace Officers Association 144
Cameron, David 171–172, 173–174
Campaña por el Aborto Legal, Seguro y Gratuito 210
Camp, J.T. 132
Canada
  anti-chattel-slavery abolitionism 13–14
  beaver fur 167–169
  chattel slavery 159–161
  eugenics 145–146
  fishing industries 169–170
  forced labour 160
  'Healing Lodge' 148
  incarceration of Indigenous people 146, 148, 190
  prisons 147–148
  protectionism 189
  slavery industrial complex 158
  Underground Railroad 161, 175
capitalism
  indifference to human life 124
  materialist underpinnings 129
  primitive accumulation 123
  punishment and labour 127
  witchcraft and Poor Laws 208
Capitalism and Slavery (Williams) 169
Capital (Marx) 123
capital punishment 140–141
'carceral abolition' 225
carceral and colonial imperatives 188
carceral chattel slavery 166
  see also chattel slavery
carceral colonial capitalism 14, 276
carceral economies 167
'carceral feminism' 202
carceral harms 223
carceral institutions 141, 223
carceral logics 71, 72
  and abolitionist voices 174–176
  defining 224
  ecological degradation 238
  labour market 131
  'reformist reforms' 289n11
carceral power 76, 174–175
Carlen, Pat 203
Casey Report 2023 231
Castillo, Pedro 251
Catholic Church 255
The Cautio Criminalis (Spee) 208

INDEX

cellular prisons 28, 31
Center for Contemporary Critical Thought 253
challenging official narratives 257
Changing Lenses (Zehr) 92
Chartist Movement 280, 289n8
chattel slavery
   Canada 159–161
   criminal legal system 164
   global systems 158
   industrial economies 158–159, 170
   Portugal 162–164
   public punishments 165
   unproductivity 12
   western Europe 161–166
   see also slavery
Chávez, Susana 204
chiasm (Merleau-Ponty) 69–70
children 188, 189–190, 232
China 262, 266n36
Chomsky, N. 249, 256–257
Christianity 85–100
   'abolition' 96–97
   and human-made laws 10
   'liberation' 87–90
   prison industrial complex 96
   reconciliation and restoration 91–92
   sacrificial atonement theology 87
   see also abolition theology
Christie, Nils ix, 26
Christmas, William Arthur 44
'cities of refuge' 92–93
'citizens' (Whites) and 'slaves' (Blacks) 44–45
City of Quartz (Davis) 51, 56
Clairvaux, France 27–29, 31–32, 33
Clark, Mark 49
Clarkson, Thomas 12
classical phenomenology 71
Cleaver, Eldridge 7, 53
Cleaver, Kathleen 51, 52, 53
climate rebels 15–16
Clinton, Bill 51, 53
Clutchette, John 44
Cohen, M. 227
Cohen, Stanley 32, 67, 68, 286
COINTELPRO (FBI) 52
Cole, G.D.H. 288n2
colonial and carceral imperatives 188
colonial carceral archipelago 183–184
colonial carceralism 185
colonial carceral power 159
'colonial inhabitation' 226
colonialism
   decentring geopolitics 176n2
   dismantling nonpenal aspects 193
   domination and control 195
   and the ecological crisis 226
   and Indigenous people 14
   as 'Janus faced' 184
   'necropower'(Mbembé) 182, 191–192

'The colonialism of incarceration'
   (Nichols) 146
'colonial matrix of power' (Quijano and
   Mignolo) 182–183
colonial power 157, 159, 182–183
colonial prisons 190–193
   see also prisons
colonization
   enforcing state of exception 184
   exploitation 226
   force as everywhere 187
   persecution of witches 208
colonizing industrial complexes 157
'colour revolutions' 247
Columbia University 57
commercial talk radio 256
Committees of Correspondence 46
communal flourishing 90–92
Communist Party USA (CPUSA) 43, 44, 46
community dysfunction 138
community organizing 236
community projects 211
Conboy, M. 248–249
concentration 32
Conditions of the English Working Class
   (Engels) 280, 281
Cone, James 87, 97
'conquering' corporate media 263, 264
Conquest (Smith) 60
consistent law enforcement 140
conspiracy narratives 255
Constante, Lena 70
contemporary inequalities 225–226
contemporary prison system 132
content controls 261
Contextualizing Angela Davis (James) 54
control prisons 151
convalescence therapies 110–111
Cooper, Afua 160–162, 166
corporate media 19, 245, 262
   20th-century exception 247–248
   Black Lives Matter movement 261–262
   'conquering' 248, 264
   emancipatory content of media 249
   internet content 250
   resistant content 251–252
   social problems sociology 263
   see also mass media; state media
corporate silos 259, 261
Correctional Services, US 144
cotton industry 227
Coulthard, Glen 193
counterhegemonic activism 245, 247
counterhegemonic information 246
counterhegemonic struggles 246, 277
Counterpunch 250
Cousins, Wayne 231
'covenant justice' 92
COVID-19 global pandemic 174

Coyle, M.J. 224, 252
'crime' 39, 209, 279–280
Crime and Punishment (Dostoevsky) 111
criminalization and shame 144–145
criminal justice system 193–194, 200, 202, 206–209
criminal law 16–18, 115, 279–280, 284
criminal physiology 108–109
criminal punishment 145, 151
criminals
  and Blackness 87
  'improbability of a cure' 112
  and the mentally ill 108–109
criminological knowledge (Foucault) 142
criminology 200, 201–202, 215n10
critical disability studies 146
critical phenomenology 71–76
critical prison studies 150
'Critical Resistance: Beyond the Prison Industrial Complex' conference 46, 55–56
Critical Resistance (CritResist/CR) ix, 47–49, 55–60, 203, 224–225, 253
Critical Resistance East (CR East) 57
'critical sociologies' 125
CritResist Louisiana conference 58
CritResist South 58–59
'cruel and unusual' punishments 70
'Cuban anti-government protests' 262
CU-Boulder conference 1998 48, 49–55, 56–57
'cultural genocide' 262

D

'damage-centred research' (Tuck) 73–74, 78
Danewid, I. 130
Daniel Morgan Independent Panel report 231
Daniels, Brandy 97, 99n18
Darwin, Australia 186
data
  femicides 212
  gender-based violence 211
  mentions of penal abolitionism 252–253, **253**
Davis, Angela Y. 8, 13, 43–61, 203
  Abolition 59
  Abolition. Feminism. Now. 59–60
  as an 'abolitionist' 44
  abolition to make prisons obsolete 76
  academic work 47
  Are Prisons Obsolete? 49, 145
  An Autobiography 45
  as a Black Panther 43
  corporate media 262
  and CPUSA 46–47
  Critical Resistance (CritResist/CR) 47
  FBI Most Wanted List 44
  Freedom Is a Constant Struggle 59
  and George Jackson 45
  Jericho movement 50–51
  mass incarceration 48
  as a political prisoner 55–56
  prison reform and development 147
  professor at UCSC 46
  'Racialized Punishment and Prison Abolition' 48
  racist criminalization 66
  States of Confinement 55
Davis, James, III 65, 70–71
Davis, Mike 51, 56
Dayan, Colin 73
Daybreak (Nietzsche) 104
  section 13 105, 113
  section 109 ('Self-Mastery and Moderation and Their Ultimate Motive') 112
  section 202 ('For the Promotion of Health') 104, 106–111, 114, 116–117
  section 235 114
  section 252 113
  section 453 ('Moral Interregnum') 109
  section 538 ('Moral Insanity of the Genius') 109
  see also Nietzsche, Friedrich
Day, Tanya 187
death 282
debts to society 141
decentralized communication 250, 251, 257, 260
decentralized information 254–255, 262, 264
decentralized meaning making 249
decentralized media 246–247, 251, 257–258, 260, 263–264
decentralized movements 253, 263
decentralized narratives 255–256, 263
decision-making 283
de Cleyre, Voltairine 38, 39
decolonial theologies 86
decolonial theory 182
defendant's soul 150
defunding the police 278
#defundthepolice 253
de Giorgi, A. 121–122, 125, 127–128
De Lara, J. 226
Deleuze, Gilles 1, 2, 8
delinquents 139, 142–145
demilitarizing law enforcement agencies 233
democracy 283
Democracy at Work 253
Democracy Now 253
Dent, Gina 59–60
depoliticizing crime 144
deportation orders 162
destabilizing information distribution monopolies 259–260
deterrence 16
developmental psychology 70
Die Linke 253
Diken, B. 187
Dillon, Stephen 149–150

direct action 278
'direct justice' (Tifft and Sullivan) 37
disciplinary power 139–141
disciplinary practices 31, 143
Discipline and Punish (Foucault) 11–12, 138–151
  approaches to punishment 141
  causes of crime 143
  genealogy of the modern soul 139
  Illegalities and Delinquencies 142–143
  see also Foucault, Michel
discriminatory policing 185–186
'disinformation' 246, 258
  see also 'fake news'
'distributive justice' 92
diverting function of prisons 128
Doctorow, Cory 257, 259
domination and exploitation 277
Donovan, K. 159–160
Dooley, Glen 186
Dostoevsky, Fyodor 36, 111
double consciousness 70
double-double consciousness 70–71
Douglas, Frederick 13
Douglas, Kelly Brown 87–88, 90–91
Doyle, Laura 69
Draper, Hal xi
drug subcultures 260
Drumgo, Fleeta 44
Dubler, Joshua 87
Du Bois, W.E.B. 70
Duncombe, T. 280, 289n8
'Dungeons and Dragons' panics (Laycock) 249
Dunlap, A. 226, 227–228, 229–230
Durham prison, UK 68
Dussel, Enrique 271–274, 281–282, 287, 288n3, 289n10
Duval, Clément 25

E

'*ecclesia* incarcerate' (Sexton) 90, 96, 98
eco-abolition 223–239
  murder of Isac Tembé 233–235
  policing and environmental injustice 225–227
  scholarship 227–228
  'spycops' case 231–233
  'Stop Cop City' (SCC) 229–231
  total liberation 235–237
'ecocide' (Falk) 16
ecological crisis 226
ecological dynamics of carcerality 238
ecological harms 223, 229–231, 235–238
ecological justice and liberation 223
economic interests 144
ecosystems and human life 282
educational reforms 212
Elizabeth Fry Society 148

Elizabeth I, Queen 162
emancipation 172, 246
  see also abolishing slavery
emancipatory knowledge 249, 274
emancipatory logic 246–247
emancipatory politics and praxis 270
Enforcing Ecocide (Dunlap and Brock) 227–228
Engels, Friedrich 123–124, 280, 281
England 123, 146, 162
English Chartist *see* Chartist Movement
English Chartist Circular 280
'English liberty' 12, 13
Enlightenment 119n5
Enns, Elaine 93, 98–99
enslaved African labour 158, 161, 166, 168–170
enslaved Africans 159–160, 164–165
environmental arguments 38
environmental justice 223, 225–227, 237
epistemological humility 98
ethical relationships 274
ethical response-abilities 274–275, 285, 286
ethical responses to voice 289n7
Eucharist 94, 98
eugenics 145–146
Europe
  abolitionist histories 175
  industry and slave-grown raw materials 166
  medieval city states 36–37
  minimizing facts of enslaved labour 175
  as a pristine white landscape 166
  racism 157
Everard, Sarah 231
exiles 29
ex-prisoners 34
Extinction Rebellion 15

F

Facebook 261
'fake news' 245–246, 251, 254, 259, 263
  see also 'anti-misinformation moral panic'; 'disinformation'
Falk, Richard 16
fallacies of punitive responses 206–209
'fallen women' 146
The Fall of the Prison (Griffith) 85–86
'false relations' (Kropotkin) 32–33, 36
Fanon, Frantz 69, 72
fatal police violence 184, 229
FBI
  COINTELPRO 52
  Most Wanted List 44
feasibility principle of socialist principles 271, 272, 281, 285–286
federal agents 257–258
Feest, Johannes 270, 287n1
Feldman, Alan 70
femicides 204–205

feminist abolitionism 46, 201, 202, 203, 214–215
feminist history 201–203
feminist judicial reform 201
feminist prison reforms 147–148
Ferdinand, M. 226
Féré, Charles 109
field punishment *see* punishment
Fight Toxic Prisons campaign (US) 223, 238
filter bubbles 257
first feminist wave 200, 201
First Nation populations 14
First Nations people 181–195
  carceral web of colonial system 189
  children 188, 189–190
  colonial domination and control 184–185, 195
  exclusion from legal rights 184
  hard labour 191
  hyperincarceration 181, 182, 189–190, 193
  law enforcement 185–186, 193
  necrocolonial power 191–192
  prison population 190
  see also Australia
First Nations sovereignty 183, 187, 284
first-person experience 64, 78
first-person introspection 68
first-person testimony 65–66, 67, 69, 70, 72, 74, 78
fishing industries 169–170
Fitzgerald, Mike 11, 132, 133
floggings 30
Floyd, George 3, 251, 277
'fool's dress' (Kropotkin) 31
'forced' and 'free' migrants (Kropotkin) 29
'forced labour' 31–32
'foreign propaganda' 251
forest defenders 230–231
forgiveness 39, 94
formal principle of socialist principles 271, 272, 281, 283–284
Fortson, Walter 253
Foucauldian genealogy of the US prison system 73
Foucault, Michel 8, 11–12, 138–151, 261
  criminal punishment 151
  criminological knowledge 142
  depoliticizing crime 144
  The History of Sexuality 142
  imprisonment and the soul 191
  limitations of analyses 150–151
  model prisons 149–150
  The Order of Things 142
  political instrumentality of prisons 145
  as a prison abolitionist 142–143
  prison abolition scholarship 145–150
  prison cycle 143
  prison reform 147
  prisons as self-evident 141

public spectacles of punishment 165
  see also Discipline and Punish (Foucault)
fourth feminist wave 200–201, 203–206, 214–215, 215n10
France 31, 68
  Penal Code 1810 119n5
Franklin, Boris 253
freedom 89, 97, 273, 282
Freedom Is a Constant Struggle (Davis) 59
free labour 13
free trade 12
free will 105–106
French Canadian slavers 159–160
Frezzatti, W, Jr. 108

G

Gago, V. 208
Gallagher, Shaun 70
Galton, Francis 109
Garland, David 126, 190
gay prisoners 147
Gaza 251
gender and crime publications 201–202
gender-based violence 201, 202, 204–205, 208–213
gender identity 203, 215n10
gender nonconforming people 146–147
gender training 211–212
Genet, Jean 45
George, Norman 186
German Empire 119n5
Germany
  First, Second and Third Reich 176–177n3
  law enforcement 251, 265n6, 265n7
Giacoia, O., Jr. 106–107
Gilmore, C. 233
Gilmore, Ruth Wilson 76, 144, 148–149, 227, 233, 262
GiP abolitionist group 11
Glissant, Eduard 1–2
Global North 127–128, 187, 201–203
Global South 14, 201, 203–206
Global Witness 233
God's action of justice 98
God's liberating/vindicating solidarity 90
Godwin, William 33, 35
Golden Gulag (R.W. Gilmore) 227
Goldman, Emma 39
Gómez Alcorta, Elizabeth 201, 205, 210, 212
'good sense' (Gramsci) 278
Gottschalk, M. 144
Gouges, Olympe de 201
government narratives and meaning making 264
Gramsci, Antonio 3, 260, 278, 280
Grassian, S. 67
grassroots movements 247–248
'great health' (Nietzsche) 106–107
Gregory of Nazianzus 10

Grenfell Tower, London 129–130
Griffith, Lee 10, 85–86, 88–89, 97, 99
Grindr 266n36
guards 30, 33
Guattari, Felix 1, 2
Guenther, Lisa 72–76, 145–146, 150–151
Guevara, Ernesto 287
Guha, R. 190
Guyau, Jean-Marie 37

H

Haan, Willem de 280
Haley, Harrold 44
Hall, Gus 46
Hall, Stuart 130
Hamilton, Hugh 253
Hampton, Fred 49
hard labour 145, 191
harms of power 277–281
Harris, Cheryl 88, 99n5
Hartman, Saidiya 73
'hate speech' 254, 259, 263
Havemann, Paul 189
Hayman, S. 148
Haymarket Books 253
healing and restoration to community 93
health 106–107
hearing (socialist response ethics) 275
Hebrew Bible 92–93
Hedges, Chris 253, 262
hegemonic knowledge 259
hegemonic narratives 259, 266n36
Heidegger, Martin 69, 70, 77
Heraclitus of Ephesus 113
Herdt, G. 249
Herman, E.S. 249, 256–257
Heynen, N. 228, 235
hierarchical modes of thought 236
"Hillsborough Law" (Labour Party) 286
The History of Sexuality (Foucault) 142
Holder, Kim 50, 51
Homeland Security Agents 258
homeless prisoners 130
House of Detention, St Petersburg 28
House of the Dead (Dostoevsky) 36
Huarte, G. 206
Hulsman, Louk ix, 280
Human, All Too Human first volume (Nietzsche)
  section 66 110
  section 88 112
  section 102 105–106
Human, All Too Human second volume (Nietzsche)
  section 33 ('The wonderer and his shadow') 115
  section 186 ('The wonderer and his shadow') 116, 117
human conflicts 280

human reproduction 282
human suffering 275
humiliations 31
humility 39
Husserl, Edmund 69, 70, 74
hybrid penal abolitionist thinking xiv
hyperincarceration 146, 188–190, 193
  see also mass incarceration

I

idleness 32
Île Royale, Canada 160, 169
illness, health and wellbeing 106
'immediatism' and abolitionist thought xiii–xiv
Immigration and Customs Enforcement (ICE) 253
imprisonment
  and 'class-based legal system' 132
  and death 10
  and restorative justice theology 95
incarceration 95–96, 127
INCITE! Women of Color against Violence 59, 60
incurable criminals 112–113
Indeterminate Public Protection (IPP) sentences 286
Indian Country Today 60
Indigenous Action Media 236
Indigenous people
  adopting traditional methods 167–169
  and buffalo and bison slaughter 226
  colonialism 14
  and ecocide 234–235
  environmental harms 204
  hyperincarceration 146
  justice traditions 188
  sovereignty 284
  state-sanctioned violence 234
Indigenous women 60, 148
'individual responsibility' 284
industrial capitalism 124
'industrial prison complex' 46
industrial revolutions 124, 158–159, 166, 226
infectious diseases 166, 174
'informants' 74
information distribution 259–260
InfoWars (website) 256
'inherited criminality' (Lombroso) 35–36
'the innocence of becoming' (Nietzsche) 106, 113–114
In Russian and French Prisons (Kropotkin) 27, 37
Inside Time 252
Instead of Prison (Morris) 203
Instead of Prisons (Knopp) 85
institutionally corrupt police 231
intellectually disabled 146
intercorporeal reciprocity of touch 69–70

International Conference on Penal Abolition (ICOPA) ix
International Criminal Court (ICC) 16, 17
International Eugenics Conference (London 1912) 36
International Handbook of Penal Abolition (Coyle and Scott) 252
International Slavery Museum, Liverpool 165–166
the internet 249–250, 259
intersectionality 203, 208
intimate-state surveillance 231–232
intimidation 258
Introduction to a Poetics of Diversity (Glissant) 1
involuntary servitude 145
Iraq War 251

J

Jackson, Andrew 53
Jackson, George 7–8, 9, 43–45, 49, 53
  Blood in My Eye 45
  letter to lawyer 65
  Soledad Brother 7–8, 45
Jackson, Jonathan 44
Jackson, Moana 188, 195
Jamaica 171–172
James, Joy 8, 13, 15, 53–54
Jericho '98 mass protest 49–55, 57
Jericho Movement 50–52, 53
Jesus 88–90, 98–99
Jewkes, Y. 28
Jim Crow Laws 145
Jim Crow segregation 49, 58
Jobe, Sarah 95
Johnston, H. 28
Jones, Alex 256
Journal of Prisoners on Prisons (NAISA) 183
'jubilee' laws 88–89
judicial punishments as revenge 114–115
justice
  'holistic' view 92
  and liberation 15
  libertarian socialism 271
  medieval city states 36–37
  principles of 36–37
'Justice Campuses' 131
Just Stop Oil 15

K

Kaba, Mariame 91, 97, 98, 99n13
Kennedy, Mark ('Mark Stone') 232
'kensey' ('negro cloth') 170
Kharkov Central Prison 32
Kilroy, Debbie 187
Kirchheimer, Otto 125–126
Klaehn, J. 264
Knopp, Faye Honey x, 85, 203
knowledge production in prisons 142
Krasnoyarsk Prison 30

Kropotkin, Peter 6–7, 9, 25–40
  abolitionism 35, 36
  'biological theory' 35
  'false relations' 32–33, 36
  'fool's dress' 31
  'forced' and 'free' migrant groups 29
  principles of justice 36–37
  prison life 29–30
  In Russian and French Prisons 27
  'wilfulness' 36
Kropotkin, Sophie 27, 37
Kunzel, R. 151

L

labelling theory 247
'Labor Market and Penal Sanction' (Rusche) 125
labour markets 125–126
Labour Party 285–286
Lacey, N. 151
Lambert, Bob 232
The Lancet 229
language of abolition 38
'Lao Tzu' 9
'the last seminar' (Cohen) 286
Latin America 209
Laustsen, C.B. 187
'lawful harms' (Tifft and Sullivan) 40
'Law, prison, and double-double consciousness' (J. Davis III) 65
Lawrence, Stephen 232
laws
  and Christianity 10
  enforcing violent social orders 123
  legitimacy of 35
  making and upholding 279
  not impartial 35
  protecting property 124
Laycock, J. 249
Lean, Tabitha 187
learning from the oppressed 274–275
Leder, Drew 67, 72
Lee, Lew Lee 50
leftist activism 19
Legacies of British Slave-Ownership project 171
legacy media 254, 262–263
legal reforms 238
Le Guin, U. 9
Lester, M. 248
letters 4–6
Levad, Amy 93–94, 95, 96–97, 98
LGBTQIA+ people
  gender-based violence 211
  moral panic narratives 249
  police targeting 232
  PREA violations 148
LGBTQIA+ studies 47
'liberal feminism' 201

liberal reform 131, 237
liberation 15, 18, 87–91
liberation-as-wholeness (Douglas) 90–91
liberation movements 2–3, 15–16, 276–278, 286
'Liberation of Political Victims' (*English Chartist Circular*) 280
liberation theology 85
liberative justice 288n4, 288n5
  ethical responses 274, 285
  and freedom 273
  love of humanity 287
  and penal abolition 272
  revolutionary praxis 276–281
  struggles for 15–19, 275–276
  subverting power 279
  unfinished struggle 272–273
  victim-centred approaches 281–286
libertarian socialism 270–289, 286, 287–288n1, 288n2
  caring for others 270
  justice 271
  participatory democracies 271
  relational values of inclusion 270
  'Socialism from Below' 270
libertarian socialists
  learning and ethical response-ability 275
  penal abolitionism 273
  punishing the powerless 283–284
  state responses to wrongdoing 278
  victim-centred approaches 281–286
life-affirming institutions 282
'Life Behind Bars' (Guenther) 145–146
Life in English Prisons (Nicoll) 25
Lindesmith, Alfred 257
Linebaugh, P. 124
lived experience in prison 64, 64–78
  Aryan Brotherhood 66
  critical phenomenologies 71–78
  phenomenological reflections 69–71
  social science research 66–69
Lloyd, Vincent 87
'lockdown America' (Robert) 87, 88
'logic of camp' (Diken and Laustsen) 187
'logics of crime' 123
Lombroso, Cesare 35, 39, 107
Long Kesh prison, Northern Ireland 70
love of humanity 287
Lowe, K. 162–163
Ludwig, A. 72
Lydon, Jason 87, 148
Lyon, France 28, 29

M

Mad studies scholars 146
Magee, Ruchell 'Cinque' 44–45, 50, 52, 53
Magnani, Laura 92, 95–96
Maher, G. 225, 236

'Maison Centrale,' Clairvaux 27–29, 31–32, 33
man-made colonial borders 157, 176n1
Manufacturing Consent (Herman and Chomsky) 256–257
Marcuse, Herbert 8
marginalized groups 249, 274–275
  see also powerless people
marijuana 260
Marin County Courthouse raid 1970 44
Maritimes, Canada 159, 160
Marshall, C.D. 93
Marxism 121–133
  abolitionist praxis 128–132
  crime and criminalization 122–125
Marxist abolitionism 11, 130–133
Marxist geographical analyses 131
Marxist-inspired liberation theologies 10
Marxist praxis 121, 123
Marx, Karl 11, 122–123
  Capital 123
Massey, D. 130
mass incarceration 48, 145, 190
  see also hyperincarceration
mass media
  and abolitionist voices 245
  and dominant narratives 260–261
  integration into corporate structures 261
  'manufacturing consent' for surveillance 249
  one-way, centralized, silo structures 248
  partisanship 256
  pressures that news is made 256–257
  top-down model of problems 249
  see also corporate media; state media
'mastership' 38
material principle of socialist principles 271, 272, 281–283
Mathiesen, Thomas ix, 11, 128–129, 133, 273, 278, 285
Mbembé, Achile 182, 191
McAllister, Laura 108
McClain, James 44
McGill University 167–168
McIntosh, Tracey 188, 194
McQuire, Amy 186
meaning making 257, 259, 261
Medhurst, Richard 250
media
  Latin America 209
  manufacturing consent 257
  postwar 248
media distribution 255
media diversity 254–259
media meaning making 264
media moral panics 262
media platforms 258
Media Sanctuary 253
medicalization of 'deviant' behaviour 35

Medium online platform 258
Medlicott, D. 67, 68
Medrado, Alice 113
Meiners, Erica 59–60
Melossi, D. 127
mental disorders 110, 130, 146
Merleau-Ponty, Maurice 69, 72
'Message to the Grass Roots' (Malcolm X) 52
Meta (Facebook) 258
Metropolitan Police 231, 232
Michell, Charlene 44
Michel, Louise 25
Mignolo, Walter 183
Mingus, Mia 91
'misinformation' 245–247, 259, 262, 263
mislabelling of knowledge 246
Mitchell, Charlene 46
modes of valuation (Nietzsche) 104, 109–110, 117–118
Mogul, J. 146
Molotch, H. 248
Montinari, Mazzino 109
Montreal, Canada 162
'moral capital' 18
'moral injury framework' (Jobe) 95
moral judgements 107, 109, 205
Moral Maze (BBC) 256
moral panics 245–246, 248, 249, 255, 263
moral panic sociology 261
'moral pollution' (Vesely-Flad) 87
moral responsibility 35
Moreton-Robinson, Aileen 182
Morris, M. 203
Morrison, Toni 45
Most Wanted List (FBI) 44
Mundine, Keenan 187–188
Muntaqim, Jalil 51, 54
murdering prisoners 31
Musk, Elon 261
Muskogee Indigenous community 230
mutual aid 33, 36, 40
Myers, Ched 93, 98–99

N

Nagel, M. 224
Nagle, A. 251
Namibia 176–177n3
narcissist and sadist guards 30
National Alliance Against Racist and Political Repression (NAARPR) 49
National Police Chief's Council 231
National United Committee to Free Angela Davis (NUCFAD) 44, 49
'The Native Scholar Who Wasn't' (*New York Times*) 60
NATO 258
'necropower'(Mbembé) 182, 191–192
negation of the negation of life (Dussel) 287

negative reforms ('non-reformist reforms') 46, 149, 286, 289n11
'negative theology of practice' (Daniels) 99n18
'negro cloth' ('kensey') 170
Nelson, Harry Jakamarra 192–193
Neocleous, M. 224
neoliberalism 127–128, 130–131
New Afrikan Liberation Front 51
New England 158, 160, 162
New France 167–168
New School 253
news narratives 254, 258–259, 262
New South Wales prisons 181–182
newspapers 249, 255–256
New Testament 93
Newton, Huey P. 45, 47, 50
New York 162
New York Times 60
New Zealand/Aotearoa 181, 187, 190
Nibert, D. 226–227
Nichols, Robert 146
nicknames 209
Nicoll, David 25
Nietzsche, Friedrich 10–11, 103–119
  anonymity of the criminal 114
  The Antichrist 104
  Beyond Good and Evil 111
  circumstances leading to crime 115
  criminal physiology 108–109
  curable illnesses 112–113
  doctor of culture 116
  Human, All Too Human 105–106, 110, 112, 115–117
  'the innocence of becoming' 106
  mentally ill as guilty people 110
  modes of valuation 104, 109–110, 117–118
  overcoming punitive culture 115–116
  penal abolitionism 103–104
  philosophy of punishment 116–117
  physiological determinism 107–108
  physiology and culture 108
  punishment (*Strafe*) 103–104
  'revaluation of all values' 104–105
  Thus Spoke Zarathustra 110
  Twilight of the Idols 113–114
  'will to power' 142
  wrath and punishment 117
  see also *Daybreak* (Nietzsche)
'non-authoritarian socialism' 287–288n1
nonhegemonic narratives 250
nonhierarchical modes of thought 236
noninstitutional, nonstate, noncorporate actors 258
nonpunitive approaches 205, 209–213, 212, 214
nonpunitive Southern abolitionist feminist voices 214
'non-reformist reforms' (negative reforms) 46, 149, 286, 289n11

Normal Life (Spade) 147
North America 13, 145, 226
  see also Canada; US
North American and Indigenous Studies Association (NAISA) 183
North Australian Aboriginal Justice Agency (NAAJA) 185, 186
Northern Territory, Australia 184, 185
Northern Territory Intervention 185–186, 192
'Not Even One Less' (Chavez) 204
'Not One More!' (*Ni una menos*) movement 204, 208
NYC Panthers 47, 50

O

obedience 36
Observatorio Lucía Perez 211
Occupy Wall Street 263
Odysee 258
Ogden, Stormy 166–167
Oliver, Kelly 275, 288n5
Olufemi, Kwame 229
On Contact (Russia Today) 253
online decentralized spaces 250
online mentions of abolition 252, **252**
online pseudonymity 259
Ontario, Canada 160
'Open Letter from Indigenous Women Scholars Regarding Discussions of Andrea Smith' (Barker) 60
oppressed voices 4–9
The Order of Things (Foucault) 142
'organic intellectuals' (Gramsci) 260
Ortega, Mariana 72
Ouida, Benin 160
Outrage (Duval) 25
Ovando, María 205
Owen, W.C. 38, 40

P

Páez, Chiara 204
Paez Terán, Manuel Esteban ('Tortuguita'/Tort) 230
Palais de Justice, Lyon 29
Palestine 258
'panopticon prisons' (Bentham) 13, 190–191
paradigm of life 281–282, 287
Pashukanis, E.V. 124–125
paternalist imprisonment 188–189
paternalist segregation 190
patriarchal violence 211
Patterson, Orlando 73, 163–164
Pavarini, M. 127
peasantry taking wood 122–123
Pedro-Carañana, J. 264
Pellow, D. N. 235
Peltier, Leonard 49, 50, 51, 53, 65

penal abolition 225
  and liberative justice 272
  and the media 253–254, 262
  and 'prison abolition' 95–96
  victim-centred approaches 283, 285
  white colonization 182
penal abolitionisms ix–x, xii–xiii, 3
  'competing contradictions' 285
  liberation movements 277
  and libertarian socialism 273–274, 286–287
  Marxist frameworks 128
  Friedrich Nietzsche 103–104
  North America 13
  revolutionary praxis 7
  social media mentions 252–253, **252**
penal abolitionists 246–247, 279–280, 281
penal abolitionist thought xiii–xiv
Penal Abolition (Ruggerio) 10
Penal Code for the German Empire 119n5
penal codes 115, 119n5
penal reformers 141, 147
penal solutions 206
penitentiaries 146
Pérez, Lucía 204–205
Pérez, M. 206
Perm region penal colony, Ural Mountains 26
perpetual serfdom 32
Peru 251
Peter and Paul Fortress, St Petersburg 27, 28
Pettit, Philip 38
Phan, T. 252, 253, 261
phenomenology 1
  abolitionist theory 76–77
  approaches to 64–72
  critical reflections 74–75
  critique of carceral power 76–77
  lived experience in prison 66–71
Philippe-Beauchamp, Xavier 72
physical violence 31
physio-psychological therapy of resentment 107
Piche, Justin 262
Pitch, Tamar 210–211
Pitts, Andrea 71, 72
plagues 166
Platonic-Christian morality 118
pleasure and *pain* (Nietzsche) 106
pluralized meaning making 249, 257
pluralized media 246–247
  see also decentralized media
Poindexter, David 44
polarizing online information 256
police abolition 86, 99n2
police and policing
  as coercive population management 226
  and colonialism 226, 238n2
  defining 224
  and ecology 227–228

and environmental injustice 224, 225–227
exclusion from rights 184
hyperpolicing Aboriginal people 186
intimate-state surveillance 231–233
use of lethal violence 184, 229
violence in US 229, 251
'policing by consent' myth (Woodman) 232
political economies of punishment 125–128
political freedoms 6
political instrumentality of prisons (Foucault) 145
political prisoners
  agency 47
  autobiographies 6
  CritResist 49
  and Angela Davis 44, 48, 49–50, 55–56
  French penitentiaries 68
  Jericho '98 mass protest 49–55
  Peter and Paul Fortress 28
political violence 261
The Politics of Abolition (Mathiesen) 11, 128
Poor Laws 208
popular resistance 140
population management 224
Portugal 158, 162–165
postcolonial theologies 86
'post-truth societies' 254, 264
postwar mass media 248
Poteet, Jennifer 72
poverty 143
power-draining function of prisons 128
powerless people
  criminal justice interventions 130
  harms of power 246–247
  lacking justice 271
  'learn to learn' from 275
  and libertarian socialists 284
  media focus 262
  responsibility for needs 275
  social harms 273
  victimizing 15
  see also marginalized groups
Pranteau, Sheri 188
Pratt, Geronimo 49, 50, 52–53
predatory subcultures 28
pre-mass-media newspaper age 249
preventing future harms 285
Prince Edward Island, Canada 160
principle of interdependence 36
principles of justice 36–37
#PrisonAbolition 252, **252**, 253
prison abolition 37–40, 95–96, 149–150, 253–254
The Prison and the Factory (Melossi and Pavarini) 127
prisoners
  enmity and antagonism with guards 33
  'foe of society' (Kropotkin) 34
  as neo-slaves 13

objects of knowledge 138
prison experience 5–6, 65–66, 74
'soumis' and 'insoumis' 33
'prisoners of conscience' 52
prison expansion 143, 150, 227
Prison for Women, Kingston, Canada 148
prison industrial complex (PIC) 51, 56, 96, 97, 166–167, 170, 203, 225
prison industry 144
Prison Memoirs of an Anarchist (Berkman) 25
prison newspapers 252
Prison Plantation System 253
Prison Radio 252
prison rape 148
prison reform 147–149
prisons
  'afterlife' of slavery 12
  as Arctic exploration 32
  assemblage of institutions 128
  demeaning and dehumanizing 32
  depredations of the poor and powerless 130
  as a 'deteriorating influence' 34–35
  draining resources from social life 131–132
  environment 27–29
  failing to rehabilitate prisoners 139, 147
  futility and iatrogenesis 202
  ideological functions 128–129
  ineffective preventing crime 138–139, 147
  'as its own remedy' (Foucault) 143
  knowledge production 142
  laboratories of violence 29–30
  monitoring communications 259
  multi-purpose capitalist tool 147
  paying debt to society 141
  policing and pollution 237
  policing gender 146
  'the power of death' 88
  producing delinquents 142–143
  as psychiatric asylums and residential homes 146
  for 'punishing the poor' 129
  racial control 87–88, 145
  'self-evident' aspects of 141
  as 'social death' 181
  surveillance and control systems 259
  transmissibility of 'criminality' 28
  'problem populations' (Box) 127
profits 166–170
'progressive' journalism 263
propaganda 251, 262, 266n41
protectionism 184, 189
Proudhon, P.J. 38
Prussian Penal Code 1851 119n5
psychiatric asylums 146
public safety 95
Puerto Rican *Independentistas* 46, 53
Pulido, L 226
'punishing the poor' (Sim) 129
Punishing the Poor (Wacquant) 145

punishment
  arguments against 39
  boys in French reformatories 31
  depriving of innocence 113
  dual-regulatory function with incarceration 127
  fallacies of punitive responses 206–209
  justification 35
  matching the crimes 141
  as a philosophical matter 103–104
  sovereign/state power 139–140, 255
  women and queer communities 210
Punishment and Social Structure (Rusche and Kirchheimer) 125–126, 127
'punitive turn' (de Giorgi) 127–128
Puritan covenant theology 87

Q
qualitative social science research 66–69
Quebec 160
queer feminism 215n10
questioning power 275
Quijano, Anibal 183

R
Raab, D. 131
racial control 87–88
racialized ghettos 145
'Racialized Punishment and Prison Abolition' (A.Y. Davis) 48
racism 157, 186
racist oppression 70
racist violence 191
Radical Alternatives to Prison 202
radical anti-carceral movements 224
  see also abolitionism
radio 'phone-ins' 256
rape 31, 148
rational approaches to conflict 280
Reagan, Ronald 43, 46, 48
real justice 271, 273
real utopian interventions 271
Rebolledo, Nuñes 206
reconciliation 90–96
Reconciliation (confession) 94
reconciliation theology 85
reconditioning criminals 150
Red Masks programme 210
Red May 253
Red (socialist channel) 266n35
reformism 37
reforms 34–35, 37, 131, 286
rehabilitation 129, 131, 150, 167, 173
Reiman, J. 130
Rembis, Michael 146
reoffending 138
reparations 171–172
Republic of New Afrika (RNA) 51, 53
residential homes 146

resistance 247
resistance content 249, 250–254
resisting injustice 6
restoration of shalom 93
restorative justice 91–92, 93, 95
restorative justice theology 93–95
Resurrection (Tolstoy) 38–40
'revaluation of all values' (Nietzsche) 104–105
'revanchist common sense' (Camp) 132
revenge 114–115
revolts 140–141
revolutionary praxis 7, 272, 275, 276–281, 283
revolutionary voices 7
Rheinische Zeitung (RZ) 122
'rhizomes' x, xii, 1–2
Rhode Island, New England 170
Rhodes, Lorna 67
Richie, Beth 59–60
'the right to exclude' (Harris) 88, 99n5
right-wing media content 249, 256
right-wing moral panics 255
Ritchie, A. 146
Ritter, Scott 258
Robert, Nikia Smith 87, 88–89, 90, 97, 98
Rodriguez, D. 147
Roebourne Prison, Western Australia 190–191
role-playing games 249
Rolfe, Zachary 192
Rome Statute (ICC) 16
Romily, Samuel 13
Rosa Luxemburg Stiftung 253
Rossi, C. 234
Rottnest Island, Western Australia 190–191
Royce Hall lecture 1969 48
Rubin, Gayle 146
Ruggerio, Vincenzo 10
rule of law 184, 185
rural communities 144
Rusche, Georg 125–126, 127
Rusche-Kirchheimer thesis 126
Russia 32, 253, 258
Russian exile system 29
'Russian propaganda' 262
Russia Today 253
Rustbelt Abolition Radio 252

S
Sacayan, Diana 211
sacrificial underclasses 87
Sakhalin, Russia 32
Sánchez, Luciana 206
Santa Cruz Women's Prison Project (SCWPP) 202–203
Satanists against Satanic moral panics (Victor) 249
Saunders, A.C. de C.M. 163, 164
school expulsions 130
Schudson, M. 248

Schutz, Alfred 69
scope of oppression 12–14
Scott, David Gordon ix, 238, 252, 262
second feminist wave 201
Second Thought (YouTube channel) 258
seeing (socialist response ethics) 275
segregation 147, 184–185, 188, 189, 191
Self and free will 105–106
'self-mastery and moderation' (Nietzsche) 112
Sennett, R. 259
sentiment analysis 252, **252**
Serge, Victor 68
'settled truth' 248
settler colonialism 182
Seven Years' War (1756–1763) 160
Sexton, Jason 90, 96, 98
sexual abuse and assaults 130, 148
sexual coercion 232
Shakur, Assata 25–26, 32–33, 65
Sharp, Granville 12
Shaw, M. 170
Shaw, Walter 186
Sherwood, Juanita 190
Siberia 28, 29–32, 111
Siberyak bounty hunters 29
Sim, Joe 11, 37, 129, 130, 132, 133
Simpson, Audra 183
Skinner, Quentin 38
'slaughterhouse approaches to justice' (Wacquant) 145
slave-grown raw materials 166
slavers 162, 171
slavery
  abolishing 38, 73, 145, 170–174
  and involuntary servitude 145
  white men's rights 172
  see also chattel slavery
slavery industrial complex 157, 158, 166–170
slaves
  as Blacks and 'citizens' as Whites 44–45
  deportation order from England 162
  invisibility of histories 162
  standardized punishments 164–165
slave trade 13
slave trials 164
Smith, Andrea 47, 60
'social death' 181, 202
social distribution of information 259
social harms 273
socialism 3, 271–272
Socialism and Man in Cuba (Guevara) 287
'Socialism from Below' (Draper) xi, 270, 287–288n1
socialist response ethics 274–277, 287
social justice and liberation 233
'social justice' (Zehr) 92
social media 253

'social murder' (Engels) 280, 281–282, 288–289n6, 289n9
social order 130
'social pollution' (Vesely-Flad) 87
social problems 247–248, 263
social relationships 32–34
social responsibility 27–28
social science education 250
sociological approaches 256–257
sociology of social problems 248
Socorristas en Red 210
Soledad Brother (G. Jackson) 7–8, 45
Soledad Brothers 44
Soledad Brothers Defence Committee (SBDC) 43, 49
solidarity 33, 59–60
solitary confinement 70, 73, 74
Solitary Confinement (Guenther) 72–73
'soumis' and 'insoumis' classifications 33
South America 235
Southern decolonial perspectives 209
Southern feminist critical movement 206
southern plantations 170
sovereign power 139–141, 284
Soviet Union 46
Soyinka, Wole 6, 7, 9
Spade, Dean 147
Spee, Friedrich 208
Spinoza, B. 10
Spitzer, S. 127
'spycops' 231–233
'stable subject' ontological conception 113
state-corporate orchestrated moral panic 246
state media 19, 245, 254, 257, 258, 261–262
  see also corporate media; mass media
state of exception 191–192
States of Confinement (James) 54–55
state violence 76, 234, 281, 286
statist social ecological order 237
Stender, Faye 45
stolen wealth 169–170
'Stop Cop City' (SCC) 229–231
Stop Ecocide International 16, 17–18
'storehouses of the living dead' (Abramsky) 151
St Paul Prison, Lyon 27, 28
St Petersburg, Russia 27, 28
street police 190
structural gaslighting 172–173
'structured dispossession' 184, 193
Struggle for Justice (AFSC) 215n8
struggles for liberative justice 15–19, 275–276
  see also liberative justice
Substack online platform 258
subversive abolitionist knowledge 282
subversive knowledge 249, 272, 279
subversive thinking 272, 278, 283
Sullivan, Dennis 37, 40

INDEX

surpluses driving expansion 227
surplus labour 126, 227
surveillance and control systems 259
survival and resistance strategies 73
Sylvester, C. 186
symbolic function of prisons 128
systems of sacrifice and criminalization 88

T

Taddei, Wanda 204
Táíwò, Olúfẹ́mi 64
Tangentyere Council Aboriginal Corporation 185, 186
Taoism 9
Tao Te Ching (Le Guin) 9
A Taste of Power (Brown) 50
Taylor, Laurie 32, 67, 68
Taylor, Mark Lewis 90
Tchaikovsky, Chris 203
Tembé, Isac 233–234
Tembé-Theneteraha people 234
textile mills, Rhode Island 170
'theatrics of counterterror' (M.L. Taylor) 90
theft of wood 122–123
theological imperative of communal wholeness 91
third feminist wave 201–203
third-person reflections 67
third-person social science research 69
Thirty Years' War (1618–1648) 176–177n3
Thomas, Gary 44
A Thousand Plateaus (Deleuze and Guattari) 2
Thus Spoke Zarathustra (Nietzsche) 110
Tifft, Larry 37, 40
Timerman, Jacobo 65, 70
Tokar, B. 226
Tolstoy, Leo 38–40
Tombs, T. 129
Tomsk, Siberia 28
Torah 92–93
Torres, Gabe 50
total liberation 224, 235–237
transcendental conditions 69
transfeminism 215n10
transfeminist-anti-prison collectives 210
transformative justice 86, 91, 288n4
transmissibility of 'criminality' 28
transmissible repressive practices 28
transparent decision making 284
trans people 211
trans prisoners 147, 209
'tree-sits' 230
'true' 245
Trump, Donald 261
Truth, Sojourner 202
Tuck, Eve 73–74, 78
Turk, J. VanSlyke 248

Twilight of the Idols (Nietzsche) 113–114
Twitter (X) 252, 253, 258, 261
tyrannical drive (Nietzsche) 110, 111
tyrannical impulses (Nietzsche) 111–112
'tyrannical instinct' (Nietzsche) 112

U

UK
  Environment Agency 129
  Health and Safety Executive 129
  Metropolitan Police 231
  Ministry of Justice 131
  Parliamentary Select Committee on Aboriginal Tribes 189
  Slavery Abolition Act 1833 13, 159, 170–174
  'spycops' 231–233
  see also Britain
Ukraine 258, 262
Undercover Policing Inquiry (UCPI) 232
Underground Railroad, Canada 161, 175
'Unfinished Liberation' conference 1998 (CU-Boulder) 48, 49–55, 56–57
United Nations (UN) 233
University of California-Berkeley (UC-Berkeley) 47
  Critical Resistance conference 56
University of California-Los Angeles (UCLA) 43
University of California-Santa Cruz (UCSC) 46
University of California (UC) 46
University of Colorado-Boulder (CU-Boulder) 47
US
  abolishing slavery 38, 73, 145
  capital punishment 140–141
  chattel slavery 170
  'colour revolutions' 247
  Correctional Services 144
  eugenics 145–146
  Indian Removal Act 1830 53
  involuntary servitude 145
  Jim Crow Laws 145
  'Justice Campuses' 131
  'mastership' 38
  police violence 229, 251
  prison expansion 150
  prison industrial complex (PIC) 167
  Prison Rape Elimination Act 2003 (PREA) 148
  racial control 87–88
  racialized ghettos 145
  rape 148
  'revolutionary era' 49
  Revolutionary War 170
  southern plantations 170
  Thirteenth Amendment 73
  and Ukraine 262

US Department of Justice, Office of Justice Programs 54–55
Uyghurs 262

V

La Vaca magazine 211
Vesely-Flad, Rima 87–88
vicious punishments 30–31
victim-centred approaches 271, 281–286
victimization and revictimization 213
'Victim-Offender Dialogues' 92
victims 114–115, 288–289n6, 289n10
  agency 278
  and compassion 287
  voices of 272, 274, 279
Victor, J.S. 249
Vieira, Antonio 12
Vietnam War 251
Viner, K. 248, 251
violence 88
  see also gender-based violence; state violence

W

Wacquant, L. 145
Walker, Kumanajayi 192–193
Walter, Maggie 193
Ward, Colin 36
Ward, Mr (Ngaanyatjarra Elder) 192
warehousing people 131
Watego, Chelsea 186
Waters, Maxine 56
Watkins, Gloria Jean (bell hooks) 202
Watson, Irene 183
Weelaunee forest, Atlanta, Georgia 229, 230–231
Weiss, G. 71
Weis, Valeria Vegh 208
wellbeing and illness duality 106
western Europe (Saleh-Hanna) 158, 161–166, 176n2
'western' (Saleh-Hanna) 158, 176n2
West India Compensation Account 171
What is Property? (Proudhon) 38
white Canadian racism 161
white colonization 182–183
whiteness and 'white space' 88
'white possessiveness' (Moreton-Robinson) 182
white supremacy 175
white Western colonialist hegemony 14

Whitfield, H.A. 159, 160–161
Whitlock, K. 146
Whyte, David 16, 18
Wife of Prisoner 4,287 (S. Kropotkin) 27
Wilberforce, William 12, 13
Wilde, Oscar 31
'wilfulness' (Kropotkin) 36
Williams, Eric 169
'will to know' (Foucault) 142
'will to power' (Nietzsche) 142
Wilson, Charlotte 38, 39
Winks, W.R. 159, 167
witches 208
Wolfe, P. 193
womanism 93
womanist theology 85, 86, 90–91
women
  abuse in prisons 130
  being raped 31
  and 'crime' as exotic 209
  criminalization 208–209
  femicides 204–205
  nicknames for female offenders 209
Women in Prison charity 203
women's prisons 33, 38, 146–148
Woodland, John 67
Woodman, C. 232
Woodward, Vincent 8
workhouses 127
work in prisons 130–131
Wray, Harmon 92, 95–96
writing by prisoners 65
wrongdoers and wrongdoing 39, 114

X

X, Malcolm 7, 52, 65
X (Twitter) 252, 253, 258, 261

Y

Ybarra, M. 235
Yo No Fui network 210
YouTube 253, 258, 261
Yuendumu community, Central Australia 192

Z

Zaffaroni, Raúl 208
Zagarin, Captain 30
Zehr, Howard 92, 95
zoological observations 142
Zurara, Gomes Eanes de 162

www.ingramcontent.com/pod-product-compliance
Lightning Source LLC
Chambersburg PA
CBHW070803040426
42333CB00061B/1809